Archaeology of Domestic Architecture and the Human Use of Space

Sharon R. Steadman

Left Coast Press Inc.
Walnut Creek, California

LEFT COAST PRESS, INC.
1630 North Main Street, #400
Walnut Creek, CA 94596
www.LCoastPress.com

Left Coast Press Inc.

ISBN 978-1-61132-282-8 hardback
ISBN 978-1-61132-283-5 paperback
ISBN 978-1-61132-285-9 consumer eBook

Library of Congress Cataloging-in-Publication Data:
Steadman, Sharon R.
Archaeology of domestic architecture and the human use of space / Sharon R. Steadman.
pages cm
Includes bibliographical references and index.
ISBN 978-1-61132-282-8 (hardback : alkaline paper) — ISBN 978-1-61132-283-5 (paperback : alkaline paper) — ISBN 978-1-61132-285-9 (consumer ebook)
1. Architecture, Domestic—History. 2. Space (Architecture)—History. 3. Architecture, Ancient. 4. Dwellings—History. 5. Household archaeology. 6. Social archaeology. 7. Civilization, Ancient. I. Title.
NA7105.S73 2015
728—dc23

2015009111

Printed in the United States of America

♾ The paper used in this publication meets the minimum requirements of American National Standard for Information Sciences—Permanence of Paper for Printed Library Materials, ANSI/NISO Z39.48–1992.

Contents

Illustrations

Acknowledgments

Family and friends are greatly deserving of thanks for their help and support during the writing of this book. I can never thank Girish and Rose enough for all they do for me. Jenni Ross and Greg McMahon have been wonderful colleagues and friends through many field seasons and scholarly projects; their support and patience with me are deeply appreciated. Without my good friend Amanda Halliwell I would never complete anything, and I thank her for her help and generosity. Jim Weinstein's friendship and encouragement these many years is also deeply appreciated. I also wish to acknowledge Ruth Tringham in whose seminars I first developed my love of architecture. Tim Matney shares my love of architecture and has been a treasured friend over the years who has inspired me in many ways. Several scholars, particularly Ted Banning and Jerry Moore, have also inspired me in the field of architecture, and I thank them for their wonderful scholarship.

Chapter 1
Social Archaeology and the Study of Architecture

Introduction: Foundations

It has taken well over a decade to write this book, or more accurately, I have been hoping to write it for that long. Other scholarly agendas seemed continually to thwart pursuit of this favored subject: the archaeology of architecture. Decades ago, I intended to write my dissertation on this topic, and even completed the literature review. However, circumstances swerved my dissertation topic dramatically to a very unarchitectural topic. When finally the dissertation process and its aftermath (publication) were completed, I returned to the study of architecture. I even managed to publish the "lit review" slated to be part of the original dissertation, and published a few architecturally based articles over the years. After being hired at my college two decades ago, I taught a course on the "Archaeology of Space and Place," which I still think is one of the best courses I have ever delivered. I intended to write this book to accompany that class.

Alas, other demands at the college again led me away from architecture and toward other academic areas. Other books were written or edited, none of them really about architecture, and an archaeological project that requires regular reports and synthetic works ate up time that could otherwise have been dedicated to architecture-based studies. At long last, I turned my attention back to my favorite and first love, the archaeology of architecture. Two years later, I am writing this introduction, with a nearly complete manuscript in its wake.

Archaeology of Domestic Architecture and the Human Use of Space, by Sharon R. Steadman, 11–21.

Had I managed to sit down and write this book long ago, it would have been very different from the one I have now produced. Mainly, it would have been shorter, perhaps to the delight of readers and certainly to the relief of my publisher. Very recently, the field of architecture, as explored through the archaeological discipline, has risen to prominence much as it did in the 1970s through the 1990s. The number of books and articles that have appeared—really in the last five years—on architecture and related topics is really quite remarkable, and very exciting. I hope my inclusion of many of them in my discussions throughout these chapters has done justice to their excellent scholarship.

Upon setting out to write this book, I did not quite know what its nature would turn out to be. I knew what the subjects of the chapters would be, and roughly what I would discuss in each, but I did not know if this book would become a highly theoretical treatise on humans and their built environment, or a vehicle in which I explored my own ideas about humans and their spaces, or turn into something else entirely. Now, having completed the thing, I can say that it is, essentially, all three, but mostly the latter. This volume is, in many ways, a "how-to" manual, a guide to understanding the rich data provided to archaeologists by the architectural record.

Chapters review the theories and methodologies employed by many archaeologists over the years and offer many case studies from very successful investigations. In many of the chapters, I offer some of my own ideas on what ancient humans might have thought, intended, needed, or wanted, when they constructed their houses long ago. Writing a book is, of course, a very different activity from building a house. However, the joy that comes from completing a long-term project—especially if the work was enjoyable and the product, one hopes, is well constructed—must be rather similar whether the actor has built a house or written a book. I offer this project to you, the reader, after many years of unintended side trips away from this subject that is so integral to the archaeological field and so foundational to the human experience.

Social Archaeology and the Study of Architecture

Archaeologists have always been concerned with architecture. It was the palaces and temples of Mesopotamia and the stone monuments emerging from the jungle that launched archaeological expeditions to Iraq and Mesoamerica in the 19th century. Interest in the vastly built has been perennial. What is more recent, and is the concern of the present volume, is the opposite of the monumental: the domestic built environment. Of course, there are many large palaces and great houses to study, some of which are discussed in the following pages, but the majority of domestic structures of the past, or in the present, are not of that ilk. Where the interest in domestic architecture came from is the subject of the brief overview of scholarship here. As Wendy Ashmore (2000) notes, interest in the small-scale built environment is rooted in the florescence of social archaeology and the aspiration to understand the non-elite people inhabiting ancient places. The following is hardly a comprehensive overview of the origins and development of the archaeological study of domestic architecture. Rather, only a thumbnail sketch is presented, as the following chapters offer far greater depth and extensive citations.

Perhaps the best place to seat widespread interest in domestic architecture is in the field of settlement archaeology as it developed in the 1950s through to the 1970s (e.g., Adams 1965; Chang 1968; Clarke 1977; Parsons 1972; Trigger 1967; Ucko, Tringham, and Dimbleby 1972; Willey 1956). At the same time, a focus on the intersection between houses and cultural structure came not from the archaeological discipline but from the architectural field. Amos Rapoport published *House Form and Culture* (1969), and followed it up with *The Mutual Interaction of People and Their Built Environment* (1976), the latter an edited volume full of cross-cultural anthropological studies. The strong connection between human culture and the creation of places had been forged; this concept was more fully developed by Rapoport in *The Meaning of the Built Environment* (1982), in which he introduced the field known as "Environment-Behavior Studies" (EBS). Rapoport has continued his investigation of the intricacies of humans and their created environments in the decades since (e.g., 1988, 1990, 2005, 2006, 2008). Simultaneously, colleagues in the anthropology and geography disciplines were also exploring the physical aspects of the houses built by living cultures, and of the spaces inhabited by them (e.g., Carsten and Hugh-Jones 1995; Cieraad 1999; Feld and Basso 1996; Low and Lawrence-Zúñiga 2003; Pred 1990; Small and Tannenbaum 1999; Tuan 1974, 1977). These innovative approaches informed the origins and development of archaeological approaches to architecture.

Kent Flannery (1972) offered the archaeological world a powerful example of what architecture might reveal about socioeconomic structure, marriage and kinship patterns, and human behavior in general. His suggestions that house form and placement could signal whether the inhabiting population practiced pastoralism or agriculture, lived in nuclear or extended families, and potentially had monogamous versus polygynous marriage patterns elicited several decades of investigations in response to his publication (see chapters 4 and 6). Just a few years later, Flannery's *Early Mesoamerican Village* (1976) firmly established Latin American archaeology as the leader in the investigation of domestic architecture in prehistoric village settings. In concert with this, however, was the focus on vernacular architecture in historical settings, as defined by Henry Glassie in his *Folk Housing in Middle Virginia* (1975).

In combination with settlement archaeology came the desire to assess population in communities. This required detailed analysis of how much space people needed and how they used it; based on such analyses, a person per square meter equation might be developed. The earliest study was offered by Naroll in 1962, with numerous responses and adjustments to his calculations over the next two decades (see chapter 3). Population estimations were critical not only for those interested in houses and communities but also for those in the field of landscape archaeology, developing largely simultaneously with settlement archaeology in the 1970s, gaining in importance in the 1980s, and becoming a major area in archaeological research today (e.g., Ashmore and Knapp 1999; Aston and Rowley 1974; Bender 1995; Butzer 1982; David and Thomas 2008a; Rossignol and Wandsnider 1992; Tilley 1994, 2009; Wilkinson 2003; Wilkinson, Gibson, and Widell 2013; and see chapter 2).

The early 1980s saw the launch of two important architecturally based analytics: proxemics and access analysis, and household archaeology (see chapters 3 and 7). Based in semiotics—the study of signs and symbols that convey meaning—proxemics examines how humans construct the space around them and what this conveys with regard to behavior and spatial needs. Rapoport drew heavily on proxemics in the development of EBS. Bill Hillier and Julienne Hanson's development of methodologies to address access analysis (1984) truly brought the fields of proxemics, access analysis, and archaeology together (see chapter 3). These tools allowed archaeologists to identify whether various behavioral codes were present in a culture simply by examining the architectural layout: Were private areas important within the household? Were boundaries between dwellings a norm? Was territoriality expressed in the community? Proxemics and access analysis have become well ensconced as viable methodologies for acquiring valuable human behavioral data from the archaeological record (e.g., Banning 2002; Brusasco 2007; Gardin and Peebles 1992; Preucel 2006).

Household archaeology, first launched as a defined field by Richard Wilk and William Rathje in 1982, quickly captured the interest of archaeologists committed to understanding prehistoric communities. In its first iteration, household archaeology was developed as a method to identify the smallest economic unit in a community. In particular, it allowed archaeologists to identify how many buildings and what types of human groupings made up a household unit, and what activities that unit engaged in cooperatively (e.g., Santley and Hirth 1993; see chapter 7). While the study of the socioeconomic unit remains fundamental in the household archaeology field, archaeologists in the last several decades have used these methodologies to examine the individuals within those households, focusing on gendered labor, status and rank, and ethnic or individualized identities (e.g., Aldenderfer 1993a; Allison 1999a; Blanton 1994; Coupland and Banning 1996; Hutson 2010; Madella et al. 2013; Roth 2010; Souvatzi 2008). Household archaeology has become one of the foundations for how any prehistorian must approach the architectural remains of an ancient community.

By the late 1980s and early 1990s, the house was increasingly recognized not just as a node of economic behavior but as a symbolic container of a culture's ideologies (Steadman 1996; and see chapters 5 and 10). Peter Wilson's *The Domestication of the Human Species* (1988) traces the many changes human society embraced as it transitioned from a mainly mobile hunting and gathering species to one engaged in cultivation in more permanently settled venues. He suggests that many of the beliefs and ideologies that were previously associated with the varied landscapes traveled by mobile peoples—deeply spiritual locations, places where ancestors rested, ritual sites—

were brought into the abode through house structure, placement, layout, decoration, and other elements. Similarly, Ian Hodder, in *The Domestication of Europe* (1990), asserts that the first houses in Europe and Turkey served to divide space between the "wild out there" and the "domesticated in here." Things inside the house could be controlled, and thus critical aspects of life—economy, religious life, ancestor veneration—were brought inside to become part of the human experience that could be managed.

Other studies in the same vein argued the house was not only a symbolic container but one that shaped the behavior of its occupants. Such studies grew out of Rapoport's EBS but also drew heavily on anthropological thinking such as structuration theory by Anthony Giddens (1984) and *habitus* as discussed by Pierre Bourdieu (1977) (see chapters 5 and 9). As humans shaped their houses, so did dwelling patterns shape behavior (Kent 1990; Rapoport 1990; Steadman 2000). Employing the field of activity area research (Kent 1984), the examination of where specific tasks were accomplished and what socioeconomic or symbolic data might be gained from such knowledge, became valuable for understanding ancient social life. Archaeologists investigated the role of architecture in *structuring* behavior and ensuring the transmission of actions, ideologies, and patterns of movement, from one generation to the next. The house as symbolic container and as reproduced actions and behavior has become firmly embedded in the way archaeologists approach the study of domestic architecture (e.g., Bogucki 1999; Bradley 2005; Parker Pearson and Richards 1994; Samson 1990). A relatively recent development derived from the ideas put forward by Giddens and Bourdieu is the field now known as "agency" (Dobres and Robb 2000; Gardner 2008; Steadman and Ross 2010; and see chapter 5); architecture serves well as a tool for investigations of ancient agency (Steadman 2010, 2011).

Ruth Tringham (1991a, 1991b, 1994) plunged into the domestic architecture field with two recommendations for archaeologists: (1) she urged them to recognize the deep connection between the individuals who dwelled within a structure, and (2) she noted that some of those people were women. The lives lived by the humans became the "life history" of the house as well; what happened to the house itself may serve as a map to what happened to the people. A prime example of this interrelation between house and occupants is the "Burnt House" at her site in Eastern Europe. What if the house, rather than being consumed in an accidental fire, was intentionally burned by its owners once the head of the household died (Tringham 1991a)? Further, if those left behind were women, where did they then go to live? Tringham, among others (Hendon 1997; Nevett 1999; Spain 1992; Wright 1996), firmly installed the study of domestic architecture as a vital part of the burgeoning field of gender archaeology, which began in the late 1980s and floresced in the 1990s (Claasen and Joyce 1997; Conkey and Spector 1984; Gero and Conkey 1991; Gilchrist 1999; Wright 1996; see chapter 8). That the built environment can reveal men's and women's spaces and their associated activities, social status, attitudes, and potentially their gendered ideologies, is now a wholly accepted area of research in the archaeology of architecture (e.g., Nelson 2006).

A major area of research regarding houses, symbolism, and human behavior was launched by Claude Lévi-Strauss in his discussion of *sociétés à maisons*, or "house societies" (1987). Here the discussion returns to the symbolic, in which a dwelling—or sometimes a collection of buildings—serves as a symbolic representation of groups of people who see themselves in cooperative relationships, whether through religious, economic, kin-based, or other ties (see chapter 6). Cultural anthropologists were the first to launch extensive investigations into the relationships between the built environment and the "house society" (Carsten and Hugh-Jones 1995; Waterson 1990), but archaeologists were soon to follow with volumes that employed ethnography to inform archaeological settings (e.g., Beck 2007a; Joyce and Gillespie 2000). Many archaeologists find the pursuit of ancient house societies through architectural remains a tricky but worthwhile challenge that yields unexpected insights into ancient social life (e.g., Chesson 2003; Paz 2012).

Architectural evidence has always been a mainstay in the search for the wealthy and powerful in a community. Beginning in the 1990s, the focus was relocated from the palaces and temples to the expression of wealth, status, and power in the domestic quarter (Blanton 1994; Crown 2000; Diehl 2000a; Moore 1996a; Santley and Hirth 1993; Smith 1987; Wason 1994), and it continues to be a critical component in measuring social and economic status within a community (see chapter 9). A continuing focus on what the domestic world can reveal about the larger society, whether it consists of hamlets or cities, will be a much welcomed addition to studies on wealth, power, and status in the ancient world.

The house as shrine or site of ritual action, already raised above, is also a major area of research (see chapter 10), as so beautifully illustrated by Suzanne Blier's research in Africa (1987). In most volumes treating the archaeological study of religion, at least one, and usually several, of the chapters will offer a case study on architectural approaches to illuminating ancient beliefs (e.g., Fogelin 2008; Hayden 2003; Insoll 2004; Parker Pearson 2000; Steadman 2009; Whitehouse and Martin 2004; Whitley and Hays-Gilpin 2008). The house as seat of all critical human cultural institutions is well demonstrated by these and other studies discussed in this volume.

The house in the urban community has also grown in importance. Decades ago, archaeologists such as Elizabeth Stone (1987) and René Millon (1976) demonstrated the usefulness of examining individual houses, clusters of dwellings, and residential neighborhoods for invaluable insights into the socioeconomy, political structure, ethnic makeup, and even ideology of residents in ancient cities. Such methodologies have continued to be employed in studies on single cultures (e.g., Cahill 2002; Cooper 2006; van de Mieroop 1999; Nevett 2010; Stone and Zimansky 2004), and recently valuable cross-cultural studies have appeared (Marcus and Sabloff 2008a; Smith 2003a; Stone 2007). In addition, the dwelling's role in the organization and evolution of prehistoric communities has also been highlighted in recent years, in part initiated by Marcello Canuto and Jason Yaeger's innovative *The Archaeology of Communities* (2000; and see Ian Kuijt's study

[2000c] on the Near East). Several other more recent contributions (Bandy and Fox 2010; Birch 2013; Düring 2006) demonstrate the continuing recognition by archaeologists that communities are of houses made.

Just prior to or during the preparation of this manuscript, a number of volumes have appeared, all either exploring archaeological studies of the architectural record or including architecture as an integral element of understanding ancient humans. Julia Hendon, a major figure in the study of Mesoamerican architecture, published *Houses in a Landscape* (2010), which recognizes that house architecture is a testament to human memory and that, if studied properly, architectural remains can be read as a type of text about an ancient society. In the same vein, Dennis Tedlock and Arthur Sze's *An Archaeology of Architecture* (2013) offers a collection of photo essays about architecture and what it reveals about its inhabitants, including what they intended in the construction of their dwelling, and perhaps the steps leading to the structure's eventual abandonment. A book that has been a tremendous inspiration during the writing of this volume is *The Prehistory of Home* by Jerry Moore (2012). Frequently cited throughout this book, Moore's volume captures many of the ideas that have been locked up in my own mind during the years that my scholarship had turned to other pursuits. Wendy Ashmore's comment (on the book cover) that Moore's "wit and personality shine throughout [the volume]" is exactly on target; Moore ably illustrates the joys of studying ancient, and modern, architecture.

Although not precisely about domestic architecture, a recent interest in architectural monumentality has generated several innovative studies. James Osborne's *Approaching Monumentality in Archaeology* (2014) takes a cross-cultural look at monumentality expressed by structures in cities and more rural landscapes. Another book, edited by Richard Burger and Robert Rosenswig (2012), examines monuments, including temples, mounds, palaces, and even agricultural fields, across the American continents. The publication of a recent workshop (Furhold, Hinz, and Mischka 2012) addresses prehistoric monuments and temporality. One of the benefits of these recent investigations is that they take the study of human-fashioned monumental constructions in new directions, beyond the standard considerations of representations of power and wealth and are a welcome addition to archaeologically based studies on architecture.

Tim Ingold's *Making* (2013) highlights the intersection between archaeology and anthropology, art and architecture. He explores, through experimental archaeology and other endeavors, the creation of the most human of items—everyday utilitarian objects, shelter, and items of beauty—and gets to the heart of what it *means* to create something. Less overtly about architecture but still of great interest is Hodder's recent *Entangled* (2012), which demonstrates the intricate relationships between humans, their things (including their built environment), and spatial and temporal landscapes. A recent volume by Stella Souvatzi and Athena Hadji (2014), *Space and Time in Mediterranean Prehistory*, explores the types of concepts raised by Ingold and Hodder at prehistoric sites across the region. The book arises out of "the ever-growing interest in space and spatiality across the social sciences . . . [and] the lack in the existing literature of an explicit and balanced focus on *both* space and time" (Souvatzi and Hadji 2014: xv). Another very recent volume, *Assembling Architecture* (Bille and Sørensen 2015), takes up the concept of temporality and combines it with other investigations, including the atmospherics of architecture, and an interesting exploration of architecture that manifests as dysfunctional. These volumes, and those in preparation that have therefore unintentionally gone unrecognized here, present the myriad directions still available in the field of the archaeology of architecture. However, in reading these volumes, it becomes clear that such innovative approaches are only possible because they have been built on the foundational research offered by scholars who pioneered the field well over half a century ago.

About This Book

This book is not based on a theoretical underpinning that drives the direction of its composite chapters. I have not taken Bourdieu's *habitus*, Gidden's structuration theory, or Lévi-Straussian house societies as overarching guides, yet all are explored for their incalculable contributions to the study of domestic architecture in prehistoric settings. As the introductory section of this chapter notes, this book is meant to serve as a combined reference volume, treatise on major theoretical and methodological developments over the decades, and platform for offering a few notions particular to the present author. It would, therefore, be counterproductive to hinge all discussions on a singular theory or methodology, brilliant though it may be. The following offers a spare "thumbnail" sketch of what the reader may find in each of the succeeding nine chapters.

Discussion in this volume rarely strays far from the domestic, but chapter 2 is one of the places where this does happen. It seemed illogical to produce an entire study on domestic architecture without first exploring why and, particular to chapter 2, where humans would create a built environment in the first place. After a brief foray into the development of the landscape archaeology field, the chapter explores the *reasons* for settling more permanently, including reasons that are imminently practical or are more symbolic. Naturally, archaeologists can never be certain what factors went into the transition of mobile people into settled lifestyles, but the evidence of what people might have felt about their built environments after settlement is explored.

Chapter 3 heads off in an entirely different direction, one that would seem to be the opposite of symbolic approaches to the places in which people live, but on close examination the relationship among symbolism, logic, and clear-eyed analysis is apparent. One of the most valuable, and elusive, things houses might be able to reveal to archaeologists is a way to estimate populations of ancient communities. Attempting such estimations, however, is fraught with difficulties, which are outlined in a historical overview of the various methodologies advanced over the years. The chapter continues on into a discussion of space syntax—that is, "reading the house." Cultures embed behavior codes in how they lay out their houses and their communities; everyone in the culture understands and largely abides by those codes. Syntactical analyses of houses can reveal some of those codes to archaeologists hundreds or thousands of years later. Related to this field is that of "proxemics" discussed earlier: What boundaries and territorial markers do people build around their houses? Once a visitor is inside a house, how does he or she know what areas are off limits? How do humans create private spaces for themselves? Chapter 3 reviews archaeological methodologies designed to answer these questions.

Chapter 4 discusses cultures termed "hunter-gatherers" and then proceeds to the nomadic pastoralist lifestyle and dwellings. There were a number of challenges associated with the writing of this chapter, not the least of which was how to offer tools for finding the dwellings of mobile peoples in the archaeological record. Their structures touched the landscape so lightly that there is often nothing left to record their passing; nonetheless, methodologies are offered and the importance of the associated material culture is highlighted. This book includes seven full chapters on the types of houses settled peoples build, but only one on mobile peoples. Thus, chapter 4 is not one of the shorter chapters in the volume, but it can claim an attempt to be fairly comprehensive in its coverage.

An equally daunting task lay in chapter 5, which picks up where chapter 2 left off, with those who left the mobile lifestyle to build their first permanent homes. The chapter explores what types of houses were first built, how permanent structures offered behavioral feedback to those dwelling in them, and how houses might have altered as people settled permanently. A significant portion of the discussion in this chapter asks about the role agency and intentionality played in the construction of the earliest houses: Can we identify ancient builders' intentions? Can we divine the decisions that went into form and style of first constructions, and the subsequent redesigns? A final section on urban housing ranges far from the building of one's first permanent house. However, in the writing of this chapter, a discussion of houses in ancient cities seemed to flow from what came before it.

With chapter 6, the book turns to theories and methodologies on how to recognize some of the central cultural institutions that are often expressed in the bones of a culture's dwellings. The chapter begins by delving deeply into the concept of a "house society" as it was described by Lévi-Strauss, first exploring ethnographic examples of house societies to understand the physical versions of the social and symbolic relationships in such cultures. It then captures the largely successful efforts by archaeologists to apply house society methodology and theory to the archaeological past. It remains, in the opinion of this author, one of the most challenging research areas in the archaeology of architecture. The chapter then moves on to discuss methods that archaeologists have employed to reveal what types of marriage patterns, kinship systems, and family structures ancient residences might have housed. Kent Flannery's early work on this subject (1972), and the avalanche of studies in response to his ideas, are explored at length, along with some key case studies. The chapter underscores the complexity of these cultural institutions and that, at best, we can only hope to see the faint outline of these systems as they are expressed in the skeletons of the dwellings within which they once existed.

Household archaeology, the subject of chapter 7, has become a permanent fixture in the archaeological discipline. The origins of this field and the early methodologies offered by its founders are surveyed in the first half of the chapter. The second half follows the development of household archaeology as it stretches its boundaries beyond the focus on socioeconomy and seeks to get at the individuals who make up the "household." Methodologies and representative case studies reveal how to get at the gender, identity, status, and religious practice of those living within the household.

A book on domestic architecture would not be complete without a more extensive discussion of gender and architecture than could be undertaken in chapter 7. Chapter 8, therefore, is devoted solely to this subject and takes on the challenge of attempting to present enough of the incredibly innovative studies on gender and archaeology from the last several decades to adequately represent the rapid and satisfying growth in this field. The first major topic explored is the subject of the sexual division of labor and how to identify gendered spaces inside and outside the house in the prehistoric past. As is made patently clear throughout the volume, the associated material record is a critical component in such studies. The second topic investigates how ancient architecture might reveal the desire to segregate or seclude one sex from the other in the house or from non-household members. The final discussion in the chapter centers on how gendered status might be recognized through the domestic remains, both architectural and artifactual, in prehistoric communities.

Chapter 9, on the subject of "power," is one of the essays where the discussion broadens from the domestic and briefly delves into the public sphere. Methodologies for recognizing power and status are first surveyed, and these are then employed in the presentation of case studies that very successfully identify emerging power structures in both domestic and non-domestic buildings. The final section in the chapter explores how architecture can express the shifting sands of power: new power regimes, colonization, emulation of new and powerful neighbors. Both domestic and public structures serve as examples in this discussion as well.

The final chapter turns to religion, perhaps of greatest interest to some readers of this volume. A few non-domestic, or at least seemingly non-domestic, structures are explored in chapter 10. Most of the discussion, however, centers on religion inside, near to, and embedded within the house. Methodologies for recognizing the practice of ancestor veneration fit well into this chapter. The practice of household ritual, briefly raised in chapter 7, is more fully explored here. The chapter would not be complete without exploration of the symbolic house, that is, the house that expresses a culture's cosmology, either in part or in its entirety. The critical role of ethnography in this discussion is made clear. The decision to put the chapter on religion last was easy to make. In many ways, the discussion of this most complicated of the cultural institutions draws on every topic raised in the previous chapters: marriage, kinship, family, economy, gendered behavior, ethnicity, and so many other behaviors encoded in human culture. It is an appropriate capstone in a book on the human built environment.

Sadly—or more accurately, happily—even as this manuscript is sent off to the printer, it is already out of date. The archaeology of architecture field is on a dynamic, upward swing, and the number of innovative studies undertaken increases with every field season. What is definitely an unhappy state of affairs is that this volume will not have captured all such studies that have already been produced. In so many places in the world, by so many researchers, the house has formed a vital component in understanding an ancient society. It is my hope that those studies not included here are highlighted in some of the very recent and notable volumes cited above and in those yet to come. There is no doubt that a book such as this one, undertaken in two decades' time, will require two, even three, volumes to even approach being a complete review of the literature. That is the sign of a robust and dynamic field.

Section I

Initial Foundations: Theories and Methodologies in the Archaeology of Architecture

Chapter 2
Choice Locations: The Power and Meaning of (First) Place(s)

There are places on the earth that have the capacity to evoke powerful feelings in the humans who visit them. Some places are in natural form, while others have been transformed by the creation of human-built structures. The feelings, emotions, and sentiments humans feel when visiting or dwelling in these places might be generated entirely by the humans themselves; many believe, however, that the power actually resides in the places. I have experienced some powerful feelings when visiting remarkable places across the earth. Some years ago in Australia, I visited Uluru; seeing the remarkable natural monolith, sacred to a number of Australian Aboriginal cultures, was a wonderful experience. The next day, I went to a nearby location called Kata Juta (Figure 2.1). While Uluru was spectacular, it was Kata Juta that held my fascination. It was all I could do not to abandon the group I was with and run into the beautiful rock formations and wander the paths between them. Kata Juta was the first natural place, aside from the desert valley where I grew up, to elicit a visceral reaction. Human creations such as the Taj Mahal and Stonehenge (to which my powerful response, as a cynical archaeology student, was a complete surprise) induced reactions that are due, perhaps, to the beauty of the structures, or the awe-inspiring labor necessary to construct them. One factor that cannot be discounted is the influence a natural place may have had on humans *prior to* the creation of any human-built form upon it. Humans choose to build their homes and communities in places that make strategic sense; however, the power and vitality of certain locations may also play a role in the human choice to place their abodes upon them.

Archaeology of Domestic Architecture and the Human Use of Space, by Sharon R. Steadman, 25–38.

Figure 2.1: Photo of Kata Juta, near Uluru, in Australia's Red Center (photo by the author).

This chapter explores those factors that may have drawn humans to specific places upon which they constructed their dwellings. The focus here is not on the dwellings themselves; it is left to the remaining chapters of this volume to treat the built environment. Rather, here the aim is to examine the unbuilt landscape that drew its first permanent inhabitants. An early and stolidly Western perspective saw the uninhabited landscape as a "wild" and even "unformed" space in the human perspective, capable of becoming a meaningful "place" only after human activity on it (David and Wilson 2002; Terrell and Hart 2008; Thomas 2008). More recent and broadened perspectives have acknowledged that the landscape can be imbued with meaning long before the human alteration of it (Casey 1996, 2008; Heidegger 2008; Thomas 2008). It is this latter perspective that drives the present chapter. While acknowledging that pragmatic choices must be made when choosing a place at which significant time will be spent, there are other factors that may have led past humans to choose one place over another. Three subjects are briefly explored here: the practicalities associated with settlement locations, the significance of ancestral places, and the power of sacred space. These may offer a starting point for anyone attempting to divine the motivation behind the prehistoric human agency of spatial choices.

First Explorations: The Archaeology of Landscape

"First explorations" in part refers to the importance of acknowledging that structures rest in a landscape and thus any study of the built environment should include an exploration of the landscape around it. A second meaning relates more directly to prehistory, referring to when people first considered places within the landscape for more permanent settlement. The aim of this chapter, the only one to consider "space" and "place" absent of human construction, is to explore pragmatic and symbolic factors that may have drawn the first settlers to a location. While elements that make locational choices imminently practical may be quite visible in the landscape, symbolic aspects may not be as easily discernable by the present-day archaeologist. For instance, since "landscape, like 'beauty,' is in the mind of the beholder" (Taçon 1999: 34), it is almost impossible to evaluate the role "beauty" may have played in settlement location; nonetheless, the power of a beautiful landscape is worth consideration when tracking the motivations for prehistoric settlement. Today, of course, one pays a premium for a "beautiful view" of landscape; might this view have appealed to humans long past as well? For instance, ancient settlers often chose to pitch their homes on a rise; such a location affords the ability to more easily evaluate who might be approaching and also avoids settlement on valuable arable or pastureland. In addition to these very practical concerns, the more attractive view available to those settling on higher elevations might have been an added attraction, if not the most vital characteristic. While we might never be able to discern what constituted a "beautiful landscape" for a prehistoric culture, we might be wise to consider that a consistent placement of settlements in view of water, or mountains, or other identifiable topographic feature may have resulted not only from pragmatic or cosmological concerns but also from a desire to awake each day to a magnificent scene.

Beyond notions of beauty, other seemingly unfathomable ancient perspectives are those deriving from the symbolic meaning the landscape may have held for earliest settlers. Here one delves into the field of cognitive archaeology (Flannery and Marcus 1998, first published a few years earlier) and attempts to tap into the "mental things" (Hill 1994: 83) of ancient peoples. For instance, it might be useful to place "mental things" into categories termed "places of power" and "shrines of the land" (Scarre 2008, drawing on Colson 1997), the former referring to natural (i.e., "unbuilt") locations where a spiritual essence resides, while "shrines of the land" refers more specifically to locations dedicated to ancestors (both real and fictive). Before addressing the mental things that affected choices in a landscape, it is useful to consider archaeological approaches to landscape analysis.

Attempting to reveal ancient motivations for where people settled and why would not be possible without the development of landscape archaeology over the last several decades (see Anschuetz, Wilshusen, and Scheick 2001; Blake 2007; David and Thomas 2008a; Knapp 1997 for an overview). The first robust archaeological foray into landscape studies was primarily from a land-use perspective in what became a productive effort to identify links between economically based activities and settled environments (e.g., Clarke 1977; Higgs 1975; Hodder and Orton 1976; Vita-Finzi 1978; Willey 1956). From these studies came approaches now standard in archaeological literature such as site-catchment analysis, nearest neighbor analysis, studies on central place theory heavily used in the Aegean and the Middle East, and a variety of explorations of land use employing quantitative spatial methods (Fish and Kowalewski 1990; Kroll and Price 1991; Renfrew and Cherry 1986; Rowlands, Larsen, and Kristiansen 1987). The intersection of settlement analysis and intrasite/intersite analysis, examining not just economic but political structure, also became an important element in archaeological landscape studies (Adams 1965, 1981; Blanton 1978; Chang 1968; Sanders, Parsons, and Santley 1979). The development of geographical information systems (GIS), which initially provided methods for the interpretation of data acquired by human means, such as survey (e.g., Aldenderfer and Maschner 1996; Allen, Green, and Zubrow 1990; Kvamme 1999; Lock and Stancic 1995; Wheatley and Gillings 2002), has today become an analytical method in and of itself, sometimes even eliminating the need for humans to set foot in the region (e.g., Kantner 2008; Lock 2000; Menze, Ur, and Sherratt 2006; Salisbury and Keeler 2007; Ur 2003; Wilkinson 2003).

Cognitive elements inherent in the ancient landscape became central to significant recent research in phenomenology, which focused on the role of cosmology in landscape studies (Ashmore and Knapp 1999; Barrett, Bradley, and Green 1991; Bender 1995; Bradley 1993; Carmichael et al. 1994; Thomas 1996; Tilley 1994, 2009; Ucko and Layton 1999). As Thomas notes, "over the last 15 years or so, phenomenological thought has come to exercise a considerable influence over the way that archaeologists address past landscapes" (2008: 300). The robust number of research methods on landscape studies now available to archaeologists is sufficiently extensive to occasion a need for compendia on this subject (e.g., Chapman 2006; David and Thomas 2008b; Robertson et al. 2006). It is by using these approaches that archaeologists can begin to traverse the landscape with a mind open to both the practical matters that concerned the ancient inhabitants and the intangible attitudes, emotions, and beliefs that the landscape evoked in them.

Earliest Settlements: Practical Matters

When first examining a landscape for potential settlement, what may have been the priorities of prehistoric peoples? As modern archaeologists, we try to understand ancient choices by theorizing that would-be settlers may have undertaken an inventory of pertinent factors not so dissimilar to the present-day family engaged in house hunting. Such priorities would include good arable land (i.e., grocery stores today), a safe neighborhood, and perhaps access to communication routes (or today, good roads to workplaces). Fortunately, priorities such as these are archaeologically visible and have thus formed the basis of significant ecologically based landscape approaches to understanding early human settlement (e.g., Binford 1982; Butzer 1964, 1982; Higgs 1975). Site catchment analyses have allowed archaeologists to answer questions about land-use and subsistence patterns of early inhabitants and to roughly calculate models for site

Figure 2.2: Photo of the author's site, Çadır Höyük, in central Turkey; a human-produced lake is in the background (photo by the author).

distributions across given landscapes (Joachim 1988; Johnson 1977; Mueller 1975; Vita-Finzi 1978). Such analyses have become basic tenets in prehistoric research. Archaeologists automatically assess what physical characteristics in the landscape might have benefited the residents at prehistoric sites in the region.

A case in point is my own site of Çadır Höyük on the north central Anatolian plateau. The earliest occupation documented thus far dates to the Middle Chalcolithic (ca. 5200 BCE); residents were engaged in farming and animal husbandry/herding (Arbuckle 2009). Çadır today rests on the shores of a dam-produced lake (Figure 2.2). In antiquity, a river flowed past the site and was occasionally fierce enough to flood the lower reaches of the settlement (C. Kuzucuoğlu, personal communication). In addition, at least one spring, just north of the site, existed in the classical period; today there are several springs within easy walking distance (one is less than 1 km away, and two more are inside 2 km). Fresh water was likely in abundance for the earliest settlers at Çadır Höyük. The surrounding landscape must have also pleased inhabitants; today the site is surrounded, literally, by agricultural fields (see Figure 2.2). Field stubble and fallow fields provide ample food for small herds of cattle, sheep, and goat, and a similar situation likely existed in the ancient landscape as well.

Beyond subsistence necessities, there are other prerequisites for settlement in a landscape: defensibility and accessibility, the latter referring to possible interest in trade interaction. The ancient Puebloans (Kantner 2004; Lekson 2007), along with the Maori (Davidson 1984) and the Urartians (Zimansky 1998), are good examples of peoples choosing strategic locations for settlement that would be advantageous in the event of attack; each culture situated its communities in places that presented the best defensive position while also giving them access to water and cultivable land. The Puebloans also placed their settlements at the center of important trade routes. Çadır once again serves as a good example of these prerequisites for settlement location. The Çadır mound stands at a height of over 30 m, but its impressive profile on the landscape stems not only from its extensive strata of occupation debris but from the fact that the earliest residents (at least in the later sixth millennium BCE) chose to settle on a natural rise on the landscape where the bedrock heaves up above the floodplain. The practical aspects of such a choice are obvious: avoidance of damaging spring floods and accentuated visibility across the landscape to keep track of expected (herding and farming) activities as well as the unexpected (approaching strangers). During the Late Chalcolithic occupation (ca. 3800–3000 BCE), Çadır rested at the center of a group of smaller sites that may have relied on Çadır for the distribution of trade goods and other materials (Steadman, McMahon, and Ross 2007). This would suggest that trade networks were either already existent or were quickly developed in the Chalcolithic of the region. Çadır Höyük, then, is a prime example of early inhabitants taking into account all the necessary practicalities in a landscape when making their initial settlement choice. Though these attractive and practical characteristics of the landscape were clearly attestable, I continue to wonder whether there wasn't something more in that landscape that attracted the first residents: possibly the high peak visible from the site, or perhaps the call of a sacred place utterly invisible to me (Steadman 2005). It is these thoughts that prompt the remainder of this chapter.

Settling the Sacred Landscape

Many pursuing the field of landscape archaeology have recognized that the surrounding environment meant far more to the ancient mind than just a place within which one might hunt, gather, drink fresh water, and rest. Tim Ingold notes that "through living in it, the landscape becomes a part of us, just as we are a part of it" (1993: 154). The key is to discern what the landscape meant to those living in it some thousands of years before. In particular, what constituted a "sacred" landscape, and how might it have figured into ancient settlement patterns?

The archaeologist seeking a past culture's notion of sacred space must start with the known—that is, what was demonstrably sacred to that culture. The ethnographic record can be a reliable source for this type of research. An excellent example of a culture that views itself as "part of the landscape" is the Ndee Athabascan speakers of the American Southwest. The Ndee do not separate their humanness from the land they inhabit (Basso 1996a, 1996b; Welch 2009).

Basso's ethnographic research provides detailed understanding of how the Ndee see themselves as inextricably linked to the land in which they dwell. Welch notes that the "Ndee are unwilling to think of themselves, their culture, or their history or future without reference to land" (2009: 151). Though the Ndee are now long settled, their connection to their landscape encourages one to imagine what a previously mobile Ndee society might have considered important with regard to the location of their first dwelling. Might the sacred places have guided placement of their first dwellings, whether near, or appropriately far, from sacred locations?

Similarly, one need look no further than Australian Aboriginal attitudes to the landscape. In traditional Australian Aboriginal thinking, there is no separation between land, kinship, inheritance, or religion (Smith 1999: 193). In the "Dreamtime" belief system, the landscape was created by ancestors and supernatural beings to whom Aboriginals have individualized connections and often a totemic relationship. Depending on one's birthplace or where certain important events occurred in a lifetime, as well as the kinship ties of one's parents, certain places are extremely sacred to that individual; they are the sites of ritual performances and are often decorated with rock art. For these reasons, though traditionally mobile hunter-gatherers, Australian Aboriginals tend to remain in the vicinity of these sacred places, since the landscape itself becomes an element of their material culture (Fullagar and Head 1999). Dreamtime tracks explain and describe the world, containing myths that recount the creation of a water source, an unusual rock formation, or some other important node on the landscape (Head 1993; Layton 1999; Taçon 1999). A recent study finds that "[f]or [Aboriginals] 'country' is spoken about in the same way that people talk about their living human relatives" (Bradley 2008: 634); the same study notes that not just the earth itself, but the material culture in it, such as a stone tool, is also considered a kin relative. While the subject of "ancestral places" in the landscape is explored more fully below, the Australian Aboriginal entwinement with their landscape serves to illustrate notions of a sacred landscape. Had organic sedentism among Aboriginals developed prior to, or instead of, European colonization, the placement of initial semi-permanent dwellings might well have been guided by attachment to sacred (ancestral) places (e.g., Fullagar and Head 1999).

Both of the examples above stem from knowledge archaeologists have gained from living informants. Mapping the sacred landscape of a prehistoric culture presents a host of possibly insurmountable obstacles. R. J. Nash (1997) argues that some landscapes are "archetypal" in that certain topographies mapped themselves on the human psyche: humans are, in a way, hardwired to find certain landscapes powerful and even frightening. One possible place to start is with landscapes featuring what Taçon calls "common features which make them recognizably special, sacred, or sublime" regardless of cultural or temporal affiliation (1999: 34). He and other scholars have found that certain landscape features seemingly never fail to evoke powerful feelings in those who call the region their home. These features are notable not just to ancient inhabitants but to those visiting the landscapes today. Places with naturally flowing waters such as streams and springs are often viewed as possessing power (Crumley 1999; Taçon 1999), as are forests, stands of trees, or areas of specialized vegetation, or indeed where such areas intersect (Carmichael 1994; Parker Pearson, Ramilsonina, and Retsihisatse 1999; Taçon 1999). Other categories of locations with features that capture attention are places with unusual rock formations or that offer a view from some type of natural rise or high place (Theodoratus and LaPena 1994). Finally, it is perhaps caves and mountains, including volcanoes, that evoke the most powerful responses (Brady and Ashmore 1999; Crumley 1999; Lee 2002; Saunders 1994; Taçon 1999; Torrence 2008). It is upon, near, or within sight of these natural features that archaeologists might likely find evidence of ancient human activity; the archaeological record offers several excellent examples of human habitation near caves and/or mountains with associated evidence that they were viewed as "sacred space" by the landscape's ancient inhabitants.

The Hohokam site of Snaketown, near Gila Butte in Arizona illustrates the importance of mountains in the cosmology of a culture and the influence such natural features have on settlement patterns. The Hohokam (ca. CE 800–1150) may well have immigrated from Mesoamerica prior to their new settlements in Arizona (e.g., Gumerman 1991; Haury 1976; see Crown and Judge 1991 for discussion) where they established irrigation agriculture, growing maize, beans, and tobacco, among other crops. It was while they were in Mesoamerica that the Hohokam may have adopted the ballcourt ceremonial system, and then subsequently transported it to their new homeland in the Gila River Valley (Whittlesey 2009). Besides the ballcourt system, the Hohokam may have also brought the Mesoamerican focus on sacred places in the landscape, the most important of which may have been the mountain (Whittlesey 2009).

In Mesoamerican belief, mountains were containers of essential things such as maize and water, both of which would also have been essential to the agricultural Hohokam. Snaketown, the largest of the Hohokam settlements, is located 5 km from Gila Butte, which stands approximately 150 m above the river valley; the Snaketown fields lay across the landscape between town and butte, and the canal that irrigated these fields drew water from the base of Gila Butte, making it a "container of water" (Whittlesey 2009). Gila Butte seems to have held multidimensional meaning for the Hohokam. For instance, schist from the butte was used as a temper in Hohokam pottery, although it offers no practical or technological properties and the glittering surface it created was often covered in paint. It was, apparently, the fact that it came from Gila Butte that made the schist important, rather than any functionality it imparted. Besides being a "container" of water, the butte may have also been considered a source of rain, as were mountains in Mesoamerican belief systems. Thus, for the Hohokam, "as an agricultural people wholly invested in the cultivation of a suite of plant food staples, rain would have been considered the source of life itself. Surely, it focused Hohokam religion and ritual . . . [and the] mountain symbolized rain and clouds to the Hohokam" (Whittlesey 2009: 87–88). Hohokam people migrated northward roughly 1,200 years ago. It is not difficult to imagine that the landscape, and particularly Gila Butte, guided their initial settlement choice. Snaketown exemplifies a place where a prehistoric people settled a particular landscape based on eminently practical concerns—readily available land and water—but also because an easily identifiable sacred place, Gila Butte, testified to the certain location of their new home.

A somewhat similar circumstance can be found half a world away in the mountainous regions that stretch from Afghanistan to northern China and Korea. Gina Barnes (1999) describes a three-stage evolution of sacred mountainous landscapes. In two case studies of locales in northeast China and Korea, she notes that the mountains had long been considered sacred in ancient Chinese folk beliefs (Barnes 1999: 104, 117). With the establishment of Buddhism, these sacred places became sites where images of Buddha were carved into rock faces, thereby transforming the landscape from a natural state to one inscribed by humans and substantiating sacrality visually. In both of her case studies, this progression led to the building of Buddhist temples on these mountainsides, near the statues and carvings of Buddha (Barnes 1999: 106–11). Barnes's work illustrates the principle of places—in this case, mountains—long believed to be sacred eventually becoming marked as such by human constructions.

The same phenomenon can be found in other places across the world. A number of researchers have argued that the spectacular megaliths built on the landscapes of Britain and Western Europe were originally natural (unbuilt) places held as sacred by hunter-gatherers millennia earlier (Allen and Gardiner 2002; Barrett 1999; Bradley 1993); further, the eventual building materials may themselves have also come from sacred locales (Scarre 2008). John Barrett makes the following argument regarding the existence of long-held sacred places: "[T]he world as it already existed will always have been imbued with meanings and have been used as a background of reference against which contemporary acts, including monument building, were played out" (1999: 155). One particular type of sacred landscape that has a ubiquitous presence in the present and likely the past is that inhabited by the ancestors.

Settling with Family: Ancestral Landscapes

One of the most powerful threads connecting the living to a particular place is the belief that ancestors inhabit that place. Ancestral places are selected for a closer look here because they constitute perhaps the most common category of sacred ties to the landscape. Such ties, what Chris Scarre and others refer to as "shrines of the land," manifest themselves in material remnants such as subterranean burials and the placement of altars or other ritual items such as statuary. Prior to these built signifiers, ties to place may have been represented by symbolic cues in the natural landscape. It is those materially invisible relationships to the land that may have been at the root of some of the earliest settlements in any given region of the world.

From the Ethnographic Records

Ethnographic examples offer us insight into the power the ancestral landscape has over the living. A return to Aboriginal Australia personifies this perfectly. Drawing on Lester Hiatt and Rhys Jones (1988; Jones 1991), Lesley Head explains that Australian

Aboriginal cultures view the landscape as inhabited equally by humans and ancestral beings (1993: 489; see also Layton 1999). Australian landscapes are strewn with meaningful places, created and built in the Dreamtime belief system that describes the creation of every inch of the continent. The supernatural actors, many of them totemic ancestors to particular kin/clan groups, were responsible for the creation of those places (David 2002; Smith 1999; Tilley 1994: 37–54). A walk with an Aboriginal across the landscape will result in the identification of many places inhabited by his or her totemic ancestor as recounted in a Dreamtime myth (Jackson 1995). In this way, Aboriginals create a "socialized landscape" that is everywhere "imbued with ancestral associations" (Smith 1999:193). Archaeologists can identify some places of particular significance by the rock art placed there; lacking the painted or etched landscape, however, the deep Aboriginal tie with particular places is wholly unrecognizable archaeologically.

Employing the premise that certain places exerted power over a particular kin group, Head and colleague Richard Fullagar compared "a particular Dreaming story from the Keep River region of northwestern Australia with the archaeological record from the Jinmium rockshelter in the same region" and suggest that "while the antiquity of the story can never be known, the antiquity of the mapped landscapes, and of perceived links with specific places, can be traced over thousands of years" (1999: 322). At the time of colonization, the vast majority of Australian Aboriginal peoples lived highly mobile lives, constructing only the most temporary of bush camps. As already observed, many remaining Aboriginals are now "settled" in today's Australia, though the sedentization process was not an organic one; if unaltered Aboriginal cultures had transitioned to more permanent settlements according to their own needs, it seems inescapable that the location of important ancestral histories would have had a significant impact on the placement of more permanent residential sites.

There are many examples of living cultures whose settlement location was indeed dictated by ancestral ties to the land. On the Melanesian island of Kanaky (New Caledonia), pre-contact Kanaks traced their lineages back to early clan ancestors who symbolically resided in earthen mounds located at the center of ancient settlements (Bensa and Leblic 2000). Kanaks, though today often dwelling in a village distant from an ancestral mound, trace their lineage spatially through the series of village mounds near which clan members have lived. An interesting variant on this model is found among the pastoralist Tandoy of Madagascar. Their oral history includes their original *arrival* into the Andoy region of the island, perhaps in the 16th century CE, and the establishment of original ancestral villages by major clan groups; ancestral tombs consist of elaborate stone constructions visible from some distance away (Parker Pearson, Ramilsonina, and Retsihisatse 1999). Since the Tandoy are highly mobile, they are today living some distance from their ancestral locations, and archaeology suggests that their oral tradition sometimes records not the original and more distant location of the original village but a second or third iteration closer to their present location (Parker Pearson, Ramilsonina, and Retsihisatse 1999: 401). The Tandoy examples illustrate not only the creation of kin-related ties to the land but that these can be lost even to present-day oral traditions.

The connection to ancestral origins in a landscape is perhaps even more clearly articulated in the Hopi culture of the American Southwest. Hopi religious tradition recounts that the first ancestors emerged onto the earth and met the god Máasaw (guardian of the earth) in what is known today as the Grand Canyon. After demonstrating their fealty to the principle of stewardship of the earth, the Hopi ancestors migrated to their traditional homelands on the mesas (Kuwanwisiwma and Ferguson 2009). The lands that the Hopi received from Máasaw are marked by Hopi "footprints" of past Hopi habitation (*Ang Kuktota*), which include petroglyphs, ancient Puebloan villages, and ancient burial grounds (all now archaeological sites), creating an unbroken tether between the living Hopi and their ancestral lands given to them by divine right (Kuwanwisiwma and Ferguson 2009: 92–97).

The ethnographic examples noted here exemplify only a few of the hundreds, or thousands, of cultures that have a deep-seated connection to an ancestral landscape. They also illustrate the range of physical evidence created by such relationships. While Australian Aboriginal rock art is quite famous, the majority of sacred and totemic locations in Dreamtime tracks are not marked in this way, consigning the myths and ancestors to archaeological invisibility. Kanak ancestral mounds might hint at the presence of sacred space, but more specific identification of their meanings might be difficult hundreds or thousands of years after their creation. Only among the Hopi are there any significant archaeological signs to indicate that specific spaces were sacred to the culture that marked or created them. The next section offers some archaeological success stories regarding the ancient ancestral landscape.

Identifying Ancestral Landscapes Archaeologically

Identifying the ancestral component in a landscape that first drew settlers would seem an impossibility, and so it may be. As the previous section demonstrated, however, there are archaeological indicators that can alert researchers to the possibility of sacred ancestral homelands. Some of the most useful sets of evidence are skeletal remains and burial locations, a subject discussed in more detail in chapter 10. A brief look here at evidence in archaeological settings offers some examples of how archaeologists have identified sacred ancestral first settlement locations.

The ancient people of Khok Phanom Di were Neolithic hunter-gatherers (ca. 2000–1500 BCE) who occupied an estuary region south of the Phraya River on the Gulf of Thailand. When they first settled the area, the estuary offered resources that included both freshwater fish and saltwater shellfish, while the mangrove and land forests provided plentiful prey (2002a: 56–78). The people of Khok Phanom Di buried their dead beneath their domestic areas; burials were distributed in clusters that may reflect kin groups, and were supplied with burial goods (for details on mortuary ritual, see Higham 2002a: 56–111; Steadman 2009: 226–31). For five centuries, Khok Phanom Di peoples remained persistently in place, even when environmental conditions altered (a decrease in marine and mangrove resources) and forced a change in their subsistence strategies. Between 2500 and 2000 BCE, rice cultivation and early farming settlements began to be established across Southeast Asia (Higham 2004). Most farming settlements were located inland, where rice cultivation strategies were more easily accomplished. The environment around Khok Phanom Di was not conducive to rice cultivation, and thus the residents established trade relationships with inland communities to acquire the quickly ubiquitous staple (Higham 2002a: 77).

The first Neolithic inhabitants were almost certainly drawn to the estuary because of its abundant resources. It is impossible to assess whether they were also drawn there because their ancestors, at least symbolically, inhabited that same place. Archaeology establishes, however, that after Khok Phanom Di was settled, kin (ancestors?) were buried there, perhaps reinforcing the symbolic importance of the region as one belonging to the ancestors and the living residents. Khok Phanom Di people remained in their estuary for the next five centuries, even when environmental conditions created less favorable resource availability; they remained even though rice cultivation was impossible in their environmental zone. The people in this location, therefore, have offered us "a site which documents interaction between a community of hunter-gatherers with deep ancestral roots in the rich, warm estuarine habitat of Southeast Asia" (Higham 2002a: 78). Whether it was ancestors that first drew people to Khok Phanom Di, it was quite possibly ancestors that kept them there through thick and thin.

In the mid-continental Illinois Valley region of the United States, the hunter-gatherers of the Middle Archaic period (ca. 6000–2500 BCE) constructed earthen burial mounds on the landscape (Buikstra and Charles 1999). This is also the period when there was a trend toward increasing sedentization, with more permanent settlements emerging in the Early and Middle Woodland periods (ca. 1000 BCE–CE 400). These valley residents built mounds that housed their dead in two primary locations: on hilltop bluffs above the river valley, and on sand ridges in the floodplain near the river (Buikstra and Charles 1999). The later Mississippian culture centers such as Cahokia (ca. CE 750–400) constructed built environments reflecting a multilayered cosmology that included layers above and below the middle level occupied by humans (Emerson 1997a; and see chapter 10). For example, the layered platforms of Monk's Mound at Cahokia may have mirrored this cosmology (Emerson and Pauketat 2008; Pauketat 2004). The cosmology itself may have been represented several thousand years earlier in the locational placement of Middle Archaic burial mounds located at high and low points. Mobile residents may have viewed their landscape as one in which certain points offered access to sacred worlds above and below, navigable by the ancestors who would provide protection to those remaining in the human layer. Sand ridge locations might mark the point where ancestors could access the underworld through water-borne passages, while burials on high bluff mounds, at the "liminal zones between earth and sky," offered passage to layers above (Buikstra and Charles 1999: 212). Earliest settlement choices in mid-continental North America were certainly dictated by economic concerns such as desirable cultivable land, but ancient ties to ancestral access nodes likely played an important role in shaping eventual settlement across the landscape.

Ancestral connections to place would explain settlement patterns at Abu Hureyra, in Syria. Abu Hureyra 1 was inhabited ca. 9500–8000 BCE by a population engaged in the cultivation and domestication of plants (Moore, Hillman, and Legge 2000). Although still somewhat mobile, the inhabitants of Abu Hureyra 1 appear to have spent a large portion of the year at the site where migrating gazelle herds and other fauna could be found and where the Euphrates River, along with the intersection of river valley and forest, offered a variety of easily obtainable subsistence items. While human remains were found in association with the Abu Hureyra 1 phases, burial methods and mortuary ritual were not clearly evident. After Abu Hureyra was largely abandoned (due to changing environmental conditions), the site lay unoccupied for a little more than 500 years until inhabitants resettled it in ca. 7400 BCE and remained there for close to 2,500 years (Moore, Hillman, and Legge 2000: 251–59). Although the Abu Hureyra 2 residents built far better houses than their predecessors, and half a millennium had passed between occupations, elements of the material culture suggested that there was a "degree of cultural continuity" stretching from the earlier to the later occupation (Moore, Hillman, and Legge 2000: 182). The Abu Hureyra 2 inhabitants practiced interment of the dead, usually under house floors or in open spaces near the houses. Such burial practices, including specialized treatment of the skulls, have been found at numerous Neolithic Levantine sites including Jericho, Ain Ghazal, and Nahal Hemar. Many scholars have interpreted such behaviors as reflecting the practice of ancestor veneration (for discussion and references, see Kuijt 2000a, 2000b; Kuijt and Chesson 2005; Steadman 2005; and see chapter 10). Did the Abu Hureyra 1 inhabitants create an ancestral place (or, alternatively, settle on one that was already ancestral)? When Abu Hureyra 2 residents settled there, possibly including members who had descended from the original occupants, did they believe they were settling on ground long inhabited by ancestral kin? The rich environmental attributes of Epipalaeolithic Abu Hureyra 1 and a newly favorable climate at the beginning of Abu Hureyra 2 are likely the primary reasons for the two settlements at the site, but the cognitive approach minimally presented here adds a further dimension for understanding the locational choices made by the region's earliest inhabitants.

While compelling, the evidence presented in this section cannot come close to proving the ancestral connection to these first human settlement locations. Such, however, is the fate of archaeology: what is inferred and subsequently offered as interpretation almost always remains in the realm of informed supposition.

Conclusion: Landscapes Untouched

Dozens of topics have been left untouched in this chapter, as a quick glance through Bruno David and Julian Thomas's excellent handbook on archaeological landscapes (2008a) will show. Territoriality may have played an enormous role in determining initial settlement strategies (e.g., Greverus 1976; Sack 1986; Zedeño 2008), ranging from defining traditional hunting grounds in the Palaeolithic (Geneste, Castel, and Chadelle 2008) to delineating lands designated for farming versus pastoralism among Neolithic settlements (Bar-Yosef 2008). In defining ancient territories and boundaries, archaeologists *may* have the luxury of ancient markers extant in the present day (e.g., cairns, rock art, even later inscriptions proclaiming the control of ancient territories). Related to territoriality, but perhaps even more difficult to access archaeologically, is the ethnic landscape: "Ethnic landscapes are spatial and temporal constructs defined by communities whose members create and manipulate material culture and symbols to signify ethnic or cultural boundaries based on customs and shared modes of thought" (Anschuetz, Wilshusen, and Scheick 2001: 180). A number of archaeologists have developed models to successfully identify ethnic landscapes (Lightfoot and Martinez 1995; Stark 1998; Zedeño 1997), and these have proven extremely productive for understanding the why and where of early settlements. Territoriality and ethnicity are only two of many factors, in addition to the sacred landscape, that may have shaped final ancient choices for permanent homes. The following chapters drill down to the "post-choice" sequence of human habitation of the landscape, to the built enjoinment and what we might learn about ancient culture from its architectural remnants.

However, it is essential to remember that under, around, and even above every brick, stone, or wooden foundation is a landscape that certainly represented deeply felt meaning to the ancient residents who settled upon it.

Chapter 3

Reading the House: Populations, Proxemics, and the Syntax of Space

The term "syntax" is most often used in contexts that involve grammatical issues, but as this chapter illustrates, there is a syntax to space that allows anthropologists and archaeologists to "read" a house as if it were a text. The methodologies discussed here offer tools to archaeologists who seek to use the house as a descriptive text for ancient society. It might have been more straightforward to title this chapter "Spatial Analysis," since that is precisely what the methods discussed here outline. However, as Robin Boast and Eugenia Yiannouli note (1986: 136), "there exist a wide range and diversity of techniques, methods of analysis, theoretical assumptions, interpretive issues, and other beliefs" under the heading of "spatial studies." The term "spatial analysis" means, for many, the study of artifact distribution at a site and what we might gain from the careful documentation of material culture analysis in its spatial context (e.g., Blankholm 1991; Hietala 1984; Hodder and Orton 1976; Kroll and Price 1991; Rossignol and Wandsnider 1992). However, the study of the architectural form and what it can reveal about past, or present, societal structure also falls neatly into the area of "spatial analysis" (Fairclough 1992).

The success of spatial analysis models lies partially in their reliance on Giddens's structuration theory (1984)—that is, the belief that space and its associated built environment are structured according to behavioral codes passed from one generation to the next. Also underlying architectural spatial analysis is Bourdieu's *habitus* (1977), or the learned behavior everyone acquires, unconsciously, within their culture. Structuration theory and interpretations employing *habitus* see residences built within certain

Archaeology of Domestic Architecture and the Human Use of Space, by Sharon R. Steadman, 39–66.

guidelines of accepted behavior; spatial organization would be at least partially predictable archaeologically once basic tenets of the culture were understood. Data such as how many people occupied a house (population estimation studies), what certain built structures might signify symbolically within a culture (semiotics), and privacy needs and boundary control within a culture (proxemics and access analysis) can be derived using these contextualized models.

Such models have been criticized in part for their inherently "structured" nature. Leach (1976, 1978), for instance, argues that an archaeological analysis of space is necessarily sterile and unable to account for social relationships and symbolic meanings that define those spaces. Another area of research, agency theory (e.g., Barrett 2001; Dobres 2000; Dornan 2002; Gardner 2004; Kovacik 2002; Robb 1999a; Steadman and Ross 2010), might also find flaws in some of the interpretive models discussed here. Agency sees individuals within a culture behaving according to how they understand their universe to operate; they make decisions within the context of their world view with expectations of what outcomes will likely result (see chapter 5). Beyond models offered by Giddens and Bourdieu, agency studies also recognize that decisions sometimes yield surprising results; alternatively, agents may intentionally defy cultural norms to achieve a unique outcome (e.g., Steadman 2010).

It is precisely *because* many models track "expected" behavior with regard to architectural renderings that the unusual is often observable in the archaeological record, though many of the cognitive aspects of the built environment—symbolic meanings, emotional reactions to space—are irretrievably lost. As will be seen in some of the case studies presented, the accidental or intended radical outcomes of architectural decisions made by individual or group agents in ancient cultures have indeed been recognized by archaeologists, and the societal alterations signified by those outcomes have become part of the overall interpretation of the (changing) built environment. Finally, the absolute necessity of consulting the ethnographic record is made clear in the following discussions.

How Many People? Estimating Ancient Populations

Archaeologists are usually quite interested in determining how many people once occupied the settlement undergoing excavation. On first review, it might seem that estimating an ancient population is one of the easier undertakings in archaeology, but the last 50 years of research suggests otherwise. This section offers a brief historical review of archaeological methods for population estimation.

A History of Archaeological Demography and Population Estimation

The 1970s saw the emergence of several books on archaeological demography (Cook 1972; Drake 1974; Zubrow 1976; followed by Hassan 1981), accompanied by a number of articles that are discussed below. The message made clear in all these studies was that population estimates and growth trends were exceedingly difficult to assess for the prehistoric past. Methods employed by archaeologists included mortuary data, material accumulation studies, ceramic distribution densities, and of course, architectural remains (Kolb 1985: 582). It is the last of these that forms the basis of the following discussion.

The 1960s and 1970s

In the early 1960s, a three-page article by Raoul Naroll (1962) kicked off the archaeological discussion centered on prehistoric population estimation. Naroll's methodology involved analyzing the allometric relationship between dwelling floor area and number of people residing in the building. He used data from 18 ethnographic cultures from quite diverse locations (e.g., Tikopia, Iroquois, and Zulu; 1962: 588). Based on his calculations, he concluded that "the population of a prehistoric settlement can be very roughly estimated by archaeologists as of the order of one-tenth of the floor area in square meters occupied by its dwellings" (1962: 588). Over the course of the decade, several more articles appeared, addressing the formula offered by Naroll. Sherburne Cook and Robert Heizer (1968) undertook an extensive study of prehistoric settlement populations, using ethnographic and archaeological data to construct a nonlinear, log-log relationship between floor area (the ordinate) to the mean number of persons in the settlement (abscissa); they argued that environment, cultural-social patterning, and other culture-specific factors affect the floor area/per person ratio (1968: 81–87). Cook and Heizer proposed a formula of 20 ft^2 (1.854) per person for the first six household residents, but for every resident above six, the formula should be 100 ft^2 (9.278 m^2) per person (1968: 114–15). Though their study was consistently cited as an example of an alternate formula, it was Naroll's earlier suggestion that was more often employed. The standard calculation for population estimates, based on necessary living space, was therefore set at 10 m^2 per person for the next decade.

In the early 1970s, several studies questioned some of Naroll's basic assumptions but then essentially confirmed his floor area/population estimation formula. Steven LeBlanc (1971) noted that the ethnographic cultures cited in Naroll's analyses were incomplete with regard to dwelling/building information and thus may have provided flawed, or at least incomplete, data. LeBlanc checked Naroll's formula against seven settlements that did provide complete architectural and population data, two in Western Samoa, two in Iran, and three in Amazonia. The two villages in Samoa provided quite different ratios of person/floor area (11.0 m^2 and 8.7 m^2) because of an under-/over-population trend in each (LeBlanc 1971: 210). In Iran, he noted that the ethnographer described many household activities taking place in the courtyard and rooftop rather than within the dwelling. Therefore, if "outside" areas were taken into account, the Iranian village data suggested a formula of 43.3 m^2 per person (1971: 210). LeBlanc's main point is that the "standard deviation of floor areas among family units suggests that any given household is unlikely to be a good indicator of the village average," and any study on developing population estimate formulae must rely on a very large sample (1971: 210). LeBlanc concludes by acknowledging that if outside work areas are discarded, Naroll's estimate of approximately 10 m^2 per person is largely accurate.

Two other studies, by Samuel Casselberry (1974) and Polly Wiessner (1974), took issue mainly with Naroll's generalized application of the formula to any type of settlement. Casselberry argues that Naroll's formula falls short when applied to non-permanent residents or to non-nuclear family dwellings (1974: 117). Casselberry suggests that the only way to achieve any accuracy in developing population estimate formulae is to analyze specific types of residential groups (e.g., nuclear family, multifamily dwellings, polygynous societies, etc.). He analyzed multifamily dwellings in which several nuclear families, or an extended family, share a dwelling. He surveyed data of such family structures from nine cultures spread across the American continents. A chart compared his findings with Naroll's formula and one offered by a third researcher; Casselberry noted that while his calculations were consistently the closest to reality, in all three cases, the formula under-predicted the population (1974: 119). Casselberry's formula for multifamily dwellings is 6 m^2 per person, but this is relevant only for specific types of family dwellings. Like Casselberry, Wiessner criticized Naroll's "one-size-fits-all" formula. She undertakes an allometric analysis of Kalahari Bushmen hunter-gatherer camps using a model that allows for different camp sizes and also assesses areas around huts as well as internal floor areas. Her study indicates that small camps of 10 persons or fewer yield a 5.9 m^2 per person result, while larger camps (approximately 25 people) yield a 10.2 m^2 per person result (1974: 349; and see Uerkvitz [1992] for additional discussion and literature review on this subject).

An important use of Naroll's formula was made by Kent Flannery (1972) in his influential study on dwelling types in which he outlined what we might learn about socioeconomic and kinship structure from circular versus rectangular house forms. Using ethnographic data from Africa and the Middle East, Flannery argued that circular dwellings organized in compounds correlated more closely with nomadic extended families practicing polygynous marriage, while rectangular houses were more closely associated with sedentary societies in nuclear family (largely monogamous) structures (1972: 29–44). In order to calculate extended versus nuclear family structures within dwellings, Flannery employed Naroll's formula of 10 m^2 per person, not necessarily to calculate population but to show the lower numbers of individuals inhabiting rectangular houses versus circular hut compounds. Flannery's study established a baseline for understanding prehistoric socioeconomic and kinship structures, particularly in Mesoamerica and the Levant, for the next two decades (see Steadman 2004, and chapter 6 for discussion).

This two-decade period was capped by Dwight Read's discussion on the subject of floor area and population. Read (in Read and LeBlanc 1978: 313–15) reviewed Naroll's formula and, like Wiessner, found it too general, noting that different communities (e.g., village versus city) need different analyses to achieve workable formulae and accurate estimations. He also questioned the use of the allometric model. His study suggested a more geometrically based model, allowing for hut and camp area (and the camp's shape) to form an important part of the equation. His own formula for hunter-gatherer mobile camps offered similar results to Wiessner's (1978: 344–47). The discussions of the 1960s and 1970s were sufficiently extensive to soon evoke a significant review of methodologies for estimating ancient population trends.

The 1980s to the Present

As noted in the introduction to this section, archaeologists use a variety of ways to calculate demographic trends (e.g., Howell 1986 on demography). Robert Schacht (1981) marshaled the research on these methods for a review article, which included a section on "Habitation Space." He noted that, up to the writing of his review, archaeologists had used two main sets of architectural data for population estimates. The first method rested on determining the number of "households"—that is, families—that existed within a settlement, yielding a population estimate (1981: 125–26; and see De Roche 1983). However, as is noted by studies employing this methodology, and by Schacht himself, when a site is not completely excavated, it is problematic to identify how many people actually constitute a "family" and how many "households" may have existed. An equally significant problem is the identification of "households": Is a household constituted by single or multiple dwellings, a room within a dwelling (e.g., one with sleeping and food preparation areas), or other indicators less archaeologically visible? This methodology is useful only if the ethnographic data are plentiful, and the identification of what constitutes a "household" area is carefully considered (Schacht 1981: 125). Further complicating this method are the variables of shifting occupation and house abandonment, and the archaeologist's uncertainty in determining which houses were contemporaneously occupied and which were unused (e.g., Schreiber and Kintigh 1996; Sumner 1989; Verhoeven 2006; Wilshusen 2002).

The other method discussed by Schacht is that outlined in the previous section: the floor area per person measurement (1981: 126–27). While he notes that this method bypasses the problems associated with estimating population on the basis of the frequency of households, he also lists all the problems associated with Naroll's general formula. He concludes his discussion with the caution that "what is needed are more statistical tests on more ethnographic data in order to determine what factors influence this [population/floor area] relationship, and how" (Schacht 1981: 128; also see Eighmy 1981).

That said, even a carefully researched ethnographic record may not be enough. Elizabeth Williams (1985) used historical accounts on Australian Aboriginal settlements and their populations as a basis for calculating prehistoric populations, relying on the total area of settlements as the baseline for analysis. However, due to a number of factors, including some particular to the nature of her archaeological data (e.g., contemporaneity of dwellings, and gaps in the historical data regarding floor/settlement area and population), she found that "it has not been possible to make meaningful estimates of actual population numbers at archaeological sites in south-western Victoria" (Williams 1985: 80). Williams's study further confirms the need for solid ethnographic data if population estimates of an archaeological community are an important goal. Her work, along with Wiessner's, shows that determining the ancient populations of mobile hunter-gatherer camps requires a very different rubric from that used for estimating populations of ancient sedentary settlements.

By the late 1980s, population estimation methods were well entrenched in archaeological considerations of the prehistoric sites in North America. Sarah Schlanger, drawing on a relatively rich ethnographic database, estimated a household population of five persons per dwelling (whether pithouses or above-ground structures) in order to measure demographic change in the prehistoric Southwest (1988: 781–84). This average did not depend on floor area but rather on averaging the number of occupants per household. In a somewhat similar fashion, Gary Warrick (1989) also discards the floor area formula in favor of estimating population by the number of hearths found in Huron longhouses. His reasons for using this method are essentially twofold. The first is his access to Huron historical and ethnographic material that documented Huron households and family size within longhouses (Warrick 1989: 278). His second reason for rejecting (specifically Naroll's) house floor formulae rests on what he feels is the limitations of the methodology. Warrick observes, as does Charles Kolb (1985), that wealthier people live in larger houses; furthermore, in some cultures, ground floor area (especially if the structure is two-storied) is occupied by animals, not people (Warrick 1989: 277). For the Huron, Warrick finds that estimating population based on the number of hearths is far more accurate than longhouse floor area.

Sherri Deaver (1989), in her study of prehistoric populations in North Dakota and Montana, rejected Naroll's floor area formula for many of the same reasons cited by Wiessner. Mobile people require far less "floor area" and use more of the outdoors surrounding their structures. Drawing from ethnographic data on lodges (tipis), as well as other research, Deaver estimates that one person requires 2.7 m^2 of floor area. She adds an additional measure by calculating the weight of tipi components (skins and poles) and how many people were required to carry the weight, in order to achieve a nuanced population count in prehistoric temporary camps (1989: 246–48). The overarching message from these studies appears to be that population estimates must be made on a culture-by-culture basis, with substantial ethnographic data for support. While such methods might be minimally available to archaeologists working in some parts of the Americas, the ethnographic database for those working elsewhere can be extremely thin.

This circumstance, however, did not deter archaeologists working in Southwest Asia from taking up the discussion roughly a decade later. The subject was not population estimate specifically, but rather issues centered on Flannery's (1972) theories regarding circular compounds, rectangular structures, and the types of marriage, family, and socioeconomic patterns each type of structure housed (see Steadman 2004 and chapter 6 for extensive discussion). Various scholars (Banning 1996; Saidel 1993) argued that Flannery's model was flawed on a number of levels, including his assignment of the number of residents per circular versus rectilinear houses based on the floor/area formula. Brian Byrd (2000) also took issue with Flannery's house form and socioeconomic/family structure model, directly addressing the subject of floor area and population estimates. Byrd drew on several important ethnographic studies carried out in villages in Iran to argue that the floor area per person ratio should be no more than 7.5 m^2, and perhaps even less (2000: 83). In Iran, factors such as the availability of building materials, outdoor usage (rooftops, courtyards), and environment (colder climates might necessitate larger interiors) affect structure size for relatively similar families (Horne 1994: 151–57; Kramer 1983; Sumner 1989; Watson 1978, 1979: 291–99; and see Hopkins 2003: 70–71 for Anatolia; Kolb 1985 for Mesoamerica). Byrd concludes that a general formula such as that produced by Naroll and used by Flannery cannot be applied universally, and furthermore it affords too much space per person; for the Near East, at least, a formula of 7.5 m^2 per person is closer to reality.

The subject of palaeodemography and population estimation continued to be of interest to archaeologists into the late 1990s and early in the new millennium (Curet 1998; Paine 1997; Schreiber and Kintigh 1996; Wilshusen 2002). In general, most concurred with the view expressed by Curet that "universal formulae" were not particularly useful and that ethnographic data were an essential component to achieving a reliable population estimate for a site (1998: 360–62).

The many books, chapters, and articles dedicated to palaeodemography, population estimation, and house form and its relationship to socioeconomy and family prompted Flannery (2002) to revisit the theories he had advanced 30 years earlier. Flannery noted the plethora of data available in the 30 years hence, including the ethnographic studies in Iran and elsewhere (2002: 423). He concurred that population estimates must be based on culturally specific indicators, including ethnography, but that Naroll's formula remains useful as a general guide to village population estimation (2002: 423). In the same year, Richard Wilshusen (2002) also argued that using roofed space, as Naroll did, is a reliable population measure in prehistoric cultures of the American Southwest.

The last few years have seen a growing interest in palaeodemography, particularly regarding prehistoric population growth and decline trends on a regional basis (e.g., Bocquet-Appel 2008; Chamberlain 2006; and an entire issue of *Human Biology* devoted to the subject which includes, but is not limited to, articles from Chamberlain 2009; Renfrew 2009a; and Shennan 2009). However, these studies examine population trends, with less emphasis on population estimates of camps or settlements, thereby leaving the matter of how to accurately gauge prehistoric occupation numbers, using architecture or other methods, largely unresolved.

The Quandary: Estimating Prehistoric Populations

There is no simple solution to prehistoric population estimation offered in these several paragraphs. Some of the following guidelines may or may not be useful, depending on the type of settlement studied and the region of the world in which it is located. While Naroll (1962) did the field an enormous favor by starting a wide-ranging discussion of this issue, as was suggested by many, it is the opinion here that the 10 m^2 per person formula he offered is too general to be applied as a norm to any and all prehistoric settlements. The ethnographic research carried out in Iranian villages suggests that a relationship of somewhere between 7 and 7.5 m^2 per person might be more reasonable for sedentary settlements—at least, perhaps, for the ancient Near East. Furthermore, the growing literature on hunter-gatherer occupation suggests that a much smaller area, perhaps as little as under 3 m^2 per person, is more appropriate for mobile cultures. What has become clear from the literature presented over the last half century is that population estimates must be made essentially on a culture-by-culture, even a settlement-by-settlement basis. This is not particularly heartening for the archaeologist seeking an answer to the question of ancient population numbers.

Perhaps one place to begin is with whether architecture is a useful guide to population at all. The opinion here is that it is indeed, but with the caveat that this may not be true in all cases. A good example of an exception is the study by Warrick (1989) in which the number of hearths within longhouses serves as a far better measure of household occupants than floor area. Furthermore, it might be wise to stay away from "room size" or "persons per room" for the simple reason that the architectural footprint available to the modern eye may not represent the actual living space. Many homes in rural Turkey are two-storied; the lower story is used for storage of surplus grains and equipment, while the second floor is the actual living space. The storage area may actually be divided into rooms, but these may not reflect the number of rooms inhabited in the floor above. Therefore, Naroll's original idea of "roofed area" is perhaps the best measure to use, regardless of the person per meter area employed in the formula.

A second point to stress is use of the ethnographic database. As noted above, those working in places such as the American Southwest have access to a relatively stable set of ethnographic data on architectural settings not totally dissimilar from those found in the archaeological record. Present-day mobile groups, such as hunter-gatherer or nomadic pastoralist societies, also serve as a rich data source for those researching prehistoric temporary camps (though such cultures are rapidly dwindling). It is the prehistoric village, with no comparable descendants living today, that presents the greatest challenge for ethnographic analogy. Nonetheless, as Flannery demonstrated twice (1972, 2002), cultures with *similar* socioeconomic and architectural patterns can offer interpretive guidelines to build at least a floor area per person range for population estimation. Such a formula might then be refined by other data sets, including refuse accumulation (e.g., Gallivan 2002), distribution and amount of utilitarian goods within dwellings, and the placement and patterning of furniture such as sleeping platforms, personal storage areas, and hearths. Indeed, undertaking this research, and correlating the data to achieve a reasonable formula for one's own site, can be daunting for something so seemingly simple—to figure out how many people lived in the village. Thus, it is not surprising that most archaeological reports avoid population estimations altogether. However, if the effort is undertaken, a variety of valuable data can be inferred in both synchronic and diachronic settings. A final factor in estimating population is one raised by Deaver (1989) in her discussion of tipi placement within a community, and that is the incorporation of proxemics analysis. The cultural patterns underlying how and why people configure their space in certain ways, including the need for "personal space" and "privacy," has a significant impact on house size and structure and, therefore, on how many people might inhabit that space. The section below lays out the many aspects of human perceptions of space and their expressions in the architectural footprint.

Semiotics: Syntax and the Built Environment

Semiotic analysis of architecture grew out of the linguistics-based semiotic studies of signs and signification in nonverbal communication analyses (e.g., Chandler 2007; Clarke 1987; Eco 1976, 1986; Foucault 1970; see Steadman 1996). Since then, it has evolved considerably from its language study origins. Architectural semiotics is based on the concept that the built environment represents culturally rendered systems of communication expressed by signs and symbols within the architectural structure. Recognizing the meaning represented by these signifiers triggers the appropriate or required behavior within each space in the structure (e.g., Eco 1980; Fletcher 1981).

One of the most thorough explanations of the use of semiotics in archaeology was offered by Jean-Claude Gardin (1992), who suggested that methodologies fall into three categories. The first category he termed the "Semiostructural Current," in which "the reference to semiology rests on the fact that the analysis of archaeological remains calls on *ad hoc* systems of signs, under various names" (1992: 88). These signs or codes are placed in distinctive and recognizable patterns, often in hierarchical order, which provide prompts for behavior from one generation to the next. The second category Gardin defines as "Logicist Trends," which do not so much represent a methodology as an explanation of how archaeologists do their work (1992: 89–90). He notes that archaeological and ethnographic interpretation relies on the existence of logical, recognizable patterns—that is, semiological systems—which result in the deposition of material culture; such patterns can be "read" as if they were written languages (or step-by-step scientific processes). Once the language is deciphered, the culture can be interpreted. Gardin's third category is termed "Hermeneutic Trends," which he identifies as being the near polar opposite of the second category. Drawing on previous work by Hodder (1982, 1986; see also Hodder 1990) and Colin Renfrew (1982; see also Renfrew and Zubrow 1994), Gardin defines this third category as one that embodies an interpretive approach based on "symbolic, cognitive, or contextual archaeology" (1992: 92). Here the patterns that include coded meanings are still present, but they are multivariate, whether within the same generation or through time. They are not "scientifically" rendered (i.e., stable and predictable), but variable, because human behavior cannot be subject to the same interpretive approach as processes and experiments in the natural sciences. Archaeologists will therefore arrive at different interpretations depending on how the patterns are "read." Gardin notes that all three categories have a "common denominator which justifies in a sense this [semiotics] label: they all tend to cast some light, in one way or other, on 'mentalities,' differently conceived" (1992: 94). He suggests that the use of the structuralist/hermeneutics approaches will yield more faithful data simply because they more accurately acknowledge the reality of human behavior (1992: 101–2). In a focused study on how archaeologists might approach the interpretation of symbols, John Robb (1998) reaffirms the necessity of a multivariate approach to reading the diverse "mentalities" that codes and symbols represent in any give context.

Robert Preucel (2006) offered a book-length overview of the use of semiotics in archaeological contexts. He agrees with Gardin that semiotics is best considered as having had its foundations in structuralism, with a heavy addition of cognitive, symbolic, and social archaeology or, more broadly, the processual archaeological approach (2006: 94–95), though post-processualism is also an important player in shaping modern archaeological semiotics. Without the addition of the processual approach, semiotic interpretations in archaeology would take on the "narrow," "logistical," and "scientific" method eschewed by Gardin. The systems theory approach in processual archaeology, recognizing interlocking systems of human behavioral patterns (including those that involve the use of space)—environment, economy, and a cognitive element—is ideally suited to a semiotics-based methodology that relies on the interpretation of coded symbols and signs. However, the danger of systems theory in a semiotics approach might be an adherence to an inflexible interpretation of the system, such as in a Lévi-Straussian structuralist approach (Lévi-Strauss 1963). To avoid this, post-processualists preferred what they considered more contextually and historically based interpretive frames such as Bourdieu's theory of practice (1977, 1990) and Giddens's structuration theory (1984) (see chapters 5 and 9). Preucel notes that post-processualism, recognizing the individuality of social groups and individuals, offers a more flexible method of analysis that is closer to "reading a text" than the strict following of the grammatical rules of a language (2006: 135–46). The use of semiotics in archaeology has yielded a methodology that allows us to identify stable patterns of symbols and codes that offer deeper interpretive opportunities for understanding cultural behavior.

Semiotics in Archaeological Context

It is in dealing with material culture (rather than architecture) that the application of semiotics-based methodologies is more commonly found. Preucel notes (2006: 168–70) that material culture patterning has many similarities to the steps involved in the process of writing. The technological aspects and cognitive steps associated with the origins of early writing include symbols, cognitive development, and prompts (through recognizable codes) for writers to create understandable written patterns (Ross 2010). Among the important facets in the manufacture of technology, whether writing, lithics, ceramics, or even the production of museum displays, are the steps necessary to achieve a viable outcome (e.g., Bauer 2002; Brusasco 2007; Castro Gessner 2010; Dobres 2000; Schlanger 1994; Sellet 1993; van der Leeuw 1993, 1994; and on the semiotics of the body, see Joyce 2005). Methodologies based on the concept of *chaîne opératoire* implicitly employ semiotic methods that "may reveal the moments at which producers followed cultural rules, rules that were socialized and instilled into their bodies, and other points when they made intentional choices to stray from or modify those rules" (Ross and Steadman 2010: 6). There is, therefore, a syntax to the production of materials; alterations in the order, or variations in the steps, can signal cultural or social changes, altered attitudes toward categories of material culture, or a variety of other factors that may be deduced by "reading" the material culture products.

Art historian Donald Preziosi made use of semiotics in a syntactical analysis of the construction and use of space in second-millennium BCE Minoan palaces (1979, 1983). Preziosi demonstrates that the palaces, while bearing differing footprints, have similar or identical patterns to the sequencing of space and the codes (walls and doors) that separate and direct passage through the palaces. While Preziosi offers penetrating insights into the structure of these Minoan palaces, his work does not significantly address the cultural patterns that both generated and then resulted from the built environment. Minoan palaces are analyzed, to use Gardin's terms, for logistics but not for hermaneutics.

Perhaps a more explicit example employing semiotics in the reading of architecture can be found in Henry Glassie's work on 17th- to 19th-century vernacular architecture in the Chesapeake Bay area of Virginia (1975, 2000), though he never explicitly states his employment of semiotic-based methods. Over a roughly 200-year period, Glassie noted that houses in the region underwent two changes from the original layout (1975). The first change occurred in the middle to late 18th century (Figure 3.1a, b). The original house plans featured a square hall, where "the front door gave access immediately to the interior . . . [W]ith one step, the visitor enters the hall, then turns toward the fire where the work of cooking and entertainment takes place"; these then altered to the "I-house . . . two stories high, but only one room deep . . . [U]pon entering, you do not stand in a room where people sit. You are in an unheated, unlit corridor . . . out of which you must be led to the sociable place" (Glassie 2000: 117). The syntax here is in the codes or symbols that are imparted to the visitor by the built structure: warmth, welcome, entrance into family space, in the former, versus cold, unlit, wait to see if entry is permitted, in the latter. The space syntax described here can also be described in the context of "proxemics" and front/back analysis (although here it is

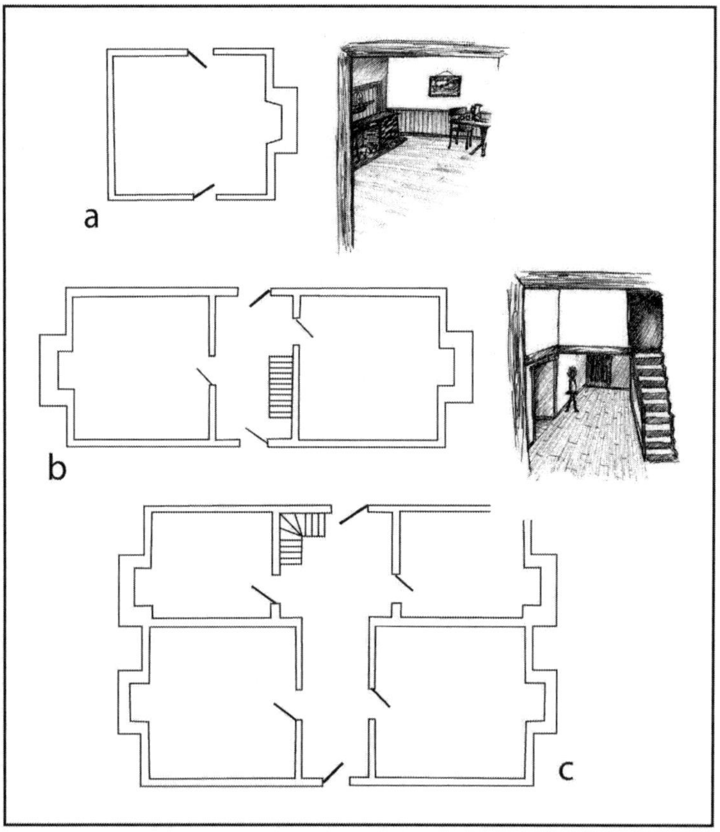

Figure 3.1: (a) Example of the "open" 18th-century Virginia house (showing entry directly into the main room); (b) example of the 18th-century Virginia "I-house" (showing entry into the hallway); (c) example of the later "Georgian manner" (plans based on Glassie 2000: 119; drawings by Corrina Petit).

front/side-to-side), subjects discussed in some detail below. Glassie advances an interpretation of this architectural change based in historical context. He notes that the "old house belonged to the little community of engagement, of constant and direct exchange" (2000: 121); recognizing that the architectural change occurred at the time of the American Revolution, he interpreted the shift from one house type to the other as material evidence of the change in social arrangements that brought the war and built the nation. Houses told of a retreat from the community of immediate experience, where people might be radicals, loyalists, or unconcerned, where differences were stiffening along lines of class and race and persuasion (Glassie 2000: 118).

Glassie also describes a third house plan based on the English Georgian house, an eight-roomed, two-story structure (Figure 3.1c), which was adopted by the new Americans for its representation of wealth and social standing, and "as a symbol of fashion and progress" (2000: 126). The Georgian house served the dual purpose of continuing to keep strangers in the hallway with no access to the interior of the house without a guide, while also symbolizing the "new American" pride in their young nation, along with a bit of self-aggrandizement. Glassie's study is an excellent illustration of a semiotic analysis that combines a "structural" approach with a hermeneutically based interpretation of architectural change.

Applications of semiotics-based methods to archaeological settings offer a variety of results. For instance, Ronald Fletcher (1984) undertook an extremely detailed analysis of spatial order at Taşkun Kale, a 13th- to 14th-century Mongol fort in eastern Turkey. The large structure was affected by fire and post-depositional processes, but Fletcher was nonetheless able to apply spatial analysis techniques to the subsequent rebuilding of portions of the fort after the fire. Near the end of its use period, the fort no longer functioned as a military installation. However, Fletcher found that those living in it nonetheless adapted their spatial use to that established by prior military structure, and thus there was no identifiable change in spatial order or "syntax" (Fletcher 1984: 221–23). At Taşkun Kale, humans adapted to a preexisting spatial order; the changes in usage of the fort were represented by material culture, not architectural alteration. A second example comes from Preucel's presentation of Puebloan architecture before and after a 1680 revolt against Spanish colonists (2000; 2006: 210–46). For nearly a century, Pueblo peoples of the American Southwest lived under Spanish rule, their villages converted to Franciscan missions and their freedom coopted by Spanish *encomenderos*, landowners who exacted tribute and labor from the Puebloans (Preucel 2006: 210–12). In a regional study, Preucel found that during and after the revolt, the mission villages were abandoned and new villages were relocated to high mesas, which offered defensive positions against Spanish incursions. However, besides their defensibility, the new villages encoded other meanings that contributed to a revitalization of Puebloan culture. Mountains were the homes of important deities, and the new villages were located nearer these natural monuments, or even alongside them. Villages were also constructed to reflect the cosmological universe, further uniting Puebloans with their religion and initiating sociocultural revitalization after a century of Spanish Catholic domination. Preucel notes that "Pueblo Revolt mesa villages can be read both as 'signed in history' and 'signs of history'" in that they both result from and are reflective of the social milieu of the several decades following the 1680 revolt (2006: 244). Codes and symbols embedded in architecture are also critical components in methodologies using proxemics and access analysis, fields that emerged in tandem and interrelated with semiotic studies of the built environment.

Proxemics: Human Spatial Organization and Architecture

The field of "proxemics" grew out of Edward T. Hall's work on the human organization of space (1959) and particularly how this differs cross-culturally (Hall 1966). He coined the term "proxemics" for this field, as "no suitable designation had been found for the study of microspace as a system of bio-communication" (1963: 1022, n. 2). To paraphrase Hall's definition of proxemics, it is the study of how humans unconsciously structure the space around them, including maintaining appropriate distances from other humans, organizing the structure and space within buildings, and even among communities (1963: 1003). Hall's work was quickly embedded in anthropological research, in part because it was so deeply intertwined with human behavioral characteristics, but also because his style was so accessible. In *The Hidden Dimension*, Hall recounts how, during his undergraduate days, he unintentionally intruded on the "private space" of a German artist, while he was attempting to chat up the artist's female neighbor (1966: 124–26). After being verbally chastised by the German artist for his infringement, Hall reports that he "felt bullied and humiliated, and even after almost thirty years, [Hall] can still feel [his] anger" at the artist (1966: 126). These anecdotes spoke deeply to all who study culture and who, numerous times, have literally committed a misstep into a place where they should not have trod, or perhaps worse, touched or approached someone they should not have, when conducting fieldwork. Hall's proxemics research was tailor made for inclusion into anthropological research (see Hall 1968, 1974).

Initially, Hall's research received a great deal of critical analysis, particularly concerning issues of personal space perceptions within and across cultures. This response was owing to the fact that much of Hall's evidence was anecdotal, based on his own experiences and observations and, to some extent, on what others had reported to him. O. Michael Watson was the first to subject Hall's proxemic theories to controlled (laboratory) testing, with results largely confirming Hall's models (Watson 1970; Watson and Graves 1966). Research on proxemics and personal space, especially among and between different ethnic groups in North America, continued throughout the 1970s (see Gillespie and Leffler 1983 for a review of literature). A refinement of Hall's models suggested that while there were general parameters of appropriate interactional space perceptions within cultures, these parameters were mitigated by various factors (see especially Altman 1975 and Ciolek 1978), with one of the most important being an individual's status (e.g., Gillespie and Leffler 1983; Henley 1973; Leffler, Gillespie, and Conaty 1982; Scheflen and Ashcraft 1976). Proxemic analysis became well ensconced in the fields of anthropology, psychology, sociology, and communications.

It was not long before proxemic analysis was applied to architectural structuring and furniture within built spaces. Hall had already introduced the concept of architecture and proxemics by creating three categories—fixed, semi-fixed, and dynamic (Hall 1968: 91)—in which walls and bounded territories are fixed, furniture is generally semi-fixed, and the interpersonal space between humans is dynamic. It was primarily Amos Rapoport (e.g., 1969, 1976, 1982) who launched the next several decades of research that integrated the concepts found in proxemics with architectural studies of cultures both past and present. In his own work, Rapoport combined concepts from proxemics and the field of semiotics to offer, along with others, a vast literature on human–environment behaviors as they are expressed in architectural renderings (see chapter 5).

Proxemics research on the built environment is most applicable in studies of human territoriality, the construction and maintenance of boundaries, and concerns regarding public and private space, as effectively reviewed by Donald Sanders (1990: 47–51). These three areas are addressed in the remainder of the chapter.

Territoriality and Boundary-Making Writ Large

The bulk of research on human territoriality, which includes the erection of physical, psychological, or symbolic boundaries, has focused on issues of personal space that are rarely detectable in the archaeological record. Norman Ashcraft and Albert Scheflen (1976: 3–4) note that humans, like animals, create particular territories that they will defend against invasion and intrusion (see also Edney 1974). This attitude ranges in applicability from a single individual's personal space to the nation-state's official borders. As has been thoroughly discussed in the literature on territories (Ashcraft and Scheflen 1976; Greverus 1976; Porteous 1977; Rapoport 1969; Scheflen and Ashcraft 1976), a physical bounding is not necessary; rather, individuals in the same culture *perceive* the proper territorial boundaries in various settings (e.g., standing together in conversation, sitting in public places). These are essentially invisible archaeologically; only territories that acquire physical, built boundaries are accessible in the material record.

Geographer Robert Sack defines territoriality as "the attempt by an individual or group to affect, influence, or control people, phenomena, and relationships, by delimiting and asserting control over a geographic area"—that is, the territory (1986: 19). Altman (1975: 105–6) describes six "qualities" of human territoriality and, after considering all foregoing scholarly definitions, offers the following: "territorial behavior is a self/other boundary-regulation mechanism that involves personalization of or marking of a place or object and communication that it is 'owned' by a person or group" (Altman 1975: 107). Territoriality is considered a natural human characteristic that includes as well as excludes others in order to provide security, the exertion of control over space or even other people, and the marking of specific space as off limits to most or all others (Altman 1975: 103–11; Lavin 1981; Lawrence 1984; Porteous 1977: 63–64; Rapoport 1969: Sack 1986: 20–22).

Most researchers divide human territoriality into spatial stages ranging from individual/personal to the perception of "public" areas (Lavin 1981). J. Douglas Porteous (1977: 28–30) offers three categories of territories: (1) microspace, which is the area around the individual that is the "comfort zone" and should not be violated by another; (2) mesospace, which corresponds most closely to the living area, including the home, surrounding yard, or even the neighborhood; and (3) macrospace, which is the area around the mesospace "home base" in which one acquires the necessities of life, such as food. The third type is a "public" area that can be used by others, who then form a group consciousness about that macrospace as "theirs" and will defend it against intrusion (a present-day neighborhood alliance to fight the arrival of a big-box company, for instance). Ashcraft and Scheflen offer a description that aptly describes the notion of macrospace (1976: 73):

> A system, or "field" of human space forces us to recognize that human territories are not simply comprised of a series of discrete and separate space, like ten separate houses on a block, but, instead, that any particular space is also a very integral part of a larger system of space, those ten houses arranged in a very definite pattern linking each house to the others on the block.

Identifying a neighborhood or community "macrospace" archaeologically would seem impossible upon first consideration, but as is described below, through the use of research methodologies such as ethnography and GIS, some success at identifying a regional "territory" has been achieved.

An additional area of human territoriality that is an extension of the "home base" in Porteous's "mesospace" category includes places where an individual spends a substantial amount of time, or in which a consistent presence is expected. Such places might include a workplace, a designated place for religious ritual, or other daily or regular spaces outside the home. This is captured by Irwin Altman's definition of "primary territories," which are "owned and used exclusively by individuals or groups, are clearly identified as theirs by others, are controlled on a relatively permanent basis, and are central to the day-to-day lives of the occupants" (1975: 112). Altman notes that primary territories include workplaces, and that a violation of this primary territory by others can be traumatic and have serious consequences for those whose territories have been intruded upon.

There is no doubt that territorial attitudes about these spaces develop even after a short period of time. Early in my career, I taught a small class of 25 students which met three times a week; as always happens, students selected their seats and stuck with those for the entire semester. The final exam was held in the same room. When I entered the room to administer the final, I was surprised to see a male student who usually sat in the back row reposing in a front row seat usually occupied by a female student. When she entered, just after me, she was brought up short to see "her seat" occupied; she asked the male student, whom she knew well, to move back to "his seat" and he refused (mainly to tease her, I suspect). After further exchange and his refusal to move, she burst into tears and left the room. The male student immediately moved to "his seat," and I went to find my female student, who explained to me that she "couldn't think" in my class anywhere but in that seat. This was a clear demonstration of a violation of her territory, a place where she felt comfortable, safe, and calm enough to successfully complete a final exam. Therefore, the concept of "mesospace" must be extended to include areas outside the home but that acquire the same territorial characteristics as one's own abode.

When humans organize space territorially there are consequences. The first and most obvious one is that the violation of that space may elicit an unpleasant reaction (e.g., the female student), up to and including violence (Ashcraft and Scheflen 1976: 138–54). A second is the imposition of spatial boundaries such as occurred in the colonization processes of the last several centuries. Robert Sack (1986: 6–15) describes the forced change in concepts of "territoriality" among the Ojibwe in the north central United States and south central Canada near Lake Superior. Traditionally hunter-gatherers, the Ojibwe were a mobile culture with an essentially unbounded macrospace and movable and relatively permeable mesospace "territories." After European colonization, and as political boundaries were imposed and the land was partitioned into parcels for sale as "private property" to Europeans, the landscape occupied by the Ojibwe in 1500 was completely changed by the 1700s (Sack 1986: 11–12). The Ojibwe were forced to alter their concepts of "territory" and to repurpose what had been communally shared lands into a "this is mine and that is yours" mentality. The Ojibwe were also faced with another consequence: that of crowding. If people in a culture have a consistent perception of "personal space," then crowding can occur. Tracking how a culture reacts to crowding is, of course, discernible in modern contexts but may also be visible archaeologically. An interesting perspective on the subject of crowding was offered by Ashcraft and Scheflen (1976: 86–87) when they asked women from differing ethnic groups and nationalities (in North America) where they went when they wanted to be "alone." While women from most groups indicated that they would go to the bedroom and shut the door, women from Puerto Rico answered that they went "home." In the first group, "aloneness" meant away from family and children for some "down time," while among Puerto Rican women, "alone" meant away from strangers and the hustle and bustle outside the home. The concept of crowding, then, is multidimensional in that researchers must consider who is "causing" the "crowding," which is often difficult to recognize archaeologically.

Boundaries and the Archaeological Record

As already noted, it is difficult, and sometimes impossible, to define archaeologically the differences between "territory" and "boundary." Boundaries define the territory of the "home," including external space around the home; internal walls may define individual territories of household members. For this reason, the subjects of territory and boundary are discussed in tandem here primarily with regard to house plans and the organization of domestic space. However, pre-residential prehistoric concepts of territory, and their impact on the origins of residential patterns, might also be detectable. For instance, Michael Rosenberg (1998) makes a strong argument that places territoriality, and the desire to control productive areas (possibly in the face of increasing population) at the heart of early sedentism in prehistoric Southwest Asia. A combination of population pressure, land degradation, and territoriality may have also resulted in behavioral changes at the Neolithic site of 'Ain Ghazal in Jordan (Rollefson

1997; Rollefson and Simmons 1987; Rollefson, Simmons, and Kafafi 1992). 'Ain Ghazal is known for its architecture, for the careful palaeoenvironmental study conducted by its excavator, Gary Rollefson, and for the subfloor burials, including plastered skulls and plaster statues (also see chapter 2). These plaster figurines with painted faces were constructed so that they could be erected on a platform or base, some standing as tall as 90 cm (Rollefson 1986; Rollefson and Simmons 1987). Rollefson notes that these statues appeared at 'Ain Ghazal when the population began to increase, with "newcomers" drawn to the settlement by its successful agricultural strategies. Possibly, these statues were a visible marker as to the "territory" already belonging to long-term residents at the settlement (see Steadman 2005 for further discussion). Or, they may have functioned as symbolic "walls," identifying which spaces were already inhabited, not just by living humans but by ancestral ones as well (see chapter 10).

An ethnographic-archaeological study of the Iroquoian longhouse and the area surrounding the settlement offers multilevel insights into territoriality within and between cultures in the eastern Great Lakes region (Wright 1979). Settlement territory was divided into two areas, the "cleared" area where cultivation was carried out, and the surrounding forest. The clearing was considered women's territory, and the forest was the male domain where hunting, trading, and fighting took place (Wright 1979: 36–37). In addition to being gendered territories, each also had a symbolic dimension: the cleared area, which included the longhouse, was the safe and secure area, while the forest was dangerous, the source of enemies and threats from the supernatural world (Wright 1979: 37). The forest was not considered a "territory" belonging to the Iroquois, but rather a type of "buffer zone" between Iroquois settlements and possibly hostile neighbors, though Iroquois men did "tame" the forest by creating trails through it and naming prominent features within it (Wright 1979: 37, 40–42). The Iroquois example illustrates the multidimensionality of territoriality and the notion of "macrospace" proposed by Porteous (1977). While the forest was considered a separate "territory," it was not one that belonged exclusively to the Iroquois, although defense of it, and therefore of the village, was essential to security concerns. Most of these Iroquoian perceptions of territoriality were not reflected in the built environment; the cleared areas were not typically fenced, and thus male/female and dangerous/secure spaces might not be rendered archaeologically. It is more common for boundaries inside and nearby the home to be more visible in the archaeological record.

Mark Leone offers an interesting view in his study of Mormon homes over the course of the 20th century (1973, 1979). He documents the emergence and growth of the Mormon way of life, and eventual Mormon success as a socioeconomic and religious entity in American culture. While there were many reasons for Mormon successes (Leone 1979; see also Lightfoot 1980), Leone argues that fence building was one very important factor. The building of fences around every Mormon house in an Arizona community, as well as around more public buildings (such as temples), was, Leone argues (1973), completely intertwined with the building of the structures themselves. Though physically unconnected, a house without a surrounding fence was inconceivable. Fences allowed Mormons to keep their religion and lifeways inside their own boundaries, free from interference from the gentile world (Leone 1973, 1979). In contrast, a study on Mormon houses in a Hawaiian town by Patricia Price-Beggerly (1981) suggested that the physical fences noted by Leone were not necessarily required by Hawaiian Mormons and that their socio-religious patterns could be maintained ideologically in remote or less crowded locations. It is possible that Mormons in 20th-century Arizona felt a greater need not only for ideological but also physical separation from their neighbors, while the Polynesian setting may not have necessitated such visual separation between believers and non-believers. Thus, the Mormon example illustrates that the needs for boundary making and territoriality may differ even within the same culture, depending on external factors and societal attitudes to potential encroachment.

Territoriality is an elusive concept in the absence of identifiable markers or ancient texts that delineate imperial boundaries. Territorial perceptions are not impossible to detect (the plaster statues of 'Ain Ghazal perhaps demonstrating such in prehistoric societies), but they do fall into the category of "difficult to access" archaeologically. Boundaries are more likely to be traceable in the archaeological record, especially if they fall into the "fixed" or "semi-fixed" categories, but the spaces they are defining may not be completely transparent to the researcher. The Mormon example is testament to a varying use of boundary markers based on the social milieu in which each community is located. When boundaries are in use near, or within, the home, there is a far greater likelihood of detection archaeologically, particularly because they are often delimiting what is considered private as opposed to what is public.

Limiting Space: Privacy and Access

Traditionally, the architectural rendering of "privacy" and the analysis of access into interior spaces belonged under the heading of "proxemics." However, there has been such extensive research into, and application of, the models employing access analysis and privacy configurations that they have essentially become their own major subfield within the archaeology of architecture study area.

Creating Privacy in the Built Environment

Separating boundary marking from the attainment of privacy is, to a certain extent, artificial, since boundaries are often meant to create privacy, as was shown above. Boundaries, however, can contain or bound any area, including an entire settlement. Privacy is a far more personal concern and is most often manifested at the individual or household level. Many argue that the human desire for privacy is not only a human universal (Sanders 1990: 50) but a human requirement (see Wilson 1988: 170–84 for discussion). The desire, or need, for privacy appears to derive from different social needs depending on the cultural structure. At its most fundamental level, cultural perceptions of privacy concepts help to create behavioral codes, whether symbolic, visual, or physical, that serve to establish appropriate individual and group conduct (Sanders 1990: 50). Some even suggest that privacy is a basic human right, "a state of human existence that makes possible the establishment, maintenance, and protection of certain necessary features of life . . . an aspect of human dignity without which a person would be impaired" (Wilson 1988: 172; and see articles in Pennock and Chapman 1971).

Wilson argues that the need for privacy emerged with the "domestication" of humans, a term he uses to describe the transition to building and inhabiting permanent dwellings, noting that "privacy, made universally possible with dwellings, provides both protection and concealment for people, their actions, attitudes, intentions, and property" (1988: 99, see also 173–74). This notion is thoroughly embedded in the anthropological and archaeological research on domestic structures: "among the most fundamental symbolic messages found in houses is the coded distinction between public and private space" (Birdwell-Pheasant and Lawrence-Zúñiga 1999: 4; and see Sanders 1990: 50 for similar discussion). A number of scholars have observed that as societies grow more complex, with greater levels of wealth differentiation, the desire for privacy controls become stronger as well (Hodder 1990; Lawrence 1990; Rapoport 1990; Sanders 1990; Steadman 2000; Wilson 1988). It is these coded messages that are often surprisingly visible in the archaeological record.

Just as there are levels of acceptable personal space boundaries, there are levels, or stages, of privacy. Wilson asserts that what he terms "domesticated privacy" (1988: 179), the need to have a private place to call one's own, exists between households, not within them, and that individuals in many cultures seek only minimal privacy within their homes (also see Sanders 1990). This is illustrated by the "aloneness" example from the territoriality section above; some women identify "being alone" as being separate from family in their own bedroom, while others see it as retreat to the household away from the outside. Cultures that seemingly have no "internal household privacy" do indeed offer such through social conventions of "not seeing" people in multifamily, open-plan houses that lack internal walls (Rapoport 1969: 66); in these types of cultures, subtle cues indicate private regions (Blier 1987; Rapoport 1982: 77, 147–52, 1988). The desire for privacy, therefore, can be expressed not only in the configuration of the house vis-à-vis other houses and generally "those outside" but also internally as well. Rapoport notes that many cultures configure their homes with the privacy of women in mind (1969: 66–68); this concern for privacy would certainly include visitors to the home, but sometimes can extend even to other household members (see chapter 6). While gender might be the most common intra-household concern with regard to privacy, other social groups, such as elders, may have their own concerns; or separation between extended or polygynous marriage family members might require privacy coding. The greatest concern for privacy will occur when strangers or visitors enter the home.

The architectural components for achieving privacy include, of course, external and internal walls, doorways and their placement, and the configuration of those rooms, walls, and doorways within the home; courtyards can also play a critical role in creating secluded locales (see BaHammam 2006; Zako 2006). One of the most common methods for creating privacy within the household is using the front:public/back:private convention (Giddens 1984:122–26; Lawrence 1984; Portnoy 1981). Salons and rooms where household members or guests are entertained are typically at the front of a house, while sleeping areas and rooms devoted to hygiene are usually found in the back:private regions (Portnoy 1981: 215; Rapoport 1982:118). Some rooms, such as kitchens, might be found in either area, depending on cultural mores and concepts of propriety (e.g., if women do the cooking, and women are to be segregated from strangers, then kitchens will be in a back:private region). Another method of ensuring privacy, especially from strangers, is to regulate "lines of sight" and the placement of doorways. Opening the front door offers the visitor a view into the interior of the home; how much of that is visible can be controlled by doorway placement. A simple illustration of this can be found in the hall-and-porch, or "megaron," style of architecture found at ancient Mediterranean settlements. The "front" door, opening into the porch, can be aligned with the doorway into the hall, affording visitors line-of-sight into the entire home (Figure 3.2a). However, a simple displacement of the porch door to the right or left limits the view to the exterior wall of the hall (Figure 3.2b), ensuring that curious eyes see nothing of the home's main room.

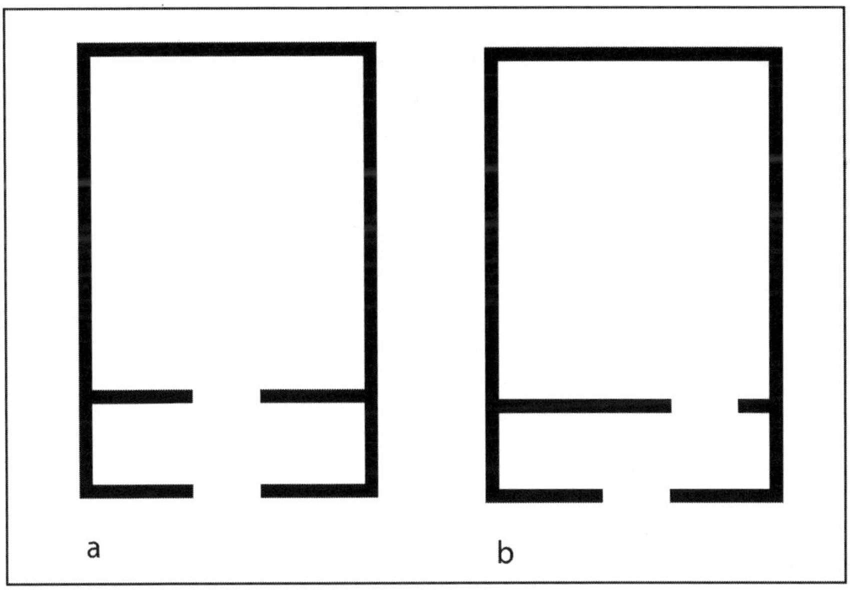

Figure 3.2: (a) Example of a megaron in which the doorway allows a "line of sight" into the heart of the house; (b) example of a megaron with a front door that limits the line of sight.

Doorway placement and line-of-sight access can also function inside a house. At the age of 13, I moved from a ranch-style house with rooms staggered off long hallways to a small house of five rooms (two bedrooms, one bathroom, a living room and a kitchen/dining area). My aunt Donna, who came to visit a month after we moved in (and who lived in a huge Victorian house with three floors), stood at the center of my new house and exclaimed gleefully, "I can see into all five rooms!" I think that, after keeping house for her family in a three-story structure, the small and compact style of our new home appealed to her aching knees and arthritic hands. Her comment, though, stuck with me all through my remaining years at home, as did the sense that my new house was not like the one I had left. It wasn't that the new house was "too small" but, rather, different in some undefined way. I now know that my new house lacked the "front/back" aspect typical of American homes; retreat to back:private was impossible for me when visitors or even family were in the house. The other factor defining my new house went beyond the lack of front/back and included the aspect of "access" even to the most personal areas of the house (bedroom and bathroom). Had I employed it, the field of access analysis would have charted very clearly the lack of transitional spaces between the public and private areas of my new home.

Crossing Boundaries: Access Analysis and the Control of Space

The field of access analysis, which has emerged as a major subfield of semiotics (Chippendale 1992; Hillier and Hanson 1984; Steadman 2000; and see Fisher 2009 for discussion and literature review), combines the proxemic areas of boundaries and privacy, and adds a measurable statistical analysis of the human built environment. Access to spaces is diagrammed, and thus a quantitative analysis identifying stages of access can be achieved. For instance, in one culture, the household's ancestral altar might typically be located in a room that requires passage through four previous spaces (four access points), suggesting that the ceremonies associated with the altar are private and meant only for the household members, or even a limited number of household members. In another culture, the altar might be just inside two access points, suggesting a much more "public" attendance at household ceremonies. This scenario is diagrammed in Figure 3.3 using access analysis methodology.

The methods used in access analysis, or "gamma analysis" as it was originally called, were primarily developed by Hillier and Hanson in the mid-1980s (Hillier and Hanson 1984; Hillier, Hanson, and Graham 1987; see also Hanson 1998). Sonit Bafna describes access analysis as a methodology based on the concept that "human societies use space as a key and necessary resource in organizing themselves.... [T]he space of inhabitation is *configured*," and one aspect of that configuration is the creation of boundaries and entrances in a pattern logical for that culture's spatial principles (2003: 17). Bafna goes on to note that the goal of methods such as access analysis "is to develop strategies of description for configured, inhabited spaces ... in such a way that their underlying

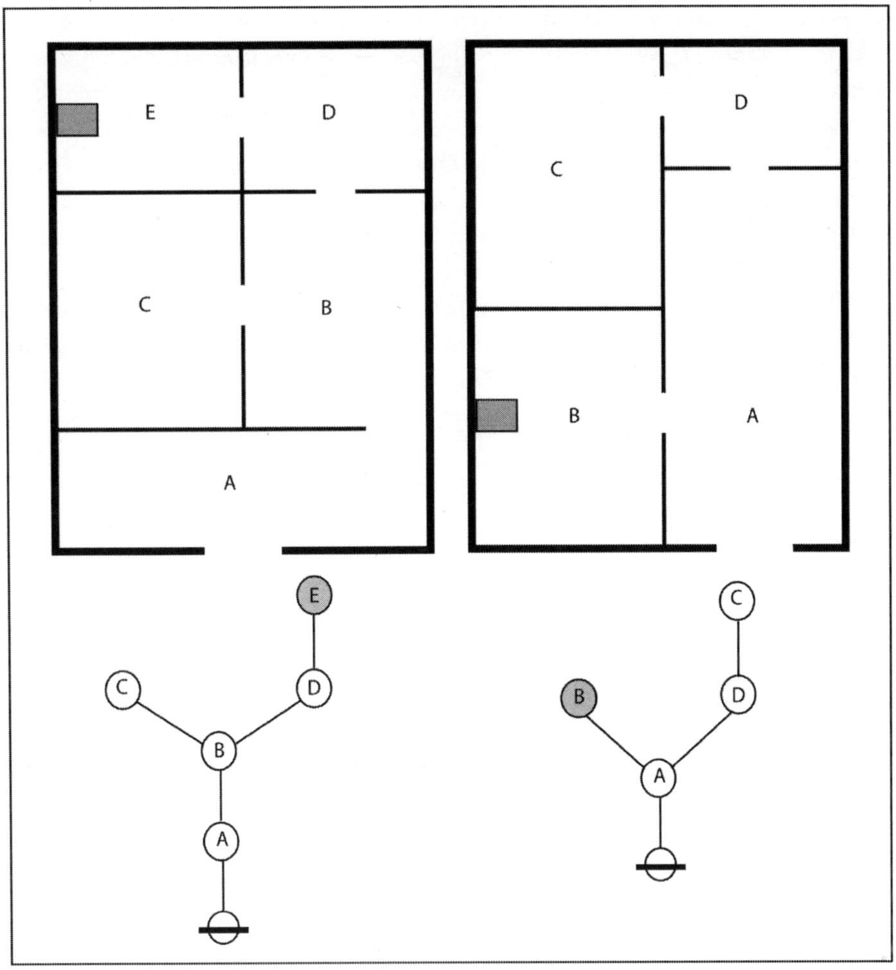

Figure 3.3: Example of access analysis diagrammed on a house.

social logic can be enunciated" (2003: 18). Because these patterns are expressed architecturally, access analysis, as Marion Cutting (2003: 3) notes, "is of interest to archaeologists because it is particularly useful in studying the social use of domestic and small settlement spaces."

A building incorporates walls and doorways not only into the building itself but also into the interior spaces. How those interior spaces are configured can reveal relevant aspects of societal norms; for instance, boundary and privacy concerns can be diagrammed as consistently represented in a community. Charles Bergengren captures the usefulness of the access analysis methodology in the following observation: "[S]tylistic elements and fashionable details [in a house] change every generation or so, whereas the most basic aspects of traditional floor plans, such as the general relation of doorway to hearth, can span centuries of time" (1994: 43). He further notes that when there are substantial changes to house form, this often results from a change in the "worldview of the people affected" (1994: 44). Bergengren's study revealed two changes in house form: In the earliest 18th-century German houses in Pennsylvania, which were based on the European Medieval house form, front doors were often left open and led directly to the hearth and the heart of the house; by the 19th century, doors were kept closed and the living area was often on the second floor (also see discussion on 18th- to 19th-century houses and Figure 3a–c, above). The architectural shift illustrates the more "modern" world view of individualism and social separation from one's neighbors and strangers (Bergengren 1994: 52–61, 71). The examples below further illustrate the usefulness of applying access analysis to the widest range of residences, from the most humble huts to royal palaces.

Access Analysis and the Archaeological Record

Access analysis methodology would seem, as noted above by Cutting, immediately attractive and applicable to archaeological remains of architecture. However, as she goes on to describe, its use is limited when certain conditions affect prehistoric remains. Cutting identifies factors that can hinder the use of access analysis, including rooftop access (no discernible doorway), lack of clear evidence as to the location of external and internal doorways, and the inability to identify room or space use (2003: 6–13). Several scholars have also noted that the methodology is not likely to yield broadly useful data unless a large area of the housing complex or community has been exposed. Even with these caveats, there are, as shown below, often sufficient architectural remains for detailed access analysis study.

It is perhaps prudent to begin with an illustration of the limitations of access analysis, using the Iroquoian longhouse, discussed above, as a case in point. In Wright's study of Iroquoian space (1979), the only built doorway(s) led into the entire interior space, which, according to the ground plan, was entirely open to visual and physical inspection; the lack of internal partitions would impede a researcher from identifying spaces denoting stages of increasingly proscribed access (see Figure 3.4). Further, attempting a traditional "front/back" analysis on the Iroquoian longhouse would also yield murky results, since the house plan suggests that the "front" is at either end of the structure, whereas Wright's study shows that the front/back positioning is really in relation to the hearth rather than the doorway (1979: 45–52). The stranger/visitor access from one family's living space/hearth to the next is through the longhouse central passageway, while the private space, where sleeping and family activities are carried out, is located at the outer wall of the longhouse, away from the central hearth. Thus, the front/back axis in an Iroquoian longhouse is perpendicular to the entryway. It was Wright's ethnographic analysis of the longhouse that revealed privacy and spatial organization; access analysis would have been of minimal use in this type of archaeological setting.

A completely different result is found in C. L. Plimpton and F. A. Hassan's study of modern rural Egyptian houses (1987), in which spatial patterns were similar to those found in archaeological contexts. Employing both access analysis and hypothesizing that the houses in this rural farming village would be organized according to Alice Portnoy's front/back public/private principles (1981), Plimpton and Hassan studied these houses as potentially representative of domestic structures in prehistoric Egyptian contexts. These houses were mostly one-storied and offered similar layout patterns regardless of socioeconomic status, illustrating an architectural "grammar" that reflected societal concepts of appropriate spatial patterns (Plimpton and Hassan 1987: 441–43). The houses had five traditional spatial areas: a hall, a sitting room (salon), a sleeping room, a latrine, and an animal enclosure (*kharga*). The hall and salon were at the front of the home and were for guest entertainment, the latrine and *kharga* were at the back, and the sleeping room was in either area but was always closed off when guests were in the house. The authors conclude that this consistency of spatial organization "reveal[s] certain rules by which a house may be mentally constructed and by which a variety of plans can be generated within the acceptabe [*sic!*] range of the domestic use of space" as well as identifies "the modalities and the norms that may be read into [domestic layouts, and which] may also be regarded as the embodiment of social and cultural ideas, values, and attitudes" (Plimpton and Hassan 1987: 446). A decade or so later, a similar study of traditional Turkish houses offered insights into Ottoman-period houses and families. The researchers identified two house types, one in which a first floor room featuring a sofa (a type of "salon") stood as the intersection between public and private space, and the second in which the courtyard fronting the house was the "public" area (Orhun, Hillier, and Hanson 1995). (In my years working in Turkey, I have been a guest in both of these house layout configurations.) In their follow-up study, the authors argued that these differing configurations signified different elements about late Ottoman society, especially

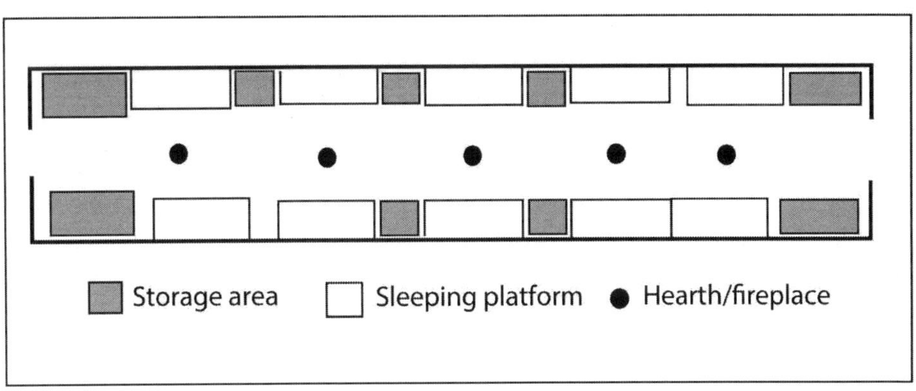

Figure 3.4: Stylized ground plan of an Iroquoian longhouse, showing application of access analysis methodology (based on descriptions in Wright 1979). Note the doorways at either end that allow direct access to living areas.

reflecting more conservative versus more liberal views in the 18th–19th centuries regarding gender relations and attitudes to strangers and visitors (Orhun, Hiller, and Hanson 1995). It is quite possible that a similar study carried out on present-day Turkish rural homes might find similar configurations and attitudes.

Spatial analysis using access and front/back studies can be applied not only at the household level but to spatial usage in an entire community. Gerald Oetelaar (1993) makes interesting use of front/back public/private analysis in his application of this method to the prehistoric (ca. CE 1100–1300) "Bridges" site in the Mississippian culture in south-central Illinois. He uses the front/back model to identify four spaces in the Bridges site: a communal front region, consisting of an open area and at least one communal structure; a family front region, which encompassed areas directly in front of houses; a family back region located inside and outside of domestic structures, including refuse and pits likely used for storage; and a communal back region, which contained a midden, work spaces, a possible footpath, and communal storage areas (1993: 672–78). By combining the front/back approach with the distribution of artifactual material, Oetelaar differentiated between public/communal activities and those more often relegated to the privacy of the home. His study also documented a long-term stability in spatial usage strategies of the Bridges occupants; deviations from these spatial patterns within the rural sites of the late Mississippian culture would be indicative of change in social and economic organization (Oetelaar 1993: 678–81).

That house plans may not only be lenses on attitudes toward privacy, but may also herald social change, has been of considerable interest to researchers (see chapter 9). Sally Foster (1989a, 1989b) used access analysis in a diachronic examination of Early to Late Iron Age Orkney houses, focusing on how the architectural configurations in homes conformed to residents' desire for privacy. Foster documented an increase in social hierarchy over the course of the Iron Age, identifying increased interest in constructing boundary controls and limiting access by strangers into home interiors (1989a: 47–49; 1989b: 45–50). The front/back, public/private differentiation became much more clearly defined by the Late Iron Age, with sleeping and storage areas eventually situated in the most difficult-to-access parts of the houses (1989b: 45). Boundary making and access control were achieved, particularly in elite homes, by the construction of additional walls (sometimes thickened) and by greater regulation of doorways (Foster 1989a: 49–50).

Also illustrating architectural adjustments to societal change, Graham Fairclough (1992) demonstrated that residents of a medieval castle redesigned access into and inside the castle, reflecting an increasing emphasis on domestic privacy and less attention to public areas. This change of attitude took place over a three-century period (ca. CE 1300–1575) and was at least partially precipitated by the declining fear of raids and the associated need to shelter during times of attack (Fairclough 1992: 362–64). Castle residents decreased the size of public areas and increased boundaries and access between public areas and their "back" private regions. Fairclough's study is important, as it illustrates that architectural change can occur in response to a variety of factors. The social change here was not that of increasing social complexity but rather an alteration in social climate: the lessening of fear of attack and the freedom to make one's elite home more private. A similar adjustment occurred in houses at Late Antique Aphrodisias when the need to more firmly establish social hierarchical rankings resulted in larger and more carefully designed audience halls in elite houses, replacing what had once been smaller public spaces from which visitors could easily glimpse house interiors and private rooms (Özgenel 2007). Architectural organization in both cases served the dual purpose of ensuring desired levels of privacy while also reaffirming social hierarchical rankings within the built structures.

As demonstrated by Fairclough, architectural analysis of access or privacy need not be limited to small-scale domestic structures. Van Dyke (1999) studied the Great House at the Guadalupe Ruin (ca. CE 900–1300), a settlement near Chaco Canyon in New Mexico. The Great House, a multi-roomed structure significantly larger than surrounding houses, rested on a butte above the rest of the community. Ruth Van Dyke was interested in determining if the Great House, whether constructed by outsiders from Chaco Canyon or by Guadalupe Ruin residents, was intended to establish authority through the control of resources and ritual activities (1999: 466). By using access analysis, she tracked access to spaces over four centuries and three phases of occupation. Her study concluded that specialized or controlled access to priority spaces such as storage and ritual areas was not apparent either in the initial building of the Great House nor through architectural alterations over time (Van Dyke 1999: 469–70). However, Van Dyke's study could not account for two critical factors (as Cutting pointed out was possible; see above): (1) the existence of a second story in the Great House, which may have controlled access, and (2) the fact that it rested on a butte above the community, so that approach to the entire structure may have been regulated (1999: 470).

In a study of prehistoric fourth- to third-millennium BCE Maltese temples, A. Bonanno and colleagues (1990) found exactly the opposite. Scholarly theories on these Maltese temples suggested that as social hierarchy increased, elites competed for control of regions and resources; temple construction symbolized power and control of larger temples correlated with greater authority (Bonanno et al. 1990: 192). The application of access analysis appears to confirm this view. Over the course of temple construction and expansion, Bonanno et al. found that "principles of exclusion began to operate" (1990: 202) as the elite hierarchy became more firmly established in the settlements. The creation of boundaries and limitations on access allowed those controlling the temple area, probably local elites, to regulate entry into the inner recesses of the central temples, areas devoted to such activities as the ritual consumption of food (Bonanno et al. 1990: 200–202). The change in temple architecture is reflective of changes in prehistoric Maltese social hierarchies, and these societal alterations can be "read" in the layouts of monumental buildings.

By comparing the Hasmonaean palaces (second–first centuries BCE) with Hellenized palaces built by Herod the Great later in the first century BCE in the Levant, Eyal Regev looked to answer the question, "What kind of rulers were the Hasmonaeans?" (2011: 45). Regev's detailed access analysis found that while the opulence of the five Hellenistic palaces seemed intended to overwhelm visitors with the importance of the palace inhabitants through grand audience rooms and vast courtyards, Hasmonaean rulers built palaces that represented themselves as "of the people," providing ample public gardens and pools and deemphasizing spaces within their own palatial abodes (2011: 63–68). Regev was able to employ the access analysis methodology to draw insight into the very nature of royal rule, and self-representation, within the complicated sociopolitics of the Hellenistic Levant.

Conclusion

The fields discussed in this chapter all seek methods to acquire specific and important data archaeologically: How many people lived there? Were they territorial? Did they crave privacy and if so, why? It is clear from the foregoing that one may indeed "read" a house, but only if all, or at least most, of the "written components" are there. Missing doorways, unidentifiable rooms, movable or invisible boundaries, and temporary occupation are all pitfalls that may trap an archaeologist into an inaccurate interpretation. In several cases, such as Wright's analysis of Iroquoian communities, ethnographic data are essential in order to achieve even a semblance of understanding as to how an ancient population used its household and community space. In other cases, as in Regev's excellent study, results can be retrieved from the archaeological record alone. The tools presented here are just that, tools that may aid in the quest to elicit data from an often recalcitrant past. And as is the case with all tools, sometimes they will be a good fit, but just as often they will be inadequate for the job.

Section II

Scales of Architecture: From Mobile Home to Cityscape

Chapter 4
The Mobile Architecture of Hunter-Gatherers and Nomadic Pastoralists

The notion of "home" is probably as varied as the number of human inhabitants on the planet. While it might be unclear whether hominids carried such a notion with them as they traveled the landscape (Sept 1992), there is little doubt that human hunter-gatherers and nomadic pastoralists had a keen sense of "going home" at the end of a long day spent gathering, hunting, or herding. Julian Thomas (2008) notes that people dwelled within their landscape and were shaped *by it* far more than they altered it when building their first dwellings. This chapter attempts to examine what types of information might be derived from the feathery light architectural footprint of mobile societies.

The Mobile Life of Hunter-Gatherers

It is the fate of archaeologists that ancient hunter-gatherer societies are very hard to study because they leave so little at their temporary homesteads. Even when hunter-gatherer habitation sites are identified and carefully excavated, the minimal levels of material culture and the light touch on the landscape present formidable challenges to interpretive efforts. This has led to a strong tradition of ethnographic research by archaeologists interested in understanding ancient hunter-gatherers (e.g., Binford 1978a, 1982; Brooks and Yellen 1987; Gould 1980; Kent 1991a, 1992, 1999; Yellen 1977). It is

Archaeology of Domestic Architecture and the Human Use of Space, by Sharon R. Steadman, 69–101.

from the work of scholars such as these that archaeologists have gained a relatively significant level of insight into the social institutions that make up ancient hunter-gatherer cultures.

Hunter-Gatherer Research: A Brief Profile

It is impossible to summarize the complex social structures of mobile cultures in a paragraph or two; an entire chapter—or better, a book—would have more chance of some success at portraying the diverse nature of these cultures. However, as anthropologists must do on a regular basis, the following discussion offers some general characteristics that will aid in the larger treatment of mobile architecture.

Anthropological descriptions of hunter-gatherer cultures have undergone substantial revisions over the last half-century. Originally, researchers assumed that these were groups of people regularly on the edge of starvation, always on the lookout for their next meal and a way to ease their stress-filled lives, who banded tightly together in small, egalitarian, kinship groups that relied on one another for survival. Several major studies published in the 1960s and shortly thereafter began to dispel these myths and attempted to describe the foraging culture based on empirical research (e.g., Lee and DeVore 1968; see Jordan 2008 for discussion). One important publication, first appearing in 1968 in Richard Lee and Erven DeVore's *Man the Hunter* but then in more developed form in 1972, was Marshall Sahlins's description of hunter-gatherers as the "original affluent society." Sahlins asserted that all their needs are met and thus they do not experience the stressors of the "modern" settled society. While not all hunter-gatherer communities have consistently rich environments to exploit (e.g., Yesner 1994), the notion that all hunter-gatherers are in constant and dire need of food resources has been largely debunked. Continued research rejects the notion of a hunter-gatherer "archetypal" social structure but rather reveals varied social and economic structures (e.g., in Bird-David 1992a; Price and Brown 1985; Rowley-Conwy 1991; Wilson 1988: 23–56). Scholars have also realized, through fieldwork, that hunter-gatherers are not always perfectly "egalitarian," do not always live in close-knit kin groups, may store acquired subsistence items, and sometimes take on wage labor work to supplement their foraging (Bird-David 1992b; Vierich and Hitchcock 1996;Woodburn 1982); all of these have an impact on their habitation patterns.

As more data were amassed, scholars began to attempt a more nuanced understanding of hunter-gatherer socioeconomic behaviors. Two studies in the early 1980s offered methods by which anthropologists and archaeologists might differentiate between hunter-gatherer behaviors with particular reference to storage systems. Lewis Binford (1980) and James Woodburn (1982) offered differing terminologies but similar analytical methods regarding hunter-gatherer behavior based on environmental settings. Woodburn (1982) categorized cultures into two basic groups: those that practiced either "immediate-return" or "delayed-return" systems. Immediate-return systems are found in "truly egalitarian" societies that consume acquired resources within hours or a few days; resources are shared, no storage is necessary, and group size is flexible, as members may come and go between different camps. In delayed-return systems, there is generally some technological aid to resource acquisition that requires labor to create or to operate (e.g., boats, trapping devices), and there is likely some additional processing of food necessary prior to consumption; resources might be stored over a period of weeks or even a season. Binford (1980) termed these groups "foragers" and "collectors," the former referring to cultures that lived where there are year-round resources, such as the tropics, and the latter to those living in more variable environments such as the Arctic region. Foragers, therefore, have no need to store resources, but collectors must do so to tide people over during the season(s) of scarcity. In delayed-return/collector societies, then, workstations and storage areas might look very different across the camp than they would in the immediate-return/ forager societies.

These studies opened the door, beginning in the mid-1980s (Price and Brown 1985), to discussion of differing complexity levels among hunter-gatherer societies, some deemed "simple" and others "complex" (see Arnold 1996a; Bettinger 1991; Burch and Ellanna 1994; Chapman 2003: 84–87; Coupland 2013; Finlayson and Warren 2010; Fitzhugh 2003; Kelly 1995; Myers 1988; Papagianni, Layton, and Maschner 2008; Prentiss and Kuijt 2004; Sassaman 2004). These studies recognized that some more "complex" hunter-gatherer societies might exhibit social hierarchies and hereditary status (Arnold 1996a), or differentially exploit resources (e.g., one group controlling marine resources, another the hunting of land mammals), which may relate to territorial or religious concerns (Kelly 1995: 293–331). As inquiry on "complex" hunter-gatherer societies increased, usage of the term "simple" fell into disuse, and foragers (whether they collected/stored goods or not) were identified either as highly mobile egalitarian groups, or emergent/already complex hunter-gatherers. Twenty years after the notion of simple/complex foragers entered the anthropological literature, Kenneth Sassaman (2004: 233) remarked that "[c]learly, the term *hunter-gatherer* does not carry the unified conceptual weight it once did. . . ." Closely tied to the exploration of hunter-gatherer complexity was a more dedicated focus on factors beyond the environment that might cause forager diversity. These included population size, contact or lack thereof with settled populations, the presence or absence of exotic and desirable non-utilitarian goods (possibly useful as trade items), and, of course, the presence or absence of storage systems (e.g., Kelly 1995; Kent 1991b). Material culture may be very helpful in identifying differing exploitation of resources across the camp (some huts might feature fish bones, others animal bones, for instance); architectural differences in hut placement, size, and presence of storage facilities might be indicators of egalitarianism or the existence of "complexity." It has become very clear that hunter-gatherer cultures are quite varied and that earlier "standard" interpretations of hunter-gatherer societies were far too simplistic.

Hunter-Gatherer Dwelling Types

There are myriad ways to describe the types of shelters that different hunter-gatherer societies construct. Norbert Schoenauer, leaving aside his sometimes terribly outdated language, divides housing structures into two major categories: "ephemeral or transient dwellings" and "episodic or irregular temporary dwellings" (Schoenauer 2000: 12). The ephemeral/transient dwelling is generally small, built of materials found nearby (branches, brush), and is typical of arid or tropical environments (Schoenauer 2000: 15–16); these shelters are used for only a few days or weeks until the group moves to a new location. Examples of such dwellings are the huts built by the Kalahari Bushmen, the (Ba)M'buti in tropical Africa, or the Arunta of central Australia (Figure 4.1a). The episodic/irregular houses are somewhat more substantial, owing to the fact that these foragers spend at least several weeks (or perhaps even close to two months) in the same location. Longer residence is in part due to the greater variety of exploitable ecozones, which may include riverine and forest resources, or, as in the case of the Inuit, the challenging climate, which requires more substantial shelter. These dwellings are also composed of natural materials, but they require more preparation than ephemeral/transient dwellings. Schoenauer's examples of episodic/irregular houses include Inuit ice houses and the Plains Indians circular lodges, the former requiring the fashioning of ice blocks and the latter the making of lodge poles and preparation of animal skins (Figure 4.1b). In each case, more labor is required for their construction. The lodges might have a greater impact on the landscape than would be the case for

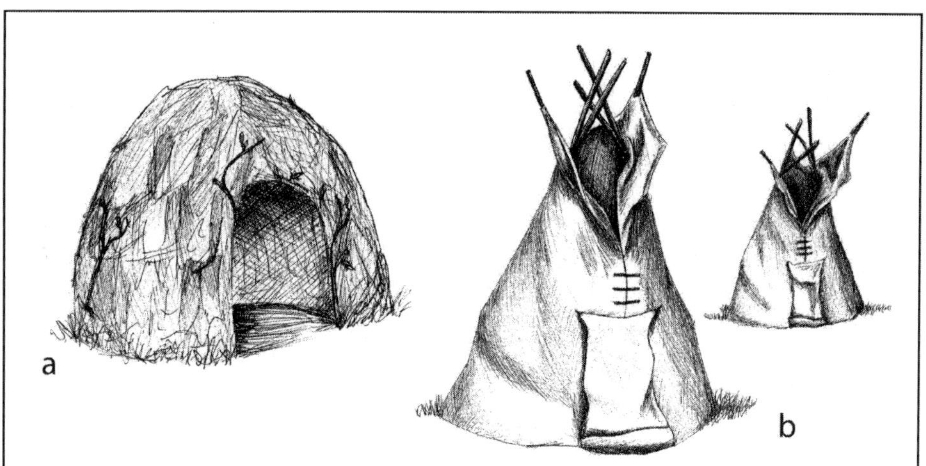

Figure 4.1: (a) Example of ephemeral/transient hunter-gatherer dwelling; (b) example of episodic/ irregular temporary dwellings (after Schoenauer 2000: 16, 18, 29; drawing by Corrina Petit).

ephemeral/transient dwellings, though the Inuit ice houses would leave absolutely no trace.

Interpreting Social Institutions from Hunter-Gatherer Architecture

Binford asserted that all cultures, nomadic or not, build shelters (1990). In nomadic cultures, shelters are commensurate with the environment not only in the materials used but in the level of sheltering needed (i.e., from hot sun, rains, etc.). Each group's degree of mobility is based on a number of variables, including the carrying capacity of the land, and whether the culture relies more on hunting (more mobile), gathering (perhaps slightly less mobile), or riverine/marine resources (far less mobile). The following discussion offers a range of information pertaining to human social institutions that might be derived from hunter-gatherer architectural remains. Social institutions here refer to the social pillars that constitute cultural structure, including economic strategy, kinship and family structures, political systems, and religion. These subjects are at the center of other chapters in this book, but the rather unique nature of mobile architecture calls for a closer analysis of them here.

Hunter-Gatherers and Subsistence Strategies

Any significant information on subsistence activities from a mobile camp will be derived more substantially from the artifactual remains than from the architecture. That said, there is some possibility of inferring subsistence "behavior" from the architecture, largely from examining the dwellings and the placement of production and consumption activities (see the discussion on household archaeology in chapter 7; and see Briz et al. 2013 and Escalera and Conte 2013). A strong indicator is the presence and location of storage systems in a hunter-gatherer camp. Most agree that storage systems are more likely to be found in environments with seasonal resources (such as arctic or temperate zones) than in tropical or arid locales. Truly egalitarian hunting and gathering, mobile societies would seem to be anathema to the notion of "storage," but Binford's (1980) "collectors"—that is, cultures that practice Woodburn's "delayed-return system"—do exist (e.g., Binford 1978b; Chatters and Prentiss 2005; Habu 2008; Morgan 2012; Speth and Spielmann 1983; Testart 1982; Zvelebil 1986; and see Fitzhugh and Habu 2002). Alain Testart (1982) argued that foragers who practice storage become more sedentary, moving toward "complexity," inasmuch as social inequality develops from resource possession. Timothy Ingold (1982), by contrast, notes that hunter-gatherers can remain quite mobile and still practice storage (leaving resources in a built structure at a camp for their eventual return), and Brian Hayden (1982, 1994) suggests that even hunter-gatherers who practice storage can be egalitarian and that, while storage *inevitably results from* socioeconomic inequality, it doesn't cause it (see also Kuijt 2008a for discussion). Ingold (1983) makes a distinction between "practical" storage and "social" storage; the former refers to the need to store resources for mutually exclusive activities (such as needing to stockpile in advance of a major celebration during which no one hunts or gathers) and the latter to the husbanding of resources due to varying availability. Neither negates, according to Ingold, mobility or egalitarian sharing. What is worth noting is that depending on the nature of the "practical" storage—that is, whether the practical need is frequent or only occasional—storage-based architecture may be quite ephemeral, whereas that of "social" storage, which may consist of seasonal or long-term structures, is more likely to be recognizable archaeologically.

Jerry Moore's work at Arroyo Hondo (2006) on the coast of Baja California is a stellar example of the challenges associated with interpreting socioeconomic behavior of hunter-gatherers based on architectural remains. Over several years of survey, Moore and his team recorded hundreds of forager sites, the earliest of which date to the early sixth millennium BCE. Moore notes, these were "small open-air camps, most probably inhabited for a single season. There are no traces of permanent houses or other structures, and dwellings were probably brush windbreaks" (2012: 28). Residents at these sites exploited marine resources (mussels, abalone), hunted deer, and gathered agave and other plant resources (Moore 2006). It is from the distribution of materials at these sites that researchers can glean some information on subsistence behavior: the presence of numerous *metates* and *manos* (grinding slabs and pestles) suggests that many group members participated, perhaps simultaneously, in processing food. A large cooking platform (Moore 2006) suggests that the processed food was cooked all at once (rather than separately by each "household"). Thus, at Arroyo Hondo sites 7,000 years ago, subsistence practices, not surprisingly, were cooperative and possibly completely egalitarian; it would seem the Arroyo Hondo hunter-gatherer culture practiced an immediate-return subsistence system without using a storage strategy. In this example, what constituted subsistence practices, and where and how mobile peoples did their work, were revealed through the placement of work-related materials such as tools and products of their work (e.g., bones). If the archaeological record is generous enough to supply architectural data—in the form of post-holes, for instance—then deeper inferences about the distribution of work (by household, performed on a group basis, etc.) might be possible.

Hunter-gatherers employ a variety of storage systems, but, as Susan Kent (1999) cautions, it is critical to differentiate between "storage" and "midden." Christopher Morgan (2012), based on his work in California, defined two main types of storage methods, which he terms "central place storage" and "caching." Central place storage refers to storage systems located at residential locales such as base camps where hunter-gatherers live seasonally or for shorter periods of time. Morgan found that central place storage systems were more closely associated with longer residence time—for instance, at a winter base camp (2012: 715, 730). He divides caching strategies into "dispersed" and "dispersed bulk," the former referring to smaller amounts of resources stored in various locales and the latter to more extensive resources that might tide a group over for a year or more, particularly in a highly variable environment (2012: 715). Morgan's study finds that residentially based storage does lead to greater sedentism, whereas caching, no matter what quantities are involved, enables mobility. Marianne Stopp (2002) used ethnohistorical and ethnographic data on the Inuit and Innu who lived on the Labrador-Quebec peninsula and on the island of Newfoundland (ca. 8500 BP to the 19th-century contact period) to examine not only types of storage systems but also the preservation methods used for the stored resources. Cultures in this region were primarily concerned with the long-term storage of marine mammal (seal), land mammal (caribou), and fish resources. Preservation techniques included dehydration or fermentation of the meat, fat preservation (e.g., oil kept in skins, probably largely undetectable archaeologically), and caching, which was a form of freezing or cold storing of resources (Stopp 2002: 306–16). Caching systems in Stopp's study area included bark-lined pits, scaffolds or cache racks, and some above-ground stone-built caches (2002: 314). Inside these, meats might be stored in boxes or other containers. Stopp also notes that caches were not always located in camps for later return but may also have been located along travel routes (2002: 319), which would make archaeological detection much more difficult. Like Morgan, Stopp stresses that caching does not encourage sedentism but instead enables mobility, in that foraging groups know that food awaits them at future camp locations or along the route.

The types of preservation methods and storage devices noted by Stopp also exist in Greenland. Sites excavated in the Disko Bay area of West Greenland (Olsen 1998) were occupied by mobile Palaeo-Eskimo societies between 2500 and 1800 BCE. Two roughly contemporary sites, Kuup Qalorsaa and Tupersuai, are of note here. Kuup Qalorsaa had only a single habitation structure, a circular tent with a central hearth. Circular tent structures known as "tent rings" were identified based on the presence of stones set in an oval or circular shape, the location of the hearth and fire-cracked rock, and the circular scatter of artifacts (Olsen 1998: 106). At Kuup Qalorsaa (ca. 2100–1800 BCE), the tent ring was accompanied by two other stone-built structures, which Olsen interpreted as caches for supplies that could be accessed during the winter (1998: 115). At Tupersuai, only the northern portion of the site was excavated; other structures observed on the surface remain unexplored. Excavators uncovered several phases of occupation, the earliest of which is described here (Structures II and III, ca. 2450–1950 BCE). Structure III was a habitation structure, ca. 3.2 × 1 m in size, built using upright stone slabs to ring the exterior (Olsen 1998: 97). Inside were a hearth, a sleeping area, and storage bins. Within 2 m of Structure III was Structure II, ca. 1.5 × 1.5 m, which the excavator identified as a rock-lined (subterranean) cache (Olsen 1998: 97). There may have been other early phase structures, possibly with associated caches, left unexcavated.

The example from western Greenland is notable for several reasons. First, the light mark that hunter-gatherer occupational sites make on the landscape is evident. Tent rings are discovered only if a hearth and artifact scatter remain; even more permanent stone-built structures are largely ephemeral. However, a second point is that what does remain suggests that the Palaeo-Eskimo inhabitants of these sites practiced "social" storage in their stockpiling for times of scarcity (although "practical" storage for an imminent ceremony is also possible). At Tupersuai, the presence of a built structure with internal hearth and sleeping areas suggests a winter base camp, and the cache may have been stocked in the fall when hunting was easier. The cache at Kuup Qalorsaa, likely a short-term hunting camp, was perhaps constructed in the summer for the provision of winter supplies (Olsen 1998: 115). The storage facilities at the Disko Bay sites support Stopp's assertion that caching does not inhibit mobility.

Subsistence strategies of "complex" foragers in temperate climates can be illuminated by examining architectural remains and associated material culture. In the case of hunter-gatherers in the eastern United States during the Archaic/Middle Woodlands periods (ca. 1200 BCE–CE 500), Andrew White (2013) finds evidence of increasing inequality between family groups. Hunter-gatherer camps offered noticeable changes in architecture: houses that had previously been roughly equal in size became variable in size and gained associated storage units. Material culture and economic data indicate that intensified resource acquisition strategies were at the root of these changes. Residents began collecting "low skill" and labor-intensive plant resources (generally seeds and nuts) that could be stored to sustain groups during the late winter and early spring season of scarcity (White 2013: 123). The development of intensified resource exploitation meant that quite young children could participate in a productive capacity, and this, according to White, led to larger, even polygynous families. Commensurate with this development were larger houses and associated storage units. These larger families, able to collect and store more resources, led to (less mobile) hunter-gatherer cultures with internal social inequality, demonstrated through material culture, architecture, and storage.

In a nearly opposite reaction to resource specialization at a Jomon-period site (ca. 3900–2300 BCE) in Japan, Junko Habu (2008) finds a complex hunter-gatherer society growing, seemingly, less complex. At the site of Sannai Maruyama, Habu examined the lithic and figurine assemblage associated with the pit dwellings spanning 12 occupational phases. The lithic data indicated that residents began to rely on specialized plant foods (likely chestnut, acorn, grass, and millet) rather than on animal products, shown by an increase in grinding stones and a decrease in scrapers (Habu 2008: 576–77). Concomitant with this was an increase in the number of huts; approximately 50 small, seasonally occupied huts, accompanied by nearly as many clay figurines (associated with rituals), populated the settlement during this plant resource specialization period. However, in the phases shortly after this period, the number of huts and figurines dropped dramatically, and the stone tool assemblage reflected a dominance of arrowheads rather than grinders (Habu 2008: 576–80). For Habu, the data indicate that plant specialization could not, in the end, sustain population growth, and thus residents returned to smaller, more dispersed groups practicing a mixed hunter-gatherer economy. Smaller numbers of people required fewer figurines and certainly fewer housing structures.

Hunter-Gatherer Social Structure: Kinship, Gender, Politics, and Religion

Flexible family configurations among hunter-gatherers, limited material culture for identifying gendered spaces, a purported lack of political structures, and ritual practices that are usually performed outdoors all cast doubt on whether the topics discussed here should even be broached. However, as these social institutions are at the core of most discussions in this volume, they are worth exploring. As the following will show, hints of them can indeed be culled from the archaeological and occasionally the architectural record.

Kinship and Family

The placement of temporary dwellings in a camp may give some information as to kinship relations, though in his study of Greenland sites, Bjønar Olsen notes that this can be rather tricky (1998: 122): "Saqqaq societies may have had the character of local bands . . . consisting of small, exogamous residential groups. . . . The need to maintain a flexible social system may have prevented close kindred residential groups as well as promoted bilateral and bilocal kinship systems. . . . " Yet, while family relationships and kinship structures in hunter-gatherer camps may be indeterminable based on architectural remains, basic social relationships might be recoverable. At the very lowest level of analysis, one might determine the number of people living together based on camp size and the number and size of huts or structures (see chapter 3, and Kent 1991b). For instance, an ethnoarchaeological study (Svoboda et al. 2011) of the Nenets in northwest Siberia offered interesting evidence suggesting that housing can correspond to nuclear family structure in the prehistoric past (Figure 4.2). The Nenets (today, reindeer herders who also practice a hunting economy) migrate and camp in nuclear family groups; usually two or three families cooperate together. Each family, generally a husband and wife with two or three children, builds a "chum," which is a circular tent with a floor made of planks and skins and a wooden superstructure covered by a reindeer skin (Svoboda et al. 2011: 33). Each chum has a central hearth and a "toss" area outside the doorway; between 5 and 10 m typically separate chums, and between them are sometimes shared activity areas, such as for woodworking (Svoboda et al. 2011: 34–37). The structure size, single hearth, and artifactual assemblage suggests that four to five people occupied a chum, and the ethnographic record reveals that these occupants consist of a nuclear family. The Nenet camp demonstrates that archaeological remains, if recoverable, can provide evidence as to family structures, if not kinship relationships.

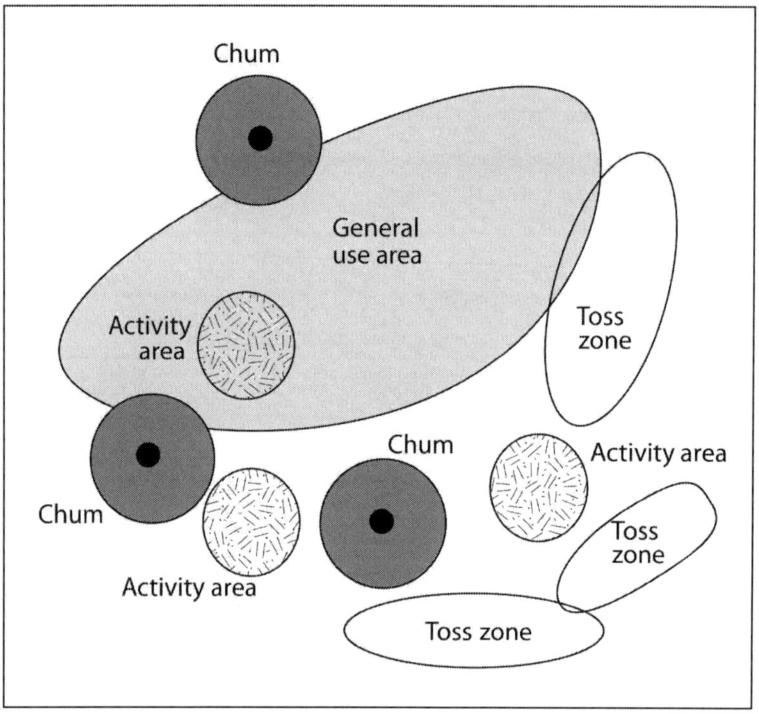

Figure 4.2: Nenet site showing distribution of housing in a hunter-gatherers' site in which "chums" likely housed a nuclear family (after Svoboda et al. 2011: fig. 5).

Gendered Spaces and Hunter-Gatherer Camps

Most gender-based discussions relevant to (both modern and prehistoric) hunter-gatherer societies focus, quite successfully, on the sexual division of labor (e.g., Claassen 1991; Gero 1991; Joachim 1988; Keeley 2010; Owen 2000; Sassaman 1998; Wadley 1998). Rock art, as discussed below (and see Parkington 2002), can also indicate women's roles in a hunting-gathering society. However, relating the artifactual remains of labor to gendered space within a camp or hut is often problematic because of the need to assign "tools" and "activities" to specific genders and to assume that hearths, for instance, were typically used by women (LeMoine 2003; Reinhardt 2002; Wadley 2000; see discussion in Weedman 2006). Add to this the possible existence of more than two genders in a society (Duke 1991) and we have an even more problematic situation. Even when there is remarkable preservation, such as at the Upper Palaeolithic (ca. 23,000–20,000 BP) Levantine site of Ohalo II on the Sea of Galilee (Nadal 2003; Nadal and Hershkovitz 1991; Nadal et al. 2004), it is possible to infer (from a wealth of material culture within the huts) what activities took place, but not who did them. There is no doubt that spatiality in hunter-gatherer camps is indeed differentiated, with some areas more commonly occupied by specific genders and others used by all (e.g., see studies in Jarvenpa and Brumbach 2006). For instance, ethnographic data indicate that, in Nenet chums, the interior is the "female" space while the exterior is the "male" space (Svoboda et al. 2011: 33). However, translating ethnographic observations to the archaeological record is fraught with difficulties (see discussion in Kent 1998a); thus, as already noted, the vast majority of archaeological information on gender in prehistoric hunter-gatherer societies derives from portable artifacts rather than from spatial analysis. Nicole Waguespack (2005) examined ethnographic societies with a predominance of male hunting activities to answer the question, "What do women do in large-game hunting societies?" Besides plant gathering, they engage in many activities, including "weaving, pottery making, butchery, house building, rope making, leather working, basketry, and burden carrying" (Waguespack 2005: 671). Waguespack could then speculate about what Palaeoindian Clovis women of the American Southwest did thousands of years ago, and where.

In her assessment of European Magdalenian (ca. 17,000–10,000 BP) women's roles, Meg Conkey notes that, aside from the spectacular cave painting sites and a few rock shelters, the "typical" Magdalenian sites, probably located near rivers, are largely archaeologically absent, and "above all, the Magdalenian period appears to have yielded a wealth of material objects" rather than habitation sites (Conkey 1991: 59). She goes on to analyze the discoveries at Cueto de la Mina, a rock-shelter site, which offered a host of material culture pointing to activities such as cordage and net construction, sewing, tool crafting, and a variety of other tasks that Conkey suggests might have been accomplished by women while men hunted (1991: 76–79). As in Waguespack's study, it is the artifacts rather than architecture (or lack thereof) that offer vital clues to gendered activities (also see Cattin 2010 for similar analyses). While ethnographic data tell us that there are frequently gendered spaces in hunter-gatherer residential units and even across the camps, unless certain assumptions about "who used what item" are made, defining these spaces is extraordinarily difficult. Though research has illuminated the vital roles played by women and men in prehistoric or present-day hunter-gatherer communities (see Brumbach and Jarvenpa 2007; Dahlberg 1981; Kent 1998b; Leacock 1978; Lee 1981, 1982; Murdock and Provost 1973), the architectural record, except possibly in a very few spectacular situations, is largely silent on gendered spaces in these types of mobile societies.

Social Inequality

Briefly mentioned above was the subject of social inequality and the possible existence of structured leadership systems within hunter-gatherer societies, which are more often present in "delayed-return system" societies that are likely sedentary for a season or longer. In fact, most anthropologists find the existence of "non-egalitarian" hunter-gatherer societies to be rather uncommon: "There are only a few ethnographic examples that fit the anthropological definition of nonegalitarian hunter-gatherers" (Kelly 1995: 302). Most cite the Ainu of Japan and societies on the North American west coast as the gold standard of hunter-gatherer societies that practiced social inequality. This does not mean that the ranks of hunter-gatherer societies spread across Africa, most of Asia, the Middle East, Europe, and the rest of the Americas were all egalitarian all of the time; individual leaders who gain respect for their oratorical skills, their age, number of wives, or other factors did and do exist. But the institutionalized social inequality that comes with "non-egalitarian" is not present across camps or through generations (see, for instance, studies in Burch and Ellanna 1994; Leacock and Lee 1982). The placement and orientation of structures in hunter-gatherer camps are more likely to correlate to individual social relations than to status. Among the M'buti of the central African rainforest, Colin Turnbull reports that "if relatives come to visit, either the house has to be enlarged or a new one built. Whenever this happens there are repercussions throughout the camp since people will have to change the entrances to their huts to avoid looking directly into the stranger's hut. The entrances also get changed if there are arguments between two families" (1961: 132). Note that a larger hut here corresponds to visitors rather than social status. Privacy concerns dictate entrance placement, as do social relations. A further example of the latter is found among the G/wi of Botswana, where the building of huts corresponds to the "temporary preference among the constituent households for one another's close company," even though "leadership in the band is apparent at all phases of decision-making," in the sense of individual prowess rather than institutionalized authority (Silberbauer 1982: 28–29). Even within a generation in which there is an acknowledged "leader," the living arrangements are far more likely to reflect who is getting along with whom rather than who carries significant status. Finally, a comparative study of Australian Aboriginal and Kalahari Bushmen camps (Gould and Yellen 1987) found that hut placement (close together in the African cultures, farther apart in Australia) was due to fear of predation by wild animals! The social equation, therefore, may be entirely missing from hunter-gatherer hut placement and orientation.

Equally challenging is the identification of higher-ranking members within a hunter-gatherer camp, though indicators used to track elite residences in settled societies (see chapter 9) can be used: dwellings, even though they are meant to be temporary structures, might be larger or built with a greater intensity of labor; stored resources may be more abundant in a high-ranking residence; dwelling contents may indicate a more consistent access to desirable goods. A good example comes from the Owens Valley in California (Eerkens 2004, 2009), where early 20th-century ethnographic data describe a non-egalitarian hunter-gatherer Paiute society. Recent archaeological work on Paiute sites that date between 1000 and 600 years ago has sought to identify the processes that led to their complex hunter-gatherer structure. The main indicator of social inequality between nuclear family household units was the possession of non-utilitarian items such as beads and more desirable goods such as obsidian, especially from diverse sources (Eerkens and Spurling 2008). The development of non-egalitarianism in the Owens Valley seems to have corresponded to a shift in resource acquisition, with individual groups specializing in seed acquisition; thus, larger family units could acquire more foods (Eerkens 2004). Commensurate with this was the ability of larger family units to develop more social networks and thus acquire a greater amount of exchange items such as obsidian and beads. At Owens Valley Paiute sites, a larger residence reflects a larger family unit, which in turn correlates to a wealthier household.

On the Kodiak Islands, Ben Fitzhugh (2003) saw a similar trend involving increasing complexity and changing house size and structure. Over the course of 3,000 years, from the Kachemak to the Koniag periods (ca. 3200–200 BP), residents of the Kodiak Islands seemingly transitioned from egalitarian to complex, non-egalitarian hunter-gatherers. In the earlier Kachemak phase, nuclear families resided in rectangular wooden houses averaging 15 m^2 in size, containing a hearth and storage pit, and were usually single-roomed and not significantly differentiated in size: "[A]ll Kachemak people lived, cooked, ate, and slept in their small single-roomed houses" (Fitzhugh 2003: 203) and cooperated in resource acquisition. By the Koniag phase several thousand years later, houses averaged 47 m^2 and were multi-roomed; the central room functioned as kitchen and living area, with a large central hearth and storage boxes, and side rooms served as sleeping quarters or special-function rooms such as sweat-bath chambers (Fitzhugh 2003: 202). These later structures were inhabited by extended families that cooperated to increase resource acquisition within the household unit instead of across the community. These changes appear to have coincided with a decrease in the availability of resources and the (successful) attempts of groups, usually kin-related, to acquire control over critical or prestige items (Fitzhugh 2003: 219–44). Co-residential family members who had access to significant amounts of resources had larger houses, more storage areas, and more influence in politics and decision-making processes. House size and storage capacity in the Kodiak Islands corresponded not just to the family size but to political and economic authority.

That current scholarship locates the predominance of "complex" and "non-egalitarian" hunter-gatherer societies in North America and Japan does not mean that they did not exist in other regions. Some "complex" hunter-gatherer cultures may have transitioned to semi-nomadic cultivators and then to settled farmers in prehistory. Indeed, scholars have engaged in significant discussion on the processes potentially involved in an "evolution" from mobile economic strategies to sedentary society (see discussions in Arnold 1996a; Jordan 2008; Layton, Foley, and Williams 1991; Sassaman 2004; Shott 2001), but this topic is well beyond the scope of this volume. Relevant here is the reality that recognizing social inequality among hunter-gatherers is possible, but difficult; architecture can function as only one of the critical lines of evidence in such investigations.

Religion and Ritual

Discovering clues to hunter-gatherer ritual and religion through architecture is rare, though not unheard of. The main obstacle is that most hunter-gatherer ritual activity depends on the use of ritual items or clothing, all of which is either composed of organic materials or requires no materials at all. Examples of hunter-gatherer rituals include the "trance dance" of Kalahari Bushmen cultures, which requires a hearth fire, some musical instruments (of organic materials), and human participants; or the *molimo* ritual among the M'buti of central Africa, which requires a hearth and includes singing and dancing and the playing of the *molimo* wooden trumpet. Many hunter-gatherer societies, including Australian Aboriginal, North American, Siberian, Kalahari Bushmen, and Palaeolithic European cultures, include rock art as an important element in their ritual performances. This art often remains vibrant in the archaeological record, and interpretation of its meaning has led to a vast literature on the topic (for discussions see Lewis-Williams 2002; Price 2001; Whitley 2001, 2006). However, rock art, even on cave or rock-shelter walls, does not really constitute the *creation* of a built environment for ritual purposes. Structures built by mobile hunter-gatherers to host ritual activity are quite rare, but among some cultures identified as "complex" they do exist; often these structures are built when cultures are seasonally stationary or are engaged in increasing periods of sedentism (see Aldenderfer 1993b). Fitzhugh's work in the Kodiak Islands recovered architectural remains that were larger and likely nondomestic in function; the ethnographic record suggests that feasting (in this region, potlatching) was the reason for the construction of these buildings (Fitzhugh 2003: 70–74). In many mobile cultures, seasonal gatherings are held at which trading, marriage partner selection, and other social interaction activities take place, and some kind of communal feasting almost always forms part of the event.

Another type of ritual architecture—or more specifically, ritual space—is demonstrated by excavations of Chumash sites on the California Channel Islands. The Chumash present a fascinating case of hunter-gatherer/marine foragers who, over the course of millennia, developed a significant social hierarchy that, by the time of contact, was referred to as "chiefdom" (Arnold 1992, 2001, 2004; Arnold, Colten, and Pletka 1997). Certainly in later prehistory, and perhaps earlier, the Chumash built *siliyik,* which were enclosures within which dancing and the playing of bone whistles took place (Corbett 2004). The *siliyik* was circular, surrounded by poles and mat screens which served to block the view of interior activities. Those allowed inside the *siliyik* were the *'antap,* who were the community's ritual specialists (Corbett 2004). Each community had a number of *'antap* who were drawn from the leading Chumash families. While the antiquity of the Chumash *'antap* specialist group is debated (some feel it developed just before or during the contact period), the *siliyik*-style dance floors and sacred bone whistles are associated with earlier Chumash sites (Hollimon 2004; Corbett 2004). Ethnographic data inform archaeologists that feasting and dance/music ceremonialism is fairly common, and architectural clues to these activities are, with luck, sometimes preserved in ancient campsites.

The Mobile Life of Nomadic Pastoralists

Nomadic pastoralism existed on nearly every inhabited continent in prehistory, even the Americas (e.g., Browman 2008; Nielsen 2009). It is best known and documented, however, in the Middle East, Central Asia, and on the African continent, with an additional substantial literature on Arctic reindeer herders. The following discussion focuses mainly on these regions because of the more extensive ethnographic, ethnoarchaeological, and archaeological data that derive from them.

Nomadic Pastoralist Research: A Brief Profile

Nomadic pastoralist research is, in many ways, far less controversial than that related to prehistoric hunter-gatherer cultures. Nomadic pastoralists herded animals and thus controversy over economic subsistence strategies is at a minimum; they were rarely egalitarian, and thus arguments about social inequality center on "how much" inequality there was in any given pastoralist society rather than on whether it existed at all. Though nomadic pastoralist architecture is often as ephemeral as that of hunter-gatherers, the generally larger pastoralist camps and greater amounts of material culture left somewhat more of an imprint on the landscape. There is, therefore, greater likelihood of finding pastoralists in the archaeological record and interpreting social structure from those remains.

Most of the scholarly debate regarding pastoralists centers not on herding but on whether herding was a precursor to agriculture and sedentism: do herders *become* farmers, and once sedentary, do they ever return to a mobile herding lifestyle? The Near East and southern Africa are areas in which these discussions flourish. The herding of sheep and goat became common in southern Africa roughly 2,000 years ago (Sadr 1998; Webley 2007). However, archaeological evidence for domestication prior to that time is lacking, prompting some scholars to argue that herding was imported into southern Africa from the north, where it was an older economic tradition (Mitchell 2002; Smith 2005, 2008). Others argue that there was no *sudden* transition to herding, but that hunter-gatherers may have adopted very small herds or flocks which, over the course of centuries, grew to sizes more commonly associated with "pastoralist" economics (Sadr 2003, 2008).

The more plentiful data in the Near East provides different platforms for significant debate regarding the role of ancient pastoralists in the emergence of agriculture. That sedentism occurred in some fashion, perhaps from hunter-gatherers engaging in early cultivation practices, is a substantial topic of discussion in Epipalaeolithic/Neolithic Levantine studies (see discussions in Bar-Yosef 2002; Bar-Yosef and Belfer-Cohen 1991;

Boyd 2006; Edwards 1989; Henry 1989, 1991; Watkins 2005). However, the transition, according to these and other scholars, may have been a "bumpy ride" (Belfer-Cohen and Bar-Yosef 2000), and most agree that the role of animal domestication was prominent. In fact, another argument suggests that Pre-Pottery Neolithic A–B Levantine residents (9th–7th millennia BCE), once settled, did not feel compelled to remain so. The pressures of population growth and the need to ensure a permanent and reliable subsistence base resulted in some returning to a pastoralist lifestyle in the Pre-Pottery Neolithic B. During this period, sedentary/farming villages appeared to have been abandoned, and new communities appeared on the arid Levantine landscape that conform to the kind that mobile pastoralists might have built (Banning 1995; Bar-Yosef 1984; Goring-Morris 1993). Herders, whose ancestors had had a taste of sedentary farming life, (re)turned to life on the open landscape.

A great deal of literature is devoted to the degree of sedentism present in a pastoralist camp. Studies focusing on this are relevant today, due to the effects of globalization and land management systems that privilege farming over pasturage (e.g., Galvin 2009; Khazanov and Schlee 2012; Khazanov and Wink 2001); such concerns were likewise relevant in prehistory, when various socioeconomic factors, including engagement in cultivation practices or trade with settled farming communities, may have encouraged increased sedentism among pastoralists (Jarno 1984; Polat 2013; Porter 2012; Rowton 1973, 1974). The degree of sedentism in a nomadic camp is sometimes simply an expression of their normal level of mobility (Tibetan nomads, for instance, stay at a "home base" for half a year or more), or may be related to specific factors such as trade or burgeoning cultivation that create the need for longer encampments. These issues are addressed below.

Perhaps even more so than hunter-gatherer studies, the archaeology of nomadic pastoralism relies on ethnographic data—even with the inherent pitfalls of using present-day cultures to aid in interpretation of ancient ones, a concern often raised (see discussions in Bernbeck 2008; Frachetti 2008; Gifford-Gonzalez 1991, 1998; Porter 2012). Despite the risks of using ethnographic analogy to interpret the past, the study of nomadic cultures of the past century goes far to enable the interpretation of architectural remnants left by pastoralists from long ago.

Nomadic Pastoralist Dwelling Types

Roger Cribb (1991) refers to all pastoral nomadic dwellings as "tents" no matter their shape or material constitution; and he is not alone in preferring this term to describe the dwellings of pastoral nomads (see discussion in Cowan 2002). Schoenauer also finds that nomadic pastoralists regularly reside in "portable tents," which he designates "periodic or regular temporary dwellings" (2000: 41; see Figure 4.3). Peter Andrews asks, "When is a tent not a tent?" and goes on to note that he has been "taken to task" for describing as "tents" Central Asian yurts and Iranian pastoralist huts that use a wattle base (1997: 3). Andrews answers his question and, for the purposes of this volume, his answer is more than adequate. For Andrews, building materials are not the key; tents are tents as long as part or all of the walls are transportable and they have a "covering which can be separated from its supports" (1997: 3). He notes that not every group actually transports all parts of the tent; in some cases, parts of the frame are left in place for eventual return or are stored at various locales along the migration route (1997: passim). That transportable materials are *not* transported does not void the structure's identity as a tent. Since the covering usually consists of something that took some effort to create, it is usually transported and placed over a new (or previously existing) frame at the next campsite.

The superstructures of most pastoral nomad tents, especially prior to the 20th century, were constructed of animal skins. Schoenauer and others note that there are exceptions to this, such as in some African cultures that construct wooden tents covered by woven mats or brush (Schoenauer 2000: 44–45; Daker 1984); Labelle Prussin finds that textiles are also used (1974, 1995). Quite often, tents are constructed of felt or skins over a framework consisting of wooden poles or even animal bones. The tent materials could be transported by herd animals from camp to camp. Andrews offers a magnificent inventory of tent types, listing their size, shape, materials, plan, and transport methods, used by pastoralists stretching from Turkey to central Asia (1981, 1986, 1997), complete with a glossary of dozens of different architectural features (1997: 18–19). Like the other materials in hunter-gatherer camps, the architectural assemblage of most tents is almost entirely constructed of organic materials that easily decay; thus, it is often only the post-holes or stone foundations and supports that remain in the archaeological record.

Figure 4.3: Example of a nomadic pastoralist dwelling modeled on Bedouin tents (after Schoenauer 2000: 47; drawing by Corrina Petit).

Interpreting Social Institutions from Pastoral Nomadic Architecture

The fact that pastoralists have more *stuff* and built more substantial structures than hunter-gatherers would seem to mean that acquiring data on social behavior is far easier. Naturally, this is not the case, because nomadic pastoralists often make as light an imprint on the landscape as hunter-gatherers, and in fact their campsites are sometimes even tidier! As noted throughout this book, architectural remains are but a tiny cog in the enormous wheel that is the archaeological record. Without the accompanying data derived from organic and artifactual remains, ecological settings, other resources such as ancient texts, and, of course, a judiciously employed ethnographic record, the architecture can provide only a faint impression, if that, about those who inhabited it.

Nomadic Pastoralists and Economic Subsistence Strategies

The overarching subsistence strategies of nomadic pastoralists revolve around herd management and the use of what has come to be termed "secondary products" (Greenfield 2010; Marciniak 2011; Sherratt 1981, 1983), meaning the fiber and dairy products that can be harvested from live animals. There is some debate as to whether nomadic pastoralists who engage in cultivation are "true" pastoralists. The focus here is on the housing built by nomads who herd animals as a mainstay of their subsistence, whether they dabble in cultivation or not.

Perhaps one of the simplest methods of getting at the economic strategies of nomadic pastoralists is to examine their architectural patterns. In other words, is their whole "kit" entirely mobile and transportable, or is some of it left behind for later return? As Claudia Chang and Perry Tourtellotte note for pastoralists in the Balkans, "there is a continuum of pastoral mobility strategies wherein, at one end of the spectrum, pastoral specialists engage in long-distance seasonal transhumance, while at the other end, village herders keep their livestock year-round on village lands" (1993: 249). The "transhumance" refers to pastoral nomads who move their flocks and homes either vertically (lowlands to uplands) or horizontally (across different pasturages) at intervals that often, but not always, correspond to seasonal changes.

Architectural strategies of nomadic pastoralists can be divided into two categories: entirely mobile (when all elements of the tent are packed up and moved), and partially stationary (when more permanent architecture is built for eventual return). Examples of both abound in the ethnographic and archaeological records. Complete mobility means that upon return to the region, pastoralists need not camp in exactly the same place as they had in the previous visit; they may be meters or even a kilometer away from previous campsites.

Many Bedouin cultures offer excellent examples of complete architectural mobility. During his years excavating in Wadi Ziqlâb, in Jordan, Ted Banning observed daily life in several Bedouin camps. When he returned to his site in 1990, a Bedouin family had erected a tent near where his excavations would take place; he reported the following activities by the woman inhabiting the tent (1993: 215):

> The woman had excavated shallow terraces in three steps down the slope, one for each tent compartment, and shallow ditches to direct any rainwater away from the living floors. . . . Shortly after our arrival, apparently prompted by our plans to excavate only a short distance from her tent, she moved the tent to the other side of the road. This operation she carried out by herself in about an hour and a half.

Banning's observations offer two (among other) insights: the slight imprint on the landscape left by the shallow ditches would not last long archaeologically, and the women had no qualms about occupying a different space than she had originally chosen. Perhaps in the following year, to avoid contact with Banning's excavation altogether, she might have chosen a spot quite a bit more distant.

Total mobility is not unique to the Bedouin of the Middle East. The Rendille of eastern Africa traditionally packed up tents, furniture, and belongings onto their camels (a process that took approximately two hours) to move between a few hundred meters to a hundred kilometers or more, depending on pasturage and water needs (Grum 1995). A similar process is found among the tent-dwelling pastoral nomads of Afghanistan (Szabo and Barfield 1991). In these types of camps, the remnants left behind after the camp has relocated are quite minimal compared with those in partially stationary camps. And yet, ethnoarchaeology has observed remains such as milking platforms and refuse scatters from household sweeping (Simms 1988), circular or rectilinear patterns of stones used to hold down tent flaps, hearths, and, occasionally, postholes. Even these seemingly ephemeral remains are sometimes detectable archaeologically.

In the second category, nomads return each year to their partially built camps. The Tibetan pastoral nomads of the Pala Plateau have a "home-base" encampment where they spend much of the winter, spring, and part of the summer, and then in the late summer and fall they move their herds to fresh pastures in "temporary" camps (Goldstein and Beall 1990: 58–64). At the home-base camp, the nomads live in tents made of heavier materials, including yak hair, to withstand the brutal winters; tents at the temporary camps are made of lighter materials, such as cloth, when summer and early fall temperatures can reach 100 °F. At the home-base, the nomads excavate down approximately 1 m in a rectangular shape, over which they can pitch their tent; around these, they construct stone or sod walls to act as windbreaks during the harsh winters (Goldstein and Beall 1990: 62). Other structures include stone-walled corrals and occasionally a small one-room sod or stone storage hut. A somewhat similar case is found among eastern African cattle-herders who build substantial "*kraals*," usually with the huts arrayed around it. *Kraals* protect the animals from predation and theft; though dwellings and their contents are moved when pasturage demands it, the *kraals* remain for eventual return. In each of these instances, there is a possibility of architecture remaining in the archaeological record.

Michael Frachetti's work at the site of Begash in the Koksu Valley of eastern Kazakhstan illustrates how the construction of the relatively more permanent structures can aid in archaeological analysis. Frachetti and his colleagues (Frachetti 2008; Frachetti and Mar'yashev 2007) documented 4,000 years of nomadic pastoralist residential history at Begash over the course of six occupational phases. The construction of cist tombs likely drew the repeated use of Bronze Age pastoralists (2460–1950 BCE), while in other phases the construction of stone-built foundations (topped by movable and organic superstructures) may have been the attraction. The construction of more durable architecture indicated to Frachetti that not only did pastoralists return to the Koksu Valley in general, but precisely to Begash, which he terms "a node in a pastoralist landscape" (2007: 224). At another site in eastern Kazakhstan, Mukri, Frachetti found what appears to be a shift from one mobility strategy to another over the course of the Phase 2–3 occupations. Nomadic pastoralists who occupied Phase 2 Iron Age Mukri for as long as two centuries (CE 440–650) built stone foundations to what were probably their mobile superstructures. That the stone foundations were reconfigured over this period suggests a reuse by the same people or culture rather than a foreign presence (Frachetti et al. 2010: 634). The labor put into the Phase 2 structures speaks to a longer-term (perhaps season- or multi-season-long) occupation. During the Phase 3 Medieval period (ca. CE 1040–1260), architectural remains were quite different; only a single course of stones, in a circular pattern, remained, which were interpreted as footings for circular tents or yurts (2010: 637). The far more ephemeral remains may have represented "the last construction of a campsite that was re-used and re-configured—seasonally, periodically or both—over the span of a few centuries" (Frachetti et al. 2010: 639). Frachetti suggests that Mukri was a desirable locale for a pastoralist camp because of its proximity to trade routes, fresh water, and good pasturage, explaining the relative permanence of the Phase 2 camp. By the Phase 3 period, however, pastoralists may have been more reliant on trade than on herds, and thus the need to stay near traders on caravan routes may have resulted in much higher rates of mobility and much lower labor investment in camp structures.

Labor and time investment in more permanent camp structures, or lack thereof, is certainly detectable in the archaeological record. At the very least, the presence of such structures likely means that, first, there was the intention on the part of a mobile group to return to the same location, and, second, that once there, they may have remained for some time. The lack of any permanent architectural structures *may* indicate a much higher rate of mobility in a pastoralist group, and that returning to *precisely* the same locale was not necessarily incumbent upon them. The reasons for employing one mobility strategy over the other are, of course, far more difficult to discern. The pastoralists in eastern Kazakhstan may have wanted either to stay near critical resources (more permanence) or to move at a moment's notice when traders deviated from an expected route (high mobility). Among the Tibetan nomads of the Pala region, the weather plays a huge role. As the snows recede in the foothills, herders from temporary camps can take herds up to fresh grasses, but lowland home-base camps protect them from frozen winter nights. Ethnography suggests that access to specific tracts of land for pasturage, provided by settled farmers, has a bearing on where and for how long pastoralists might settle. Likewise, in prehistory or early historic periods, as cities developed, pastoralists may have chosen to camp for longer periods near settlements in symbiotic exchange relationships (Khazanov and Wink 2001; Porter 2012; Rowton 1973, 1974).

Animal enclosures are another architectural clue to economic strategies. It is generally the case that livestock is "owned" by family or cooperative units rather than shared equally by the members of a pastoralist camp. In this way, herds function as "fields on the hoof" (Ekvall 1968), a specific resource for which the care and feeding falls to those who control them. Herd sizes vary widely across cultures and regions, and even from camp to camp. Sheep/goat herd sizes can vary from 50 to 100 per household in the Middle East to flocks of up to 600 sheep/goat in the Balkans (Chang and Tourtellotte 1993; Cribb 1991: 25–26). In part, herd size is based on what is necessary for minimal subsistence of the economic unit; annual mortality rates also affect herd size. For instance, among pastoral nomads living in the Pala Plateau of Tibet, the sheep/goat/yak herds are significantly larger than the average herd size in the Middle East; the annual mortality rate can be as high as 50% of the herd due to severe weather and predation (Goldstein and Beall 1990; Naess et al. 2004). In Arctic societies, reindeer herd sizes vary greatly, and the risks to the animals are enormous, ranging from snowstorms and wolf attacks to "the huge wave of wild reindeer migrations, since domestic animals have a tendency to run away and join their wild relatives" (Ventsel 2012: 47). Overall, then, it may be quite difficult to determine herd size archaeologically, but where they were kept might be attainable.

There are two major strategies for herd management in the camp, each with enormous variation in style: a communal fold or pen where all animals are kept, or small pens, yards, or herd lines (posts connected by ropes to which animals may be tied) associated with each tent or a small group of tents. The different spatial layout of these two strategies can be seen in Figure 4.4; in 4.4a, the herd is penned at night into a central yard bounded by the fencing and structures. In Figure 4.4b, the sheep fold or pen is associated with the tent, either next to it or actually covered by the tenting material. The animals owned by everyone in the camp are penned together in the first example, whereas in the second, each household keeps its animals separately from the others. There can be many reasons for choosing one strategy over the other within a culture or even in a particular camp. Ethnography and ethnoarchaeology have helped to identify some of the reasons behind these herd management choices.

The far more common strategy appears to be the construction of one centralized pen to house the animals at night. Those of us who have worked in places where herding is common have seen the various methods that owners use to mark their animals.

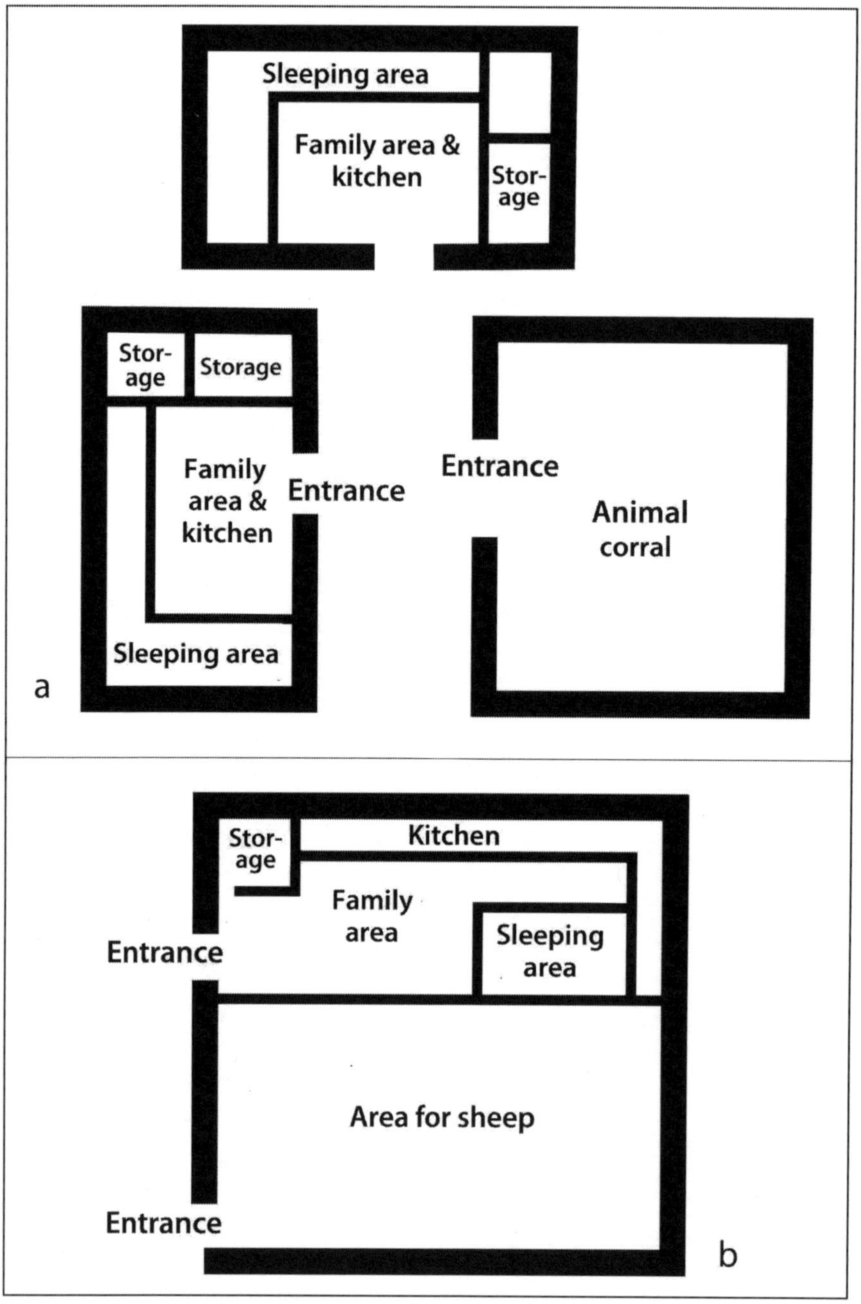

Figure 4.4: (a) Example of a nomadic pastoralist camp with communal herd management; (b) example of a nomadic pastoralist camp with individualized herd management (after Cribb 1991: 102–3).

In the village where I have worked for over two decades, a quickly spray-painted colorful spot on the rump or side of a sheep identifies the animal as to owner (I have seen the same done to geese as well). Thus, a shepherd may be caring for a herd of sheep that bears three or four different color marks. The markings may aid in delivering the proper sheep back to their owners at day's end but would also identify ownership of sheep penned together at night. Among the Türkmen pastoralists of Anatolia, tents are usually placed to encircle or at least oversee the sheepfold where all the sheep are penned at night. A typical spacing between tents is 10–15 m apart, but when the situation is less secure (as during a rise in thievery), tents might be more numerous and placed as close as 3 m apart (Andrews 1997: 53). In areas where predation or theft by competing groups is a problem, such as among the Maasai in eastern Africa, dwellings are built in a circular pattern, creating an outer boundary; the inner central court functions as the cattle enclosure (Marshall 2000; Shahack-Gross et al. 2004).

Another reason for penning the combined herd relates to management tactics. Nomadic pastoralists in the Kerman province of Iran, for instance, "manage their animals together to support each other and to share the cost of different livestock activities including shepherding, feeding, milking and health care. For example, joint management allows adult and young animals to be herded separately" (Ansari-Renani 2013:6). Herds taken to pasture each day are therefore not separated by household but by age or other characteristics that do not reflect individualized ownership of animals. In these cases, co-residential tent-householders rely on one another to care for and manage the entire herd. Among the Brahui of Baluchistan, though each tent-household sees to its own meal preparation and other production and consumption activities, herds from tent-households are combined (up to 500 sheep can be herded by a single shepherd), which frees men of the tent-household for other activities (Swidler 1972). Thus, the spatial layout of a camp, particularly with regard to where pens are located, may reflect a camp of tent-householders that may be engaging in greater levels of cooperative livestock management economic strategies.

The alternative is to pen the animals inside or near the tent, in individual enclosures, as among the Al Murrah of Saudi Arabia (Barfield 1993; Cole 1975) and the Basseri in Iran (Barth 1961). Al Murrah camel-herding tent-households keep their animals separate from those of other tent-households for two main reasons. The first is their tradition of household autonomy in which "[e]ach household remains responsible for its own animals whether camped within a group or on its own" (Barfield 1993: 72). Household herds are managed by the males within the tent-household and are typically not combined either at night or in the pasture with other herds, even though they may be camping together. The other reason for this separation, which is related to the first, is that the Al Murrah are highly mobile and often camp as a single tent-household (or *beyt*) (Cole 1975). They will occasionally join with another *beyt* for a shorter or longer period for companionship or protection (Barfield 1993), but due to the *beyts*' mobility and autonomy, the herds remain separated. The Basseri offer a slightly different model, in which several tent-households might combine their herds in an area surrounded by their tents: "Within this group, where there are three or more tents, their relative positions are generally constant. . . . [T]his reflects the ties of kinship and economic dependence within the herding unit, and not in the camp as a whole" (Barth 1961: 42). In a Basseri camp, then, there may be several "herding units" that correspond to tent-households, with close family ties and a cooperative economy between them. These herding units may stay together for long periods but also may combine with different herding units over the seasons. Thus, while among the Al Murrah it is each tent that controls its own animals, in the Basseri culture one might instead find several tents set close together surrounding a pen, with identical clumps of tents and pens elsewhere throughout the camp (as Barth notes, at least 20–30 m away "to avoid the mixing of the herds" [1961: 42]). The difficulty for archaeologists here is that unless excavation (or survey) is wide-ranging on a site, some tents and their associated enclosures might be missed. A site may look as if it held only one or two tent-householders when, in reality, there were eight dispersed across the landscape.

Identifying pastoral nomadic sites, especially the animal pens, is incredibly challenging archaeologically: "[B]ased on ethnographic observations, pastoralists tend to leave few material remains in their abandoned sites" (Shahack-Gross, Marshall, and Weiner 2003: 439). This is borne out by other ethnographic studies that comment on nomads' tents being even "cleaner" in their interior than those of hunter-gatherers due to frequent (daily or several times daily) sweeping (Banning 1993). As mentioned above, unless non-organic materials are used to build the pens (e.g., stone, mudbrick, etc.), the likelihood of finding ancient pens once bordered by brush is essentially nil. Nonetheless, several examples from the archaeological record offer just these types of data. In fact, E. B. Banning and Ilse Köhler-Rollefson (1992: 195) caution that "[i]n contrast to the expectations of many archaeologists, who view pastoral camps as ephemeral sites without substantial traces that would enter the archaeological record, most of the tent sites we surveyed boasted a wealth of architectural features." Banning and colleagues have investigated a number of Bedouin camps in Jordan and elsewhere that offer circular or rectangular patterns of stones, used to hold down tent flaps, with areas within these stone patterns flattened, smoothed, and swept clean (Banning 1993; Banning and Köhler-Rollefson 1983; Simms 1988). Recent work in southeastern Turkey found the remains of campsites in which great effort went into the building of animal enclosures (Ur and Hammer 2009; and see Hammer 2014).

The enclosure-based patterns outlined above were observed in the archaeological record in sites discovered in the Negev, the Sinai, and the Arabian Peninsula. Juris Zarins (1992), using ethnographic research conducted in Oman (Janzen 1986), noted patterns of two types of campsites, one in which huts were arranged in a circle, with cattle kept in a communal central court at night, and one in which individual compounds included a dwelling (tent) with animal pens nearby or attached. Zarins then examined the archaeological record and found examples of these camp layouts at sites dating back to the fourth and third millennia BCE. He found a number of examples of the "communal" camps, in which tents (demonstrated by the patterns of stones possibly used to secure tent flaps) were arranged around a central area where animals could be kept. This camp layout is also present at a number of sites in Southwest Asia (see, for instance, Beit-Arieh 1981; Betts 1982). Also in Southwest Asia, Zarins found the type of camp that he terms "agglutinative groupings interspersing residences with cattle dwellings of different sizes" (1992: 233). These "groupings" would, he believes, consist of a dwelling, a "mature" (adult) animal pen, smaller pens for calves, and other structures perhaps associated with storage. It is possible that these camp layouts reflect a more individualized approach to herd management.

A camp layout that features either a "communal" or "individualized" pen for animals provides at least a starting point for investigation into economic strategies that might have been pursued by a prehistoric group. The accompanying material record is the vital "superstructure" that helps to build the past from its bare foundations.

Nomadic Pastoralist Social Structure: Kinship and Marriage, Gender, Politics, and Religion

It would be gratifying to be able to say that acquiring data on social institutional structures such as kinship, religion, and gender is easier when examining the architectural remains of nomadic pastoralists than it is for hunter-gatherer sites. Sadly, such a statement would be untrue. In some circumstances, however, these types of data can be acquired for nomadic pastoralists with some level of certainty, especially when ethnographic analogy can be prudently employed as a guideline.

Kinship and Family

The ethnographic record suggests that the majority of nomadic pastoralist groups who live and cooperate together are kin-related, usually based on a unilineal descent structure (Barfield 1993; Barth 1961; Cribb 1991; Krader 1963; Prussin 1995). In Andrews's (1997) compendium of pastoralist tent types across Turkey and Central Asia, the majority of co-residential tent-householders are patrilineally related, with sets of brothers and their families, fathers and sons, brothers and cousins, and other combinations of male relatives serving as the kinship threads that weave together a pastoralist grouping of anywhere from 2 to 15 or 20 tents. The same is generally found in Africa (Prussin 1995; Shahack-Gross et al. 2004); kinship relations are also usually at the heart of Arctic reindeer-herding camps and among pastoralists of Central Asia. The association between architectural form and the family/marriage unit became a major topic of discussion after the publication of Kent Flannery's 1972 study, mentioned in chapter 2, in which he equated round huts with polygynous extended families, and suggested that square houses occurred more commonly in nuclear and monogamous systems. This analysis launched a decades-long discussion, mainly centered on Near Eastern architecture, regarding the notions of round versus square houses and the family structures they contained. Flannery and associated scholars were focused more particularly on the first houses built by initially sedentary populations rather than mobile groups, and thus the debate is not entirely apropos here; it is, however, a very fitting topic for the "kinship" chapter (chapter 6), where it is explored in detail (and see discussion in chapter 3).

It is largely impossible to determine marriage patterns from the architecture at ancient nomadic pastoralist sites. This opinion is based on both the common sense of pastoralists themselves and on the ethnographic record. The very nature of tents, their construction, and their transport necessitates a "smaller is better" norm. Hauling around a felt or goat-hair cover for a larger-than-necessary space is simply not practical, and most construct tents for precisely the size they need. For this reason, most tents house what can be considered "nuclear" families which occasionally include several spouses or an extra family member, such as an unmarried brother or cousin, a widowed parent, or a long-term guest. Therefore, using methods such as those proposed in chapters 3 or 6 of this volume will not work well in attempting to interpret clues from nomadic architecture. For instance, a tent that houses an adult male and his two wives and associated children will likely not boast two hearths or two sets of cookware. A mobile people would not cart around two sets of identical cooking kits, nor would they build a tent large enough to house two hearths if only one was needed. More likely, the women's work between the co-wives would be divided as to seniority. Occasionally, an archaeologist may discover, with a shiver of excitement, the presence of sleeping platforms at a tent site. That excitement fades, however, when the discoverer recalls that other adults besides a second or third wife might be a household member (e.g., unmarried siblings, widowed parents, guest, etc.). A study seeking to document how to recognize polygyny in the archaeological record identified three indicators: wife's quarters, hearth types, and domestic structure arrangement (Chase 1991). Only one culture in the study practiced nomadic pastoralism (the Maasai), and though each wife had her own hut and hearth, the Maasai studied were somewhat more sedentary and thus built structures rather than tents or temporary huts.

The ethnographic record throws a real wrench into the mechanics of detecting marriage practices in nomadic pastoralist houses. Among the Tubu in Africa, a man and woman may be married, but the wife lives in her own tent near her family for several years until she produces the first child; only then might she move her tent to her husband's camp and live with him (Prussin 1995: 108–23). The camps built by the Mahria in Sudan are perfectly illustrative of the dangers of attempting to define marriage practices from tent size and placement. A winter camp consisting of six tents includes the following: three belong to the co-wives of one man (he resides in one of the tents with the youngest wife); the eldest wife pitches her tent near her grown son and his wife rather than near her husband; the eldest wife's son has a second wife who has her own tent, pitched between her mother-in-law and the tent of her father-in-law; the sixth tent houses a woman and her children, including a married daughter who has not yet gone to live in a tent with her husband (Holter 1995: 124–33). In the same culture, a man who has several wives who do not get along will locate his wives in different camps; he travels between the camps and spends several days with each (Holter 1995: 128). Among the Al Murrah of Saudi Arabia, monogamy is the norm, but the tent-household in which Donald Cole lived included the male elder and his wife, their second son and his wife and child, and an unmarried son (1975: 65). Archaeologically, would the separate conjugal families be detectable, or might space and artifacts suggest that a polygynous family inhabited the tent? The situation is further confused, at least among historic-period pastoralists in the Middle East, due to the practice of lineage endogamy in which males marry daughters of their paternal uncles. Among the Brahui, for instance, two tents with overlapping guidelines (indicating economic cooperation and/or kinship ties) may house two related females (Swidler 1972), each of whom has her own tent-household and husband. Archaeologically, however, the setting may look like two wives of the same husband. It is quite difficult enough to distinguish marriage practices in sedentary societies (see chapter 6); identifying them in highly or even partially mobile tent-households may turn out to be, for the archaeologist, a true exercise in futility.

Gendered Spaces and Nomadic Pastoralist Camps

That tents feature gendered spaces is an absolute given in most pastoralist societies. The ethnographic record presents many a culture that considers the entire tent as the "women's area" or, perhaps, more commonly, that cedes specific areas of the tent to one gender or the other. Among the Mahria culture, Uta Holter notes, "Although the man is the head of household and the main decision maker, the woman is the almost exclusive user of the tent" (1995: 129). As was the case with hunter-gatherers, most of the literature involving gender and pastoralism revolve around the sexual division of labor (e.g., Martin and Voorhies 1975). This subject becomes especially important in pastoralist societies because of their dependence on the secondary products derived from the animals, products for which women are often responsible (Crabtree 2006; Dyson-Hudson and Dyson-Hudson 1980). Thus, activities such as milking, processing of dairy products, and fiber/textile production often (but not always) fall to women, who accomplish these activities inside or near their tent home. The more "standard" tasks such as food processing and cooking also generally fall to women in pastoralist societies (but see Rasmussen 2001, who describes the many other activities carried out by Tuareg women). To take the Mahria tent as an example (Figure 4.5a), the sleeping area serves the entire family, and the features and artifacts in the tent and just outside of it would correlate with Holter's statement that women are the "exclusive users" of the tent. However, the layout in a Rendille tent (Figure 4.5b) indicates the more gendered spatial assignment, in which women's space is always to the north and men's to the south (Grum 1995: 158). If identifying men's and women's work spaces in a pastoralist camp

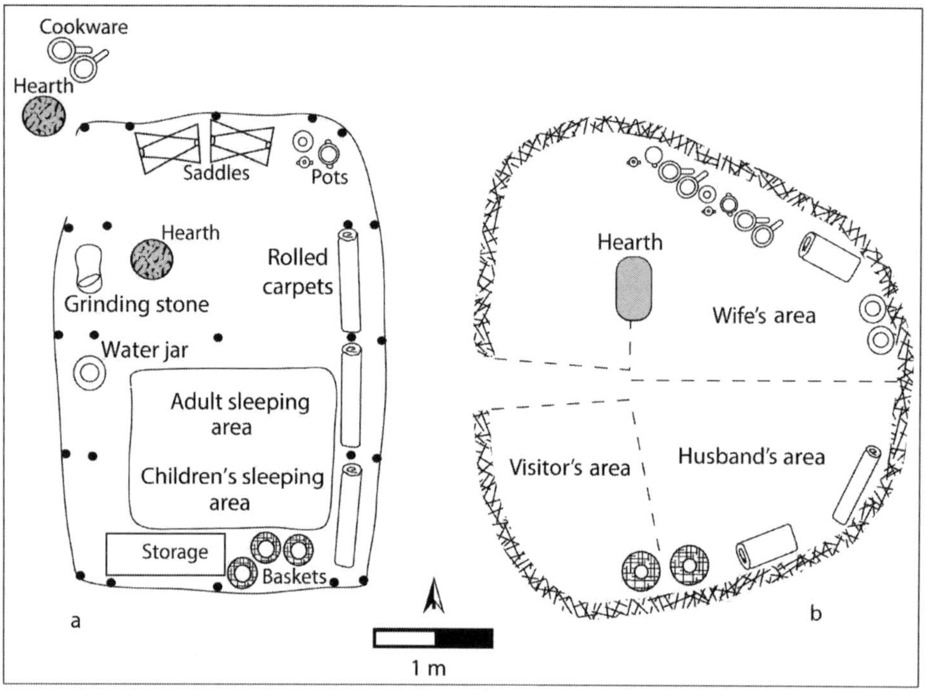

Figure 4.5: (a) Example of the Mahria tent and gendered use of space in which the interior and doorway areas are primarily used by women (after Prussin 1995: 132, fig. 7.4); (b) example of the Rendille tent and gendered use of space in which the northern half is used by women and the southern half by men (after Prussin 1995: 158, fig. 8.6).

is the archaeological goal, then studies must concentrate on artifact scatters, sweeping/refuse areas, and work areas, such as areas for milling (e.g., Simms 1988). To accomplish this type of investigation, an initial assumption about who performs which tasks must preface the assignment of spaces based on the location of artifacts and features. In such cases, architecture provides only the backdrop for defining the work areas (see chapter 8).

Though gendered spatial segregation might seem difficult to achieve within a tent, the placement of poles and a judiciously hung curtain is more than sufficient in many cases. An ethnographic description of a Bedouin tent in the Wadi Rum of Jordan is illustrative of this. In a recent study, Mahmoud Na'amneh and colleagues (Na'amneh, Shunnaq, and Tasbasi 2008: 150) describe the Bedouin tent:

> The Bedouin tent lies at the heart of the Bedouin lifestyle. Indeed, it is more than a simple shelter and place to sleep or meet guests. It is a whole sphere where sociocultural values are constantly produced and reproduced . . . the physical features of the tent re-

flect many aspects of the Bedouin socioeconomic realms and reveal many elements of the Bedouin culture in general.

The tent is divided into two separate spaces (see also Young 1995), consisting of the men's section, which is also the public receiving area (generally for male guests), and the women's section, where food is prepared, including bread (Na'amneh, Shunnaq, and Tasbasi 2008). Up to three poles may be used to support the superstructure. When only family members are present in the evenings, everyone may gather in the public/men's area, never in the women's area (if men are present). A similar situation is found among the Al Murrah of Saudi Arabia. The long black tent, usually about 40 feet in length, devotes up to a third of the area to the "men's area," where all male social time is spent and where male guests are entertained (Cole 1975: 64). The rest of the tent is designated as the women's section and is demarcated by a *ru'ag,* which is a tapestry divider, and also by the piling of household items and supplies. As was also the case in the Wadi Rum Bedouin tent, the men's section has a fire dedicated to coffee/tea-making, while the women's section has an area for food preparation and cooking.

In today's Middle East, there is almost always a gendered division of space in a nomadic pastoralist tent (given that the vast majority practice Islam); and, in African societies, the entire tent area is often considered the "women's space," though men obviously enter it on a regular basis. As noted above, the objects used in daily tasks may be more productive than the tent's architectural footprint as indicators for identifying gendered spaces. Despite the physical division in the Bedouin and Al Murrah tent, the curtain (*ru'ag*) would certainly be a non-factor in any archaeological site, and the tent poles that might have supported it would simply look like the regular supports for the tent itself. The analysis of gendered spaces in any architectural context is a challenging but fascinating endeavor.

Social Inequality

Nomadic pastoralist societies typically exhibit some level of social stratification, if only in the number of animals a household owns. Significant wealth sometimes translates into camp leadership, although kinship usually plays a substantial role in camp politics as well (see Salzman 1967 for discussion on political structures in pastoralist groups). For mobile pastoralists, some of the determinants of wealth found among sedentary types, such as possession of exotic or finer-quality goods (see chapter 9), may be impractical, since carrying delicate or numerous goods would be burdensome in such a lifestyle. Besides the number of animals, wealth may be detected in a few other ways: the possession of jewelry or other smaller but costly items is the most common. Wealth through the ownership of animals is expressed either in pure numbers of animals, or in types of animals, or both. Among the Tibetan nomads of the Pala Plateau, for instance, the number of yak a household owns is much more illustrative of wealth than how many sheep or goats make up the herd; even more notable is the ownership of horses, which are costly to keep because they provide little in return (such as milk or fiber products) (Goldstein and Beall 1990). Architecture is potentially useful in identifying social stratification and perhaps even political leadership within a camp, but it can also create misconceptions.

If animals represent wealth, then corral size would identify a wealthy tent-householder. The foregoing discussion, however, has identified the pitfalls of such a strategy, in that an entire camp's animals are often penned together, or several households may cooperate and use a single corral. If the pastoralists under study do keep individualized pens near their tents, then this strategy could be successful under various conditions: if *all* the tents are excavated in an entire camp; if everyone keeps the same types of animals (i.e., fewer cattle might require a larger pen than far more sheep/goats . . . who is more wealthy?); and if other indicators such as material culture possession bear out the corral-size interpretation. Tent size, unlike house size, is also a weak indicator. As noted above, pastoralists build tents according to need; possessing a larger and more ostentatious tent is far more work to transport and erect than most would deem worth the effort. Thus, larger families require larger tents; this does not necessarily correlate to wealthier families.

The location of tents within a camp is a potentially useful guide to status and position. Ethnographic and archaeological data offer two possible locations where one might find a leader's tent: at the camp's entrance or at the most optimal camp location. In African camps such as those of the Rendille, in which the habitations form a circle (inside of which the animals are kept), the house of the senior family is located near or next to the main entrance to the camp (Grum 1995). In physically "small" societies, such as nomadic pastoralist camps and smaller towns, when social stratification is present it is not uncommon to find the camp or town leader occupying a residence near the main entrance to the settlement (Steadman 2011). Reasons for this are myriad but often have to do with being visible, being able to tap into the trade and transactions that take place at or near the gate, and being in the midst of the action to keep one's finger on the pulse of the settlement. Thus, if there is a particular pattern to a pastoralist encampment (i.e., circular around a central enclosure, in "clumps" but always in the same pattern, etc.), it might be possible to detect where the "entrance" to the encampment is, and an investigation of the closest tent-household may yield other evidence of wealth and social status.

This is precisely the case at the southern African site of //Khauxa!nas, where 18th-century nomadic pastoralists, in the throes of dealing with a new colonial presence, made their home (Kinahan 1996). At //Khauxa!nas, located in Namibia, a pastoralist Khoi group built a settlement that featured several stone-built buildings (the structure of which was likely influenced by colonial contact) and a significant stone perimeter wall built to a height of 2 m, which served to enclose the encampment and its animals. In a careful analysis of the camp, John Kinahan (1996) determined that the public entrance to the camp, where visitors and traders would have entered, was situated at the southern perimeter. Visitors would then have entered one of the rectangular stone buildings which Kinahan believes served as a public meeting place. Quite nearby both this stone building and the main entrance was house "M," which Kinahan believes belonged to the senior resident/leader of this Khoi group (1996: 238). Besides the evidence of placement, the extra labor used to build the house (stone walls), together with its larger size, are indicators for Kinahan that this house belonged to the group leader. While the Khoi were more of a "settled" pastoralist society than the more mobile cultures discussed in the majority of this chapter, the location of the possible group leader at the site of //Khauxa!nas is still illustrative of how a more mobile camp might locate its highly ranked tent-householders.

Another possibility is to identify the tent that is set apart, perhaps at a "special place," at a site: is one tent-household in an optimal spot? Cribb describes a Kosan Kabile camp in eastern Turkey that demonstrates this principle (1991: 140–49). This encampment had quite a number of tents because the chief owned much of the area and thus pasturing a large herd was not a problem. Most of the 60+ tents were set in relatively close proximity to one another. The Kosan Kabile chief's tent, however, was located several hundred meters away from the main encampment, with easy access to pasturage and stream. Besides the main tent of the chief, a tent housing a bath and satellite tents for the chief's shepherds made up the complex (Cribb 1991: 149). Cribb writes (1991: 147), "A stratified nomad community should exhibit hierarchical rather than modular organization [of tents]," and he notes that this arrangement is found in a number of societies (see also Marsden 1976). However, it is not always the case that the leader or senior member lives apart from the main camp. Lawrence Krader notes that, in general among Mongol and Turkic nomads of Central Asia, it is indeed the leader who chooses the camping spot and pitches his tent first. Then the other tents are pitched in a specified array according to the location of the leader's, either forming a circle or an arc (1963: 335–37) that renders the chief's tent largely undetectable. In contrast, Frederik Barth describes the migration process of the Basseri in which the leader stays behind to make sure everyone packs up and leaves; and those who left earliest then choose the next camp location and "disperse over the chosen area to stake out their claims to the better localities for their own tents" (1961: 43). Since the leader is likely bringing up the rear, he does not get to choose the best location for his own tent.

Identifying social stratification and hierarchy in an ancient nomadic pastoralist site is a hit-and-miss situation. If recognizable factors such as tent placement (near the "entrance" of the camp, in a prime location, away from the main tents in a prime location) can be paired with other indicators, such as material goods possessions, access to special features (such as the Kosan Kabile "bath house" tent), and possibly larger tents and/or corrals, then identifying camp leaders or the wealthier families within the camp may be possible.

Religion and Ritual

Detecting religion and ritual in nomadic pastoralist sites is much the same as described for hunter-gatherers: most of the evidence comes not from architecture but from items that tend to be perishable. When there are permanent structures, these may be "visited" or part of a pilgrimage but not part of an encampment. For instance, the Basseri, according to Philip Salzman (1967: 122), "practice few religious duties other than the profession of faith" (requiring a carpet and possibly some beads); they also visit the tombs of saints, which would constitute the types of permanent religious sites mentioned above. An archaeological example of this is outlined below. Perhaps the best advice that can be offered here is that any archaeologically discovered structure that cannot be attributed to domestic use, storage, or animal pens may have been devoted to non-domestic and non-utilitarian activities. Possible functions include as a meeting place for the camp members, for ritual activities, or to receive guests (though, in this latter case, cooking materials might be present). In the Rendille camp, there is a central stone enclosure where the elders meet; it is considered the "religious center" of the settlement, and a fire is constantly kept alight there (Grum 1995: 150).

Of course, sometimes even ritual structures may be undetectable. The Arab Bedouin cultures of Mauritania construct a "marriage tent" for a newlywed couple, which is used only during the first nights of the marriage (Boulay 2007). The pitching of a tent specifically for marriage is quite common among pastoralist groups in Africa (see Prussin 1995) and is found elsewhere as well. The utterly ephemeral nature of marriage tents, usually present for only a few days, likely means they are largely undiscoverable archaeologically; however, they fit the category of "apparently non-domestic" structures (since a marriage tent would be small and would have few if any daily task paraphernalia), and if such structures are present at a site, they could potentially be interpreted as relating to ritual behavior.

Finally, the structure of the camp itself might yield some clues. Anders Grum (1995) notes that the Rendille orient all their doors to the west (though the reasons for this are not clearly stated). As is described in chapter 10, the placement and orientation of houses in villages often signifies religious beliefs. There is no reason the same would not be so in the layout of tents, though topographic factors might interfere from time to time if a specific placement were needed. On the other hand, the foregoing discussion has made clear that, in many cases, tent-pitching has to do with kinship relations, herd management, and social stratification, rather than an intention to organize the camp according to religious symbolism. Religion in a pastoralist camp, if expressed materially, is most likely to be found among the artifacts and features located within a tent or at a more permanent monument located somewhere in the landscape.

An example of the latter is found in northwest Kenya. Here stone pillar sites, sometimes including cairns or stone circles, appear to have been built by the first herders living near Lake Turkana over 4,000 years ago (Hildebrand and Grillo 2012). The researchers determined that building these pillar sites was a cooperative effort. First, a stone platform was built, as large as 500 m^3; then the massive stone pillars (ca. 800 kg) had to be transported over several kilometers and finally erected on the platform, along with the other stone architecture (cairn, stone circle) that sometimes accompany them. Hildebrand and Grillo speculate that as herding began in the area (either brought by immigrants or developed by locals), these pillars filled a social and possibly economic or religious need. The artifacts found in association with the pillars suggest that some might have functioned as mortuary sites (human bone remains), but "others accommodated periodic meetings for non-mortuary activities such as initiations, social negotiation, exchange and/or loans of livestock or ceremonies" (Hildebrand and Grillo 2012: 348). East African herders from over four millennia ago, rather than build temporary religious "places" in each camp, spent extensive time and effort to create stone monuments for a variety of purposes, some of them religious. Though architecture of a rich religious life may be undetectable within a nomadic pastoralist camp, the landscape may occasionally offer up a few surprises.

Conclusion

The reader may have noticed that this chapter is one of the longest in the entire volume. This is ironic, given that the majority of the discussion centers on what we *cannot* learn from mobile architecture rather than what can be discovered. Nonetheless, the preceding discussion perhaps clarifies both the tremendous insights that can be gained from the fleeting presence of mobile architecture while simultaneously illustrating the capriciousness of its presence in the archaeological record.

Chapter 5
From First House to City Suburb

The previous chapter offered some detail on the types of homes built by mobile peoples both past and present. Beginning roughly 12,000 years ago, some humans began to build more permanent shelters, which sometimes led to the establishment of small communities. Initially, causes of sedentism were laid at the door of the domestication of agriculture, but further archaeological work has demonstrated that many prehistoric peoples settled before they farmed, and farmed without sedentism. Answering the why of sedentism is far beyond the purview of this book. Asking *where* people first settled, addressed in chapter 2, might be more productive and can, in fact, sometimes partially answer the question of why as well. Perhaps the most answerable is when; archaeology has done a fairly effective job of tracking the emergence of settled communities across the world. Most pertinent to architectural questions is not the when but the how and what of first settlement. Specifically, how did becoming sedentary impact humans, what types of more permanent houses did humans first build, and what do they reveal about them?

James Deetz (1977) defines "vernacular architecture" as homes built by those who will also inhabit them. While vernacular architecture is the main subject of this book, the goal in this chapter is to understand the motivations involved in building the earliest permanent homes. The first section surveys the impact of permanent settlement on human thought and action. The second profiles what we know about first houses and earliest communities and what these tell us about human agency, intentionality, and

Archaeology of Domestic Architecture and the Human Use of Space, by Sharon R. Steadman, 103–138.

behavioral structure. The final section examines what happens to architecture at the advent appearance of social complexity and as communities become towns and cities.

Settlement and Its Impact

Does settling more permanently change the way humans think and behave? It would seem that it should, and several book authors address such changes in significant detail (Finlayson and Warren 2010; Hodder 1990; Ingold 2013; Moore 2012; Wilson 1988; and see chapters in Bandy and Fox 2010; Brück and Goodman 1999). Discussed here are some possible alterations in human thought and action as previously mobile peoples, as Matthew Bandy and Jake Fox put it (2010), "become villagers."

The Way Humans Think

Mobile peoples certainly built shelters, or sought shelter in places like caves. Built shelters may have been constructed of easily obtainable materials such as branches, or through considerable labor, such as processing animal skins. Did the humans who built these shelters feel, once inside of them, "separated from the outside," shielded from nature in all its manifestations? In other words, did the built walls of a temporary shelter, or the rock walls of the cave, symbolically set humans apart from their surrounding natural world? Ian Hodder suggests that humans did not see themselves as "separated" from the machinations of nature until they began to build more permanent settlements. He uses the terms *domus* and *agrios* (1990, 1992) to define the differences in human perception between the "home" and the "outside world." He argues that the earliest permanent structures in Neolithic Europe allowed humans to differentiate themselves from the outside, to achieve "human domestication," and even to gain control of wild nature, all within the confines of the home: "The domus as defined here is the concept and practice of nurturing and caring, but at a still more general level it obtains its dramatic force from the exclusion, control and domination of the wild, the outside . . . the 'agrios' . . . " (Hodder 1990: 45). Tied to permanent shelter is the notion of controlling the agricultural fields and thus gaining empowerment over one of the most important of human endeavors, nutritional subsistence. Hodder develops this notion in more detail (1992: 208):

> Palaeolithic caves or elaborate houses on the Russian steppes presumably defined home against outside in some sense. But with the origins of agriculture the opposition was used and emphasized by, for example, bringing the wild into the house and transforming it. This bringing in and opposing was done both economically (by domesticating some plants and animals), and symbolically (by, for example, lacing representations of wild animals in house walls or by surrounding the cooking and presentation of food in elaborate decoration).

Hodder also asserts that ritual activities near the hearth, and the burial of ancestors beneath house floors, is further testament to the notion of domesticating human space and triumphing over the uncontrolled outside world. By bringing food production (processing), ritual behavior, and burial of the dead *through* the doorway from the outside and into the home, humans took control of their world and saw themselves as separated from nature on a number of levels. The house walls formed the boundary between nature and human space. Thus, in Hodder's analysis, the world view of humans shifted: the building of permanent house walls, accompanied by the activities within them, created a concrete division between the wild "out there" and the domesticated "in here," a differentiation that was permeable or entirely absent when preceding generations inhabited caves and temporary homes.

The next step, perhaps, after taming the space inside the home is to make the home, and possibly the community, cosmologically symbolic. Among others, Peter Wilson (1988) and Trevor Watkins (2004a) both argue that once humans got the hang of building permanent residences, the structures soon became representative of vital cultural beliefs. Wilson asserts, "The adoption of the house as the permanent context of social and economic life also marks a major development in cosmological thinking . . . the house is appropriated to mediate and synthesize the natural symbols of both the body and the landscape. At the same time it provides the environment and context for social life" (1988: 58). Much of Wilson's statement is reminiscent of the "domestication" notion offered by Hodder. Indeed, there are similarities but Wilson's ideas are at the same time broader and more specific. Hodder begins with a division between wild and domesticated, while Wilson suggests that building permanent houses had an impact on specific areas of human behavior, including the symbolic representation of the universe and social behavior—that is, how humans interacted with one another: "[T]he house, and often the village. . . . [embody] the spiritual beliefs of people and contributes the setting, and sometimes the text, of their religious lives" (1988: 66). Wilson is neither the first nor last to recognize that the built environment is often reflective of a culture's cosmology; numerous scholars have addressed the cosmological patterning of home and community (see discussion in Moore 2012, and in chapter 10). What Wilson wishes to delineate is that this trend began at the very moment that humans settled permanently. They who once used the natural world to represent the cosmos, perhaps in the location of mountains and topographical features, the stars in the sky, or in the shadows that appeared on the landscape at sunrise and sunset, transitioned to recognizing such symbols in the placement of structures, the layout of communities, and the shadows cast upon walls inside a room. The cosmos had been brought down to earth; in effect it had been "tamed."

In a brilliant essay on the earliest permanent houses in the Epipalaeolithic and Neolithic Near East, Watkins (2004a) acknowledges the arguments offered by both Hodder and Wilson but takes them a step further. He asserts that psychologically, humans were *primed* to translate the natural and cosmological world into material representations. He suggests that humans undergo "cognitive-cultural co-evolutionary revolutions" that change the way the species thinks; one example is the development of modern language abilities, which certainly impacted human behavior (Watkins 2004a: 103). As humans settled permanently, they were ready to use the built environment as "an especially powerful mode of external symbolic storage," which coincided with the experimentation in plant cultivation and the need to engage in physical storage systems (Watkins 2004a: 105). Humans were prepared, even eager, to make the leap from a symbolic world "out there" to one they could materialize in walls, floors, courtyards, and other built surroundings. Symbolic representations could be embodied in permanency that could be seen, felt, and smelled, from one generation to the next. The built environment effectively altered human experience, affecting the way people saw, and navigated, their world.

It can also be argued that permanent architecture became a part of cultural identity. Addressing cultural and social identity in the archaeological past is a significant area of research (Emberling 1997; Fowler 2004; Gardener 2007; Graves-Brown, Jones, and Gamble 1996; Jones 1997, 2008; Meskell 2001; Shennan 1994) and indeed a controversial one. First, it must be recognized that each human carries multiple identities simultaneously; these may be class-based, embedded in one's gender, sexuality, or physical disability, derived from kinship relationships, or stem from ethnicity and perceived nationality (Clark 2005; Ingold 2007; Jones 1997; Kane 2003; Meskell 2002; Shennan 1994; and see Díaz-Andreu et al. 2005). Material culture is most often used to define ethnic and class-based identities, though there has been recent work on recognizing gender- and sexuality-based identities as well (Ashmore 2006; Dowson 2006; Lyons 2009; Meskell 1999; Stockett 2005; Voss 2000).

However, controversy revolves around whether material culture is an accurate measure of identity, ethnicity, and the ancient creation of social boundaries (see discussions in Kramer 1977; Meskell and Preucel 2007; Rowlands 1994; Stark 1998; Van Gijseghem and Vaughn 2008). If an element of material culture can signify ethnic or social identity, does its occurrence outside its normative "culture area" indicate the presence of that social or ethnic group? René Millon, who worked at the great Mesoamerican city of Teotihuacan, employed material culture as the vehicle for identifying the presence of numerous ethnic neighborhoods across the vast settlement (Millon 1976). Archaeology would lose a tremendous tool for understanding the past if material culture were ever deemed a poor indicator of social or ethnic identity. The trick is to discern when such material signifiers—ceramic decoration, jewelry styles, tool embellishments, and other characteristics—are present through trade (and thus the original makers are elsewhere) or copied (because such signifiers represent power, or an attractive ideology or trait) at an archaeological site.

Fortunately, when it comes to domestic architecture, archaeologists can be fairly certain that the buildings were not transported, and it is generally the case that people tend to build their homes in formats and patterns familiar to them (Aldenderfer 1993a; Oliver 1987; Rapoport 1969; Van Dyke 2003; though see the discussion on architectural emulation in chapter 9, and discussions by Baydar 2004). Architectural styles can be described as "conservative" (Steadman 2010) in that they are generally long-lasting; building forms and internal layouts remain consistent through multiple generations, over centuries and even millennia, and in many cases houses are rebuilt in precisely the same place as were previous iterations (Steadman 2005). Though colonialism can have an impact on architecture (see chapter 9), it often has far less influence than one might imagine. John Scarry and Bonnie McEwan (1995) found that the Spanish colonization of the Apalachee cultural region of northern Florida had little impact on Apalachee circular and oval architectural styles; nor did the Spanish alter their residential patterns even though they were settling a new territory with a different environment. Architecture, then, because of the archaeologist's ability to attribute it to builders from particular social or ethnic groups, is a key element in recognizing "identity" in the archaeological past as well as in the present. This concept is demonstrated by a proposed museum project in Connecticut dedicated to the Mashantucket Pequot culture. Architecture students were tasked with using Pequot architectural styles, considered "a conveyor of cultural identity, as both a repository and a generator of cultural meaning" (Atkins and Krinsky 1996: 237), to help determine how both the external and internal layouts of the museum should be constructed. The architectural layout was as vital a conveyor of the culture as the artifacts contained within the structure.

At what point did architecture become a purveyor of cultural identity? It is suggested here that houses, once they became symbolic embodiments of the cosmological universe, took on shapes, formats, and decorative techniques that were representative of, and recognizable by, their builders. The built environment and, in many cases, the entire physical community, became a signifier of cultural identity, just as smaller elements of the material culture had already become or were destined to be. Symbols in a landscape that had once been home to mobile peoples were partially or wholly transmuted into structures built by human hands. In many instances, particular landscapes remained critical to cultural identities; the built environment simply reflected, reinforced, and sometimes reinterpreted the cosmologies embedded in the landscapes. Architectural structures represented a combination of utilitarian needs and unique symbols of beliefs and behaviors. Specific forms, styles, and formats, instantly recognizable to those who built and lived within such buildings, became markers of cultural/ethnic/social identity through generations of occupation. This ideological process, long in the making, had its inception in the first expressions of permanent houses.

The Way Humans Act

On many levels, this entire book is evidence that building permanent houses affects the way humans behave: suggested here is that the very act of living in one place, inside walls, generated alterations in human social action. New behavioral patterns emerged, in part, not just from permanent habitation but through more permanent interaction with *other* humans.

The acquisition of "stuff" seems an inevitable outcome of living a more permanent lifestyle. Hunter-gatherers "own" very few belongings—in general, only what they can easily move from one camp to the next. Nomadic pastoralists certainly have more possessions, in part because they often use their animals to move them. Only in taking a months-long backpacking trip across foreign continents can a present-day traveler come close to experiencing "stuff" like a mobile people. I did this twice in my youth, for four months and then for two, and twice (so far) during my professional life for two-month treks across parts of the Asian continent. In my youth, to fill my single backpack, I agonized over every item I would take: what did I truly *need*, and what did I absolutely *want*? In my two more recent trips, I had a backpack (smaller) and a rolling duffle which allowed me to take more belongings, but this still did not alleviate the pre-trip anxious decisions about what to pack. In each case and, of course, during every summer when I leave for the field with my single case mostly full of equipment, intellectually I know I could purchase anything forgotten or suddenly needed. The point here is that in any endeavor that involves significant time away from home, the issue of "stuff" is pervasive. When did "stuff" become an important concept for humans? When they begin building places to store it?

Jerry Moore's recent book (2012) has a chapter titled "Durable Goods" in which he tells a story similar to that in the previous paragraph, though far more elaborate. Moore and his wife, both archaeologists, moved a total of 13 times over a period of six years (2012: 50), for fellowships, jobs, fieldwork, and research. In all their peregrinations, it was their "stuff" that loomed large as an issue; at one point, they considered renting a storage unit somewhere in the middle of the United States, figuring they would pass through that region at least every few months! When people today prepare to move households, they often go through their "stuff" and throw out things they no longer want or need. However, once ensconced in the new home, the stuff factor begins to increase, perhaps even exponentially if the residents feel they will not have to move again.

There is little controversy over the notion that when humans settle permanently they acquire far more belongings than their mobile forebears; Moore's "Durable Goods" chapter exemplifies the consensus on this. What is debatable, or at least worth considering, is what other human behaviors stem from the acquisition of stuff. It can be argued, for instance, that the human traits of individualism and competitiveness were either born from, or enhanced by, the increasing ownership of goods kept within one's residence. Stephen Sanderson (1999) suggests that it was the initial settlement of farmers and the early acquisition of commodities that eventually led to modern capitalism. While Sanderson's theory is quite far-reaching, it is not much of a leap to suggest that systemic inequality is also a by-product of not only permanent settlement but also the acquisition of belongings, including lands on which one produces necessary sustenance. This is not to suggest that permanent settlement is the single cause of something as hugely complicated as social inequality in human societies. The vast literature on this subject addressing multiscalar causes (e.g., Ames 2008; Arnold 1996b; Clark and Blake 1996; Johnson and Earle 1987; Price and Feinman 1995; Upham 1990) is proof enough of this. However, it is possible to argue that permanent residence is *one* critical factor in the birth of institutionalized social inequality, no matter what the other circumstantial causes might have been.

Ofer Bar-Yosef's (2001) opinion, in his overview of the transition from mobile hunter-gatherers to sedentary foragers and finally to "village hierarchies" in Southwest Asia, suggests that a variety of factors, among them climate and permanent settlement, are integral to the rise of social inequality in the region. He profiles the emergence of social differentiation among Natufian/Neolithic sedentary foragers by assessing burial goods and the decoration of the burials and skeletal remains. Late Natufian (ca. 11,000–9500 BCE) mobile populations buried their dead in simple graves with few goods and little decoration (Bar-Yosef 2001: 15). By the more sedentary Pre-Pottery Neolithic A (ca. 9500–8000 BCE), burials were much more elaborate and architecture reflected social inequality in the form of storage capacity, the presence of specialized buildings and ceremonial centers, and the evidence of organized labor to build large public structures (Bar-Yosef 2001: 18–19). Social hierarchies had become institutionalized.

It is not only in Southwest Asia that social inequality seems to emerge concurrently with more permanent settlement. Brian Hayden offers extensive discussion of individuals, or sometimes corporate groups, that he labels "aggrandizers" (Hayden 1995, 2001, 2003: 221–27). He asserts that aggrandizers are members of society who consistently strive "to promote their own self-interests above the interests of others"; such individuals or groups are spurred to action when resources become scarce or fluctuating (2003: 221). Once resource conditions stabilize, aggrandizers can indulge in activities that further cement their leadership positions in the community. Such activities might include organizing labor to construct public buildings, and ensuring that their own buildings (houses, tombs) are recognized as belonging to important personages. Hayden argues that the building of megalithic structures and tombs in the British Isles exemplifies aggrandizers demonstrating both their ability to organize labor and to protect their lands by advertising the presence of the ancestors buried there (2003: 226–48). The notion of using the built environment to trumpet one's societal position is necessarily tied to permanency of place and the building of long-lasting structures.

An exceedingly careful study of the Keatley Creek site in British Columbia nearly pinpoints the moment at which residents of the village began developing institutionalized inequality (Prentiss et al. 2007). Keatley Creek was occupied for roughly 750 years (ca. 1614–747 cal BP; Prentiss et al. 2007: 303). During the first several hundreds of years, residents practiced hunting and gathering and relied on salmon fishing as their subsistence base. Until ca. 1200 BP, residents prepared food in outdoor locations, and though house sizes varied, food types and access to prestige resources (such as obsidian) did not vary dramatically. After 1200 BP, patterns changed at Keatley Creek. Food preparation moved from public to more private intra-household locations, suggesting that sharing and cooperative patterns were eroding. Smaller houses were abandoned, and larger houses began to exhibit greater access to prestige items and to substantial food supplies, the latter being important because climatic conditions caused a decrease in salmon and other resources, Anna Marie Prentiss and her colleagues (2007: 321) write:

> The biggest payoffs went to those with the largest and best organized groups since they could produce more products for internal use and for exchange, more effectively protect themselves and their resource collection locales, and simultaneously forage over a wider landscape. . . . Inequality became institutionalized as elders from "old money" families sought to protect their original social positions by passing on rights of property, resource, and ritual to their children.

At Keatley Creek, it was not the building of permanent houses that *caused* the social inequality; environmental factors played a significant role during the critical periods. However, without the architectural and spatial adjustments that took place, social inequality might have been largely a non-starter. Permanent houses are indeed a necessary component for institutionalized inequality in human society.

Another potential area of behavioral change associated with the first permanent homes is in the realm of privacy. Using architecture to effectuate privacy was discussed in some detail in chapter 3. The intention here is simply to note that the building of more permanent walls offers the *ability* to create consistent privacy from one's neighbors. Certainly, there are examples of houses that feature no "privacy" in the Western sense—for instance, the longhouses of many Native American cultures in which several families live in full view of one another. The ability to create private places within one's abode is also tied to the processes associated with increasing individualism, competition, acquisition of wealth, and the eventual institution of social inequalities, discussed above. The example at Keatley Creek in which food preparation moved from open accessible areas to the interior of compounds is precisely a function of "privatizing" an activity. No one need know just how much food, or other belongings, you might have, and what other activities you might perform once you move daily life behind walls. While the desirability and feasibility of "aloneness" are culturally variable (see chapter 3), it is certainly the advent of permanent architecture that made standards of privacy and personal space available to humans.

Wilson (1988) notes that permanent homes change social interaction codes. He terms mobile hunter-gatherers "open societies" and notes that their composition is typically quite fluid (1988: 28–34). A number of ethnographies show that highly mobile hunter-gatherers "vote with their feet" when there is social tension or stress within the group. Among partially mobile societies, such as the M'buti of central Africa, architecture can be used as a social distancing device; Wilson notes that when the M'buti build their huts, they angle them away from people with whom they are engaged in disputes, thereby avoiding conflict (1988: 62). Once people are "domesticated" and settled into a permanent community, the "exit" or "avoidance" options are unavailable. Permanent homes force social groups to incorporate behavioral codes that will allow them to exist, long term, side by side. Part of this is having a place to retreat to in order to avoid conflict: one's house or room. He suggests that "village life provides the facilities for an enriched or heightened social life at the same time as it offers the means and instruments for keeping that social life under control, preventing it from getting out of hand by assembling people within boundaries and separating them by partitions" (1988: 60). At a very basic level, the building of permanent homes in a community results in the cementing of cultural mores and codes of behavior that allow individuals and groups within the community to live together.

Tent to House: First Settled Homes

Before these ideological and behavioral changes could take hold, first permanent homes had to be built. This section examines these homes and villages and asks some interesting but perhaps largely unanswerable questions about them: What did the first builders intend to build? Did they *know* they were building a permanent house? Did they consider the consequences of such actions? A more archaeologically answerable question is, What did the first houses look like? Southwest Asia and North America are particularly forthcoming on this subject. Confidence decreases, however, when the question turns to *why* first houses took their shape, form, and pattern. Inferences, one of the lifelines of archaeology, can be made, however, and perhaps some answers to questions related to why can be deduced.

Agency, Intentionality, and the Construction of First Permanent Homes

When mobile peoples put in the first stake or baked the first brick for their more permanent house, what was in their minds? Were careful calculations made about size and arrangement of the construction, given that this was meant to be a longer-term structure, or were the ramifications of more permanent habitation not yet relevant? Asking such questions brings the archaeological discipline face to face with discussions of human intentionality. Originally emerging in the discipline of philosophy (Brentano 1995; Crane 1998; Papineau 1987; Searle 1983; Thau 2002), intentionality was concerned not so much with what someone "intends" but rather what the mind perceives, conceptualizes, and understands on a symbolic level; it explored how the mind fathoms representation of things, concepts, ideas, situations, states of affairs. In the archaeological realm, discussion of intentionality led to several theoretical lines, including a reinterpretation of the initial concept and a consideration of agency in the past, and next to cognitive archaeology and neuroepistemological systems. This last field addresses the actual brain functions that deal with choice, reaction, and belief—generally, the neural correlates that produced actions and objects in the past (e.g., Abramiuk

2012; Cochrane and Gardner 2011; de Beaune, Coolidge, and Wynn 2009; Renfrew, Frith, and Malafouris 2009). The discussion here focuses on intentionality and agency, which offer a closer fit to the attempt to understand the mental and physical precepts behind early home construction.

Whitney Davis accurately captures the archaeological interest in "intentionality" quite well (1992: 336):

> As mental directedness, Intentionality is the way in which the mind directs itself toward its objects—for example, in perceiving something, referring to it, imagining it, desiring it, believing in it or commanding it. Logically, Intentionality is the relation of mental "aboutness", because perception, reference, imagination, are about their objects in the world.

Davis notes that retrieving ancient intentionality is an imperfect process, recognizing that not everything done, created, or acted upon in the past was, in fact, intended (see also the discussion of "agency" below). Obviously, unintended actions would skew an archaeologist's attempt to identify intentionality and the meaning behind human behavior. Thus, ascribing intentionality to past things and actions does not capture the entirety of the ancient mind. A decade later, archaeologists again grappled with notions of intentionality. Lynnette Russell offers some concrete suggestions for addressing intentionality. While an archaeologist might be able to apprehend an ancient intention to make a cup, the use for which the cup was intended might not be immediately discernible: was it for drink, to give as a gift, to hold pens? Use-wear analysis, suggests Russell, might help identify not only the intention to *make* the cup but also how it was used (2004: 64). A caveat, however, is that while the maker might have had an intended use for the cup, other users might have had other ideas: a cup given as a drinking vessel might instead have ended up on the receiver's desk as a pen holder. The total recovery of intentionality in the past is impossible in such instances. Bruno David states this conundrum succinctly: "[W]hile the existence of a cultural object may allow us to say that an artist or other cultural being intended to *create* something (materially manifest as the object accessible to the archaeologist), it does not of itself allow us to determine the intentionality of the 'work' or life of the object following its creation" (2004: 67). Tim Ingold (2013) takes these issues into the architectural realm, asking questions such as, What did builders intend to build, and when is the building finished? Did builders of the earliest houses consider the ramifications of structure permanency before they began building or in the midst of construction? Were adjustments made before, during, or after construction to account for more permanent residence? In such questions, we find the intersection of intentionality and agency: humans who intend an action that conforms to societal structure but may adjust those actions based on a variety of reasons.

The subject of agency and the built environment was raised in chapter 3, but a more thorough exploration is offered here. The concept of agents and agency evolved from the interpretive frameworks within structuration theory, developed by Giddens (1979, 1984), and behavioral patterns shaped in Bourdieu's notion of *habitus* (1977, 1990). Bourdieu's "practice theory" stipulates that an individual's behavior is structured by people's practices within a given culture (1977: 164–66). They acquire their own behaviors through "doxa" (shared knowledge regulating behavior), and this results in *habitus*, the repetition of practices and behaviors through time. For Bourdieu, *habitus* is so deeply ingrained in individual behavior (i.e., the "doxa" of behavioral patterns) that individuals who deviate from such patterns would do so unthinkingly—in other words, without intention (see Smith 2001). The import of practice theory and *habitus* to the concept of archaeology is the assertion that humans generally behave generationally in predictive patterns, which can be recognized in the material culture. For Giddens, humans behave according to a "practical consciousness" and "discursive consciousness" (Giddens 1979: 5, 57). Practical consciousness refers to actions we learn by rote and do almost unthinkingly, such as typing on a keyboard. Discursive consciousness refers to actions undertaken with knowledge and even forethought. Like Bourdieu's *habitus*, Giddens's practical consciousness acknowledges that these actions are routinized practices developed according to cultural beliefs, styles, and actions over succeeding generations. However, because these practices are, in effect, "by rote," actors who understand the reasons for their behavior can then use that awareness for their own means (Giddens 1984: 284), thereby employing discursive consciousness. It is in such instances that the concept of "agency" arises.

Agency theory explores the decisions individual agents, or groups, might make in order to effect a particular outcome, or perhaps to prevent one, given the agent's understanding of "how things work" within her or his cultural framework (Dobres 2000; Gardner 2008). In other words, based on societal and historical knowledge, individuals might select a particular course of action intended to result in a particular end point, such as their own elevation to a position of greater power (Steadman 2010). Such actions, however, may in fact result in entirely different, and unexpected ends, which may or may not benefit the agents responsible for the decisions (Archer 2000; McCall 1999; VanPool and VanPool 2003). This does not necessarily mean that desired goals are not achieved, or that the different outcome is not positive; it is simply recognition that humans, even when guided by cultural behavioral codes, do not always react in a predictable fashion.

An important question is whether individual agents can be recognized in the archaeological record. The simple answer to this question is yes, as thoroughly explored by a number of books and articles (e.g., Dobres and Robb 2000; Dornan 2002; Gardner 2004; Robb 1999b; Spencer 1993; Steadman and Ross 2010). Contained in these and other publications are investigations of agents and their manipulation of material culture, especially through technology (e.g., Dobres 2000) and mortuary behavior (e.g., Gillespie 2001), but also in more seemingly unlikely archaeological remains such as those related to subsistence practices (e.g., Russell and Bogaard 2010), or even art (Feldman 2010;

Gell 1998; Layton 2003). In some cases, the process by which specific agents became the ultimate leaders of their societies can be traced using material culture (Flannery 1999; McMahon 2010; Porter 2010). The crucial element in the usefulness of agency models in archaeology is that the evidence of the decision-making must be visible to the archaeologist. Architecture, then, would be an ideal vehicle for investigating agency in the archaeological record (Guengerich 2014; Steadman 2010). As has been shown throughout the present volume, architectural patterns are typically culturally ordained; certain building materials, structural patterns, and settlement layouts become archaeologically recognizable cultural traits. This leads to a discussion of identity: in the archaeological realm, agency and identity can be, and often are, closely allied (Díaz-Andreu et al. 2005; Meskell 2001; Ross and Steadman 2010; Steadman 2010). In the fashioning of one's first more permanent abode, and then throughout the process of making adjustments to this initial structural plan, it can be inferred that elements of both intentionality and agency, and the construction of identity through architectural rendering, have some traction.

First Permanent Houses

In profiling the earliest known (semi)permanent houses, the intentionality involved in building the structure and the choices made about its size, form, and style, can all shine light into the prehistoric housebuilder's mind, if the archaeologist can successfully can follow the lines of interpretation. Randall McGuire and Michael Schiffer offered (1983), over 30 years ago, a very good starting point for interpreting house structure. They suggest that housebuilders design houses with three goals in mind: (1) managing the production of the house; (2) managing the maintenance of the house; and (3) structuring the house properly for anticipated use. They posit that the goals of production and maintenance are often in opposition to one another (McGuire and Schiffer 1983: 282). The builder wants to build the most cost-effective (in energy expenditure and cost of materials) house; however, a house that will maintain its integrity over a long use-life might require more expensive materials and careful attention to detail during the construction process. Consider the necessity of building stilted houses in areas prone to flood (Figure 5.1), which would require a balance between expenditure and maintenance. Reaching the happy medium may take some experimentation over several iterations of house form.

The third goal, structuring the house for anticipated use, has two trajectories, one utilitarian and one symbolic (McGuire and Schiffer 1983: 280; see also Rapoport 1980). Utilitarian functions include providing a barrier to the outside world, and serving as a place to perform activities necessary to daily life. The symbolic functions are far less easy to identify; these accommodate beliefs and ideologies as well as the needs resulting from community social structure (McGuire and Schiffer 1983: 281). These two trajectories may also come into conflict; while a square or rectangular house may more

Figure 5.1: Stilted house at Kampong Phluk village near Tonle Sap Lake, Cambodia. Residents must build houses high enough to avoid flooding during the monsoon season but balance this with efficiency and maintenance costs (photo by the author).

easily accommodate the performance of necessary activities, an oblong or round house may satisfy ideological concerns. The way in which a housebuilder might negotiate these conflicting concerns reflects both intentionality and agency. The discussion of North American and Near Eastern cultures below employs McGuire and Schiffer's use goals as a framework for identifying elements of intentionality and choice (agency) in the construction of first permanent homes. In general, the following examples are drawn from small settlements in which archaeological evidence indicates a nearly year-round occupation, perhaps with only seasonal mobility (e.g., in the spring or summer) for the purposes of maximum resource acquisition. The "first homes" discussed, therefore, are those built to last for most of a year, or for the repeated return on a yearly basis for long-term, if not precisely year-round, occupation.

North America: Longhouses and Pithouses

The first strong evidence for Iroquoian longhouses appeared in the St. Lawrence and southern Ontario regions after the ninth century CE (Chapdelaine 1993, 2012; Warrick

1996, 2000; Williamson 2012). There is very little information on pre-longhouse dwelling styles from this region. Sites dating to earlier centuries have been located mainly on the basis of material culture such as lithics and ceramics (e.g., Chapdelaine 2012; Gates St-Pierre and Chapdelaine 2013; Morin 2001) as well as palaeobotanical and faunal remains in middens. At sites such as Princess Point Site, on Lake Ontario, domestic structures in the pre-longhouse periods were small circular or oval structures measuring between 3 × 5 and 4 × 6 m in size; each house could hold one or perhaps two families, depending on the number of hearths inside the structure (Kapuches 1987, 1990; Smith and Crawford 1997; Warrick 1996, 2000; Williamson 1990). That so little is known about earlier domestic structures may reflect their largely ephemeral nature. Beginning in the eighth century, evidence of longhouses emerges and they become the "norm" for Iroquoian villages in succeeding centuries (Figure 5.2). Debate concerning the reasons for the appearance of longhouses, built by a culture that comes to be identified as the Iroquois nation, revolves around a number of controversies, one being whether this was an "in situ" culture or one that migrated into the region from elsewhere (e.g., Crawford and Smith 1996; Gates St-Pierre 2004; Pendergast 1975; Snow 1995, 1996; Williamson 2012). A second debate involves the origins of agriculture in the region and whether Iroquois peoples began building permanent housing, in longhouse form, to accommodate their cultivation cycles (e.g., Chapdelaine 1993; Hart, Anderson, and Feranec 2011; Hart and Means 2002). Whether or not the (proto-) Iroquois migrated into the region by the ninth century, their residential requirements necessitated the construction of semi-permanent and then permanent longhouse structures. In general, the literature on cultivation strategies suggests that there was a tangential connection between cultivation and more permanent settlement.

There is general agreement among scholars that the construction of longhouses was designed in part to accommodate the matrilineal and matrilocal kinship and residential structures practiced by the Iroquois from the late 10th century on, thereby identifying an essential use goal for longhouses. Building a longhouse took considerable effort and likely many hands to complete it in a timely fashion. This suggests a collaborative investment of time and energy from the initial stages of permanent housing. The Early Iroquoian longhouses (ca. CE 1000–1300) were shorter (ca. 10–15 m) than those constructed in the later Contact period (Warrick 2000: 434–36). After several decades of permanent longhouse-living, structures had grown to remarkable size, stretching an average of 48 m but extending to as much as 124 m in length (Warrick 1996). Thus, the initial labor investment, though significant, was far less than in later decades, when permanency was the norm and population had increased. However, a recent study by John Creese (2009) suggests that these early builders did take environmental needs into consideration in longhouse construction (snow, ice, etc.) and included a total of four rows of posts (rather than two, which is the more common assumption) to support the roof. Creese believes that learning to build a successful longhouse was "risky in terms of the scale of wasted labor and the dangers associated

Figure 5.2: Artistic rendering of an Iroquoian longhouse structure and internal layout (drawing by Corrina Petit).

with structural failure. In such a situation, we should anticipate that years of apprenticeship were involved in learning to build safely and consistently" (2009: 65). With respect to the "maintenance" aspect of the McGuire and Schiffer model, it is hard to determine, given that the archaeological remains consist only of post-holes. It appears that early villages were occupied for 10 to 50 years before abandonment, relinquished perhaps because of deterioration of the houses that made habitation uncomfortable or impossible (Warrick 2000). A significant amount of labor and engineering acumen had to be put into designing and building the first longhouses, suggesting that builders may have sacrificed expediency in favor of building a more long-lasting structure with fewer maintenance needs.

In terms of the "use goal" for Iroquoian longhouses, the oblong structure may have served utilitarian and symbolic needs equally, as noted by Bruce Trigger (1985), who suggests that during a more mobile lifestyle early Iroquoian residence was patrilocal, but that matrilocality, and possibly matrilineal descent, became the norm concurrently with the adoption of agriculture. This is echoed by Claude Chapdelaine (1993: 198):

> Sedentarization was accompanied by important social changes among the Iroquoians and there is good reason to believe that this process was probably related to the crystallization of maternal lineages. . . . This new arrangement would have highly visible consequences such as the choice of new settlements for summer base camps, an increased

> sedentariness resulting in an increased familiarity with the growth of plants, as well as a new kind of house which is built in accordance with a new form of solidarity between women.

If longhouses were built to accommodate a new, or even preexisting, kinship and residential pattern based on Iroquoian women, then the creation of that structured space would have served to cement those patterns and ensure their reproduction through the generations. The building of longhouses established more permanent cooperative groups: those living within the longhouse developed close social, economic, and political relationships with fellow longhouse residents. Jodie O'Gorman sees longhouses as "the real and symbolic location of kin, entailing one's rights, responsibilities, and obligations among that kin" (2010: 575). She argues that the establishment of the longhouse created a community within a community: a close-knit group of people inhabiting the longhouse was the first and foremost level of relationship, and longhouse membership was an important element of social identity and world view (O'Gorman 2010: 576). In this way, she connects the social and symbolic construction of the Iroquoian longhouse with Lévi-Strauss's notion of a "house society" (see chapter 6). The initial building of the early Iroquoian longhouses, then, may have "captured" a new form of kin and residence patterns emergent with significant cultivation practices, and then reinforced these patterns through time. The longhouse simultaneously forged socioeconomic ties and more symbolic threads that wove residents into a close-knit community that shared a common identity, fostered by the walls of their earliest homes.

The architectural characteristics associated with earliest settlement in the American Southwest offer both similarities to and differences from the process in the Northeast. The similarities are in the several-centuries-long process in both regions, from the first substantially built home to essentially permanent residence. The differences are in the style of houses built, and in the circumstance in the Southwest that the residential structure changed long after initial settlement rather than contemporaneous with it. Like their counterparts in the Northeast, builders in the Southwest combined elements of technological strategy with both practical and symbolic needs.

A number of archaeological projects have focused on the correlation between the agricultural and architectural sequence of early residents in the upland Mogollon region in New Mexico (Diehl 1996; Rocek 1995; Stokes and Roth 1999). Though there is disagreement regarding elements of timing, most scholars see a correlation between a rising dependence on maize agriculture and more permanent settlement. During the later Archaic period of this region (ca. 2000 BCE–CE 200), people built temporary shelters, mainly engaging in hunting and gathering and experimenting with maize cultivation (Fish and Fish 1994; Huckell 1996). Just under 2,000 years ago in the Mimbres River area, a culture by the same name, part of the larger Mogollon region, began building more substantial pithouses. This ushered in the Early Pithouse (CE 200–550) and Late Pithouse (CE 550–1000) periods. Beginning in the ninth or tenth century of the

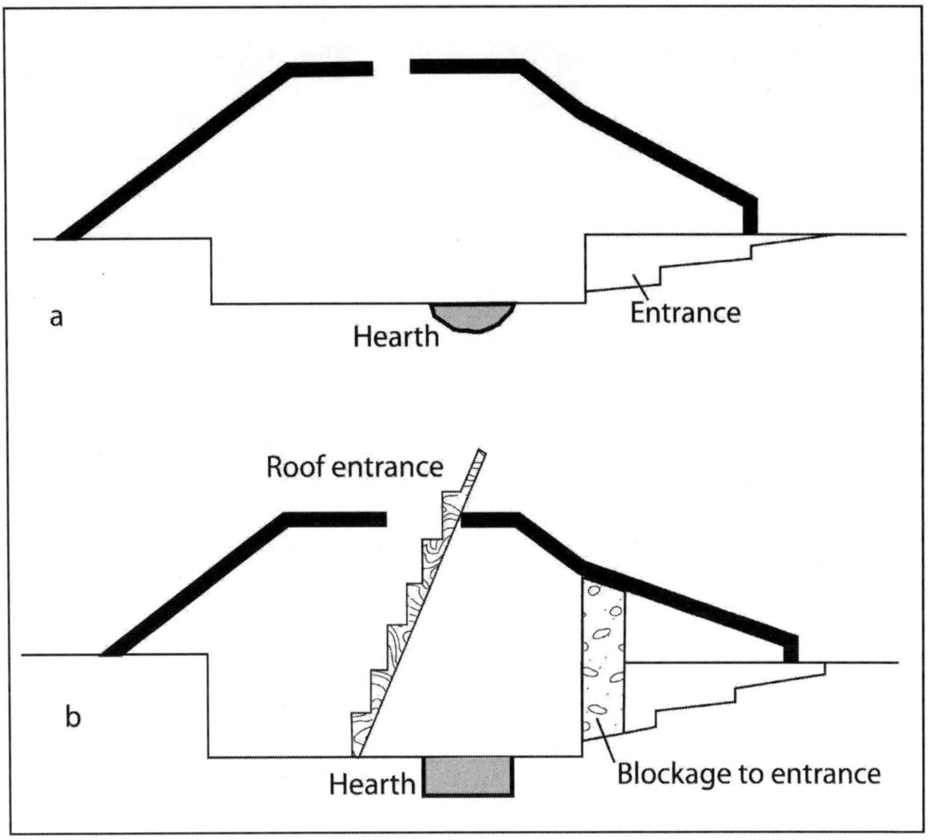

Figure 5.3: (a) Example of an earlier Mimbres pithouse with shallower depth and "basin" hearth; (b) a later Mimbres pithouse with more labor investment and built-in hearth (after Shafer 1995: figs. 3, 12).

Late Pithouse period, residents began building a new type of house, the pueblo; by this time, they were wholly sedentary agriculturalists.

In the Early Pithouse and earlier Late Pithouse periods, Mimbres residents built semi-subterranean pithouses that were circular or oval in form (Figure 5.3a); they tended to be located on higher elevations overlooking streams or rivers (Shafer 1995). The pithouses tended to be dug to rather shallow depths, with virtually no masonry used to support the walls; the interiors of the rooms were rarely plastered, and a minimal number of posts were employed to uphold the superstructure of branches (Diehl 1997). Each Early Pithouse structure had a simple "basin" hearth that was constructed on the floor of the house in a shallow pit. Entrance into the pithouse was through a ramp beginning at ground level and leading down via steps into the center of the house. Though builders of Early Pithouse–phase structures may have been involved in cultivation, archaeologists suggest that this was only one of a number of subsistence strategies employed at this stage. Pithouses were probably abandoned for at least one season during the year. Michael Diehl notes (1997: 189) that there was little in the way of renovation or remodeling of these houses, suggesting that residents may not have returned to them on a regular basis. Patricia Gilman (1987) suggests these structures were mainly winter residences, a season when shelter was more necessary and foods could be stored in a stable location.

Between CE 550 and 750, these circular or oval pithouses began to look substantially different from the earlier phase. One change involved location: Late Pithouse settlements were now located at lower elevations near the rivers, perhaps suggesting the need for water for cultivation. Much more labor was invested in the houses, including increasing the depth of the floor to an average of 124 cm, compared with 74 cm during the earlier phase (Diehl 1997). House form transitioned from circular to more square-shaped but with rounded corners (Stokes and Roth 1999). Masonry was used more frequently to support walls, the number of posts to support the roof nearly doubled from the earlier phase, and interior plaster was far more common (Diehl 1997; Shafer 1995). Two other architectural shifts are particularly notable (Figure 5.3b). Rather than hearths being on the floor, by this later phase hearths were built in the floor. In other words, a deep pit was excavated, often lined with stone slabs, and given an adobe collar to create a "formal" and well-built hearth. The other change involves the entryway. The ramp entrances were blocked, and entry was via a ladder through a hole in the roof. This required the construction of a sturdy roof that could bear the weight of humans traversing it. The rate of renovation and remodeling was higher in these later phases as well (Diehl 1997), suggesting repeated returns to these homes perhaps after a season, or less, away. By the Late Pithouse phase, Mimbres residents were living more sedentary lives than in the previous phase. They had contributed far more labor to the construction of their houses, perhaps necessitating less maintenance upon yearly return. Given that the structure and layout (excepting the entrance) remained virtually the same for 700 years, the use goals must have been largely met by these types of homes.

A change in the architectural footprint began around CE 900, leading to a new house form still built today. Mimbres residents began to abandon the rounded pithouses and instead built above-ground, rectangular pueblos, sometimes detached but more often contiguous, creating "apartment-style" housing (Figure 5.4). By this time, Mimbres residents were entirely sedentary and engaged in consistent farming activities. One of the most frequent explanations for this substantial shift in agricultural style is the growth in population that occurred at this time (Diehl 1996; Gilman 1987; Kohler et al. 2008), perhaps due to the increasing sedentarization and the food staples being provided by the crops (a roughly contemporary process occurred to the north in the Mesa Verde region of southern Colorado [Wilshusen and Potter 2010]). Entry into the houses continued to be roof-based, and the hearths were still very well built. Harry Shafer (1995) suggests that some of these architectural changes reflect adjustments in Mimbres cosmology and world view. He notes the ubiquity of the be-

Figure 5.4: "Apartment"-style housing construction in Pueblo/Mimbres settlements, exemplified here by the Bandelier site (photos by the author).

lief in a multilayered cosmos in both prehistoric and present-day cultures in North America and Mesoamerica in which residences symbolically represent the universe. He suggests that the relocation of the doorway to the roof may have approximated the doorway within a multi-tiered world; the space within the house was "this world," the one inhabited by humans, and the hearth (dug deeply into the earth) and the doorway in the ceiling symbolically represented the passageway between the upper and lower worlds in the Mimbres cosmos. The rectangular form is representative of the cardinal points in a "four-cornered universe," which is also a common component in Native American belief systems. Thus, according to Shafer, "it follows that a major shift in house design could signal a change in either the cosmology or the way their world view was materially expressed" (1995: 42). He notes that the later practice in the Classic Puebloan phase, CE 1000–1130, in which residents placed burials under house floors, may have been meant to allow ancestors easy passage from one layer to another using the access points within the home.

The Early and Late Pithouse phases provide a fascinating accounting of which "goals" were paramount in which phases of architectural construction. As so clearly laid out by Diehl (1997) and Gilman (1987), the Early Pithouse structures were built with an eye to minimal labor and utilitarian use. Little maintenance was accorded these structures, and they may have offered only one or a very few "use-lives" on a seasonal basis. Our available data do not allow us to know whether "symbolic" goals were met by the construction of these early pithouses. By the Late Pithouse phase, when residential patterns were likely much more sedentary, construction and use goals had changed. Far more labor was invested in the initial construction, and remodeling and maintenance was carried out more frequently. Utilitarian use of these structures may have remained the primary use goal, although recasting the entrance, making a more formal hearth, and possibly squaring the house corners may reflect the desire to bring the residence into conformity with the symbolism of Mimbres cosmology. A minimum of effort in the first stages of sedentism transitioned to a maximization of labor to build substantial and symbolically relevant homes when full sedentism was in force.

The Levantine Neolithic: Circles and Squares

As in North America, a transition in architectural forms is found in the Near Eastern southern Levant. While much research has been devoted to whether sedentism and agriculture coincided in the Levant (Bar-Yosef 2002; Bar-Yosef and Belfer-Cohen 1991; Belfer-Cohen and Bar-Yosef 1989; Boyd 2006; Byrd 2005; Goring-Morris and Belfer Cohen 2011; Rocek 1998), this is not the primary focus of discussion here. As noted in chapter 2, the transition was a lengthy and multiphase process.

Some of the earliest architecture in the Levant is found at Ohalo in the Kebaran period (ca. 18,000–12,500 BCE). Residents here built circular or kidney-shaped structures using mud and botanical materials suitable for temporary housing during the summer and/or fall (Barker 2009: 104–13; Nadal 2003). It is in the following periods, known as the Natufian (ca. 12,500–9700 BCE), and particularly in the Pre-Pottery Neolithic A (PPNA; 9700–8500 BCE), when a more substantial data set of architectural remains suggests Levantine foragers were transitioning into more sedentary settlements. At Natufian sites such as 'Ain Mallaha, Hayonim Cave, Wadi Hammeh 27, Beidha, Nahal Oren, and elsewhere, houses were oval and generally semi-subterranean (Banning 1996; Bar-Yosef 1998; Byrd 1994; Kozlowski 2006), not dissimilar to the pithouses of the American Southwest (Rocek 1998). Structures ranged in size from 2.5 to 7 m in diameter, and unlike those at Ohalo, Natufian structures employed stone foundations, suggesting a greater investment of labor (Boyd 2006), perhaps due to longer-term habitation. Nonetheless, most recent interpretations of Natufian sites identify these structures as representing seasonal occupation, with some perhaps serving as base camps to which residents returned on a yearly basis (Bar-Yosef 1998; Belfer-Cohen 1991; Belfer-Cohen and Bar-Yosef 2000).

In the PPNA, people continued to build semi-subterranean circular structures, with stone foundations and superstructures of unbaked mudbricks. Studies suggest a more formalized use of space, such as the development of refuse management systems and the creation of specific activity areas (Kuijt and Goodale 2009). In addition, small silos at PPNA sites suggest the need for seasonal or longer-term storage (Bar-Yosef 1998; Belfer-Cohen and Goring-Morris 2011). Subsistence data and other elements of material culture suggest to archaeologists that residents were spending far longer in their PPNA settlements than they had in the preceding Natufian period, and that PPNA domestic structures were built by the first nearly or wholly sedentary settlers in the region.

The following PPNB period can be divided into an Early/Middle PPNB phase (ca. 8500–7500 BCE) during which a *koiné* PPNB village type develops, and Late/Final PPNB (ca. 7500–6400 BCE), when "mega-sites" with hundreds of residents emerged, At the close of the PPNB, community dissolution occurred, prompted by various factors, including overpopulation, climate change, and disease (Belfer-Cohen and Goring-Morris 2011; Goring-Morris and Belfer-Cohen 2010; Kuijt 2000c). It is during the earlier "*koiné* PPNB" period that a type of Near Eastern community and residential structure emerges that is quite distinct from its PPNA precedents: Near Eastern residents begin building rectilinear rather than circular houses, above ground, and strong enough to support a second story or rooftop activities. These rectangular houses are often divided into several cells or rooms, with a central passage running through the structure and a doorway at the end. A hearth sits in the central and usually largest room, and mudbrick, stone, or wooden posts or piers along the sides serve not only to hold up the roof but to delineate space (Byrd 2000; Byrd and Banning 1988).

The site of Beidha (Byrd 1995; Kirkbride 1966), in southern Jordan, offers the best example of this PPNA to PPNB architectural change. In the PPNA Phase A layer (Figure 5.5a), residents built semi-subterranean oval structures that were often connected to each other, with several adjacent doorways that opened into the same courtyard space (Byrd 1994: 647). Space inside the Phase A houses was largely undifferentiated, and external spaces were not delineated per house but rather shared between several. In the later PPNA Phase B (Figure 5.5b), houses had become more truly circular and were built above ground; they were no longer agglutinated but were more often separate. A single doorway offered more restricted access to Phase B houses, and interiors were slightly more differentiated as to activities and the use of space. Brian Byrd notes that "more energy was invested in [Phase B house] construction and maintenance than in Phase A, as the buildings were slightly larger than previously and contained plaster floors that were replastered a number of times during their use lives" (Byrd 1994: 652).

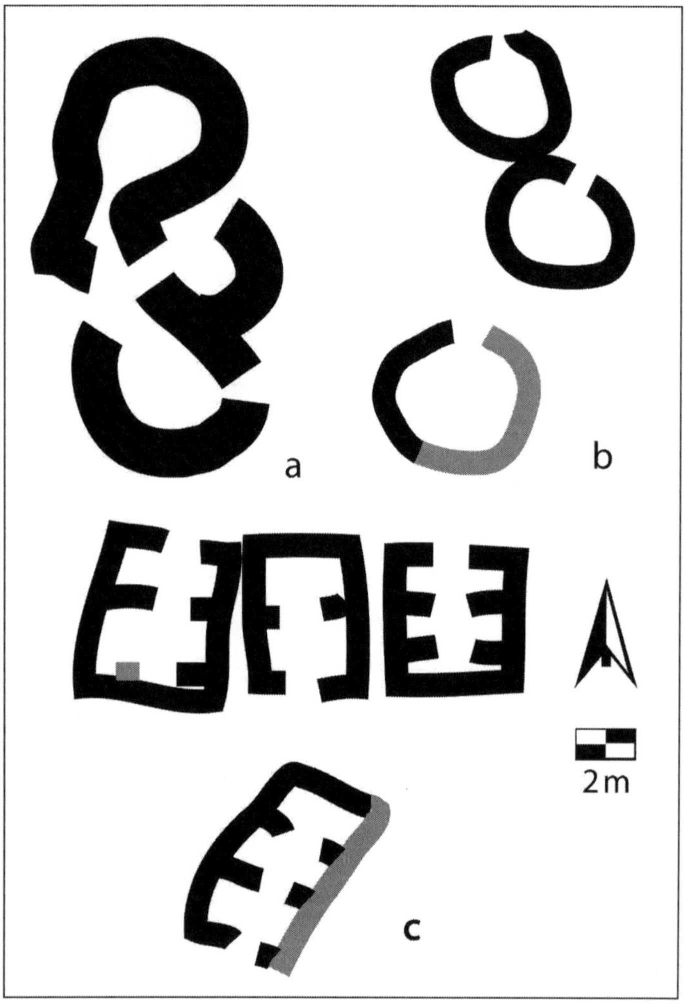

Figure 5.5: Examples of housing styles from (a) Beidha Phase A; (b) Beidha Phase B; (c) Beidha Phase C (after Byrd 1994: 649, 651, 653).

It is in the PPNA Phase C level that a radically different residential plan emerged (Figure 5.5c). Agglutinated rectilinear two-story houses were built above ground and were larger than their previously circular counterparts. Substantial investment of labor, including the internal buttresses or piers separating rooms/cells, ensured the use of the roof or second story, and allowed for compartmentalization of activities and greater privacy (Byrd 1994: 656). Phase C Beidha residents probably occupied their homes on a year-round basis, while Phase B inhabitants were likely on the threshold of permanent residency. Why, then, the switch to rectilinear architecture, not limited just to Beidha, but a Levantine-wide PPNB phenomenon?

On the practical side, the new space offered greater flexibility for task performance; a larger space was more easily differentiated. Storage capacity was also increased, and items could be tucked away behind a wall rather than in a basket easily visible from a doorway. More spacious rectangular houses allowed for the housing of a larger or extended family, possibly necessary in a more intensive farming-based economy. In general, while a circular structure is easier to build out of pliable materials (e.g., skins), a rectangular structure may provide a more efficient use of space once permanency in residence commences. However, practicality may not have been the only motivator for house form choice in the Levantine Neolithic.

E. B. Banning and others suggest that archaeologists working in this region should not be too quick to ignore the role symbolism may have played in house structure (Banning 2003; Byrd 2005; Watkins 1990). Researchers on the PPNB period note an increase in ritual objects present in and around houses, including human skulls (some specially treated), plaster and clay figurines, and human burials placed under house floors (Banning 2003; Kuijt 2000b; Goring-Morris 2000; Verhoeven 2002); these coincide with increasing population and sedentism (Kuijt 2000c). Ancestor veneration is usually the explanation for such rituals, a practice suggesting a strong attachment to place and possibly to house (see chapters 2 and 10). Changing from circular to rectilinear may have served practical (maintenance, space use) needs, but it may have also dovetailed with the desire to establish permanency—in a prominent two-storied structure that visually demonstrated the presence of *that* family in *that* space. Perhaps a religious connection to place, and house, documented through the placement of ancestors beneath the floors and in above-ground household altars, had developed by the PPNB as Levantine residents created long-term homes in their growing villages. The investment of labor to build bigger and more sturdy structures was rewarded by the opportunity for long-term occupancy; thus, all three goals were met: significant investment in construction achieving fewer maintenance issues, and a well-built home capable of housing both the living and the dead, for generations.

While expediency may have suited builders of very early (semi-)permanent houses, attention to what was necessary for more long-term, or repeated occupation—after seasonal absences—soon became important. Also soon emerging was consideration of the more symbolic functions of the house, perhaps representing cosmology, kinship, ancestors, or other ideologies and beliefs. Using McGuire and Schiffer's (1983) guide to understanding the earliest permanent homes allows archaeologists to witness a progression of utilitarian to more symbolic needs as permanency becomes a norm.

From Sedentism to City

The discussion here offers an overview of what happens when domestic dwellers find themselves living among increasing numbers of neighbors in growing communities. How architecture might reveal the development of socioeconomic complexity is a major topic explored. Also touched upon, but too vast a topic to fully cover, is what "urban houses" might look like in a prehistoric city.

Finding Social Complexity in the Architectural Footprint

As the hamlets created by early sedentary settlers turned first into small villages and then into towns, social structure often necessarily altered in order to handle the more complex social, political, and economic behavioral codes of larger populations living in crowded conditions. Architectural adjustments in such circumstances might include the increased segmentation of interior space and the creation of "private" spaces—already present in PPNB Levantine houses discussed above. Another common appearance after permanent settlement was the creation of public spaces or buildings.

Sue Kent and Amos Rapoport pioneered studies on the correlation between domestic spatial segmentation and increasing social complexity (Kent 1984, 1987a, 1990, 1991c; Rapoport 1982, 1990; see also Oswald 1987). Using a combination of ethnoarchaeological and archaeological data, Kent noted that house interiors become more ideologically and physically segmented as household members have increasing numbers of tasks to perform. Walls and partitions create necessary spaces, which become, archaeologically, activity areas (Kent 1990: 127, 1991c: 439–45). Kent therefore sees a direct relationship between societal complexity and the shape of the house: "[A]s groups become socially and politically more segmented (complex), their use of space and architecture also becomes more segmented" (1990: 150). The physical division of space reflects ideological and behavioral changes in an increasingly complex society.

Kent's model dovetails with Rapoport's work on the interaction between humans and their built environment. Rapoport builds his model on the premise that architecture encloses human behavior, and thus it is a physical representation of that behavior (1990: 9–10). "Activity systems" that occur in particular spaces within the built environment require "cues," which may be tools or other portable items, as well as furniture, in the space apportioned to the specific activities (Rapoport 1990: 13). Anyone entering that space who is acquainted with the socioeconomic activities of the household in that community would recognize the cues and immediately understand the association of space and behavior. As more tasks are necessary within a household (commensurate with increasing social and economic complexity), the number of cues and spaces would increase, thereby requiring more area within a household or a decision to specialize in fewer and more specific tasks suitable to the household. A growing community (in size and complexity) would feature increasingly segmented houses—more rooms or partitioned spaces inside the house or compound—and more differentiated cues in houses across the community as certain household turned to specialized activities (Steadman 2000). Often, physical expansion of the house's footprint is difficult, if not impossible, because space was allotted in previous generations and simpler times. Increasing population may even decrease space allotment per dwelling (impinging on exterior spaces such as alleys and courtyards). In these cases, residents might give up some interior space by building thicker walls, and then constructing a second story, thereby nearly doubling the space that can be used for an increasing number of activities (Steadman 1996, 2000). Alternatively, when population exceeds sustainability, villages may fission if ecological and social environments—the availability of arable land without resultant conflict—allow such a process (Bandy 2004, 2010; Cameron and Duff 2008; Duffy et al. 2013; Kohler and Varien 2010). If neighbors leave, then spatial expansion on a horizontal plane might certainly be possible.

The increase in partitioned space, as well as the construction of additional stories, can also help create another architectural trait found in increasingly complex societies: private spaces, dealt with in detail in chapter 3. As societies become increasingly stratified, households often acquire surpluses and competition for social positioning occurs, generating a desire to protect material possessions from easy access (Hall 1966; Rapoport 1982; Sommer 1969). In more egalitarian settings, entry often gives access to all spaces within the house, either physically or visually. From the doorway or just inside of it, a visitor may be able to see every portion of the house interior and all the belongings in it. A good example of this is the Bhunga homes in the Kutch region of Gujarat, India, circular homes into which one can see the entire abode from the doorway (Figure 5.6).

Figure 5.6: Round Bhunga house in the Kutch region of Gujarat, India, in which the front door opens into the entire interior of house (photo by the author).

As more possessions "to protect" are acquired, architectural boundaries can be used to prevent non-household members from having physical or visual access to sensitive places and valuable goods. To achieve a more private location, residents might employ an increasing number of boundaries or access points to reach storage rooms or private spaces, archaeologically discernible through the use of syntactical analyses of space and access analysis (Chippendale 1992; Hillier and Hanson 1984; Hillier et al. 1976; see chapter 3). Alternatively, house footprints might be recast to achieve a "front/back" organization, making frontal areas more public, and back private "no-go" areas for guests (Giddens 1984:122–26; Portnoy 1981; Rapoport 1982: 118). Just such a restructuring was found by Denise Lawrence-Zúñiga (1999) in her study of recently built homes in Portugal. Houses built by wealthier families introduced a salon or parlor located at the front of the house where guests could be entertained; another innovation was the front garden, separating the house from the street both physically and visually. The "front/back" differentiation in these Portuguese houses was firmly established over the span of several decades as the economy improved and more significant social stratification developed (Lawrence-Zúñiga 1999: 166–73). The creation of private spaces throughout the house, or the clear "sealing off" of a portion of the house, is a very strong indicator of social change within a community.

A final indicator of increasing social complexity involves the construction of non-domestic structures. The impetus to build such structures varies depending on the agency of the builders, the goals of construction, and the norms guiding social relations in the community. A shortcut to understanding the myriad motivations for building non-domestic structures involves dividing incentivized actions into two categories: those in which individuals use networking strategies and those involving cooperative corporate goals. Network or more individualized strategies are "associated with heavily personalized or centralized forms of leadership" (Feinman, Lightfoot, and Upham 2000: 453) in which increasing wealth and power become consolidated into fewer hands through overt actions such as controlling crafts and trade, access to important places, and controlling surplus (Costin 1991; D'Altroy 1992; Earle 2001; Pauketat 1994). As noted elsewhere, Hayden and others refer to these types of actions as "aggrandizing," allowing one or a few to capture higher political and economic positions in society (Hayden 1995; and see Clark and Blake 1996). "Aggrandizers" engage in networking strategies with other prominent community members in order to solidify their own power base and secure influential allies within and beyond the community. The building of non-domestic structures is one avenue to demonstrating power and influence; for instance, a specialized structure built for feasting purposes serves networking opportunities and also demonstrates the luxury *to* feast (Helwing 2003; Pollock 2003; Stanish 2009). Public architecture also demonstrates the ability of an individual or political entity to exert control over people's labor and burgeoning sociopolitical complexity (Clark and Blake 1996). An aspiring leader, purportedly for the betterment of the community, will seek to coerce, cajole, or otherwise convince village residents to participate in the creation of public works

(Arnold 1996c; Feinman 2000a). In this case, the placement of public monuments is often near the leader's residence. The control of ritually important areas, expressed by physical proximity or by limiting access via gates or doors, can also be a means of demonstrating sociopolitical power (Potter 2000).

In contrast, cooperative groups may pool resources to construct ritual and public areas (Feinman 2000b) where no overt spatial relationship between particular households and public areas is likely to exist, and public access to important areas is easily attained. The cooperative/corporate model works on a more decentralized basis, creating sociopolitical heterarchy—namely, in making use of available relationships through extended family contacts as well as in supra-kin settings (Arnold 2000; Chesson 2003; Feinman 2000a; Hayden and Cannon 1982; Rodning 2009; Schachner 2010). In such systems, there is far less emphasis on the individual and much more on the success of the overall community. The ingredients of power structures are present, but exist rather in a pan-village occurrence of surplus accumulation and craft production, participation in trade networks, and shared labor input into public works and meeting spaces in an equal spatial distribution throughout the village (Costin 2001; Crumley 1995; Feinman 2000a: 38–40; Renfrew 2001). Cooperative units may consist of kin groups but may also cross-cut family lines to stretch across neighborhoods or other sociopolitical units (Chesson 2003; Crumley 1995). Public structures would be built in areas accessible by the cooperative groups, or might be in a centralized location available to all community members. Structures might be religious, economic (for surplus), or political (for public gatherings). The social organization involved in funding and building the structures, and the need for them, speaks to an increasingly complex sociopolitical and economic organization across the community.

Case Studies in the Americas and the Levant

The indicators of increasing social complexity described above can be found in the houses built in various localites across the Americas and during the Levantine later Neolithic. The presence of public buildings in the early Pueblo phase of the Mimbres culture is, according to Gary Feinman and colleagues (Feinman, Lightfoot, and Upham 2000), a prime example of the emergence of cooperative corporate groups pooling resources within a community. As semi-subterranean detached circular pithouses transformed into above-ground attached rectilinear structures (ca. CE 900), these complexes incorporated storage areas accessible to household units in the complex but not beyond; the circular semi-subterranean structures—now called *kivas*—had become the religious spaces and the burial locations for important members of the cooperative group (Anyon and LeBlanc 1984; Feinman, Lightfoot, and Upham 2000; Schachner 2010; Shafer 1995). Each of the residential complexes expressed differing levels of wealth in the investment of labor in the structures, their size, and their contents. Motivations for the emergence or reification (from earlier patterns) of these corporate groups may have been related to scalar stress created by population growth, external forces such as the growth of politically aggressive systems in neighboring regions, or, most likely, a combination of variables (Creel and Anyon 2003). In the Mimbres case, the creation of public spaces for communal ritual was concomitant with increasing agricultural intensification and emergent socioeconomic and political complexity.

A study of "first towns" in various places in the Americas (Clark, Gibson, and Zeidler 2010) offers architectural insights into the creation of public spaces that feature greater controls to access and that likely reflect individual or small group networking (aggrandizing) strategies. Excavations at Real Alto in Ecuador (ca. 2900 BCE), Paso de la Amada in Mexico (ca. 1650 BCE), and Poverty Point in the southern United States (ca. 1700 BCE) show the aggregation of population and a corresponding change in settlement layouts. At Real Alto, the population of roughly 600 in Phase 2b expanded to 1800 in Phase 3; new public architecture emerged in the form of a plaza, and mound structures on platforms offered significant evidence of ritual functions. Some houses were three times larger than in the previous phase and demonstrated greater labor investment, "indicative of status differences" (Clark, Gibson, and Zeidler 2010: 214). A similar process occurred at Paso de la Amada, where a collection of domestic structures housing approximately 250–400 people around 1900 BCE gave way to large residences on platforms, a plaza, ballcourt, and a "chiefly residence" by 1650 BCE (Clark, Gibson, and Zeidler 2010: 220). Mounded concentric rings at Poverty Point were not only cosmologically important, but also delineated social status, with the innermost rings commanding a higher and more prominent position at the site, supporting fewer houses than the outer, lower rings. The mounds constructed at Poverty Point were not used for burials but rather were likely associated with ritual activity. In each of these towns, architecture makes manifest the development of public ritual and secular spaces, perhaps designated for use by only a portion of the town's population, with significant social stratification shown by house size and location, burials, and goods. Leaders marshaled labor and resources from town dwellers to build public places ostensibly for the good of the entire population but also serving the need of highlighting the accomplishments of these new leaders.

Similar needs for space and privacy are found at American Southwestern sites dating to the last millennium. At Pot Creek Pueblo, near Taos, New Mexico, a small community of pithouses in the early 1100s transitioned, by the early 1300s, to a large settlement of above-ground attached pueblos surrounding a plaza, arranged in room blocks. After the advent of pueblos, and following a population increase, not only did housing units increase in size, but the number of doorways into housing units decreased significantly, with 53% of rooms featuring doorways in the 1270s and only 13% in the 1310s (Crown and Kohler 1994: 107). These two architectural adjustments to "town" living are interpreted as a "greater concern with protecting food stored in ground-floor rooms" (Crown and Kohler 1994: 111), explaining the decrease in the number of doorways and expressing a greater desire for privacy and areas for task performance (Dohm 1990; and see Dohm 1996).

During the later Natufian period in the Near Eastern Levant, the Phase C houses at Beidha, described above, exemplify the creation of segmented space, in part to separate activities in a more economically active household (Byrd 1994). It is not only at Beidha where the "pier" houses appear but at sites all over the Levant (Byrd and Banning 1988). In some settlements, the practice of using courtyards to regulate access to houses afforded some wealthier residents the ability to engage in "privacy practices"—that is, to publically display some elements of wealth but to also block visual and physical access to others (Banning 2011a). As residents of the Neolithic Levant engaged in a greater variety and intensity of economic activities, and as differentiations in wealth possession developed, houses began to reflect the desire to create defined spaces for specific activities—occasionally these spaces were rooftops—and to recast their architectural footprints to create spaces hidden or inaccessible to the casual visitor or passer-by.

The Neolithic Levant also witnessed the construction of public structures not long after permanent settlement. The most famous example, perhaps, is the tower at Jericho, dating to the mid-ninth millennium. This conical tower stands over 8 m high and has a circumference of up to 2 m, with an interior staircase allowing access to the top of the tower. It was a feat of engineering requiring forethought and a great deal of labor. Initial interpretations suggested it was built for defensive reasons, while later interpretations argued for a function related to flood control in this well-watered region of the Jordan Valley (Bar-Yosef 1986, 1998; Kenyon 1957). More recently, archaeologists have argued that the tower was not suitable for either of these tasks but rather must have had a deep symbolic significance for the inhabitants of Neolithic Jericho, perhaps serving as a type of observatory related to the change of seasons (Barkai and Liran 2008; Liran and Barkai 2011; Naveh 2003). The effort exerted to build this monument (several thousand working days at the minimum) suggests that labor was controlled, or at least organized, by some group in the community and that many participated in the tower's construction. Other public architecture, such as large round subterranean buildings at the site of Jerf el Ahmar in Syria, date to the PPNA–PPNB transition (Stordeur 2000; Stordeur and Abbès 2002). One building was divided into radiating cells with internal benches, while the other was simply a large open room, also with benches. Both structures contained human remains. The excavator suggests these were multifunctional buildings, offering a place for meetings, storage, and ritual (Stordeur 2000). In Phase C at Beidha, two large buildings were likely public in nature. Both were rectangular, with painted walls and courtyard, but neither contained the normal furniture or artifacts associated with domestic residences (Byrd 1994). Earlier phases at Beidha have also produced buildings that were likely non-domestic, but those in Phase C, when the community was truly sedentary, were significantly larger and located in the center of the community: "[W]ith the shift to sedentary villages, the need arose for more community regulatory mechanisms to hold social units together as a dynamic system. These buildings represent an expression of this demand and were built as a venue for conducting suprahousehold meeting and decision-making activities, and possibly related ceremonial or ritual activities" (Byrd 1994: 657).

While sedentism is not the only circumstance in which large public structures are erected, it does seem to go hand in hand with changes in the architectural footprint. Greater efforts to segment space, create private or at least visually unavailable spaces, and provide public and/or communal places seem to be some of the next steps in building a community shortly after full sedentism has been achieved.

Urbanism: Living in the Suburbs

A short section within a chapter cannot sufficiently describe the structure and form of houses in ancient cities. The reasons for the rise of cities, their layouts, and their "suburbs" are as varied as are the cultures that constructed them. The first problematic issue is the simple definition of a "city": when is an ancient settlement an "urban" center? Such questions have been recently addressed with regard to urbanism and the city (e.g., Cowgill 2004; Harmanşah 2013; Marcus and Sabloff 2008a; Smith 2003a), and in terms of the process of community aggregation, which may lead to urbanism or, as noted above, to fissioning (Bandy 2004, 2010; Bandy and Fox 2010; Birch 2013). When entire books seek to define the nature of a city, a simple description here is untenable and, essentially, unnecessary. Rather, outlining a few useful parameters of the city landscape, germane to the discussion of domestic units in an urban setting, will suffice.

Many scholars have broached the subject of the emergence and eventual structure of ancient cities. Joyce Marcus and Jeremy Sabloff (2008b) offer a historical summary of the attempt to define a "city," thereby well illustrating the difficulties scholars from a variety of disciplines have had capturing the many aspects of what an urban center might be. George Cowgill (2004: 526) offers a general guideline: city residents have behaviors, "practices, experiences, identities, and attitudes" that differ "significantly from those . . . who identify most closely with 'rural' lands outside such settlements." Thus, in Cowgill's estimation, an urban center cannot and does not exist without a hinterland with smaller communities. Spiro Kostof (1991, 1992), well known for his work on past and present cities, focuses on the unique elements each city possesses: social hierarchies, in part created by the differentiation in crafts and work within a city (i.e., bread maker versus priest), paired with spatial variety, including public quarters, domestic areas, markets and other economic establishments, and defensive architecture. All these create a place on the landscape that is complex, full of energy, and unique from any other.

Monica Smith (2003b) concurs with Cowgill that a city stands in contrast to rural settlements and also acknowledges Kostof's assertion that differential spaces are critical to the definition of a city. In fact, it is precisely these that allow us, according to

Smith, to suggest that there are some elements of cities that are predictable and expected. She notes that V. Gordon Childe's "10 criteria" for defining civilization (Childe 1950) remain a useful set of characteristics by which one may determine whether a settlement is indeed a city (Smith 2003b: 9). These criteria, including craft specialization, monumental architecture, and class structure, implicitly include the differentiation of city from hinterland, and the spatial and economic diversity within its physical limits. As Michael Smith (2009) also notes, though there have been many more recent attempts to characterize "urbanism" and state formation, most still incorporate the majority of Childe's criteria in some fashion. Marcus and Sabloff include many of Childe's criteria in their list of elements typically found in the definition of a city, paraphrased here (2008b: 13):

- A heterogeneous collection of people, work, and social statuses.
- A variety of public buildings devoted to religious, economic, and administrative activities, some monumental in size. The most sacred or highest ranking areas will be spatially distinct with limited access.
- The skyline will offer a profile with the tallest/highest buildings located in the center with height decreasing toward the margins of the settlement.
- Crowded residential and non-residential buildings will form modules or city blocks separated by streets or spaces, some of which may be public.

Monica Smith perhaps offers the best procedure for defining the notions of city and urbanism: "In sum, the definition of cities in both the modern and premodern world is subject to a variety of criteria whose applicability depends on the particular questions asked of the data set" (2003b: 11). In other words, as she notes earlier in the same chapter, we "know one when we see one" (2003b: 9).

Some of Childe's 10 criteria for urbanism also lend insight into what types of information can be gained from archaeological investigation of domestic quarters in urban centers. The methodologies for several of these form the backbone of other chapters in this volume. For instance, "class structure," by which we can also infer social stratification, is eminently detectable in the investigation of different neighborhoods or domestic quarters within a city. Chapter 9 explores in depth how one recognizes "power" in architectural renderings, which, in part, encompasses identifying houses of the wealthy as opposed to those belonging to societal members possessing far less. Closely related to social stratification are socioeconomic pursuits within the domestic quarter: Is craft specialization a household affair or a communal one? Do households produce their own utilitarian crafts or specialize, necessitating inter-household trade? What are the production and consumption activities within and across households? All of these, and particularly the latter, are investigated within the rubric of what has come to be called "household archaeology," the subject of chapter 7. Temples, palaces, and other public monuments may yield a wealth of data on what items elites obtained through trade and tribute; excavation of the domestic or non-elite areas, however, provide the most critical data on how the day-to-day economy of the city operated.

Childe's ninth criterion for urbanism is "regular 'foreign' trade over quite long distances" (1950: 15). While this does not overtly state that cities will have "foreign residents," this circumstance would interface well with his first criterion, that cities are densely populated (1950: 9). The fact that different ethnic groups lived in some ancient cities has been proven, for instance, in the excavations at ancient Teotihuacan (Cowgill 2007, 2008; Millon 1976) and Kültepe-Kanesh in Anatolia (Kulakoğlu 2010, 2011; Özgüç 2005). In both cases, residents of these "ethnic neighborhoods" were there to facilitate trade relations with their home regions. While there are certainly obstacles to identifying ethnicity archaeologically (Emberling 1997; Jones 1997; 2008), a compendium of data—including house style and form and house contents, especially in a defined area that contrasts to that found in other domestic areas—can often be sufficient to assert the presence of various ethnic groups. A correlation is the existence of "neighborhoods" in domestic quarters. If neighborhoods are identifiable, delineated by streets, courtyards, or natural boundaries, investigating who lived in those neighborhoods and why can offer fruitful data on the sociocultural and socioeconomic structure of the city as a whole (see Foster 2012 for an excellent example of this). Besides the abodes of ethnic groups, neighborhoods may be populated by kinship groups, a subject discussed in chapter 6; neighborhoods may be occupied by those engaged in similar economic activities; and, as already noted above, neighborhoods may be differentiated by societal position and wealth possession. The importance of neighborhoods in the analysis of urban living is addressed in detail below.

Finally, urban planning can be more clearly revealed by investigating the domestic quarter rather than monumental or public spaces, the latter possibly built upon the eradication of previous houses or other structures. Childe (1950) did not specifically address urban planning in his criteria, since he felt, like Kostof in his argument regarding cities, that urban patterning was essentially unique in each case, and that there was no "one characteristic" to define how cities formed. Scholarship on the urban planning of ancient cities has investigated many methodologies, but most proceed on the basis of identifying whether an ancient city was "planned" (in advance of building the domestic quarter) or "unplanned." If a city was planned, as were the ancient Harappan cities of South Asia, then this speaks to the social organization of labor and the possible existence of a preexisting leadership structure intent on "building" a civilization. If unplanned—that is, built in what Kostof (1991) refers to as a more "organic" style, the city might well have begun as a village, developing according to a variety of factors (A. T. Smith 2003). Michael Smith (2007) suggests that even cities that appear "organic" have "planned" aspects that might reflect leadership structures at various levels. Investigating urban planning can provide clues to the origin of the city and its sociopolitical, economic, and social structures.

The Urban House and Neighborhood

While the majority of this book focuses on individual houses, often in comparison with one another, this section advocates the examination of *neighborhoods* as the method likely to reveal the most information about city residents. This does not mean that individual houses are not relevant; indeed, such would be the basis for understanding the daily life of those residents. However, identification of "neighborhoods" and what makes them so will also yield bountiful data about city life and structure.

One of the best studies to explain why identifying neighborhoods in cities is critical, and how one should go about doing so, was offered by Michael Smith (2010). Smith points out that "finding neighborhoods is a subset of the study of urban spatial organization" and also that "neighborhoods seem to be universal attributes of cities in all time periods" (2010: 138, 139). Given that neighborhoods are standard to city structures, he then offers brief guidelines for identifying them (Smith 2010: 145–46):

- look for "areas bounded by physical features" that are either natural or created by humans;
- look for "areas of social distinctiveness";
- identify "spatial clusters of buildings or spaces."

Smith fleshes out these identifiers in case studies. He affirms that neighborhoods can be particularly helpful in identifying social groupings within a city, based on ethnicity, religious affiliation, occupation, or status (2010: 150). He also discusses urban development as often a "top-down" or "bottom-up" process, with one usually predominating over the other (2010: 150–51). He offers interesting points of discussion on how these oppositional processes might counterbalance each other. For instance, a "top-down" urban center within which a significant amount of urban planning structured the city's layout may see part of that planning go awry if the city suddenly receives a considerable migration into its neighborhoods. New houses, perhaps built in a nonconformist, more "higgledy-piggledy" fashion, might skew what once looked like a planned urban setting. Alternatively, pressure from the "state" to urbanize might be resisted by some neighborhoods but accepted by others (Greenberg 2002; Paz 2012). The variables involved in understanding a city's layout are numerous, if not innumerable.

Garth Bawden's study (1982) of the Moche period city of Galindo in Peru employed the principles outlined by Smith's review. He identified four neighborhoods, labeled Areas A though D, surrounding the city's ceremonial and administrative center. Each neighborhood was separated by topographical features, with two located in less than ideal circumstances (rocky slopes) and two on relatively level ground in more advantageous positions. Galindo houses were homogeneous in their composition, each possessing a living area (*sala*), a kitchen, and storage areas (Bawden 1982: 169). What differentiated the houses was the size of the *sala*, the contents of the houses, and their spatial access to the city center. Bawden was able to delineate the neighborhoods as to wealth and social status while also determining that all residents likely came from the same ethnic group (based on the homogeneity of the house types and contents). Neighborhood Area B was the poorest, featuring the smallest houses and a lack of luxury or exotic goods. It was located on a steep and rocky hillside, far from sources of water, and was barred from the ceremonial center by the placement of a large wall. Bawden described Area B as "a crowded barrio" (1982: 175). In contrast, Area D had the largest houses, sometimes possessing two *salas* with elaborate interior furniture, large quantities of luxury and exotic goods, and easy access to the ceremonial center. Areas A and C fell between these two, displaying enough differentiation to suggest that residents in Area A were quite well off, while those of Area C had similar living circumstances to residents in the poorest Area B neighborhood (Bawden 1982: 176–78). Bawden identified neighborhoods based on both natural and human-built barriers that created clusters of buildings; within each, he found class-based social homogeneity. Residents of Area D were, according to Bawden, the city leaders, while residents of Area B were at the socioeconomic bottom of the society. The substantial divide between the wealthy inhabitants of two neighborhoods and the relative poverty in the other two gave Bawden very useful insights into how ancient Moche society was structured. Though subsequent research at Galindo suggests that these neighborhoods were perhaps not as differentiated as Bawden initially inferred (Bawden 1990; Nash 2009), his methodology is sound, and elements of it have been employed very successfully at similar South American settings (e.g., Janusek 2004; Lau 2010; Moore 2003).

Wealth possession is, of course, not the only factor that causes humans to delineate neighborhoods. Ethnicity and religion can be powerful motivators as well. As Michael Smith (2010) suggests, consider the Christian, Jewish, and Muslim neighborhood arrangement of Old Jerusalem: the architectural footprints, house contents, and physical separation (through walls and partitions) between these neighborhoods are clear signifiers of the differing peoples inhabiting them. An ethnographic study of Iranian cities (Mazumdar and Mazumdar 1997) illustrates what might be learned archaeologically about attitudes and treatment of ethnic and/or religious groups. People practicing the ancient religion of Zoroastrianism in Iran have essentially become a separate ethnic group. Zoroastrian houses can be identified by certain characteristics, many of these being the *absence* of Muslim architectural features such as arches and elevated ceilings designed to cool houses in hot weather—an architectural convention that would require taller houses; Zoroastrians were not allowed to build houses that stood above those belonging to Muslims (Mazumdar and Mazumdar 1997). Zoroastrian houses also had single-leaf rather than double doors—again, a rule imposed by the dominant culture. Architectural impositions on Zoroastrians caused them to create smaller, unpretentious houses that featured large rooms, with pools of water to cool the air, and also to include secret spaces to hide sacred artifacts and sacrificial activities. These houses featured very thick walls with minimal windows in order to prevent home invasion by foreign marauders or members of the dominant culture (Mazumdar and Mazumdar 1997). Zoroastrian neighborhoods were recognizable not only by their differing houses but by their location. Zoroastrian neighborhoods were typically on the periphery of the city—hence, the fear of marauders, a constant threat in the 19th century (Mazumdar and Mazumdar 1997). Identifying which religious or ethnic group occupied which type of houses and regions of the city may provide a researcher with an immediate glimpse into inter-ethnic/religious relations and issues of dominance and subordinance in an ancient city and society.

A fine example of neighborhoods—or, more accurately, small cities—organized around craft production, can be found in ancient Egypt. Kathryn Bard (2008) offers an excellent review of the planned cities close to major Egyptian building projects. Two towns near the famous temples of Giza were broken up into areas, or neighborhoods, based on occupation (see also Lehner 2002). These towns were built with the express purpose of housing those involved in building and providing for the pyramids. Larger houses were likely occupied by administrators, while craftworkers lived in the smaller, more unassuming houses. Another area, called the "Gallery Complex," a dormitory-style residential area, was tentatively identified as the temporary housing for as many as 2,000 contingent laborers (Bard 2008: 169). The 14th-century BCE royal city at Tell el-Amarna offers some insights into workers' lives. Two areas of the city were dedicated to housing craftworkers and laborers. In the southern suburbs of Tell el-Amarna, residents had workshops for sculpture, ceramics, and glass-making built into their houses (Bard 2008; and see Kemp 1989). Residents here had their own grain storage, suggesting that they did not need to depend on the state for their sustenance. In contrast, the other area was occupied by tomb workers. This was a far more organized neighborhood, planned in six blocks with approximately 70 houses (Bard 2008: 179). Some crafts were carried out on the ground floor, and living spaces were likely upstairs; water, grain, tools, and other supplies were provided by the state. An overseer's house was also located here. Clearly, the state had a vested interest in controlling the living spaces of those designated as tomb workers, especially in this later age of "secret" tombs which replaced the stone pyramidal edifices of earlier ages.

In contrast to the planned cities and neighborhoods of Egypt are the more "organic" or "bottom-up" neighborhoods of third-millennium BCE Mesopotamia. Elizabeth Stone set the standard for studying Mesopotamian neighborhoods in her book *Nippur Neighborhoods* published several decades ago (1987). Since then, scholars have investigated the residential quarters of several third-millennium Near Eastern settlements (Keith 2003; Nishimura 2007, 2012; van de Mieroop 1999). Some clear characteristics have emerged: the similarity of houses and house contents suggests a largely homogeneous population; and individual residents sometimes had shops attached to their homes, such as bakeries, workshops (gold, leather, reed), carpentry shops, and even taverns and cookshops (Keith 2003: 71). In other words, third-millennium BCE neighborhoods were much like what we, in the West, mean by the same term: the area where we live, shop, and often work. A stroll through third-millennium Nippur, on the most basic level, might correlate with a stroll through a Manhattan neighborhood today—the very different sights, smells, and languages notwithstanding. It is once again worth noting that the ability to discuss "neighborhoods" in ancient cities stems from the close investigation of the houses within them. The goal of this section on the "urban house" was not meant to draw the reader away from the importance of the individual dwelling in any archaeological setting but to emphasize that the house within its larger context—in this case, the urban neighborhood—has as much to offer as the individual rooms in the singular abode.

Conclusion

A single chapter in a single book on the transition from first permanent house to city dwelling is hardly a sufficient review of these topics. Offered here is only an overview of some approaches taken by leading archaeologists and anthropologists. Nonetheless, the methods and results achieved by these scholars exemplify how much can be learned through the examination of human habitation at every stage of its construction.

Section III

Houses as Vessels of Social Institutions

Chapter 6
House Societies and the Identification of Kinship, Family, and Marriage in the Architectural Record

In most societies, the home is the physical container of the family, whether or not constituted by individuals who see themselves in a cooperative kinship relationship. The first part of this chapter discusses how the home may function as the symbolic container of families or groups of people who identify themselves as related through a house-based association. In fact, the built structure itself, or the idea of it, may serve as a focus of social organization in a community. The second half of the chapter is a bit more prosaic; it reviews methods used to identify what family, kinship, and marriage structures might have existed in an ancient community.

House Society

In a series of lectures delivered in France over four decades ago, Claude Lévi-Strauss laid out his conception of "house societies," or *sociétés à maisons*, in past and present cultural structures (Lévi-Strauss 1987). The "house society" is one in which the physical structure is far less important than the symbolic one. The "house" is a structuring principle for individuals who see themselves in cooperative relationships with one another; these relationships can and often do cross-cut traditional kinship lines within the society (Beck 2007b; Carsten 2003; Gillespie 2000, 2007). Lévi-Strauss saw his introduction of the "house society" as a solution to the ambiguities that anthropologists often faced when discovering the lack of coherency between kinship relationships and

Archaeology of Domestic Architecture and the Human Use of Space, by Sharon R. Steadman, 141–161.

the transmission of property; he urged anthropologists to see the house as "a social category, and not merely an architectural form or the locus of a household" (Gillespie 2000: 26). He was inspired to undertake the construction of this interpretive model by the travails of earlier anthropologists such as Franz Boas, who worked with the Northwest Coast Kwatkiutl, and Alfred Kroeber, who studied the Yurok foragers in California, both of whom encountered contradictory (to standard kinship rules) practices regarding property transmission and perceptions of who was considered a member of the larger "household" or family structure. Lévi-Strauss built his model to serve as a way to understand intricate relationships through a wider lens than that provided by the strictures of standard kinship structures described in the anthropological discipline.

House societies define social relationships between people who might not physically dwell together but who can rely on one another for various "kinship-style" behaviors. Robin Beck notes that Lévi -Stauss's *sociétés à maisons* "provides a flexible alternative to traditional kinship categories. These categories, bound by fixed, formal rules of descent, are static governing principles that ideally specify (among other relations) succession, inheritance, exchange of marriage partners, and postmarital residence" (2007b: 5). House societies provide other ways to understand family relationships and property inheritance, beyond traditional lines of corporate kinship descent (e.g., strict patrilineal or matrilineal lineage).

However, as Susan Gillespie notes, "The definition and descriptions of 'house' and 'house society' introduced by Claude Lévi-Strauss are not as straightforward and unproblematic as he might have believed" (2000: 22). Paraphrasing the English translation of Lévi-Strauss's original French definition (1979: 47) yields the description of a house society as one in which a person or group possesses land (house) and material wealth as well as the symbolic essence of "householder"; transmission of physical and symbolic wealth, status, and community position follows legitimate descent lines that may be based on kinship, affinity, or alternative lines that are harder to trace (Lévi-Strauss 1982: 152, 174, 1987: 152; and see Gillespie 2000: 27). Lévi-Strauss cites the institution of marriage as critical for creating affinal ties that become part of the larger symbolic grouping, thereby putting the "house" (both actual and symbolic) at the center of all real and fictive relationships (Gillespie notes that Lévi-Strauss effectively "fetishizes" the house as a representation of all these relationships [2000: 30–31]). Gillespie (2000: 32) sums up the Lévi-Straussian definition of *sociétés à maisons* as one that confounds the usual classificatory efforts of anthropologists, in that (1) it is a "moral person" but not a corporate group delimited by rules of descent, inheritance, or residence; (2) it is better perceived in operation as the objectification of relations rather than as a substantive phenomenon; (3) it can exist at what we recognize as various societal levels; (4) it unites what anthropologists consider to be antithetical and mutually exclusive principles of kinship, marriage, residence, and succession, principles that themselves are actually illusory; and (5) it thereby transcends the categorical distinctions among different types of societies that have been distinguished using those principles.

A further complicating factor is that Lévi-Strauss did not limit the application of *sociétés à maisons* to non-complex societies. Though inspired by his colleague's difficulties in understanding property transmission and kinship in foraging groups, he used familial structures in medieval Europe and feudal Japan to construct his model, thus suggesting that *sociétés à maisons* could be applied to any societal type. A house society, then, can have many constructs; the parameters of what might constitute it are flexible, even ambiguous. Anthropological identification of a house society often boils down to "you know it when you see it."

Although he was concerned with the transmission of property, Lévi-Strauss did not offer guidelines on what the physical house might look like in a "house society." In fact, in the complicated relationships that might embody this type of social unit, not every residence is necessarily the nexus of a group, nor is every social unit connected to a particular physical house (Gillespie 2007: 29). Because the social unit is flexible and sometimes vastly complicated, it cannot always be contained by, or closely connected to, a physical residence. Ron Adams (2007: 344) notes that "the cohesion of the households associated with the 'house' is of critical importance for the long-term maintenance of house societies . . . when they represent groups of individuals spatially dispersed." He goes on to say that caretaking of the house and its properties (including heirlooms and animals), the carrying out of rituals, and shared identities through genealogies or house-based association are key elements in recognizing a house society.

The variability in Lévi-Strauss's model garnered some criticism in the anthropological discipline, and the lack of clarity on the possible appearance of the physical structure in a house society would certainly seem to confound anthropological and certainly archaeological attempts to identify such communities. Nonetheless, a number of books (e.g., Carsten and Hugh-Jones 1995; Helms 1998; Joyce and Gillespie 2000; Macdonald 1987; Waterson 1990) and a plethora of articles have successfully applied the Lévi-Straussian model to living cultures; more recently, archaeologists have undertaken the challenge of attempting to identify ancient house societies (e.g., Beck 2007a; Chesson 2003; Moore 2005).

There is perhaps no better example of the necessity of using ethnographic research to understand archaeological material remains than in the use of *sociétés à maisons* as an interpretive model. Several anthropological ethnographies profiling living house societies described below offer insight into the relationship between the symbolic and the physical "house." These are followed by several archaeological studies that seek to identify the presence of house societies in ancient communities.

House Societies in the Ethnographic Record

It is perhaps best to begin with a cautionary tale: a discussion of living house societies whose homes offer no physical trace of human relationships and would thus be undetectable in the archaeological record. Vanessa Lea's study of the Mẽbengokre in central

Brazil offers just such a case. The Mẽbengokre view their social organization as consisting of a specific set of "houses" roughly corresponding to kinship groups (which include both blood and affinal relations in a largely matrilineal/matrilocal system). Actual dwellings are differentiated only by size, which reflects the number of inhabitants (Lea 1995: 207–8). There are no physical features associated with Mẽbengokre houses that signify the existence of house groups associated with them. Rather, in each village every house group occupies a particular position in the community vis-à-vis the east–west orientation, and new villages will be built in exactly the same format. Unoccupied spaces may be left in a new village for the future building of a house group that does not presently reside there (but may be present in other villages). There is, therefore, a strong spatial aspect to the social organization of the house groups in the Mẽbengokre culture. Besides the location of the physical and symbolic house within the community, the main characteristics that distinguish house groups (besides members) are *nekrets*, which are non-material rights—that is, what personal names might be given to children, and particular prerogatives such as what adornments might be worn, what pets might be owned, and what foods may be consumed (Lea 1995: 208–14). Thus, the Mẽbengokre demonstrate what Lea finds to be a very clear Lévi-Straussian "house society," but the material remains of such would be all but invisible in the architectural or even the artifactual footprint.

Roxana Waterson, in her study of Indonesian cultures, their dwellings, and their house-based social structures, offers some hope that archaeological detection of house societies is possible. Waterson's examination of the Sa'dan Toraja, who live in the highlands of South Sulawesi, suggests that Lévi-Strauss's model is best applied to stratified societies, where the model's defining characteristics will most likely also be reflected in the architecture (1990, 1995). The Toraja practice a bilateral kinship structure wherein children descend equally from mother and father and have rights of inheritance from both; however, the kinship relationships are even more complicated than this, as each individual is also considered descended not only from parents and grandparents but from other ancestors who may be harder to discern from outside the culture (Waterson 1990: 163–64). Each individual, therefore, may belong to a number of houses based on the location of the birth of parents, grandparents, and ancestors. The members of "origin houses" established by earlier ancestors view themselves as "siblings within the origin-house" (Waterson 1995: 55), though they do not live together nor perhaps even in the same village. Upon marriage, men often go to live with their wives but retain a strong association with the house(s) of their parents. Before death, each individual must choose one "origin house" with which to associate for purposes of burial (Waterson 1995: 55).

The Toraja are stratified into ranks of nobles, commoners, and those freed from slavery, the former being the primary owners of agricultural fields (Waterson 1995). In the Toraja culture, the "origin-house siblings" choose one family to live in the actual origin house and serve as keeper and protector of both the physical and the symbolic "house." The actual dwelling, particularly in the noble rank, may be significantly larger than is necessary to house those living within it; its larger size reflects the need to house any chosen family, no matter the number of members, and also to accommodate the many members who attend the rituals, including feasting and presentation of offerings, centered at the origin house (Waterson 1990: 165). In houses belonging to the nobility, the physical structure can be quite elaborate both in size and decoration, demonstrating not only the wealth of the origin-house members, but also their ability to marshal labor to build and decorate the structure, and maintain its upkeep. The Toraja rebuild their houses in precisely the same place even if the house is not in need of repair or reconstruction; rebuilding the house represents a "renewal" of the origin house and demonstrates the wealth and security of house members (Waterson 2000). Among the Toraja, as well as in other Southeast Asian societies, physical clues to the presence of a Lévi-Straussian "house society" include the potential residential structure's size as far larger than necessary to house actual residents, repeated rebuildings in identical locations, and the material and spatial accommodation for ritual activities potentially attended by a significant number of people.

Among the Tanimbar culture of eastern Indonesia, Susan McKinnon (1983, 1991, 1995, 2000) has found another semi-permanent physical attribute of a house society: an altar. The Tanimbarese culture practices precisely the type of kinship and inheritance structure that Lévi-Strauss envisioned in his model. Kinship practices generally follow a matrilineal system, but there are patrilineal elements involved as well (Waterson 1990; McKinnon 1995). Houses in traditional Tanimbar dwellings held ancestor altars or *tavu*, sometimes consisting only of a shelf with a few items; in the noble houses, or in the houses occupied by the leader of the social unit, the *tavu* could be quite elaborate. The altar to the ancestor was placed in the center of the house so that one faced the altar upon entry (McKinnon 2000: 163). These large altars consisted of carved wooden panels or posts, usually portraying an image of the ancestor (Figure 6.1). The *tavu* altars usually functioned as a roof support, and thus the ancestor was effectively built "into" the house (McKinnon 2000: 175). The *tavu* served as "a kind of bridge or pathway between the past and the present, the ancestors and their descendants, the root and the tip" (McKinnon 2000: 169).

A final ethnoarchaeological example comes from Kodi, on the Indonesian island of Sumba. Ron Adams's work (2007) describes a culture in which ancestral houses, *uma*, have clan-based members (*parona*) that may number in the dozens or hundreds. The *uma* are the largest and most elaborate buildings in the villages, identified by their peaked roofs and internal central pillars which have spiritual designations. In the Kodi region, "the *parona* (clan) and its constituent *uma* (ancestral house groups) traditionally formed supralocal house society polities with social ranking" (Adams 2007: 349), with members living in the central ancestral villages and outlying hamlets. Uniting the *parona* are feasts of up to several hundred attendees that take place in or next to the *uma* (Adams 2007: 350). Household groups in the *parona* all contribute food and

Figure 6.1: Artistic rendering of a *tavu* in a Tanimbar ancestral house (based on McKinnon 2000: figs. 8.2, 8.3, and 8.4; drawing by Corrina Petit).

supplies to the feast, which serves as "an expression of clan unity and solidarity . . . [and] failure to engage in the obligations associated with clan feasts can even result in one's being completely phased out of clan rituals," according to Adams (2007: 350). Thus, feasts are the primary social mechanism that unites members of the Kodi house society, confirming their continued adherence to the *parona* and *uma*. Similar to their counterparts among the Toraja, house societies in Kodi require spacious houses, a feature possibly recognizable in the archaeological record.

House Societies in the Archaeological Record

The foregoing illustrates some of the challenges for archaeologists who seek to identify house societies in the archaeological record. Nonetheless, a growing number of archaeologists believe that their data represent cooperative units formed on foundations beyond those of straightforward kinship ties. The mainstay of Lévi-Straussian house society research is based on the cultures of the Austronesian region, such as those discussed above. The rich record of ethnographic data demonstrating the presence of *sociétés à maisons* among many of these island cultures (e.g., Carsten and Hugh-Jones 1995; Schefold, Domenig, and Nas 2003; Waterson 1990; and see above) has allowed Jennifer Kahn (2007) to draw on ethnography as a resource to help her interpret house remains in the 'Opunohu Valley of Mo'orea in the Society Islands. Of the four dwellings (Houses 170 and 171a–c) and associated open spaces in the settlement, two made up the original settlement, built in the 15th century CE. The largest house was constructed on the highest ridge (House 170), and the smaller house was downslope (House 171c) (Kahn 2007: 210–15). Over the next two centuries, two additional houses were built, House 171a being the second largest and located closest to 170.

Ethnographic data throughout the region demonstrates that "height" is a symbol of status and rank, suggesting that House 170 was inhabited by the most important members of this social unit. Kahn believes that House 170 was the "origin house" of the house society founders, with residents of House 171c representing a more junior "branch" of the family/social unit (2007: 215–16). House 170, as an origin house, attracted settlement from other members of the social unit who then built Houses 171a and 171b, with House 171a representing a family of higher rank than those in 171b and 171c. Besides the location and size of House 170 (for the importance of these characteristics, see chapter 9), Kahn's evidence includes the locations of production areas, ritual areas, and associated material wealth. Residents of House 170 appear to be the only ones involved in adze production, which indicates their access to preferential raw resources (Kahn 2007: 213–14). Further, while all houses had small food preparation and cooking areas connected to the dwelling, House 170 had two areas, one set away from the dwelling; House 171a had the largest food preparation and storage facilities. The spatial evidence suggests that community feasts took place in the area near Houses 170 and 171a. The archaeological evidence in the 'Opunohu Valley corresponds to the characteristics of a suprahousehold "house society" that features an "origin house," perhaps occupied by the leading ancestral (and wealthiest) family. The associated households were united in ritual activities at prescribed locations near the origin house.

The Gallaecian culture of Iron Age Iberia (ca. eighth–first centuries BCE) offers good evidence of a house-based structure. In his study of this region of northern Portugal and northwestern Spain, Alfredo González-Ruibal identified, based on his analysis of Lévi-Strauss's work, nine elements that are typically found in a house society: ranked/hierarchical society; indistinct (from the outside) kinship relationships; houses serving as key symbols of ritual activity; labor investment in houses; the existence of family names as found in an aristocratic system; heirlooms; accentuated importance of women; defined territory; and houses functioning as social units (2006: 146). Using a trio of evidence, including written sources (mainly Roman), artifactual remains, and architectural data, the author identifies the presence of all of these elements in ancient

Iberia. Gallaecians lived in hillforts (*castella*) consisting of walled compounds in which each largely nuclear family built a circular house with outlying storage buildings. Differences in the number of non-residential buildings, labor investment, house decoration, and material possessions suggest that Gallaecian society was ranked as to positions of wealth, status, and power (González-Ruibal 2006: 155–57). Rather than identifying oneself through kinship ties, ancient Gallaecians apparently saw themselves as tied to territory, to their *castellum* and their household compound; while some members of the same *castellum* were certainly kin members, others were not and yet all were bound together as a social unit through their association within the same hillfort.

Architectural evidence suggests that at least one residence (in small hillforts, possibly several in larger ones) served as a type of "core house" (González-Ruibal 2006: 169) or, as others would term it, an "origin house." This was typically the house that would be "named" (represented in written pacts of cooperation with other *castella* or named houses) and would display the most decorative elements and feature the largest compound. All hillfort houses featured elements evocative of places of important ritual, including votive deposits in the house foundations, decorated hearths, and elaborate stone carvings on architectural elements; these were particularly prominent in core, or origin, houses (González-Ruibal 2006: 158–162). Textual accounts of heirloom and property inheritance suggest that elements of a matrilineal system were in play and that women had significant inheritance rights, but goods certainly passed from one male hand to the next as well. González-Ruibal finds that the house society model serves as an appropriate vehicle to explain the archaeological and textual evidence of the Iron Age Gallaecian society of Iberia.

Meredith Chesson (2003) uses a variety of evidence to suggest that inhabitants of prehistoric (third-millennium BCE Early Bronze Age) communities such as Arad and Bab edh-Dhra' in the Levant operated on a house-society basis. In analyzing architectural data in the walled settlement at ancient Arad (Amiran and Ilan 1996; Philip 2001), Chesson notes that the apparent lack of a ruling class (there are no palaces or elite houses in these communities) and the presence of public architecture (e.g., administrative buildings, ritual structures, and fortifications) suggest that "corporate" groups, likely based on kinship, best explain the societal structure of Arad and other communities (2003: 90–96; see also Philip 2001). Residential neighborhoods, arranged in sectors and groupings, were likely occupied by people who were not only kinship-related but who also participated in shared production and consumption activities and participated in ritual activities together (in part based on ethnographic data from present-day villages in the Middle East). Members of an Arad "house" may have had access to particular stored goods and materials, to work certain parcels of land, and to inherit heirlooms such as cylinder seals (Chesson 2003: 90). Chesson suggests that the mortuary evidence at Bab edh-Dhra' is a strong indicator of the existence of a house society: its residents buried their dead in above-ground charnel houses that resembled residential structures;

some were larger, containing vast numbers of grave goods, and some were smaller with fewer goods (Chesson 2003: 96; and see chapter 10). Chesson asserts that "we envision the power-sharing and corporate nature of EBA life as structured by houses, corporate estates whose members recognized a shared sense of kinship or affinity and who worked cooperatively to ensure the survival and growth of their house's material and immaterial wealth in the future" (2003: 97); "house" members could thus be buried together in the neighborhood charnel house. Although architectural data may be a stronger indicator in the search for ancient house societies, Chesson demonstrates that mortuary data can be a valuable investigative resource as well.

Clues to House Societies in the Archaeological Record

The foregoing has presented the difficulties inherent in securely identifying a house-based society in the archaeological past. Nonetheless, there are some architectural clues that might lead an archaeologist to speculate that an ancient culture was organized according to Lévi-Straussian house-society principles. Among the Toraja, the origin house is regularly far larger than the small number of occupants who live in it might require. Regularly present in such houses are ritual areas, such as was found among the Tanimbar who build their origin houses with an ancestral altar as part of the architecture. Also important to the Toraja (as well as in Kodi) is the practice of feasting in and near the origin house, which brings together all members of the house for community and ritual events. Finally, Waterson noted that consistency of place for origin (or actually all) houses was critical in house symbolism among the Toraja, and that the rebuilding of the house, in that place, renewed the house-based bonds. Even the Mẽbengokre, who leave no architectural trace of a house society, give us a clue: specialized possessions, or heirlooms, are passed down as important inheritance items.

We see in the archaeological examples the use of these clues for the identification of ancient house societies. Kahn found that the presence of a large house acted as the anchor, perhaps an origin house, attracting other residences into the 'Opunohu Valley in Mo'orea; designated areas for feasting were an added indicator. In Gallaecia, the large and elaborate decorated house compound, plus territoriality and the presence of heirlooms, were clues that coincided well with the written record hinting at a house-based social structure. In Chesson's analysis of ancient Arad, the walled compounds and heirlooms are critical factors in her methodology. None of these clues is sufficient in isolation as an indicator of an ancient house society: large and elaborate houses may simply suggest social stratification (see chapter 9); altars may simply be evidence of ancestor veneration (see chapter 10); consistency of place may simply imply ownership of land; and feasting and heirlooms may have a host of explanations unrelated to *sociétés à maisons*. However, taken together, such clues may serve as valuable evidence for a complicated, archaeologically elusive but perhaps quite pervasive social structure in the ancient past.

Marriage, Kinship, and Family

In Thomas Gieryn's article "What Buildings Do," he notes, "Buildings stabilize social life. They give structure to social institutions, durability to social networks, persistence to behavior patterns" (2002: 35). The remainder of this chapter discusses several of the social institutions mentioned by Gieryn: marriage, kinship, and family. It shows how archaeologists can use a range of tools, including empirical data such as house size, location, and shape, combined with inferences based on the ethnographic record, to speculate on whether families lived in extended or nuclear structures, whether they had multiple-spouse marriage practices or were monogamous, and how one might define the type of kinship system that could have been in place. As these institutions rest at the center of house societies, methodologies to identify ancient marriage, kinship, and family structures are important for recognizing house societies in the past.

Shaping the House: Family Structure and Household

Upon first reflection, it might seem an easy task to determine whether nuclear or extended families inhabited an ancient settlement. One would need only to examine, perhaps, living areas within a house, and then assess how many individuals might have dwelled together. If the number per house regularly exceeded the norm for a nuclear family, then extended family it must have been. Nothing in archaeology is ever that simple. As chapter 3 discussed, even determining square meters per individual is subject to debate; moving from that basic calculation to how many family members might have lived together is a giant leap. This hasn't, of course, stopped archaeologists from undertaking such leaps in their attempts to decipher prehistoric family structure in a given community.

The question of nuclear versus extended families became a major subject of interest beginning in the 1970s and in following decades, initially with the publication of the previously discussed article (in chapters 1-4) by Kent Flannery (1972) on the subject of round and square houses and their relationship to socioeconomy, marriage, and family structure. Flannery examined houses of the earliest sedentary communities in Early Formative Mesoamerica (ca. 1400–900 BCE) and Neolithic settlements in the Levant (ca. 9700–6700 BCE). He suggested that communities featuring circular dwellings built in clustered formats (as are found in earlier Levantine sites) were inhabited by people living in extended family networks who likely practiced polygynous marriage systems and who were still partially nomadic (also see the discussion in chapter 4). Conversely, settlements with rectangular houses, as are found in Mesoamerica and later Neolithic Levantine sites, housed more fully sedentary people who lived in nuclear family structures and practiced monogamous marriage systems (1972: 29–44). Flannery based his inferences on ethnographic studies, a person per living area formula (see chapter 3), and artifact activity areas in the archaeological sites. In the decades following Flannery's publication, there was an extended scholarly debate on the efficacy of his model, particularly with regard to the Levantine Neolithic sites (see Steadman 2004 for references and discussion).

One of the major points of contention was whether the basic equation was correct: that round houses indicated extended, polygynous families, and square houses signified potentially nuclear and monogamous social structures. Leaving aside for now the marriage patterns (which are discussed in more detail below), it is possible to construct models to predict nuclear versus extended family structure, though they do not really depend on house shape in any significant way. Scholars with expertise in the Levantine Neolithic addressed Flannery's suggestion that round houses, which later yielded to rectilinear architecture, reflected a shift in Levantine social structure from extended to nuclear family structure (and polygynous to monogamous marriage).

E. B. Banning, in his study of Epipalaeolithic/Neolithic Levantine houses (1996), does not specifically address floor area per population estimates but rather investigates the nuclear versus polygynous/extended family structure and house form issue raised by Flannery. Banning uses proxemics and access analysis (see chapter 3 and below) to argue that the more circular structures of the Epipalaeolithic Levant, which gave way to more rectilinear houses in the Neolithic, "differ little" in their organization or even, to a large extent, in floor area (1996: 170). He disputes, therefore, that circular versus rectilinear can be an accurate indicator of family structure. At the same time, Benjamin Saidel (1993) also argued that the shift from circular to rectilinear had less to do with family size than it did with sedentism and wealth accumulation. Though scholars did not agree with one another on all points, some argued that family structure was nuclear throughout the period (Banning 1996, 1997, 2002; Byrd 1994, 2000; Wright 2000; also see Banning and Byrd 1987) and others that a variety of factors ushered in house form change (Bar-Yosef 2001; Kuijt 2000c; Saidel 1993; and see Garfinkel 2006; Kuijt and Chesson 2000; and Banning 2011a for extensive discussion); all agreed that it was not a shift in family structure, or marriage practices, that resulted in the round-house-to-rectilinear architectural shift in the Neolithic Levant.

All scholars recognized that the crux of the matter was not round or rectilinear houses but rather what socioeconomic forces were in place that pushed ancient Levantine (or any other culture) toward one family structure over another. In general, family structure is extended when necessary for the daily subsistence practices and basic survival of the household. For instance, Hayden and Cannon mount an argument for why "corporate groups" form, which they define as "those which have come into being as a result of strong economic or environmental pressures, and which, as a result, exhibit a recognizable degree of residential coherency among two or more nuclear families within the community" (1982: 134–35). While these scholars specifically reference the combination of nuclear families, the "residential corporate group" might also include multigenerational members, with the nuclear family at its core. Physically, residential corporate groups may all live in the same structure, or in conjoined structures such as in a compound (Hayden and Cannon 1982: 140–47). (A third type is "neighborhoods," but these are not relevant to the present discussion of nuclear versus extended family.) Hayden and Cannon go on to argue that only economic, defensive, and environmental forces are strong enough to encourage residential corporate groups. One of the primary factors behind the creation of corporate groups/extended families is critical resource scarcity or competition (limits on land, hunting grounds, water sources, etc.); ensuring that at least one member of the extended/corporate family has access to that critical resource, perhaps through inheritance or position in the community, is a powerful motivator for maintaining extended residential ties (Hayden and Cannon 1982: 150). The second main reason for the formation of extended/corporate groups has to do with the need for labor. If basic subsistence activities, such as farming or herding, require a consistent and substantial labor force, then an extended/corporate family system will almost certainly exist (Hayden and Cannon 1982: 151). Similarly, Burton Pasternak and colleagues identify "incompatible activity requirements" as a reason for the existence of extended family: "In some societies there are activities that seem incompatible in the sense that they have to be undertaken at the same times and therefore the person responsible for those activities cannot get them done without help" (1976: 114). A textbook example is childrearing and agricultural work: a mother who is also responsible for work in the field needs an elder to care for the children while she completes her field labors. In such societies, multigenerational or related nuclear families, or both, may reside together in order to cover all necessary daily duties to ensure survival for all.

The question of round versus rectilinear houses becomes even less relevant in reviewing Gary Coupland's study (1996) of multifamily houses in prehistoric British Columbia. Two different villages erected architecture for multiseason or year-round habitation; in each case, residents built pithouses, usually in two rows, into the river terrace. At the Paul Mason site, ca. 1000 BCE, residents built rectilinear pithouses ranging in size from 45.7 to 72.6 m^2, which Coupland suggests were sufficient to house 12–13 people (1996: 124). Each of these houses had two hearths, one near the front and one farther back. The Katz site dates to about 500 years later than the Paul Mason site; here residents built rounded pithouses in the river terrace, again in two rows, again with an area similar to those at the Paul Mason site (Coupland 1996: 125). Two hearths in the Katz pithouses were located at the sides. Coupland argues that the same type of family structure—multifamily or extended family—lived at both settlements, regardless of house form. At the Paul Mason site, residents had to compete with other villages and families for prime salmon fishing locations, which necessitated cooperative extended family households. At the Katz site, it was the need for intensive labor, using dragnet fishing methods, that required many hands and thus the extended family structure (Coupland 1996: 126). For Coupland, the socioeconomic requirements, area size of the residences, and number of hearths were the keys to identifying multifamily (or extended family) co-residential structures.

In terms of the architectural footprint, as Flannery originally argued (1972) and reiterated 30 years later (2002), family structure is most clearly indicated by the area of habitation and the number of hearths (see chapter 3). The fact that, in the Levant, circular residences coincided with extended/polygynous (pastoral nomad) cultures whereas rectilinear houses belonged to settled nuclear family farmers was a bit of a red herring in the scholarly debate: what Flannery and others have really been trying to understand is the intersection between economy and family structure, not whether a round house suits one family type and a square house another. Flannery's 2002 reevaluation of his original 1972 publication still argued that circular huts, built in clusters, correspond more closely to extended mobile families, but his data more firmly seated his assertions in the realm of socioeconomic undertakings; he rectifies any original confusion in the following:

> In my 1972 paper I mentioned associations between circular houses and impermanent settlement and between rectangular houses and permanent settlement. Unfortunately, this led some readers to believe that the geometric shape of the residence was the crucial variable. In fact, my main distinction was between (1) societies where small huts are occupied by individuals and storage is shared and (2) societies where larger houses are occupied by whole nuclear families, and storage is private. (2002: 420–21)

Embodied in Flannery's studies, and as described by the statement above, is the field of "household archaeology" (see chapter 7), also emerging in the 1970s and focused on examining the production and consumption activities in a household as a vehicle for understanding family and larger societal structure. A few examples here are illustrative of the principles addressed above.

Lynne Sullivan (1995) studied the household organization of settlements in three Mississippian phases in the American South: the Dallas phase (14th–16th centuries CE), the Mouse Creek phase (15th–16th centuries CE), and the Overhill Cherokee sites (18th century CE). She examined the ethnographic record of Cherokee communities in the same area to acquire a baseline for understanding a person per space ratio and the usage of winter and summer structures; she then turned to the archaeological data from sites in the three phases (Figure 6.2). All sites exhibited roughly similar domestic structures, with one of the main differences being in the size and shape of the winter versus summer structures. In the Overhill Cherokee phase, the winter house was circular and the summer house rectangular, whereas in the Dallas and Mouse Creek phases, both houses were rectilinear (Sullivan 1995: 104–14). At each settlement, a hearth was located in the center of the winter dwelling, and post-molds around the perimeters suggest the presence of furniture and possibly partitions. Summer houses were light constructions, as shown by single lines of post-molds for walls. Summer dwellings had no hearths, and cooking likely took place away from

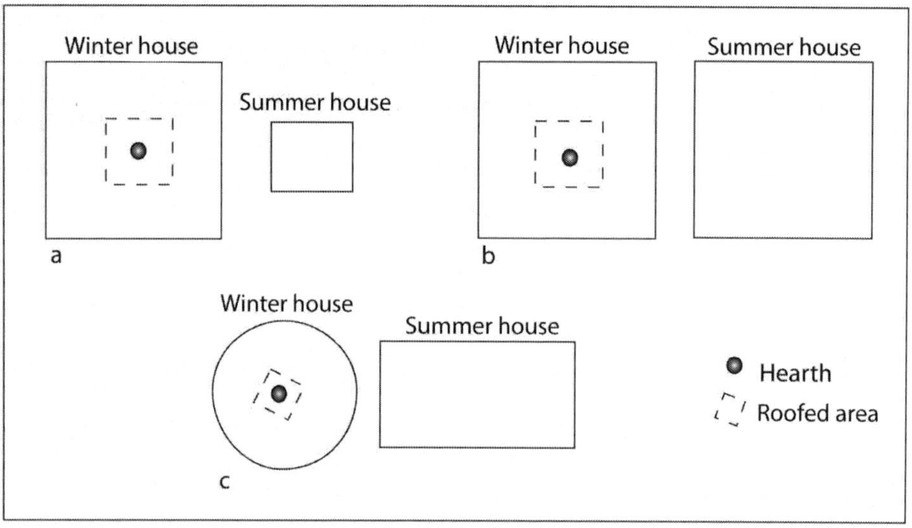

Figure 6.2: Schematic examples of houses from different phases in the Mississippian culture: (a) Dallas; (b), Mouse Creek; and (c) Overhill Cherokee (Sullivan 1995: figs. 5.2, 5.4, 5.6).

the structure. Sullivan also evaluated burial data at many sites, which suggested that household composition across dwellings was fairly consistent with regard to the age and sex of household residents (Sullivan 1996: 111–13).

Sullivan's final set of data included floor area for each structure. Here there was some differentiation, with Overhill Cherokee sites featuring houses ranging in size from ca. 30.5 to 40 m^2 (5–7 household residents), Dallas phase structures ranging from ca. 30 to 84.5 m^2 (5–14 household residents) and Mouse Creek period houses from ca. 26 to 110.5 m^2 (3–28 household residents) (Sullivan 1995: 112–13). Among other arguments, Sullivan offers two major conclusions that are relevant here. Using the ethnographic and archaeological data, including structure area and number of hearths, she suggests that extended families occupied these houses (likely multigenerational) during all three phases. A second argument, based on household contents (artifactual and ecofactual), suggests that the Mouse Creek and Dallas phase settlements featured a more highly stratified society where elite families could build and maintain large houses and households (1995: 122). Thus, as Coupland found, the shape of the house (rounded or rectilinear) was not as important as area, number of hearths, and other data, such as burials.

Another interesting example comes from Neolithic China (Yangshao/Banpo phase, spanning the fifth millennium BCE) and the site of Jiangzhai in the Yellow River Valley. Here over 100 structures within a circular village surrounded an open courtyard nearly devoid of artifacts. The village was bordered by a wide ditch (perhaps for flood control), beyond which was the village cemetery. Houses at Jiangzhai were either round or square, all built of timber with a wattle-and-daub superstructure with thatched roof;

most structures were semi-subterranean, but some were built entirely above ground (Peterson and Shelach 2012). In addition to the 122 residential structures, excavations revealed 259 hearths (both inside houses and outdoors) and 297 storage pits (Lee 2007). Two studies conducted exceedingly careful analyses of all elements of the Jiangzhai settlement, including the architecture, floor area, hearth and storage placement, and artifactual presence (Lee 2007; Peterson and Shelach 2012). Using essentially identical data, the two studies produced different interpretations of the socioeconomy of the Neolithic Jiangzhao residents! Nonetheless, they do have some points of agreement, which are highlighted here. Both acknowledge that the spatial layout of the village yields five residential "districts," featuring a larger structure accompanied by numerous smaller ones; and both acknowledge that each of these five districts likely corresponds to kin-related household groups. Furthermore, both studies use living area, placement of hearth, and location of storage facility to identify whether structures housed small (nuclear) or larger (small extended) families. Thus, for the purposes of the discussion here, the argument is that indicators such as one hearth in a single structure, accompanied by living-space calculations (both studies use ca. 4 m^2 per person), are sufficient for ascertaining the family structure in a dwelling. One scholar (Lee 2007: 654) closely examined the floor contents of several houses, determining that the available sleeping space (i.e., the area devoid of other artifactual/activity area scatter), combined with dwelling area size, yielded a household consisting of two adults and two children—the quintessential nuclear family.

Of course, the very general tools for identifying family structure advanced here—house area, number of hearths, and other minor supporting data such as burials or house placement—cannot be complete guides to identifying prehistoric family patterns. For instance, in her ethnographic study of two Turkish villages, Ayla Çevik's interest was to determine "to what extent do the size and composition of the household relate to the size and composition of the household cluster?" (1995: 45). She found, as did Carol Delaney before her (1991), that the makeup of a household depended on the presence of a "hearth" or central cooking area; each independent household had one. She also documented that there is a Turkish "domestic cycle" followed in most Turkish villages (a cycle I have also observed during two decades of living and working in a Turkish village). This domestic group cycle, all occupying the same dwelling over time, has the following pattern (1995: 46):

an extended family that includes two married brothers and their families

a nuclear family with young children

a nuclear family with an elder

a nuclear family and their grown children

an elderly couple or single elder

As male children grow up and marry, one, several, or all of them may bring their wives into the parental household for a short or extended time; however, most eventually depart to establish their own "hearth" household. The original household then shrinks from extended to nuclear family size and may eventually house only one or two of the family elders (Figure 6.3). Thus, one hearth, and whatever dwelling area is constituted by the house, sees an expansion and contraction of residents through the Turkish domestic cycle without any alteration of house size or number of hearths.

Bleda Düring and Arkadiusz Marciniak (2006) present an equally vexing situation for archaeologists seeking to identify prehistoric family structure. The Turkish Neolithic site of Aşıklı Höyük offers the type of agglomerated architectural plan common on the prehistoric Anatolian plateau (see also Cutting 2006b). At Aşıklı, clusters of rooms sharing a common wall form a type of "neighborhood" separated by open areas such as courtyards, alleys, and passages (Figure 6.4). An assessment of the living areas of the single- or multi-roomed structures suggested that the average size of the single-room structures was 9 m^2 and that of the multi-room structures was 12 m^2 (Düring and Marciniak 2006: 172). Eschewing the use of a "per person" assignment of living space, the authors determined that the average living areas of 9–12 m^2 were sufficient to house up to five people, acknowledging this was not particularly revealing as to family or household structure. While a range of perhaps three to five people per dwelling might point to a nuclear family structure, the placement of hearths at Aşıklı

Figure 6.3: Photo of a typical Turkish village house that may have housed a generation or two of the "domestic cycle" but never changed in size or shape (photo by the author).

completely derails such an assumption. Hearths were well built and typically found in the corners of rooms (Özbaşaran 1998). However, rather than in every dwelling, hearths were distributed only irregularly across the neighborhoods with some single- or multi-roomed dwellings having no hearths at all. It is impossible to determine, using only living area and hearth placement, whether Aşıklı families typically lived in nuclear or extended settings, in both, or in neither: "[H]ouseholds were probably spread across the neighbourhood in a pattern no longer discernible to us. . . . [H]ouseholds at Aşıklı Höyük were clearly bounded neither in terms of residence nor in terms of separate activity areas. . . . [They] were not autonomous in a manner that makes it possible to define them archaeologically" (Düring and Marciniak 2006: 174).

This discussion has attempted to establish two premises regarding the identification of ancient family structure: (1) the shape of the house should not serve as a critical determining factor; and (2) more essential determining factors should be the dwelling area and the number and location of hearths/cooking areas. As is made clear in chapter 7, a close look at economic elements, particularly production and consumption activities, is also a vital step in identifying what makes up a "household"

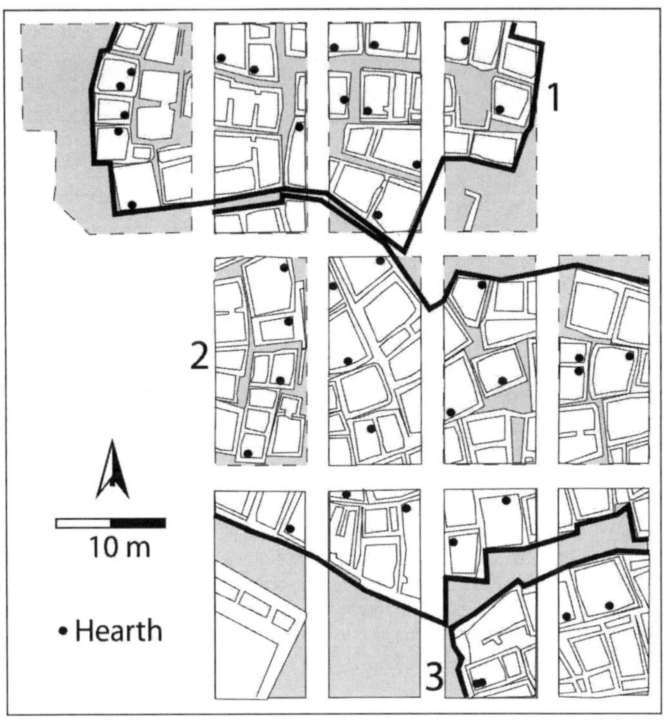

Figure 6.4: Sketch plan of Neolithic neighborhoods at Aşıklı Höyük in Turkey; the placement of hearths indicates possible communal food processing and cooking (after Düring and Marciniak 2006: 172, fig. 2; 174, fig. 4).

and family; the architectural footprint alone tells only a fraction of the story. However, in spite of the caveats illustrated by the studies on both ancient and modern Turkey, it is often possible to obtain a baseline understanding of how many people might have occupied a hearth and home, and whether such numbers might correspond to a singular nuclear family or to a more extended structure.

Elusive Institutions: Marriage Practices and Kinship Structures

As challenging as identifying family structure in prehistoric societies might be, even more problematical is determining what marriage pattern or kinship structure might have been in place. The first disconcerting fact is that it is essentially the same indicators, floor area and number of hearths/cooking areas, that might help determine how many spouses might exist in a household or, conversely, how many related families (patrilineal or matrilineal in kinship structure) dwelled together. Of course, the multiple nuclear families living in the same household, each with its own hearth (as was the case in the prehistoric British Columbia sites in Coupland's 1996 study), can be simultaneously extended and unilineal (patrilineal or matrilineal) in structure. Thus, how does an archaeologists distinguish between multigenerational (and non-unilineal) nuclear families present within the same household, and patrilineal or matrilineal sibling-based nuclear families cooperating in the same household? Furthermore, how might either of these be distinguished from a single male with multiple wives, each with her own hearth but living cooperatively in a single dwelling?

The answer to these questions is, unfortunately, not very effectively. The best approach is to draw upon the ethnographic record, as did Flannery (1972, 2002) in his attempt to capture family, marriage, and kinship. The occurrence of unilineal descent kinship structures is quite prominent in today's living societies, and there is no reason to believe it was different in antiquity. It is often the case that kin groups, related either through the male or female line, live and work cooperatively, perhaps for successful subsistence purposes or because of joint resource/property ownership, or both. A brief look at some ethnographic data offers a few basic tools that might help with archaeological determinations.

In 1972, Flannery used a selection of settlements in African societies practicing small-scale horticulture and animal husbandry to argue that circular huts situated on compounds corresponded to extended family structures practicing polygynous marriage with unilineal (usually patrilineal) descent. In 2002, he returned to an African example, the Hadza hunting-gathering culture, to further support his arguments. Households were arranged in the following manner: a cluster of structures (generally circular huts) were of varying sizes, with some housing a single individual, such as a widowed parent; others were large enough to house a wife and her children. House contents reflected either a male tool kit, a female tool kit, or both (Flannery 2002: 418–20). The spatial relationship of the houses situated in a cluster could therefore correspond to a man, his one or more wives, and singular individuals such as parents or unmarried brothers (in a patrilineal system).

A careful review of all the architectural clusters in a village might yield even more data, such as a relationship between greater wealth and the regular occurrence of multiple wives. The notion that co-wives might have separate houses is not all that far-fetched. Again, the ethnographic record demonstrates that in societies in which non-sororal polygyny is practiced, each wife tends to have her own house sufficient for herself, her children, and the part-time residence of the husband (who may have his own house as well, or rotate between spousal houses) (Chase 1991; Divale 1977; Ember 1973; Murdock 1949). The flip side to this is that in societies that practice sororal polygyny, separate houses are not typically built for the sibling wives, though each might have her own hearth. In this case, then, it might be more difficult to distinguish between a polygynous marriage system and multiple nuclear family households.

The takeaway from this discussion of "finding marriage" in the architectural record is necessarily vague and therefore essentially unsatisfying. The essential tools for recognizing a potentially polygynous marriage system in the archaeological record are the assessment of whether houses occur in "clusters," the size of the houses within those clusters, and the tool kits contained in the houses. Another important component is whether production and consumption activities are shown to be cooperative within the house cluster.

It might be said that determining the presence of a unilineal descent group is somewhat more feasible. Stephen Hugh-Jones (1995) studied an Amazonian culture's architecture, the *maloca*, built by Tukanoan-speaking peoples who live in Brazil, the Guianas, and Colombia. The *maloca* (Figure 6.5), apsidal at the back end and straight at the front, with a length of roughly 100 feet, stands as much as 30 feet high, with a width of about 40 feet (Hugh-Jones 1995: 227). The men who dwell within it construct the wooden structure, sponsored by the man who is the "owner" of the house and leader of the group building it. At the "owner's" death, so dies the house and a new *maloca* must be built. The people who live within the *maloca* are kin-related brothers, their associated wives and children, and unmarried siblings; the elder parents may also live there (Hugh-Jones 1995: 228). Each nuclear family has a "compartment" at the back (apsidal area) of the *maloca* where they sleep and store goods, with the owner having the prime position at the very back on the right. Though each family acquires food individually, consumption is shared in the communal area at the center of the *maloca*. There is a communal hot plate for baking bread and provision of warmth, and a manioc beer trough at the *maloca* center. Hugh-Jones notes that tensions can arise and that this may cause fission and even dissolution of the *maloca*, but in general, "the emphasis is on the unity of the household as a group linked by co-residence, kinship, co-operation and especially, by the sharing of food.... Sharing is crucial to the maintenance of group cohesion; when sharing stops this is a sure sign of tensions and divisions" (1995: 231). Archaeologically, it would be difficult to deny that the architectural footprint of a *maloca* offers what

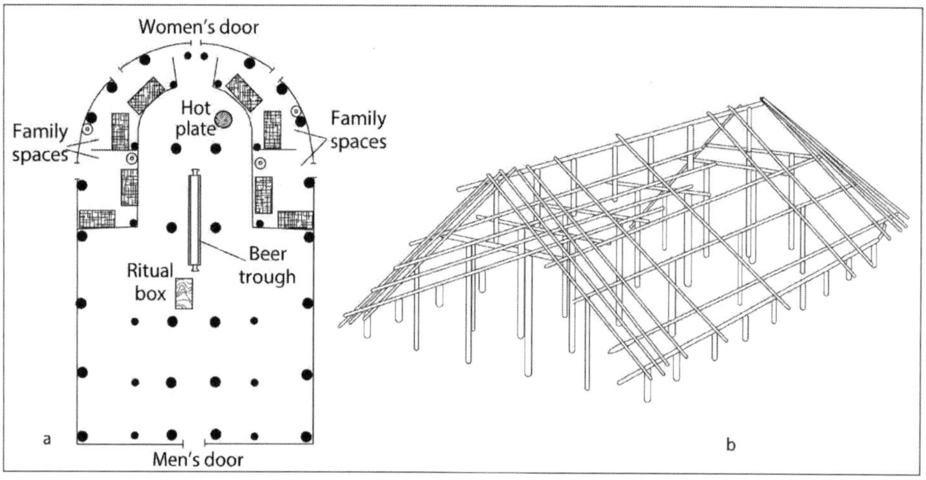

Figure 6.5: (a) Ground plan of Amazonian Tukanoan *maloca* (after Hugh-Jones 1995: 230, fig. 11.1); (b) sketch plan of internal architecture.

would pass as a textbook profile of a structure in which multiple families, likely related, live cooperatively in an extended, and possibly patrilineal (or matrilineal) setting. Ironically, the *maloca* is both "round" and "square," symbolically representing, at least for the discussion here, that once again, the shape of the house is not as important as the layout within it.

While ethnographic examples are, of course, far easier to interpret with regard to kinship organization, architectural footprints in the archaeological record may be equally informative. A good example of this is found in the residential areas at the ancient Toltec capital Tollán (ca. CE 900–1200) in central Mexico. Here, Dan Healan (1977) excavated a number of residences built in clusters that he termed "house groups." The houses, rectangular single-story structures built of stone adobe, had single entrances into their interior; not all houses had hearths or cooking areas (though portable braziers may have served houses lacking hearths). House groups consisted of three to five houses arrayed around the central courtyard, forming "distinct residential compounds" (Healan 1977: 145). All houses in a group either faced or had access to their central courtyard; entrance to the house group from the outside was by a single narrow pathway between houses. A house group was essentially "closed to the outside by the juxtaposition of its houses and the occasional use of free-standing walls to close an open side" (Healan 1977: 148). Much of the domestic activity of the houses took place in the courtyards, where residents of the houses shared space for cooperative tasks. People could freely move in and out of houses in the house group, though movement *between* house groups was much more restricted. Healan believes that house groups were kin units "consisting of a series of related households" (1977: 149), perhaps of patrilineal brothers and their spouse(s) and children or a similar unilinear-based collection of nuclear households cooperating together. Interestingly, houses within the same house group were differentiated by decorative techniques, size, and accouterments, suggesting that some families in the group were more economically successful than others (see chapter 9). The key element in the Tollán excavations was the distinct nature of house patterns arrayed around a courtyard that limited access from the outside. This has a correlate to Flannery's arguments about (circular) compounds as indicative of extended family and possibly unilinear family structure. This is not to suggest that such house patterning always reflects nuclear or extended households practicing a unilineal kinship system; bilateral systems, or non-kinship relationships, may also be the norm in any given community. However, the ethnographic record does give a slight nod toward the unilineal structure as being the most likely interpretation.

Conclusion

As is the case with every subject addressed in this book, the architectural footprint can serve as only one entry in the evidentiary checklist; the material contents of the architectural frames are usually not just as important, but more so, in the attempt to answer questions regarding social structure. Further, as has been noted repeatedly, ethnographic research is a vital tool in the archaeologist's kit. Whether looking for house societies or marriage patterns, how humans today structure their built environments is an indisputable set of evidence to such in the prehistoric or early historic past.

Chapter 7

Household Archaeology and Architecture: Socioeconomy and Beyond

The "household archaeology" field was introduced into the archaeological discipline in the 1970s as a reaction to the previous focus on elite residences and monumental architecture. Hungry to get at the small-scale perspective, archaeologists turned to the investigation of household activities and economy, striving to define the smallest unit of production and consumption within a community. Over the decades, household archaeology has come to encompass questions of gendered labor, ethnicity, symbolism, and status as expressed within a household and in the community. The main emphasis in this chapter is on the original intent of the household archaeology field: methodologies that allow archaeologists to define household socioeconomic pursuits. The latter portion of the chapter goes beyond socioeconomy, examining methods to determine sociopolitical ranking across households, as well as more socially based questions about gender, religion, and ethnicity. The exploration of these latter topics is brief, as most of these form the basis of discussion in other chapters within this volume.

For several decades, a focus on sites in the Americas formed the nucleus of dedicated household archaeology studies (Ashmore and Wilk 1988; Carballo 2011; Hendon 1996; Nash 2009; Pluckhahn 2010; Rogers and Smith 1995; Santley and Hirth 1993; Van Gijseghem 2001). Indeed, sites in the Pacific Northwest and in the American Southwest serve as valuable case studies in the discussion below. In the last decade, in part with the florescence of microarchaeological studies, household archaeology has

Archaeology of Domestic Architecture and the Human Use of Space, by Sharon R. Steadman, 163–192.

become an important mainstay in the investigation of European and Near Eastern prehistoric and early historic settlements (see below for references). These more recent studies benefit from the years of research conducted in the Americas and elsewhere, employing a variety of methodologies to great success. Examples from studies conducted in a Near Eastern context are paired with those from the Americas to present a full range of methodologies applicable to household archaeological investigation.

Origins and Development of the Household Archaeology Field

The household archaeology field was essentially launched by Richard Wilk and William Rathje (1982) in an article titled by the same name. Though some archaeologists (e.g., Clarke 1972; Flannery and Winter 1976; Hammel 1980; B. D. Smith 1978), and certainly a number of cultural anthropologists (e.g., Bender 1967; Glassie 1975; Goody 1972; Löfgren 1974; Yanagisako 1979) had begun analyzing cultures at the individual "family" unit level, it was Wilk and Rathje's publication that captured widespread interest. Wilk and Rathje noted that the archaeological field had progressed from units of analysis that spanned entire civilizations, to the investigation of smaller settlements. "The time has come," they asserted, "to move downward in specificity, to the household unit" (1982: 617). The publication was followed by an entire volume on the subject (Netting, Wilk, and Arnould 1984), in which some of the issues raised in the original article were explored in depth.

One critical issue includes how one defines a "household," a topic also explored by cultural anthropologists. J. Daniel Rogers (1995: 8) defines the dilemma succinctly: "Part of the problem in understanding the household is a tendency to conflate form and function. . . . The form of the household is embodied in the kinship relations, while function is an amalgam of the range of activities specific to the household participants." At this early point, household archaeology was less concerned with the identity of household members than with how to identify a "household." Wilk and Rathje grappled with the notion of how households *function*—that is, what their purpose is. Shortly after, Wilk, along with Robert Netting, decried the word "function" and instead suggested that archaeologists needed to be more concerned with how households "act" (1984: 5). Members of a household cooperate in economic activities related to production and consumption, they produce and socialize the children, and they ensure the transmission of the household holdings from one generation to the next. While only the first two, production and consumption, specifically involve the actual architectural remains, all will be discussed below.

The first step, however, is to examine what, spatially, is meant by "household." One point emphasized by Wilk and Rathje is that not everyone living under one roof is a member of the same household (see also Carter 1984). By the same token, members of a household might dwell in several buildings, perhaps in close proximity, but are still separate (Wilk and Rathje 1982: 620). The trick is to determine whether domestic structures situated close to one another each constitute individual households, whether several are cooperating as a single household, or if, in fact, all of them are. The key to determining this is the analysis of the material culture and the common spaces between and within the houses. Employing specific methodologies can then define ancient households that act as the smallest unit of a cooperating group within a community (Hammel 1980, 1984), and engaging in productive activities, the distribution of goods, the transmission of the property, and the reproduction of the household.

In household archaeology, "production" is one of the important actions performed by a household. By production, Wilk and Rathje (1982: 622) and others (e.g., Ashmore and Wilk 1988; Hendon 1996; Rogers 1995) refer to the practice of food acquisition and processing. All those cooperating in this endeavor, whether under the same roof or in adjacent dwellings, are likely part of the same household. Activities associated with production involve "scheduling" in that they can be simultaneous or linear, simple or complex (Wilk and Netting 1984). That is, in some cultures, the tasks associated with food acquisition and production might be quite simple, performed one after another and thus by a single person. For example, a woman in a horticultural society goes to the nearby garden and collects some of the garden products, carries them back to the house, and processes (cuts, grates, cooks) them for the evening meal. Simultaneous tasks require several people, working at the same time, to perform different activities in order to acquire or process the food. In the former case, the household can be quite small, but the latter may require a larger household. While defining production in a household falls largely within the realm of activity area research (Kent 1987b; Rapoport 1990) in which tasks are identified based on the location and distribution of material remains, it does include a spatial component. Activity areas are "found" in and around the dwelling that make up the household. Repeated spatial patterns across individual houses or clusters of dwellings can be signals to the archaeologist as to how the cooperating households are arranged in the community.

The definition of consumption—or "distribution," in Wilk and Rathje's treatise (1982: 624)—involves the movement of resources, either in the form of "pooling" them for distribution within the household or through exchange with other corporate units. "Consumption" refers more specifically to access to produced goods by members of the household—that is, to those who are allowed to consume them. The pooling of resources requiring long-term storage could well involve architectural elements in or near the dwellings.

The final two actions of the household as defined by Wilk and Rathje are "transmission" and "reproduction" (1982: 627–31). These two actions are more social than economic; the transmission has to do with the transfer of property from one generation to the next. This process may be largely invisible to the archaeologist unless there are signifiers indicating the same kinship or household group retains control of the built unit(s) over time. The practice of reproduction refers to the socializing of children, which includes child care, education, and engagement in the labor force. Children may have two major archaeological implications for the use of space; the first may be the requirement of the primary care givers (usually the women) to remain closer to the dwelling units. The second is the potential need for a large number of children; depending on the subsistence strategy, and the need for complex simultaneous tasks in the production activities, greater or lesser numbers of offspring might be necessary for an efficient household, impacting the size of dwellings.

Wilk and Rathje's 1982 publication, and the book on the same topic that quickly followed (Netting, Wilk, and Arnould 1984), launched a concerted and continuing investigation of households in the archaeological record. Initially, the focus was on archaeological evidence from the Americas (e.g., Rogers and Smith 1995; Santley and Hirth 1993; Wilk 1989; Wilk and Ashmore 1988); Richard Blanton (1994) then offered a comprehensive and insightful comparative analysis of households on a worldwide basis (see discussion in Steadman 1996). By the mid-1990s, the field was well ensconced in the archaeological discipline, appearing in the *Annual Review of Anthropology* (Hendon 1996) and in the publication of James Deetz's *In Small Things Forgotten* (1996) as an established area of research. In the last several decades, household archaeology has become a prominent methodological approach to archaeological sites in Europe and the Near East (e.g., Bianchi 2012; Gilboa, Sharon, and Zorn 2014; Hofmann and Smyth 2013; Nevett 2010; Parker and Foster 2012; Souvatzi 2008; Yasur-Landau, Ebeling, and Mazow 2011; Zubrow, Audouze, and Enloe 2010; and discussions by Goring-Morris and Belfer-Cohen 2013; Hardin 2011; Routledge 2013) and in comparative analyses (Allison 1999b; D'Altroy and Hastorf 2001; MacEachern, Archer, and Garvin 1989; Madella et al. 2013; Matson 1996). It also continues to be at the basis of much of the research that takes place in the Americas (e.g., Aldenderfer 1993a; Barile and Brandon 2004; Carballo 2011; Nash 2009; Pluckhahn 2010; Robin 2003; Sobel, Gahr, and Ames 2006). There are two major aspects found in more recent household archaeological studies that differentiate them from the original research in the 1980s. The first is that household archaeology has become such a standard approach in archaeological work that it is no longer "highlighted" in the titles of books or articles about research within a community. This demonstrates the importance, and the success, of the basic methodologies offered well over three decades ago.

The second difference is a shift in the methodological goals of household archaeology. The earliest studies focused on the "function" of the household through its material culture. These methods identified the household group through the location of artifacts and spaces that were signifiers of production and consumption activities. What they did not do, however, was allow archaeologists to delve deeper into the identities of the household members. Julia Hendon, in the *Annual Review* article, wrote, "Household archaeology's focus on the dwelling unit reveals much of what households did but has not contributed as much as it should to our understanding of who did what" (1996: 48). She and others (e.g., Aldenderfer and Stanish 1993; Allison 1999a; Blanton 1994; Cutting 2006a; Souvatzi 2008) argued then and since that households are not just productive units but are symbolic structures as well, full of individuals with differing goals, requirements, desires, interpersonal tensions, and responsibilities. This perspective has led to the use of household archaeology as a lens on more symbolic (rather than functional) components of co-residential members, including a focus on, among other things, gender, ethnicity, power, and politics. It has also been recognized that households are intrinsically critical to studies involving class and inequality in a community. More recently, households have become a vehicle to understanding cultural cosmologies and belief systems (see below and chapter 10). Though many of these approaches are explored in depth in other chapters within this volume, a few case studies from an explicitly "household archaeology" point of view are illustrative here.

Household Archaeology and the Architectural Record

Since the emergence of the household archaeology field, a variety of approaches have been pursued. For the purposes of the discussion here, the categories described by David Carballo (2011) and Donna Nash (2009) will be useful for surveying the intersection between architecture and household archaeology. Carballo (2011: 134) characterizes the archaeological study of households as falling into three categories. The first might be considered the most "traditional," comprising units of production and consumption in the format originally outlined by Wilk and Rathje and including craft production as an important element. Carballo's second category for investigating households is one in which members "serve as coordinated political actors that strategically negotiate their group's position within a social hierarchy" (2011: 134). Here, some household activities, which might include craft production beyond intra-household needs, would play a role in allowing households to maintain or gain increasingly important social and/or economic positions in their communities. Other factors such as the development of cooperative kin networks, identifiable through household archaeology methodologies, could compete with other corporate groups for social positioning. Third, Carballo notes that households contain individuals who create social units; these groups conform to, and create, human behavioral codes that serve to satisfy the needs of residents and community. It is within this approach that more symbolic aspects of the household can be addressed such as gender relations, ethnicity and identity, and ritual and belief.

Nash (2009: 207) refers to the four areas defined by Wilk and Rathje—production, distribution, transmission, and reproduction—as a "materialist approach." She observes, as have others, that this essentially economic approach to understanding the household does not accommodate an "individualized" approach to household membership, but that it is an important building block to allow such investigation. For Nash (2009: 207), the examination of extra-household activities with a view toward social position is a "political" approach that employs neoevolutionary models to "describe households as building blocks or units at the foundation of polities irrespective of size or complexity." The household provides the keys to understanding the emergence of leadership strategies, the increases in the production of surplus goods, and the labor that build a complex society. Archaeology at the household level, particularly in comparative analysis, can be a critical element in understanding the evolution of sociopolitical organizations. Finally, regarding the individuals who constitute the household, Nash employs a "structuralist model" (2009: 206), one that studies households to "show how houses can be cosmograms . . . [and] can represent the complementary relations between genders in the family or the social hierarchy of the entire society." The house and household generate, contain, and transmit embedded social structures, behavioral codes, and ideologies.

The categories and characterizations offered by Carballo and Nash, which were built on major works in anthropological and archaeological thought (e.g., Bourdieu 1977; Deetz 1982, 1996; Earle 1997; Flannery 1998; Giddens 1979; Rapoport 1969), provide the framework for the following discussion. The emphasis here is on the first, "materialist" socioeconomic approaches, as these stand at the heart of the household archaeology subdiscipline. The other "neoevolutionary" and "structuralist" approaches, addressed in more detail elsewhere in this volume, receive a brief overview regarding some of the innovative approaches accomplished by archaeologists using the household archaeology models.

Household Archaeology, Architecture, and Socioeconomy

It is production and consumption activities, as outlined above, that are the focus in the discussion here, termed by Carballo as a "traditional approach" and as a "materialist" perspective by Nash. Questions considered include how many dwellings make up a "household," whether nuclear or extended families constitute the household, and whether everyone who lives in the dwelling is necessarily part of the same household unit. Finally, through several case studies, we explore the role of production and consumption activities in the potential differentiation of wealth and status in a community.

How Many Structures?

It is Richard Wilk himself who offers a primer on determining the household group. In his study of the Kekchi Maya of Belize (1984), he notes the necessity to avoid equating a "household" with a single dwelling, contrary to what had been argued by others (e.g., Laslett 1972). Wilk makes a distinction between a single dwelling unit and a household cluster, the latter housing separate groups that may all cooperate as a single unit. He uses ethnographic data from the Kekchi Maya to inform his model for identifying a household in the archaeological record. The Kekchi Maya present three different forms of household units: a single dwelling, which may house a nuclear family plus possible additional residents such as a widowed parent; a "tight" household cluster; and a "loose" household cluster (Wilk 1984: 225). The first two types are more easily discovered archaeologically; the "loose" cluster might be entirely invisible archaeologically, looking more like completely individualized units (Figure 7.1a–c). The Maya household unit shares meals and child-care duties, cooperates in maintaining the house and associated structures, and shares in domestic chores; members fully cooperate in all production and consumption activities. Wilk notes that the sharing of resources and the placement of houses in a tight household cluster are critical clues to defining a

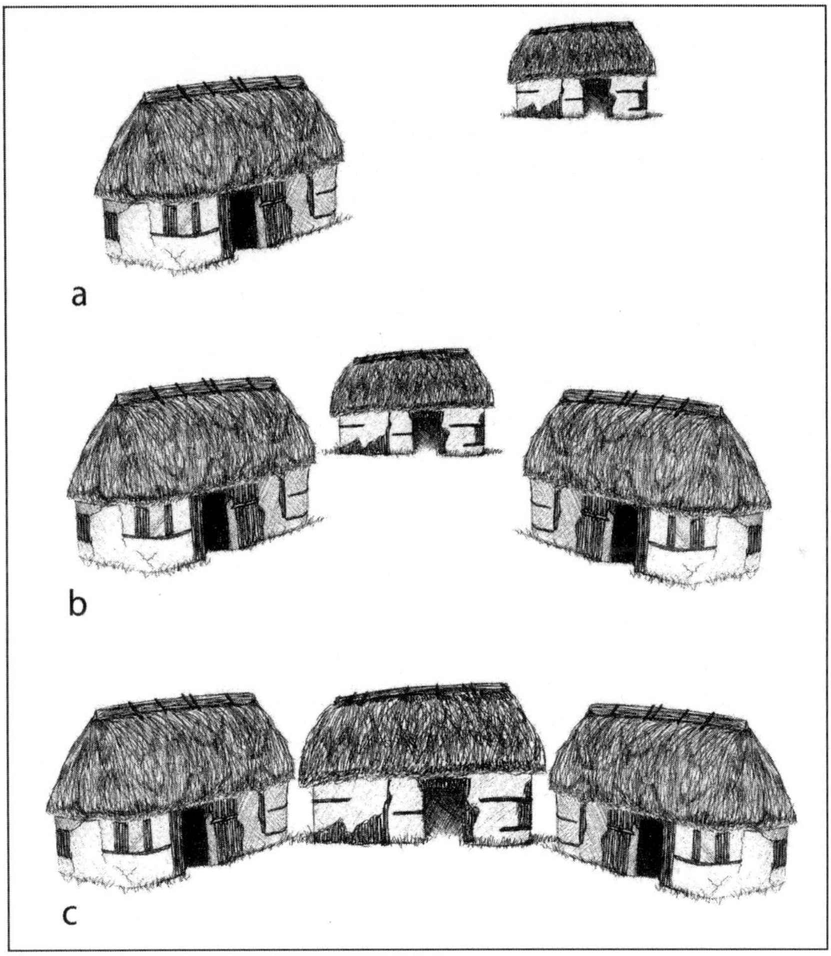

Figure 7.1: Artistic renderings of household units: (a) individual; (b) loosely clustered; and (c) tightly clustered. Note that the loosely clustered units could easily be interpreted as individual nuclear homes (drawing by Corrina Petit).

multi-dwelling household unit. Evidence of a shared processing and cooking area, along with shared storage facilities, are strong indicators of such a cluster. Dwellings in close proximity to one another, touching or nearly so, and sharing an open space between them are an "overt symbolic expression of the relationship between inhabitants" (1984: 226).

Aaron Brody (2011) used precisely these techniques in his analysis of a cluster of buildings at the Iron Age (ca. 1000–700 BCE) site of Tell En-Naṣbeh, north of Jerusalem. Brody used the combination of architectural layout and the distribution of ceramics and small finds to assess whether the household unit at Tell En-Naṣbeh consisted of single dwellings or a tight cluster of dwellings; he determined that the latter was the case. Brody examined five structures lining a street, sharing common walls (Figure 7.2). The first (H1) and most northerly was two-roomed, with one larger rec-

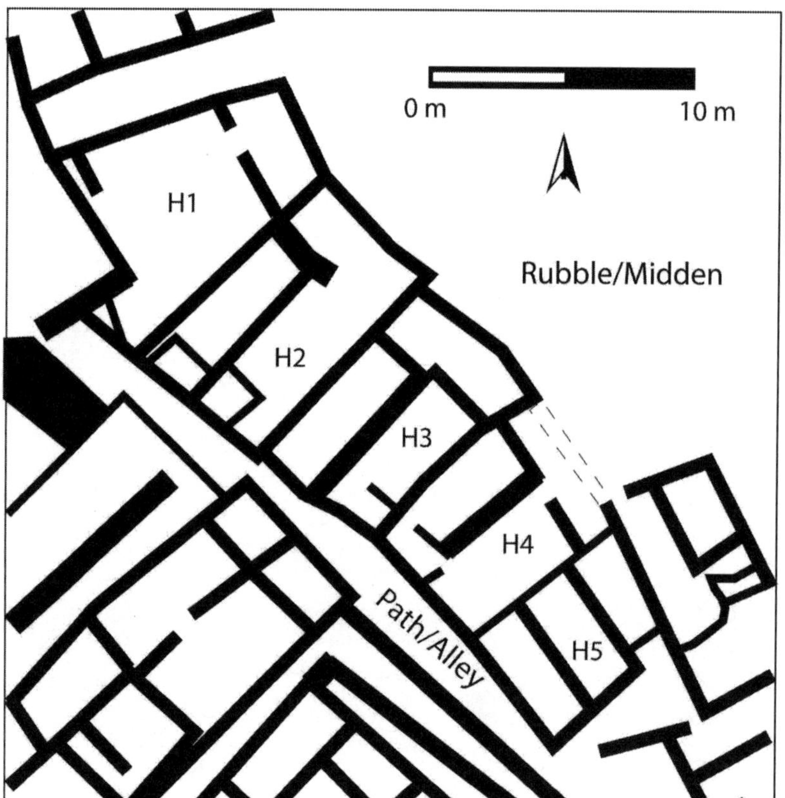

Figure 7.2: Tell En-Naṣbeh household units (after Brody 2011: 241, fig. 1).

tilinear space at the front interpreted as a courtyard, and a "broad room" at the back. The next three structures (H2–4) were three-roomed pillared houses, each sharing a wall between them. Each of these houses had a broad room at the back and two oblong rooms in the front, separated by pillars. Some of these oblong rooms featured very small walled-off spaces toward the front (near the street). The fifth structure (H5) was an "atypical" three-roomed building featuring three broad rooms; two cisterns were in this complex, one toward the more northerly rooms and one in the more southerly section (Brody 2011: 240). Based on his analysis, Brody suggests that this complex housed three nuclear families that cooperated in production, consumption, and storage activities. He identified two kitchens based on the presence of cooking vessels. One to the south in a broad room of the atypical H5 structure was likely the outdoor "summer" kitchen (a typical practice in the Middle East); this cooking area was near a doorway leading to the southerly cistern (Brody 2011: 249). The winter kitchen was likely located in the most northerly house (H1), in one of the oblong rooms that contained the other cistern. The presence of serving and consumption vessels were found evenly distributed in oblong rooms of two of the houses; Brody speculates that one more of the oblong rooms in the central house(s) (H2–3) served as the living area (2011: 249). Brody's study presents a picture of three cooperative groups or families cooking together in a single kitchen but then spreading out to their respective houses to consume the meal. Since the oblong rooms in the house were fairly small, they may not have been sufficient for all members of the household unit to gather together for meals.

Brody also analyzed the presence of storage vessels across the five structures. The majority rested in the structures at northern and southern ends of the complex, and some storage vessels were also found in the central three-roomed dwelling (Brody 2011: 250). Brody analyzed the presence and location of craft-based tools and items. He suggests that the larger oblong room in the most northerly dwelling was a dual-function craft production space, alternating between olive pressing during the harvest and sewing and weaving activities in the off season (Brody 2011: 251). In the larger oblong room of the southernmost dwelling, the presence of five tools of various types and a modified animal tusk suggests to Brody that this room functioned as a workshop. The residents of the three dwellings appear to have cooperated in both the storage and production of goods, as well as in the production and consumption of food. The two storage areas, presumably accessible to all residents of the dwellings, demonstrate the "pooling" of critical resources for the entire household. The scheduling of craft production activities may have been linear in that all workers cooperated together on the same tasks, changing activities according to season; alternatively, task performance may have been simultaneous and complex, with some deployed to the olive press, others to textile production, and another group to the workshop. However the craft production activities were accomplished, the products of the work appear to have emanated from the entire collection of residents in these adjacent dwellings and associated buildings—that is, the household unit.

Rana Özbal (2012) found a different situation in her examination of sixth-millennium BCE Tell Kurdu housing in southeast Anatolia (Figure 7.3). Excavations on the north mound area revealed six residential compounds, some consisting of numerous roofed and unroofed spaces. Özbal's detailed analysis of Area A shows that a single structure, consisting of at least ten contiguous spaces, constituted both a single dwelling and a single household unit. To reach this conclusion, she examined architectural features and layout, room contents, and the chemical composition and micro-archaeology of room floors. There was only a single entrance to this complex via a gated courtyard; upon entry, another gated doorway led to an interior unroofed central space (Room 7) in which many serving vessels and grinding slabs were found (Özbal 2012: 336). In the adjacent Room 5, more grinding slabs, workbenches, a storage bin, and an oven indicate that this was a kitchen; soil chemistry revealed high concentrations of iron in the floor soils, suggesting long-term use of basalt grinding stones (Özbal 2012:

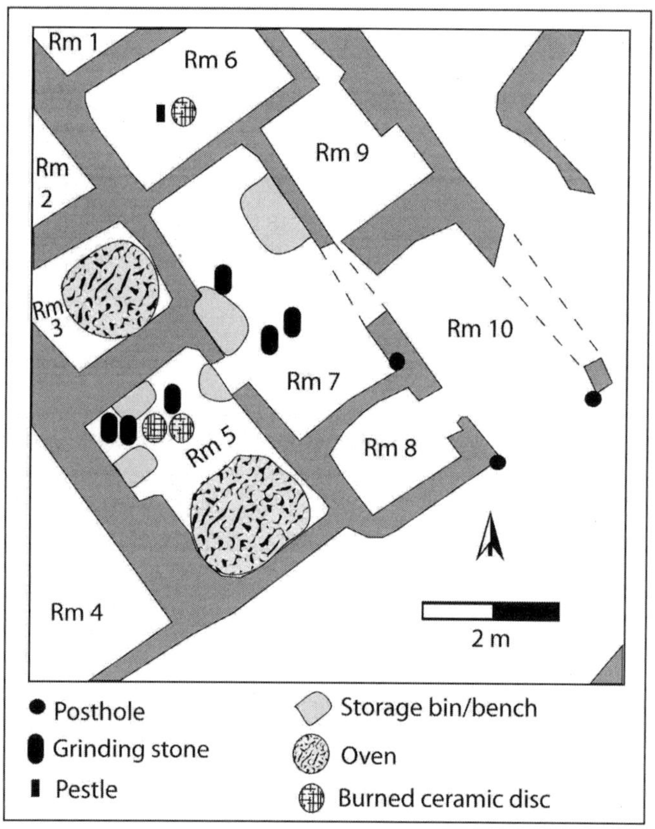

Figure 7.3: Tell Kurdu housing compound consisting of a single household unit (after Özbal 2012: 336, fig. 10).

336–37). Microartifactual analysis indicates that flint-knapping took place in Room 7. The other rooms in this structure were identified as living rooms or storage rooms. One living room revealed two subfloor burials; mitochondrial DNA analysis reveals that these were kin-related individuals. Özbal concludes that "the inhabitants of Household A were an independent group that prepared, cooked, and consumed their own food within their private compound. The restricted access, their personal kitchen and living areas, and the ancestral ties provided by the DNA data give the impression that this was a long-lived exclusive household complex" (2012: 338).

The spatiality of structures and the placement of critical features such as workstations and kitchens are some of the most important keys to determining how many structures, or dwellings, make up a single household unit. Another important factor is extra-domestic work areas, such as agricultural fields or pasturelands. Wilk (1984) as well as others (e.g., Chesson 2012; Ciolek-Torello 1996; Scarry 1995) note that one important indicator of a cooperative household unit is whether those living in the separate dwellings work in their own fields or pasturelands, or if they cooperate in the same shared area. Archaeologically, identifying ancient agricultural or other human-altered landscapes is difficult, to say the least; even if they are discovered, matching them to particular clusters of dwellings is likely impossible. Until technology and methodology exist for this seemingly impossible task, the techniques discussed above for equating singular or clustered dwellings with household units must suffice.

The Nuclear versus Extended Household Unit

Another goal in household archaeological studies is discerning the nature of the group represented in a household unit. Archaeological representations of "nuclear" and "extended" family structures is a topic thoroughly investigated by Flannery (1972) and discussed here in chapters 4 and 6. In addition, it should be noted that an "extended family" household unit may really consist of a set of nuclear families, probably but not necessarily related to one another. Nonetheless, scholars have been very successful at defining the family structures at the heart of ancient household units.

Richard Matson (1996) investigated dwellings and household units in two areas of the western United States, in the Southwest and on the Northwest Coast. He found that the type of family household unit established—nuclear versus extended—was closely related to resource acquisition strategies. A second important factor was whether social ranking and competitive elites were present in the community social organization. In the Basketmaker II period (200–400 CE) in Utah, pithouses of 25–30 m^2 in area (with internal storage) probably housed single families (Matson 1996: 108–9). Contemporary with Basketmaker II communities, Northwest Coast houses at the Paul Mason site were substantially built and were probably occupied for most of the year; they were rectangular, with two hearths and an average area of 6.5–10 m^2. It is estimated that up to 13 people may have occupied these structures, and that the two hearths represent two nuclear families. Matson stresses that house size is not necessarily indicative of nuclear versus extended family structure; Southwest pithouses are larger than the Paul Mason houses, but the former may have housed only a single nuclear family while the latter contained two. Over time, the Southwest houses shrank in size to 12–20 square meters in area, in part due to the movement of storage facilities to external locations. House size and layout then stayed consistent in the Southwest for centuries, reflecting the continued single nuclear family household unit in this region. However, major changes developed in dwelling form in the Northwest Coast.

By 2000 BP, Northwest Coast houses had altered substantially. Large "plank houses" (built with cedar planks and posts) found at Paul Mason and at another site, Gitsaex, were of substantially different sizes. Paul Mason houses averaged 62 m^2, and Gitsaex houses were over 100 m^2 in area; this suggests varying levels of wealth and resource control at the two sites (Matson 1996: 110–11). Paul Mason houses may have held two to four nuclear families, while the Gitsaex houses could hold twice that many. Archaeological investigation at Paul Mason discovered no indication that separate "family sections" were described within the dwelling, suggesting that all house occupants cooperated together as a single unit (Matson 1996: 111). These data are consistent with ethnographic studies of 19th- to 20th-century "plank house" inhabitants. Matson explains the differentiation in house size between the two Northwest Coast sites as "consistent with a rank society, some households controlling more resources than others and thus able to maintain larger groups of distant relatives and, possibly, slaves" (1996: 111). Northwest Coast houses contained household units consisting of multiple nuclear families and associated kin, and possibly non-kin occupants, all cooperating in production and consumption activities for the good of the unit.

The differing household structures in the Northwest and Southwest regions are, according to Matson, based on the available resources in each area. Residents in the Southwest relied on maize agriculture, something that could be undertaken anywhere that offered arable land and sufficient water. In addition, tending to the crop might require the labor of only a single nuclear family, some members undertaking cultivation tasks and others the processing activities at the dwelling. In contrast, the major subsistence resource for Northwest Coast populations was salmon, available only at a very particular time of the year and in specific places. The household unit size on the Northwest Coast was in direct proportion to control of territories that offered salmon runs and the number of people who could both harvest the salmon and be supported by the amount acquired (Matson 1996: 113–16). Those living in Gitsaex controlled more valuable resource areas than those who occupied the Paul Mason site. Competition for control of Northwest Coast resource areas was associated with the development of social ranking in the region, whereas the relative availability of arable land in the Southwest did not facilitate large household competition and allowed for smaller nuclear-family-based household units to remain the norm for millennia.

In ancient urban settings, even determining which room goes with which dwelling can be a challenge, as Yoko Nishimura (2012) experienced when tackling a detailed analysis of the residential area of ancient Titriş Höyük (ca. 2300–2100 BCE), located on a tributary of the Euphrates River in southeastern Turkey. Using a combination of architectural, spatial, and activity area analyses, she investigated the architecture of two excavated areas of the city. All houses were in a contiguous format, with every house sharing a wall with a neighbor and all arrayed along streets and alleys. Using ethnographic evidence from the Middle East (e.g., Horne 1994; Kramer 1983; Watson 1979), Nishimura postulated the existence of eight different types of rooms: entrance, reception, living, workshop, food preparation and processing, kitchen, storage, pantry, and mortuary (2012: 353). To identify room function, Nishimura used room size, accessibility via number of doorways (see chapter 3), the types of built-in and largely immovable features present (including fire installations, tombs, large storage jars, mortars, etc.), and the artifactual evidence for activities in each room. All the houses had a majority of the room types identified ethnographically, and some had multiple examples of the same room type.

The typical Titriş house consisted of at least one entrance room, sometimes two. These also doubled as small task rooms, judging from the artifacts found on their floors. The entrance rooms, located on the street side of the house, always led either to a reception room or an open courtyard, thereby keeping guests out of the family living quarters. Many houses had central courtyards, which functioned as workshops and food processing and preparation spaces. Some houses had only one kitchen, and houses featuring two or more often had multiple living rooms as well; multi-kitchen houses also had more rooms and spaces devoted to storage (Nishimura 2012: 364). Mortuary rooms were identified based on the presence of a cist tomb or pot burial; interestingly, though these were often quite large rooms, artifactual evidence indicates few, if any, activities took place there. Mortuary rooms seem to have served as the family crypt and a type of sacred space. The largest rooms, averaging $10.4 \times 48\ m^2$, included the courtyards, workshops, kitchens, and mortuary rooms; the smallest, roughly $0.5 \times 5.6\ m^2$, were devoted to entrance and storage; the medium-range rooms, $5.72 \times 10.22\ m^2$, served the other house functions (Nishimura 2012).

Based on the ethnographic studies, Nishimura suggests that some houses at Titriş held extended families (perhaps multiple nuclear families), and others housed a single nuclear family, perhaps with additional kin members (widowed parents, unmarried siblings). Houses with multiple kitchens and living rooms but one mortuary room suggest a cooperative household unit, especially if the workshop area for the entire dwelling was the central courtyard area; some consumption independence is reflected in the presence of separate kitchens. Nishimura's goal was not to determine whether houses contained single or multiple nuclear families but to assess whether there was socioeconomic differentiation among Titriş households. She concluded that though some were larger and had more storage and others were smaller with less, households were fairly similar in terms of activities carried out and possession of material goods: "The consistency of patterning in spatial organization and domestic activities further indicates homogeneity in economic status within these residential sectors, . . . [T]here were no clear qualitative differences in the household activities that point to differences in wealth distribution of social class" (Nishimura 2012: 365). Thus, Nishimura not only provided a methodology for identifying family structures in an urban neighborhood, she outlined the steps needed to assess whether such households were engaged in competitive status acquisition or, as she found at Titriş, were largely homogeneous regarding social differentiation.

James Hardin (2012), in another study in the same volume as Nishimura's (Parker and Foster 2012), uses a similar methodology to determine the socioeconomic activities and family structure in the Levantine "four-room house" in Iron Age Israel. Like Nishimura, Hardin draws on ethnographic data; to this, he is able to add textual evidence mainly from the Bible, which offers descriptions of family and economic pursuits from this period. Hardin examined a single house at the site of Tell Halif in southern Israel. The rectangular dwelling contained four rooms, though the largest, Room 5, was partially divided (Figure 7.4) (Hardin 2012: 527). The house is approximately 11 × 9.5 m in size, giving an area of roughly 100 m^2, and may have had a second story or rooftop usage, based on the number of pillars within the house. Like Nishimura, Hardin used artifacts to determine activity areas; he also examined room layout and built-in features such as pits, bins, floors, large storage vessels, and the hearth. His analy-

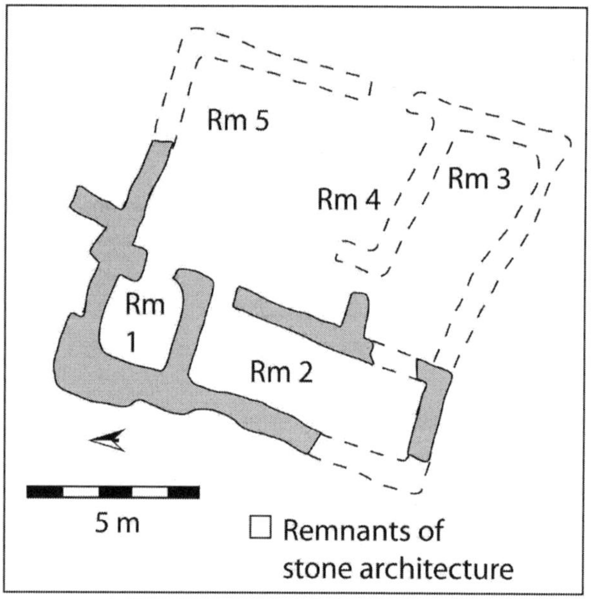

Figure 7.4: The "four-room house" in Iron Age Israel (after Hardin 2012: 527, fig. 4).

sis found that occupants of the house fully cooperated in every aspect of production and consumption, including food preparation and cooking, and task performance, which involved textile production and wine making. All meals were shared, and evidence of trade items in the dwelling suggests that they were involved in the regional exchange network. Hardin notes that others who have studied the Iron Age four-room houses (e.g., Schloen 2001) have shown that these houses were inherited, involving the transmission aspect of the household unit outlined by Wilk and Rathje. As for the occupants, the size of the houses and wide variety of tasks performed within the rooms leads Hardin to suggest that a multigenerational family formed the household unit (2012: 546). The house size and range of necessary tasks certainly suggests that more than just a single nuclear family occupied the Iron Age Levantine four-room houses.

The case studies here review several critical architectural indicators that aid the archaeologist in assessing the constituents that made up a single household unit: structure and room sizes, and room or space functions, especially with regard to the number of kitchens, storage areas, and living (and sleeping) spaces. However, task performance, particularly the production of crafts or the acquisition of important resources, is also a valuable determinant regarding the number and relationship of residents necessary to accomplish those activities.

Cohabitation and Cooperation: Not Necessarily a Matched Set

It might be tempting to assume that once one has determined that several nuclear or multigenerational families occupied a single dwelling, that all members could then be seen as constituting a household unit that was fully cooperative in all production and consumption activities. However, after a brief moment, a researcher will usually recall that humans form incredibly varied groupings that are often contrary to what would at first glance seem to be a logical socioeconomic structure. Brian Hoffman's (1999) work in Alaska demonstrates that those who occupied a single dwelling did not necessary equate to a single household unit on every productive and consumption-based level. Residents of Agayadan Village on Unimak Island in the Aleutians (CE 1300–1750) built 20 semi-subterranean winter dwellings in a longhouse format. The above-ground superstructure consisted of driftwood or whale bone interwoven with grass mats, sod, and packed earth, creating a well-insulated abode for the powerful winter storms and low temperatures. Hoffman refers to these built structures as "nuclear-satellite complexes" because of their layout (1999: 148). A central long oval or rectangular room, usually between 6 and 15 m in length, had 20 cm depressions along the side walls and small satellite rooms reached by short tunnels (Figure 7.5). The central room served as communal space for daily life, cooking, eating, the production of tools and crafts, and so forth. The small depressions along the side walls were generally used as sleeping areas for the families inhabiting the longhouse, and the satellite rooms were used for storage (Hoffman 1999: 155).

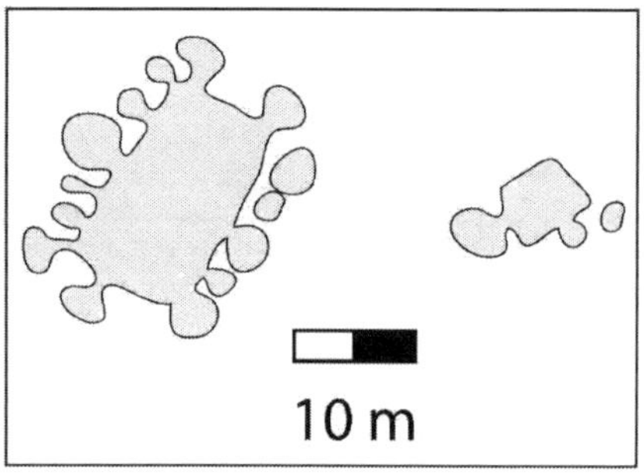

Figure 7.5: Example of house forms—large on the left, small on the right—in Agayadan Village (after Hoffman 1999: 152, fig. 3).

The number of hearths in each house depended on the size. Smaller houses (ca. 6 m in length) had a single hearth at the center, while medium and large-sized houses (up to ca. 15 m in length) had two hearths at each end of the central room. Each dwelling housed multiple nuclear families, ranging between two in the smallest house and four in the largest (Hoffman 1999). Two other notable features in the houses were rock-lined basins, which Hoffman believes were roasting pits, and storage pits found in the communal area. The distribution of hearths, roasting and storage pits, and activity areas, in combination with the satellite rooms and sleeping areas, offers Hoffman a fairly clear picture of cooperative groupings among residents in each Agayadan house. Hearths served to heat the entire structure, which was essential in an Alaskan winter and difficult in a place that featured few fuel sources. The co-residents cooperated in acquiring and using the heating fuel in the hearths for the benefit of the entire dwelling. The two hearths also served as cooking stations, and thus if there were only two hearths and four families inhabited a dwelling, then either "turns" were taken at each hearth or there was cooperation in food preparation. The roasting pits were also located in areas that lent themselves to communal use. They were not placed near tunnel entrances but instead near the communally used hearth areas. Hoffman suggests that successful large-scale winter hunts, perhaps performed cooperatively, were the source of communal roasting and feasting events which helped to strengthen the social bonds of co-dwellers (1999: 159).

The placement of storage pits, activity areas, sleeping quarters, and tunnels tells a different story about levels of cooperation. Storage pits and workstations were spatially separated within the longhouses, placed near the tunnels and the sleeping quarters (Hoffman 1999: 159–60). Nuclear families in the dwelling may well have acquired (produced) and consumed subsistence resources independently from co-residential families, with the possible exception of large-scale hunts. The tools and crafts they produced may also have been used exclusively by the family that made them, rather than being shared across the entire dwelling. The layout of the house, in combination with internally built features and artifactual positioning, allowed Hoffman to determine that Agayadan residents in single dwellings cooperated when it benefited all (e.g., heating the household, consuming a resource that had a short shelf life), but acted as multiple single household units living within a single dwelling on most other levels of daily life.

Bleda Düring (2006), in his close analysis of Neolithic Anatolian households, found a fascinating socioeconomic strategy at the site of Aşıklı Höyük (ca. 8200–7500 BCE), located in the Lake District on the central plateau (see Figure 6.3). A residential area with densely packed structures featured numerous single and multiple-room units within neighborhoods divided by streets and alleys (Cutting 2006b; Düring 2006; Esin 1996; Esin and Harmankaya 1999). Düring identified at least 26 single-room units averaging 9.3 m^2 in size; 23 multiple-room units, generally 13 m^2 in area, were identified based on the presence of shared walls and internal doorways (2006: 81–82). To identify household units, Düring examined the spatial arrangement of hearths and artifact scatters (mainly lithics) and the location of burials. Given that Anatolian plateau winters can be quite harsh, it is remarkable that hearths were not more plentiful across the Aşıklı settlement. Only 77 hearths were found, occurring in approximately 35% of the Aşıklı rooms, almost always in single-room units (Düring 2006: 84). Several dozen burials, in subfloor contexts, held males and females of all ages, including children; some revealed evidence of having been partially burned, and many burials contained jewelry or tools. Burials were almost always located in rooms with hearths. Finally, the majority of artifact scatters were found not in the interior rooms but in external areas identified as "middens" by the excavators; these may have been open courtyards used for task performance and refuse disposal. Storage bins appear to have been clustered in various locations, often near hearths, but preservation of bins and storage features was minimal.

Aşıklı, in Düring's analysis, presents a fascinating socioeconomic structure of shifting cooperative units within three distinct neighborhoods. Though single-room and multiple-room units had distinct walls, they do not seem to correspond to individual autonomous household units, since many do not possess hearths, storage bins, or domestic equipment. For instance, three single-room units had four hearths, while two large three- and four-room units had none. Cooperative units at Aşıklı appear to have been at the *neighborhood* level (Düring 2006: 89–101). Residents within a neighborhood may have used any of several hearth locations for the processing and preparation of food; all members of the neighborhood may have performed tasks such as craft production in the same open-air location. Burials of selected family members may indicate a group's "loyalty" to a particular area of the neighborhood, or may suggest an important "nodal" household. Future DNA testing identifying whether multiple burials in the same area contained non-kin or kin-related individuals would help distinguish between these scenarios.

While family structures almost certainly existed at Neolithic Aşıklı, these do not seem to have equated to the primary household units involved in cooperative production and consumption activities. Neighborhood residents may have had shifting and flexible cooperative arrangements, processing and preparing together and then dispersing to one hearth or another depending on a variety of factors. How food was acquired and stored may have been equally flexible. The examples from Agayadan and Aşıklı (and see Kafafi 2006 for 'Ain Ghazal) are fascinating snapshots into a past in which individual and group needs and alliances are represented spatially and architecturally, painting a picture of societies that had alternatively very specific and very flexible patterns of cooperation, the latter shifting on a frequent, perhaps even daily, basis.

Households and Socioeconomic Differentiation

The strategies for identifying differing levels of wealth and status across a community have been discussed in several different chapters of this volume; the methods associated with examining socioeconomic cooperation in a household unit can therefore be briefly explored here in a single but comprehensive case study. A single occupational phase presents a "snapshot" of socioeconomic strategies and differentiation in a community and offers the opportunity to compare and contrast elements such as house size, labor investment, and contents demonstrated in houses and constituent household units across a community (see Blanton 1994, and chapter 9, this volume, for extensive discussion on these strategies). A diachronic perspective can also be very informative, especially for identifying new strategies that household units may have had to develop in order to tolerate external, or internal, changes in their social arena. Stella Souvatzi (2008, 2012) cautions archaeologists not to assume that households simply *react* to external changes imposed upon them; it is sometimes, and perhaps often, the case that social change emanates from the households themselves, forcing adjustments at the community level.

Meredith Chesson (2012; and see Chesson and Goodale 2014) offers an excellent example of household units making adjustments to social forces at work over the course of two centuries of occupation inside the Early Bronze Age walled settlement of Numayra (ca. 2850–2600 cal BCE) in Jordan. Chesson's close examination of two phases of the settlement, Phase 2A and 2B (Figure 7.6), indicate that household units reorganized their dwelling spaces to adjust to, or promote, greater control over their production and consumption activities. In the earlier Phase 2A, Chesson identified two household units (nos. 1 and 2 in Figure 7.6), each consisting of at least two roofed rooms and a substantial unroofed space that functioned as an associated courtyard. Each of the residential units contained the normal items associated with domestic behavior, including hearths and tabuns (ovens), food preparation tools and paraphernalia, silos built of clay or stone, storage vessels and pits, and various types of stone tools (Chesson 2012). A third architectural unit in Phase 2A was identified as a ritual area (Area

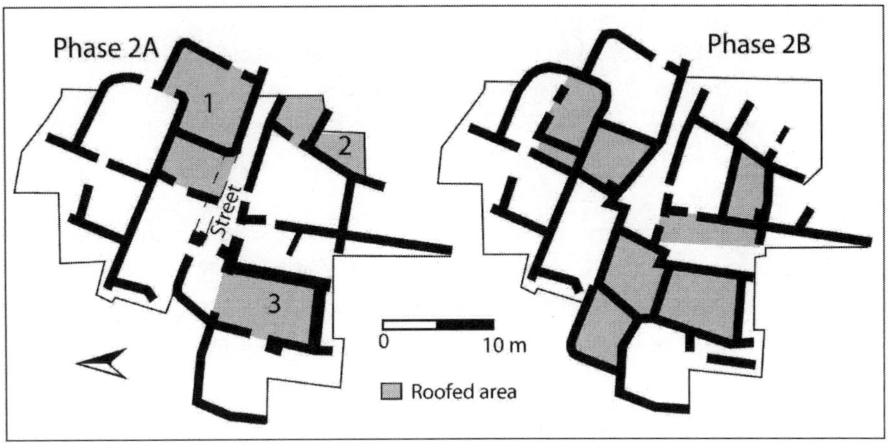

Figure 7.6: Plans of Numayra Phases 2A and 2B, showing the adjustments in roofed and unroofed room locations and alteration in living space (after Chesson and Goodale 2014: 123, fig. 4; 124, fig. 5).

3) consisting of a roofed structure with four pillars, and three unroofed spaces to its east and south; this structure contained no cooking installations or materials in the Phase 2A level, nor other indicators such as tools or silos suggesting domestic residence (Chesson 2012: 59). Chesson does not discuss household family constitution at Numayra, but the dwelling spaces are sufficient for the housing of extended or multiple nuclear family co-residents.

In the slightly later Phase 2B, the ritual complex was converted to a domestic unit. A new floor was installed, as were tabuns, storage vessels (sunk into the floor), mortars, and storage pits. In Phase 2A, the roofed room had a wide doorway leading off a courtyard that accessed a street. In Phase 2B, access to the street was blocked, the courtyard was roofed, and a new roofed room was built to the south. In addition to the cooking and storage areas introduced into this unit, a significant collection of stone tools appeared (Chesson 2012: 59–60). In the other two Phase 2B residential units, architectural changes were also undertaken. In both cases, previously unroofed courtyard areas were wholly or partially roofed, while areas that had been roofed in Phase 2A were converted to courtyard spaces. At least one new room was created in each remodeled unit within the complex (Chesson 2012: 67). Furthermore, the relocation of the roofed spaces removed them from direct access to the street or courtyard entrance; doorways into roofed areas were moved to the point farthest from public access.

In addition to the conversion of the ritual space to a domestic unit, there were two other major changes between Phases 2A and 2B at Numayra. The first concerns the ratio of roofed to unroofed space: in Phase 2A, there were five roofed rooms equaling an area of approximately 160 m^2, and 12 open spaces covering approximately 360 m^2; in Phase 2B, roofed area increased to eight rooms and ca. 230 m^2, and though unroofed spaces increased to 14, area decreased to ca. 315 m^2 (Chesson 2012: 69). The number of roofed spaces increased somewhat, and the area that was roofed became substantially greater. The other notable change was in the location and type of built-in storage receptacles.

Numayra residents built three main types of storage devices: pits that usually held sunken ceramic vessels; clay or stone silos; and above-ground bins built of stone and mudbrick. The number and area of storage pits decreased substantially from Phase 2A to 2B, and the use of silos and bins increased greatly; the number of bins grew from three to eight, and the area of silo storage increased from 4.83 to 6.76 m^2. In addition, storage facilities, especially pits containing vessels, were moved to roofed areas in the Phase 2B period (Chesson 2012: 69–70). In general, the only types of storage facilities regularly found in the unroofed areas were either pits without vessels or the occasional clay bin. There are several possible interpretations for these changes. Chesson notes that the social structure of Early Bronze Numayra has been interpreted as largely heterarchical (2003, 2007) in that social differentiation was present but status levels were not dramatically divergent. The changes in the roofed/unroofed spaces and storage practices may indicate a growth in population and a subtle shift in community relations and the strategies involving the sharing of resources (Chesson 2012: 70). An arrival of migrants might have initiated the desire to more visibly define ownership of surpluses and to protect storage areas containing more valuable commodities and foodstuffs. While this household response would have been to external forces (the arrival of migrants), it also reflects internal behaviors: the reorganization of the architectural and built storage spaces. The latter could be the first steps in the emergence of more systematic social differentiation; those who had greater surplus may have begun storing it in less accessible places, and those who had less might have felt an even greater need to protect their belongings and resources. Several other studies (Greenberg 2002; Joffee 1993; Paz 2012) indicate these types of phenomena were occurring in the Early Bronze Age across the Levantine region.

The Numayra example offers insight into how one scholar examined, at the household level, changes in socioeconomy and possibly in wealth differentiation in a community undergoing a transition to greater population and internal complexity. The following section focuses specifically on methodologies to determine whether ranking and status differentiation exists within a community, expressed at the household level.

Households: Determining Rank, Status, and Wealth Differentiation

The use of architecture in the quest to define differing levels of social status in a community is discussed in great detail in chapter 9. For this reason, methods for determining rank, status, and wealth at the household level are only lightly explored here. This discussion corresponds to the notion of the household as a "political entity" as advanced by Carballo and Nash, above.

Jeanne Arnold (2006), drawing on Richard Blanton's (1994) major work on households, describes the indicators of rank that can be expressed in domestic structures. These would include, as described in chapter 9, the amount of labor invested in building the house, the size of structures, the extra elaboration of public areas of the house such as entrance areas or interior areas that may not be visible to visitors (but is clear that elaboration is *there* whether visitors see it or not), and the location of the house. For instance, in Pacific Northwest Coast plank house settlements such as those described above, larger houses in strategic locations nearer the beach or rivers are likely homes of high-ranking members of the settlement such as the chief. Arnold also reminds readers that equally important indicators of status and wealth are the household contents (2006: 274). As an example, she cites her own work on Chumash houses on the Channel Islands off the California coast. As determined from ethnographic and archaeological data, these communities of complex hunter-gatherers featured residents with hierarchically ranked status. Houses, however, were not built for permanent use but were pole-and-thatch huts without substantial elaboration. Those that were larger did not necessarily belong to the higher-status members but may have simply housed larger families. Wealth and status was displayed in the form of beautifully crafted canoes and household contents of trade goods and valuable foods (Arnold 2006). As Arnold's study shows, the architectural evidence may be the least important in determining rank among households in a community.

Lynne Sullivan (1995) asks some of these questions about 14th- to 17th-century CE communities in eastern Tennessee, also discussed in chapter 6 in regard to kinship structure. The thrust of her argument revolves around whether houses and households can be significant diachronic indicators of changes in social stratification and ranking in communities. Sullivan examined sites in three partially overlapping cultural phases in the Tennessee valley regions: the Dallas phase (14th–16th centuries); the Mouse Creek phase (15th–16th centuries); and the largely egalitarian Overhill Cherokee phase of the 18th century. Scholars have devised two models to describe the patterns of social complexity over these centuries and phases: the "developmental sequence" and the "political complexity" models (Sullivan 1995: 101). The developmental sequence sees the Mouse Creek phase as transitional between the more socially and economically hierarchical Dallas phase and the more egalitarian Overhill Cherokee. The political complexity model sees the Dallas and Mouse Creek phases as generally similar with regard to ranking and hierarchy, and as linked components in a larger chiefdom in the region.

Sullivan examined several lines of evidence at sites in the three phases, including house styles, sizes, contents, and location, the presence and location of public buildings, and burial data. While burials were an important indicator, the architectural evidence was actually of great use in determining which model might best explain potential cultural change. In all three phases, populations built two adjacent residences, a summer and a winter structure. Though there was some differentiation in shape—Overhill Cherokee sites feature circular winter houses and rectangular summer houses, whereas Dallas and Mouse Creek sites feature rectilinear structures for both seasons—most houses across the three phases were similar in labor investment. Production and consumption activities and use of space suggest that each set of paired structures constituted a household unit; the more spacious houses contained larger extended families, and smaller ones may have housed groups more in line with nuclear families with a few additional kin members. Though there was some differentiation in house size, particularly at Mouse Creek sites, Sullivan notes that the house contents, locations of houses, and labor all suggest that dwelling size was reflective of family size rather than wealth or status in the community (1995: 109–14). An exception to this is some dwellings at the Dallas phase type-site of Toqua.

The strongest indicators of socioeconomic differentiation across the phases are the location, size, and contents of a set of dwellings at Toqua and the presence and location of public buildings at sites in all three phases. At Toqua, structures were built atop two mounds; Mound A and an adjacent structure sit in the western half of the community next to a large open plaza. The structures on Mound A and those adjacent are interpreted as public buildings or "dual-purpose" structures that served as high-status residences and public gathering areas (Sullivan 1995: 116). Further, a group of houses at Toqua, located near Mound A, were on average larger in area and contained better cuts of meat, greater quantities of corn, and burials with greater numbers of high-status goods (Sullivan 1995: 114). The larger and smaller houses at Mouse Creek sites appear to equate more to the number of household members than to wealth and status. A single exception to this was a winter structure at a Mouse Creek site known as Ledford Island (with no associated summer structure); this was the largest of the dwellings and had a prepared floor along with a greater number of painted ceramics (Sullivan 1995: 114). It is possible that this dwelling belonged to a higher-ranking family at Ledford Island. At Overhill Cherokee phase sites, there was little differentiation in the size of winter/summer dwellings and no evident elite houses. A "summer pavilion" at one site was located near the central plaza and appears to have been open and entirely public in nature (Sullivan 1995: 105–16).

For all three phases, Sullivan was able to use comparisons of house sizes, in combination with house contents and location, to assess the relative level of socioeconomic differentiation. The presence and location of public buildings were also an important factor. Sullivan concludes that the developmental sequence model best describes the three phases: the Dallas phase was more stratified, featuring elites who lived in high-ranking houses in a defined area of the community and possibly controlled public/ritual space; this gave way to less socioeconomic differentiation in Mouse Creek settlements, in which perhaps only one or two moderately higher-status households existed but were not located adjacent to public buildings. By the time of the Overhill Cherokee phase, very little differentiation in household ranking existed, and community areas were open and available to all. Though house contents and burials were critical lines of evidence, the full range of social change throughout these three phases could not have been as fully discerned without the significant architectural evidence.

Lily Singer-Avitz (2011) uses some of the same types of data streams to assess the level of social stratification at eighth-century BCE Tel Beersheba in the southern Levant. Like the roughly contemporary site of Tell En-Naṣbeh discussed above, a typical house is either a four-roomed or three-roomed structure. Public buildings stand at the center of Tel Beersheba, and the entire city is surrounded by a significant defensive wall. Singer-Avitz examined houses, including their size, layout, and contents, in most residential quarters of the city as well as in the city center. The four-roomed houses had far greater variations in size (generally 60–100 m^2 in area) and contents (both in terms of built-in features and portable material items) than did the three-roomed structures (Singer-Avitz 2011). Some of the four-roomed houses had staircases suggesting the use of the roof, or possibly a second story; one house showed evidence of ceramic production, including a kiln, and many houses contained tools associated with weaving and spinning. All four-roomed houses had evidence of food preparation and consumption. Singer-Avitz was able to determine, therefore, that four-roomed houses corresponded to individual household units engaged in production and consumption activities. She then examined the ceramic assemblage in each of the four-roomed houses, paying particular attention to the number of serving vessels; the selection of these specific vessel types rests on her assumption that wealthier households would engage in more frequent hosting activities (2011: 297–98). Singer-Avitz found a correspondence between the larger four-roomed houses and a higher number of serving vessels, suggesting that there was a differentiation in social status in these household units. Furthermore, two of the larger houses containing the greatest number of serving vessels were in the city center, near the public buildings; many of the smaller four-roomed houses, with fewer serving vessels, were at the settlement's periphery resting against the city wall. Singer-Avitz notes that in ancient Near Eastern cities, elites often lived in houses near the city center (see Steadman 2011 as well).

Equally interesting was Singer-Avitz's analysis of the smaller three-roomed houses, most of which were roughly 30 m^2 in size. With the exception of only two structures close to the central quarter, these houses featured little in the way of storage vessels and contained no built-in features associated with cooking or baking; nor were there grinding stones or other items associated with food preparation (Singer-Avitz 2011: 290). The ceramic assemblage consisted of a few storage jars and a basic number of serving bowls. There were no items associated with textile production, and none of these houses featured stairways. Singer-Avitz believes that these houses, all located along the outer city wall, were not inhabited by standard household units but instead served as housing for servants of the city, perhaps soldiers or other functionaries whose food and other needs were provided by the government (2011: 290). The evidence of consumption only, with no signs of production, was ascertained by the analysis of housing size, style, layout and location, and room contents. At eighth-century BCE Tel Beersheba, some houses—the smallest ones—were meant simply as "containers" for those serving the city.

The Social Household

As noted above, one of the complaints leveled at the household archaeology methodologies developed in the 1980s was the focus on socioeconomy without consideration of the many elements that constitute a household, including gendered labor, ethnicity, religious practice, and identity (Allison 1999a; Chesson 2012; Hendon 1996; Souvatzi 2008). The methodologies so appropriate for defining production and consumption ignored the presence of the individual household members; households appeared static and lifeless rather than composed of men and women of all ages with different agendas and needs, a range of responsibilities, and perhaps desires for a different life. Beginning in the 1990s, a wide-ranging new literature began to emerge that took into account the gender, ethnicity, religion, and other social elements of household inhabitants. This section treats the more symbolic (Carballo 2011) or "structuralist" (Nash 2009) elements within household archaeology—namely, the attempt to reveal the individual household inhabitants.

Gender in the Household

Issues of gender have inspired the largest numbers of studies treating social issues within the household unit. Ruth Tringham (1991a, 1991b), among others, brought to light the need to inject gender into the archaeological study of households and human behavior, and many archaeologists followed suit. It became clear that "finding" gender in the household includes only one or two steps beyond the definition of production and consumption activities. Most household and gender studies seek to acquire the following types of information: what spaces in the household were typically occupied by different genders; what types of labor were performed by different genders (and where); and what contributions to the production and consumption activities of the household did these offer (e.g., Hegmon, Ortman, and Mobley-Tanaka 2000; Hendon 2010; Nelson 2004; Wright 1991; Yanagisako 1979; and see chapter 8). Related to these is the question of whether production activities were limited to subsistence actions relevant only to household inhabitants, or consisted of more specialized crafts traded across the community and beyond (e.g., Brumfiel and Earle 1987; Costin 1991, 1996; Crown 2000; Nelson 2004; Nelson, Glowacki, and Smith 2002; Wright 1996). By recovering what women and men did within the dwelling and for the household unit, archaeologists not only can create "households with faces" (Tringham 1991a) but can address, at least at a basic level, gender and status within a community and society.

Singer-Avitz (2011) demonstrated the importance of gender-based analysis in her study of Tel Beersheba households (discussed above). At a basic level, she inferred that three-roomed houses were not inhabited by traditional household units and may have been the abode of single-gender occupants, likely males, based on the absence of food processing and production tools and spaces. In the four-roomed houses, she noted that such equipment and spaces, including grinding stones and ovens, were not located in a single room or at the back, but were sometimes in the central large room, in side long rooms, or in front rooms (2011: 287). This implies that women, if they were associated with these tasks, were not relegated to particular (segregated) spaces in the dwelling but had free range within it. Her analyses offer insight into the gendered use of space across the eighth-century BCE Tel Beersheba household unit.

In an earlier study, Hendon (1997) had similar success in identifying women's spaces in a Maya settlement and in assessing women's relative status within the household based on their level of contribution to the economic success of the household and community. Using Maya depictions of women's work on ceramic vessels and in other art forms, Hendon was able to identify two major types of female-based productive activities at the site of Sepulturas in the Copan Valley of Guatemala (ca. CE 600–1000). Women were responsible for food preparation activities, and thus the location of grinding stones, ceramics associated with cooking and serving, and cooking aids such as griddles and braziers were key indicators for these activities; women were also the textile producers, making spinning and weaving tools such as whorls and needles important indicators (Hendon 1997). Most of these domestic tasks took place not within the dwellings but in the patios adjacent to them.

Hendon examined three separate areas at Sepulturas, one consisting of 15 residential compounds, a second with three, and a final one with a single compound (1997: 35). In all three areas, items associated with food production were found in widespread locations across the patios and other residential areas; there did not seem to be a precise area designated for food preparation or cooking. Tools associated with textile production were also found across the external areas of the compounds, although not in as wide a distribution; and they were not found in the residential area consisting of a single compound. Two other sets of data provided Hendon with insight into women's status and the importance of their activities at Sepulturas. First, food and textile-related tools were found in areas where stone tool production and shell and bone working evidently also took place; these activities may have been carried out by men or women depending on the task. Second, extensive evidence from archaeological, pictorial, and ethnographic sources attests to the importance of food and textiles in Maya ritual activities (Hendon 1997). These data allowed Hendon to assert that women in the Maya Sepulturas community were not confined to interior spaces but had their choice of work spaces in more public and exterior places. She also suggested that the women in multiple compounds containing textile production tools were of higher status than the women in the single compound, who lacked such tools (1997: 44–45). In a similar vein to Hendon's work, a variety of studies in the Americas have very successfully employed the combination of spatial and material culture analyses to differentiate between gendered activities in the household and to assess changes in identity, status, and power between men and women in prehistoric settings (e.g., Brumfiel and Robin 2008; Hastorf 1991; Hendon 2002, 2007; McCafferty and McCafferty 1998; Sweely 1999a; and see studies in Nelson 2006; Roth 2010).

Following the proliferation of work in the Americas, the pursuit of household and gender data in other regions of the world has emerged in Europe and the Near East (e.g., Bolger 2003, 2008; Nevett 1999; Souvatzi 2008, 2012; Webb 2002; Zubrow, Audouze, and Enloe 2010). At the Bronze Age site of Marki on Cyprus (ca. 2350–1850 BCE), archaeologists investigated changes in social relations as a community faced socioeconomic changes and increasing population (Frankel and Webb 2012). Over the course of this period, nine temporal phases were identified, and at least 33 different household units existed at various stages within these occupational levels. When Marki was first settled in ca. 2350 BCE, the community consisted of perhaps a few dozen people. Early on, the placement of ovens and storage facilities in outdoor and unroofed areas, and the location of food preparation tools such as grinding stones, suggest that several dwellings, probably inhabited by related kin groups, cooperated as a single household unit (Frankel and Webb 2012: 490). By 2300 BCE, however, this more communal use of space had begun to change, with ovens, storage devices, and food preparation materials moving into enclosed courtyards or even into interior spaces. By 2100 BCE, in the middle phases of the occupation, when the population may have quadrupled, the amount of unroofed space was shrinking while enclosed interior space was increasing (Frankel and Webb 2012: 487). Single dwellings equated to single household units; no longer were the occupants of several dwellings cooperating in either production or consumption activities. All storage facilities had been moved indoors by ca. 2100 BCE, and even when ovens were in outdoor but enclosed courtyards, screens or partitions served to further block lines-of-sight by passersby (Frankel and Webb 2012: 483), effectively concealing what, and how much, was being cooked. Also changing were the numbers of activities undertaken in each household; in addition to food-related tasks, crafts such as textiles, stone tool production, wood working, hide preparation, and ceramic production were carried out within the dwellings. Some of these activities, in the early phase of the settlement, may have been communally based, but by the middle phases, each household engaged in its own production and consumption activities.

Frankel and Webb note that these changes in household structure and the use of space had ramifications for tasks performed by both men and women, but perhaps particularly for women involved in food-based and textile production activities (2012: 489–91). What once may have been cooperative activities across several houses became individualized and privatized within each dwelling and household unit. Tasks were also moved indoors or were blocked from public view, more effectively segregating public from private space but also limiting social interaction among households. As craft production activities increased, there may have been a growing requirement of women's (and men's) labor, demanding longer work hours to complete a growing number of tasks. Frankel and Webb do not necessarily equate these changes in the use of space and performance of gendered labor with a decrease in women's status. As craft specialization became a normal and perhaps necessary element in the successful household unit, women's labor may have become more rather than less important, and their relative position in the household may have remained stable or even been elevated.

Interestingly, the appearance of anthropomorphic figurines in Marki houses around 2100 BCE suggests some change in the social identity of women. Most figurines depict females in attitudes of work or with infants; representations of women in two of their important roles, as producers of subsistence and of progeny, may speak not to a decrease in their status but rather to the recognition of their essential role in household survival. Frankel and Webb stress that the movement of women and their activities into interior spaces does not necessarily signal the segregation of their activities from other household members or the diminishing of their social status and household position (2012: 491). The interior spaces in which women performed tasks were places where other activities, such as stone working possibly performed by males, also occurred. The figurines that feature women's work rather than men's speaks to a well-defined sexual division of labor and perhaps to the primacy of women's work in the Bronze Age Marki household.

Revealing Ethnicity, Housing Religion

As noted several times, identifying ethnicity and retrieving identity in the archaeological past is a very tricky endeavor (see studies in Casella and Fowler 2005 and Ross and Steadman 2010 for discussion). However, it is in the area of household archaeology, in which architecture and material culture form critical components for understanding the basic household unit, that ethnicity and sometimes associated identity might be best studied (e.g., Aldenderfer 1993a; Van Gijseghem and Vaughn 2008). Yuval Gadot (2011) demonstrates the potential usefulness of architecture alone in his very detailed analysis of the houses and households at four sites in the Yarkon River valley located along the central coastal plain of Israel; only three sites are discussed in depth here. All sites date to the Iron Age I period (ca.1000–700 BCE) and sit at the intersection of three attested ethnic groups occupying the region at this time: the Philistines to the south, the Canaanites to the north, and the Israelites to the east. Excavations show a mix of material culture from all three ethnic groups at each site, thereby negating the usefulness of this type of evidence for determining ethnic identity. Gadot examined a variety of architectural characteristics, including the placement of dwellings and courtyards, the interior layout of houses, house location within the settlement, and dwelling size and building materials (2011: 160–61). In the earlier phase of the Iron Age I period, dwellings at the site of 'Isbet Ṣartah are arranged around a shared courtyard; all of the structures are one-roomed with adjoining walls and are of roughly the same size (ca. 30 m^2) and configuration. At nearby Aphek, the architectural configuration is very different. A single structure with internal divisions creating at least three spaces—including back rooms—has individual walls and an associated courtyard of roughly 30 m^2; the structure itself has a floor area of ca. 48 m^2 (Gadot 2011: 168). Gadot believes that the multiple dwellings at 'Isbet Ṣartah represent one household unit consisting of an extended family, cooperating in production and consumption activities. At Aphek, the single structure may have also housed a (perhaps smaller) extended family as a single, individualized household unit.

Slightly later in the Iron Age I period, structures altered substantially at 'Isbet Ṣartah. Larger floor areas range from ca. 37 to 50 m^2 for most houses; the largest—with a floor area of 120 m^2—rests at the settlement center. Structures are now of the "four-roomed" style discussed above, and have internal courtyards; most have individual walls, though they are arranged in a belt around the settlement perimeter. The 'Isbet Ṣartah houses likely continued to house extended families. An open courtyard next to the largest central structure has storage silos clearly associated with this house (Gadot 2011: 169, 175). At contemporary Tell Qasile, the largest of the settlements analyzed, two residential areas feature four-roomed houses, the size and placement of which suggest socioeconomic ranking: in Area A, houses ranging from 50 to 64 m^2 in area are located along a street on a hillside; Area C houses range in size from 77 to 92 m^2 and are located near the temple area, with one of the houses sharing a wall with the temple (Gadot 2011: 170). A single structure quite near the temple has a floor area of nearly 140 m^2 and an inner courtyard. The excavators believe Tell Qasile was a pre-planned community while that at 'Isbet Ṣartah grew organically.

Based on the architectural data alone, Gadot suggests that Aphek and Tell Qasile were occupied by a different ethnic group than that at 'Isbet Ṣartah. The earliest settlement at 'Isbet Ṣartah exhibits a very different architectural preference from the other sites: multiple structures arrayed around common courtyards versus individualized homes and courtyard areas. In the earlier Iron Age I period, residents at 'Isbet Ṣartah preferred to live in large extended family household units with separate "living" structures but operating as a single production/consumption unit in most other respects; at Aphek, by contrast, smaller extended and possibly even nuclear families operated as single household units within a single structure. In the later part of the Iron Age I, the introduction of the four-roomed house altered the dwelling structure at "Isbet Ṣartah, but not, according to Gadot, the ethnic makeup or cooperative behaviors of the residents (2011: 180–81). A single family living at the center of 'Isbet Ṣartah was clearly higher ranking than those living at the periphery; this family's ethnic identity may have differed as well. The pre-planned Tell Qasile town had a far greater differentiation in social ranking and demonstrates a significantly different "flavor" in style and layout of houses than was present at the organically developed 'Isbet Ṣartah. Based on previous research at these sites and others in the region, Gadot suggests that Aphek and Tell Qasile were occupied by Philistines; the ethnic identity of 'Isbet Ṣartah may have been Israelite or Canaanite but was, he asserts, different from that of the other two settlements (2011: 181). The Yarkon River settlements demonstrate that a reliance on architectural data alone can be very illustrative in defining ethnic groups as household units in a prehistoric settlement.

Religion as practiced in and around a house or household is discussed in great detail in chapter 10. A single example of religion, as practiced in the now common "four-roomed house" in Israel, demonstrates the significant expansion of traditional "household archaeology" beyond the bounds of socioeconomic analysis. Beth Nakhai (2011) examined household shrines in Iron Age I houses at various sites in Israel and Jordan (and see Nakhai 2001). What is interesting about the ritual installations is that their placement can be, like the location of ovens, hearths, and storage facilities, an indicator of residents in several dwellings cooperating as a single household unit. Furthermore, Nakhai notes that the household shrines existed to address two areas of greatest concern to these ancient inhabitants: sustenance and economic survival, and ongoing health and successful reproduction of the family and lineage (2011: 350). The former is directly related to the basic function of the household unit—production and consumption. In the second case, particularly in the concern for reproduction, we can see another important function as outlined by Wilk and Rathje (1982), that of transmission—in this case, of the house, household, and economic concerns.

Iron Age "cultic corners" in Levantine four-roomed houses are recognized by the presence of built-in furniture such as benches, alcoves or niches, and possibly the placement of stone altars or offering stands. As also noted by Singer-Avitz, above, the presence of figurines depicting women or animals may be present; occasionally, a small clay model of a building that is likely a shrine, in which the deity was considered to dwell, may also be found (Nakhai 2011: 352). Cult corners were not present in every house; according to Nakhai, a cult place in one structure within a cluster of dwellings belonged to the elders of an extended kin group. The kin-based residents of the other houses in the cluster cooperated in rituals, just as they did in production and consumption activities in a multi-dwelling household unit (2011: 355). The location of cultic corners in multiple dwellings, especially independent houses near one another, may thus denote household units with single dwellings. Household shrines in a community may be invaluable indicators of how many dwellings constitute a household unit and perhaps may even help us to discern whether cooperative groups are based on kinship or other relationships.

Conclusion

The preceding discussion illustrates how the field of household archaeology has developed far beyond its original intent of defining the size and spatial configuration of a prehistoric household unit engaged in socioeconomic production and consumption activities. The archaeological quest to delve more deeply into finding the individuals who inhabited those ancient households has been an exciting and often successful journey. In many cases, the discussions coming up in chapters 8 through 10 on architectural approaches to gender, power, and religion are based on more recent investigations into these areas from the household archaeology perspective. It is the recommendation here, then, that the archaeologist interested in architecture and the household not stray too far from the original basic ideas behind the field that came to be known as "household archaeology." The foundational principles in household archaeology are just that, foundational; upon these we can be built an enormous database of individual, household, and community relationships present in the dwellings inhabited by ancient cultures of every age.

Chapter 8
The Gendered House

If this chapter had been written 30 years ago, it would have focused primarily on finding *women* in the archaeological record and secondarily on a more concentrated search for women's spaces. Commensurate with critical works by cultural anthropologists on subjects related to gender issues (e.g., Ardener 1993; Massey 1994; H. Moore 1996; Rosaldo and Lamphere 1974; Sanday 1981; Spain 1992; and ethnographic sources cited below), the field of "gender archaeology" came into full force in the early 1990s (e.g., Gero and Conkey 1991; Gilchrist 1999; Hays-Gilpin and Whitley 1998; Sørensen 2000; Sweely 1999b; Tringham 1991a, 1994; Walde and Willows 1991; Wicker and Arnold 1999; Wright 1996). A short time later, those working in the architectural field engaged in explicitly gender-based studies of buildings and spaces (Ahrentzen 2003; Durning and Wrigley 2000). Gender studies today recognize the presence of women *and* men and that not all cultures (perhaps very few cultures) have a strictly binary view of gender, instead incorporating anthropologies that might include third or androgynous genders (Ashmore 2006; Dowson 2006; Gero and Scatollin 2001; Russell 2005; Stockett 2005; Voss 2000). That archaeological conditions rarely allow investigators to identify *any* type of gendered spaces has not deterred archaeologists from attempting to engender the past. As is the norm in archaeology, it is the material (e.g., artifactual) culture that is the most telltale in endeavors to seek out gendered behavior of the past. The biological record, in the form of botanical and faunal remains, and especially human burials, are also very

Archaeology of Domestic Architecture and the Human Use of Space, by Sharon R. Steadman, 193–218.

fruitful in yielding results regarding men's and women's roles, statuses, and identities. Architecture, then, is not the usual lens through which archaeologists view the gendered past; rather, the material and biological remains associated with the architecture provide the fullest picture. However, architectural settings can sometimes provide startling insights into gendered activities, ideologies, and behaviors, as is shown in this chapter.

Gendered Spaces

For many, including the present author, it was reading Pierre Bourdieu's study of the Berber House (1973) that ignited a full-blown desire to track gendered spaces in the archaeological record. Bourdieu's analysis delved into issues of gender ideology, symbolism, status, and spatiality, all of intense interest to archaeologists working on gender archaeology in the 1990s and later. He described both the male and female areas of the house, contrasting the two in terms of light and darkness, dry and wet, higher and lower. At the seeming intersection of the two sits the weaving loom, an important household symbol and the site of women's work.

Another theoretical framework put forward by Bourdieu, that of *habitus* (1977; see chapter 3), is vital in the search for ancient gendered spaces. *Habitus* suggests that the daily activities and practices carried out by humans create a structure that is passed on from one generation to the next. It is an unconscious shaping of appropriate behavior, including what takes place where, and often dictates when and why activities are carried out in particular contexts at specific times. Thus, spaces become "gendered" because some are where women work or spend time, and others "belong" to the men; there are gender-neutral spaces, private spaces, and so forth, and everyone is aware of these and how to categorize them, not only in their own houses but across their community. The built environment is ideal for the creation of *habitus*, essentially "what buildings do" (Gieryn 2002), since "space serves as a stage for gendered performance: the daily and seasonal repetition of tasks, routines, conversations and personal exchanges" (Gilchrist 1999: 100). This structured space speaks to inhabitants through the generations, producing diachronic norms of behavior (Bille and Sørensen 2015; Donley-Reid 1990; Giddens 1984; Steadman 2010).

If the *habitus* concept—which is not limited to gender, but includes the behavior of groups such as age grades, visitors/residents, differing social ranks, and many others—is consistently applied across the culture and through the generations, the chances of identifying gendered (and other specific) spaces increases exponentially. This chapter focuses on gender and the built environment with an eye to three different areas: the sexual division of labor, gendered seclusion or specialized gender-based buildings, and gender and status, all of which may become archaeologically visible through the generational practice of *habitus*.

The Sexual Division of Labor: Gendered Work Spaces

Tracking the sexual division of labor spatially would seem to be one of the most straightforward of endeavors, since the vast majority of nonindustrial (and industrial) settled cultures possess a sexual division of labor, and tasks are often spatially differentiated. In fact, it is generally the case that space is the facilitator and reinforcement of the sexual division of tasks; it serves to dictate who should work where, and do what. However, though space and gendered tasks are intricately tied, rarely is it the architecture itself that offers the clues to the identity of gendered persons and their work. In fact, some argue that identifying gendered spaces in societies such as hunter-gatherer camps is well-nigh impossible (Isaac 1989; Kent 1998a; but see, e.g., Brumbach and Jarvenpa 1997; Jarvenpa and Brumbach 1999). In general, it is actually the artifacts associated with the tasks and their performers that not only serve as the clues to present-day archaeologists but that also imbue the ancient spaces with their gendered functions. This does not mean that spaces are not constructed in ancient villages without gendered labor in mind (Lawrence and Low 1990); naturally they are, but those spaces often cannot speak to the archaeologist of their gendered nature without the contextual artifacts in place. It is therefore the case that most discussions of gendered spaces and the sexual division of labor rely on activity area research and household archaeology methodology (e.g., Allison 1999c; Ault and Nevett 1999; Hegmon, Ortman, and Mobley-Tanaka 2000; Hendon 2006, 2010; Lawrence 1999; Nelson, Glowacki, and Smith 2002).

The assignment of gender to activity areas and architectural or open spaces requires a first step of allocating certain tasks to specific sexes or genders, the two not always being equal. A great deal of work on this subject (see citations above, and Arnold and Wicker 2001; Crown 2000; Hamilton, Whitehouse, and Wright 2007; Nelson 2004, 2007, 2014; Nelson and Rosen-Ayalon 2002) has identified certain tasks as belonging overwhelmingly to one sex or the other, leaving aside here societies that recognize persons of third and multi-genders, as well as tasks that are variable depending on the culture. A significant amount of cross-cultural ethnographic research (Lowell 1990; Martin and Voorhies 1975; Murdock and Provost 1973; Spain 1992) links food production with women's work, and activities such as hunting and warfare with males. By the same token, activities such as textile, jewelry, and pottery production can be considered "flexible" in that they fall to women in some cultures and to men in others (e.g., Barber 1994).

The arguments for some of these more "universal" sexual divisions of labor are diverse and enduring, and a brief review of some models is useful to the extent that arguments involve spatial assignments. Some of the earliest explanations for what appeared to be a more-or-less universal sexual division of labor rested on biological grounds. The two major biological factors regularly cited were that men possessed greater strength and aerobic ability, and that women were, of course, the bearers of children. Therefore, tasks requiring strength and endurance, such as hunting, warfare, and possibly construction work, were relegated to men, while women performed work associated with child care (Brown 1970; Friedl 1975; Murdock and Provost 1973). Women, therefore, became the processors of food and keepers of the household fires. Another biological argument revolved around expendability; women, who provide the next generation, were less expendable than men, and thus the latter could do more dangerous work such as hunting or fighting (Brown 1970; White, Burton, and Brudner 1977). Other arguments for the sexual division of labor involve "efficiency," in that a balanced diet (plants and meat) ensured reproductive capability and healthier offspring; and as it was difficult for one person to be responsible for both dietary requirements, meat acquisition fell to men and plants to women (Hurtado et al. 1992; Lee and de Vore 1968). Agriculture has also been cited as a cause: intensive farming required extensive labor, which was accomplished by males; the considerable secondary processing of field crops after the harvest was carried out in the home by the women (Boserup 1970; Burton and White 1984; Ember 1983; Martin and Voorhies 1975). There is another area of scholarly debate, kicked off by discussion appearing in Michelle Rosaldo and Louise Lamphere's book *Women, Culture, and Society* in 1974, that suggests the sexual division of labor, and women's association with the domestic sphere, emanates from cultural structures rather than biological ones, and that male domination and women's inferior status plays a large role in such spatial assignments. This is discussed in much greater detail below in the "Gender and Status" section.

The several case studies offered here demonstrate the importance of reliable ethnography and ethnoarchaeological work (Weedman 2006) when attempting spatial analysis based on the sexual division of labor. While it might be "safe" to infer that domestic items such as tools associated with food production and storage, or artifacts considered as "typically feminine" such as jewelry, or items associated with beautification such as unguent jars or cosmetics paraphernalia unambiguously define female space within a structure, there are many activities that cannot automatically be assigned to one gender or another. Quite challenging is the archaeological investigation of "gray area" tasks and whether they fall naturally to one gender or the other.

The production of clothing, cloth, and other fiber products (such as baskets and mats) for use within the household is often attributed to women, especially since the materials associated with textile production are usually found in or near the home (Figure 8.1). Elizabeth Barber (1994), using a host of archaeological data, attributes textile production almost solely to women beginning with the European Palaeolithic age and extending down to the Bronze and Iron Ages of the Mediterranean cultures. Palaeolithic "fiber arts," with the possible exception of hunting nets, are attributed to women by other scholars as well (Adovasio, Soffer, and Page 2007). In Mesoamerica and South America, pictorial and ethnographic evidence establishes fairly firmly that women were the textile producers in the ancient cultures of these regions (Brumfiel 1991; Costin

Figure 8.1: Artistic rendering of weaving inside the home, a use of space that perhaps made this area the "women's space" within the built environment (drawing by Corrina Petit).

1993, 1996; Hamann 1997; McCafferty and McCafferty 1998). Sarah Nelson (2004: 84–87) summarizes some of the worldwide evidence for the association of textile production with women's work. At this author's own site in Turkey, Çadır Höyük, evidence suggests that textile production took place on the roof of the house and in the partially covered courtyard; in the mixed herding and agricultural economy of prehistoric Çadır (ca. 3600 BCE), it seems logical to infer that the time-consuming activity of weaving fell to the women, who were more likely to be spending longer hours in the household.

Another of the "gray areas" of activity attribution is that of ceramic production. In many cultures, this is considered women's work, particularly as pots are so closely associated with food production. Charles Higham's work at the Southeast Asian site of Khok Phanom Di (ca. 2000 BCE) suggests that women were the potters in this hunting and gathering culture (Higham 2002a, 2002b; and see Marshall 1985 on the Lapita culture). His evidence for this comes not from domestic architecture but from the burials: women's burials contained complete pots as well as the tools associated with ceramic production. Male burials contained other artifacts that appear to have been associated with their hunting activities. The terrible preservation conditions at Khok Phanom Di made the recovery of significant architectural data impossible; the burial evidence might have allowed Higham to assign the pottery production locations as "women's work areas" had they been preserved. However, the attribution of ceramic production to one gender over another can be quite complicated, as the production of pottery is a multiphase process, beginning with the acquisition of the clay, the shaping and subsequent decoration of the pot, and the firing of the vessel. Both genders may cooperate in these activities (Wright 1991), and thus assuming ceramic production is a single-gender activity may not reflect the total picture in many cultures.

At Çadır Höyük in Turkey, for instance, the courtyard south and east of the one mentioned above contained the elements of what is likely a handmade pottery production process, including a pit full of raw clay balls, burnishing stones, ocher for decorating the pot's surface, and a kiln (Steadman et al. 2013). Given that these were located in a courtyard that also held cooking vessels and hearths, it is tempting to suggest that the household ceramics at the site were made by the women who also produced the food. However, who acquired the clay? And further, in the next courtyard over. there was evidence of lithic production (Steadman, McMahon, and Ross 2007), which, if stone tool production was a male task, would highlight courtyard areas as spaces where both genders spent significant time. Might women have been cooking while men produced the ceramics? Unlike the burial data from Khok Phanom Di, the evidence at this site does not yet speak loudly enough to assign specific tasks to specific genders.

Hide-working would perhaps seem to be a task that might naturally fall into the realm of males, given that men are usually the managers of the herds and draft animals. However, there is ample evidence that this is yet another of those "gray areas" (Figure 8.2). In fact, a fairly extensive literature demonstrates that hide-working is a female task in many cultures (see Frink and Weedman 2005; Weedman 2006). Kevin Gilmore (2005) offers a concise description of the various steps involved in hide processing among the prehistoric (ca. 3350 BCE–CE 1190) Great Plains hunting groups in Colorado. Using ethnographic data and the location of hide-working tools at a prehistoric site, Gilmore argues that primarily men hunted the large game, but women produced the stone tools necessary for hide-working (mainly scrapers) and were the main users of these tools. He traces the entire sequence from initial hide preparation to the sewing of moccasins as belonging to the women's task list (2005: 18–31). Lita Webley (2005) found that among the pastoralist Khoekhoen of southern Africa, women were not only traditionally the hide-workers but that they reaped great economic benefit and social status from their work. As scholarship on the sexual division of labor has moved beyond the "assumption" phase in which all work with animals was automatically relegated to males (Hodgson 2000), it has become clear that hide processing often fell to the women of the settlement, as did, on occasion, the fashioning of the associated tools.

Textbooks and museum displays tend to assume that a task that "naturally" fell to males was the knapping of chipped stone tools. Not so, says scholarship of the last several decades (Bird 1993; Conkey and Spector 1984; Frink and Weedman 2005; Nelson 2004; Sassaman 1992; Weedman 2005, 2006, 2010). Kathryn Weedman (2010; and see Brandt and Weedman 2002) uses the Konso women of eastern Africa, skilled flake stone tool producers, to suggest that archaeologists need to rethink Palaeolithic stone tool production as possibly falling into the realm of women's work. Joan Gero (1991) offered a strong argument that prehistoric women made some of the stone tools used in tasks

Figure 8.2: Artistic rendering of hide-working at the author's site of Çadır Höyük (drawing by Mary Jean Hughes).

typically considered women's work, such as in food preparation, textile (and hide) production, and in some cases pottery production, because they knew what they needed and how it should work. Gero makes the further point that flint-knapping can happen in or near the household (1991: 171), as is certainly the case at Çadır Höyük, where someone, perhaps in the winter, knapped tools in the courtyard near the hearth, with his or her back leaning up against the house wall (Steadman, McMahon, and Ross 2007).

Gero examined the spatial distribution of various types of stone tools at Huaricoto in Peru over the course of the 2,500 years of occupation (ca. 2000 BCE–CE 600). She noted that earlier in the occupational sequence, there was a significant percentage of bifaces and projectile points, many made from imported sources, found in the ceremonial complex. Later in the sequence, when the ceremonial complex was no longer a functional factor in the community, flake tools of local materials (made with expedience rather than detail) predominated in village houses. Based on careful statistical and spatial analyses, Gero (1991) suggests that the larger and more ceremonial tools may have been fashioned by men for use or presentation in rituals held at the ceremonial center; the smaller, expedient, local-resource tools used in household contexts may have been made by Huaricoto's women to assist in their daily tasks. In sum, then, the assignment of a lithic production activity area as "men's space" should no longer be considered a "given" in archaeological methodology—yet another demonstration of the difficulty of undertaking the spatial assessment of the sexual division of labor in the archaeological record.

Margaret Nelson and colleagues (Nelson, Glowacki, and Smith 2002) used ethnographic data to help identify gendered task performance in prehispanic Maya households of Guatemala. Present-day San Mateo Ixtatan is a farming community located near salt mines that contribute to the village economy. In the past, San Mateo residents eschewed agriculture in favor of reliance on income from the salt resources, but this became too risky after the 1960s (Nelson, Glowacki, and Smith 2002: 134). Now households rely on maize agriculture supplemented by black beans, eggs, some meat, and a few other subsistence goods. Maize is processed by the women using manos and metates within the dwellings; farmlands are typically located next to the house, with occasional additional fields located farther away from the village. In addition to food production, women engage in the production of crafts, which are sold (usually by men) in local markets. Crafts produced include textiles/embroidery, ceramics, various foods, and candles (Nelson, Glowacki, and Smith 2002: 136). The processing of salt and food occurs inside the dwelling, while ceramic and textile work may take place either inside the house or just outside on the patios. Tools associated with each of these activities are found in the locations where they are conducted. Using the ethnographic data, "women's spaces" could be identified in archaeological sites based on the artifactual remains. Certain interior areas of the house and possibly part or all of the patio may have been devoted to women's labor, occupied primarily by women of the household. The goal of Nelson's study was to determine whether "high-volume" craft production households were wealthier than those engaged only in farming, thus showing how identifying the sexual division of labor beyond just acquiring the knowledge of "who did what where" contributes to the understanding of ancient societies.

As noted above, defining the spatiality of the sexual division of labor comes not from the architecture itself, or rarely so, but from the material culture contained within the walls. Deciding which sex or gender practiced a particular task can entail quite a leap of faith. The use of ethnography, as demonstrated consistently here, is invaluable if direct analogy or even indirect analogy between a living population and an archaeological one is possible. Burial data can also provide insights, as was demonstrated by the allocation of ceramic production tools to the women at Khok Phanom Di. Goods that would seem gender-specific (e.g., weapons of war? unguent jars?) in spatial association with task-oriented tools might also offer clues as to gendered labor. Caveats are everywhere: consider the very specific women's versus men's spaces in the Berber house, but the location of the loom would seem to defy the gendered spatiality (Bourdieu 1973). Even when supporting data are favorable, the sexual division of labor and its spatial delineations are a challenging endeavor archaeologically.

Beyond the "gray area," tasks that vacillate from one gender to another depending on the culture, there is the archaeological bias of what is excavated and thus analyzed. As Julie Lowell (1990) and others have pointed out, it might often look as if women do all the work and men none of it. If men's work is in the agricultural fields or pastures, the mines and quarries, the surrounding forests and waterways, and women's work is in and near the dwelling, archaeologists are far more likely to see the latter's work than that of the former; men's work places can then only be speculated upon, not confirmed. Eighteenth-century colonists who first encountered Cherokee villages in the summer months believed the women to be enslaved to the men; men's work of hunting had largely been completed by the warmer months, and women's work of agriculture and craft production was at its peak intensity (Purdue 1998). By the same token, some might argue that women do indeed perform the majority of work! Jane Peterson's book (2002) on the Near Eastern osteological record suggests women accomplished a variety of activities while men performed a more narrow range of tasks. Another study on the osteological record of skeletons retrieved at Çatal Höyük in Turkey and Abu Hureyra in Syria examined "sitting and lounging patterns" (Molleson 1994, 2007). Evidence suggests women were often posed in task-oriented positions—for instance, on their knees poised over grain grinders—while men's skeletal details showed "lounging" attitudes in which they squatted flat on their feet in a resting position (Figure 8.3). Regrettable as it is to write, architecture may be the least useful type of evidence when attempting to define the sexual division of labor. Fortunately, this is not the case for all gender-based spatial analyses, as the remainder of this chapter demonstrates.

The Architecture of Sexual Seclusion and Segregation

Beyond the spatial elements associated with the sexual division of labor are the spaces designated as male or female for more symbolic or ideological reasons. These include, for instance, buildings dedicated to childbirth and menses, men's houses into which women may not enter, sexually segregated homes, and the seclusion of women within the home. The reasons behind prescriptions for sexually separated space are manifold and are briefly discussed below. In many cases, sexual seclusion and segregation is dictated by cultural beliefs that revolve around perceived attributes accorded to men, women, or both, that require regulation through the physical separation of the sexes. In other cultures, the desire to protect women from culturally inadvisable social interaction (e.g., between women and non-kin males) led to architectural designs that precluded contact and even visual interaction within a dwelling or compound.

Figure 8.3: Artistic rendering of women's work at prehistoric sites such as Abu Hureyra in Syria, where osteological analysis indicates that women were often in work positions and the men in lounging positions (drawing by Corrina Petit).

Women's Structures

The existence of separate structures to which women retired during their menses or for childbirth is rather common, according to the ethnographic record (Buckley and Gottlieb 1988; Douglas 1966; Montgomery 1974; Ortner and Whitehead 1981; Paige and Paige 1981; Sanday 1981; Schlegel 1972; van de Walle and Renne 2001). Ethnography has largely eschewed the notion that menstrual seclusion, serving as a tool of male domination, placed an unwanted burden on women; in fact, menstrual structures appear commonly in matrilineal and matrilocal societies (Galloway 1997; Gottlieb 2009; Powers 1980; Stewart and Strathern 2002). The reasons behind the practice of menstrual seclusion differ depending on cultural beliefs. Mary Douglas (1966) and others characterize the practice as a manifestation of "purity" versus "pollution," in that women, during childbirth or their menses, exist in a separate category within their cultures. This condition has been described variously as possessing a powerful magic or aura that might affect male performance (in daily tasks, warfare, etc.) or could otherwise affect societal members who are not in the same category. Menstruating or postpartum women are therefore excused from their usual tasks, commonly for a few weeks (Sanday 1981: 104–6), and they reside in a structure designated for this purpose. The ubiquity of menstrual restrictions and actual seclusion in the present-day ethnographic record suggests that similar symbolic and spatial behaviors existed in the past, although for a variety of reasons, the existence of such structures go largely unremarked in the archaeological discipline. Only a handful of archaeological reports, several noted here, specifically describe the possible existence of menstrual huts (see also Crown 1985). In part, identifying structures as specialized specifically for women's uses can be difficult, as such structures may look largely domestic and thus no different from a "regular" dwelling; another challenge is that such structures might be located some distance from the main residential area outside the excavation area.

Jesse Morin's study of the Keatley Creek site in western Canada (2010; and see Hayden 2000a, 2000b) intentionally examined structures at the settlement's periphery in order to determine their possible ritual use. The Keatley Creek culture dates to the Plateau Horizon (ca. 2400–1200 BP) and consists of complex hunter-gatherers (Hayden 2005; Morin 2010; and see discussion in chapter 4). Morin used a set of criteria developed by Hayden and Adams (2004) to analyze whether any of the peripheral buildings might have served as menstrual seclusion structures. The criteria for defining these structures were developed based on ethnographic research in the area and archaeological data from sites excavated in worldwide contexts (Hayden and Adams 2004; Morin 2010). As regards Keatley Creek–style menstrual seclusion structures, Morin expected a small building (ca. 3 m diameter) with a central pit, ritual artifacts, evidence of a limited diet, a location far from the village center, and limited evidence of domestic activity (2010: 614). Morin then chose a specific structure (ST 106) at the settlement's periphery for close analysis and found that the artifacts and size of the structure more closely corresponded with a location dedicated to ritual feasting than to ritual seclusion. There is the distinct possibility, however, that peripheral structures other than ST 106 might have served women during their menses. While this example offers a case of "negative evidence" for the identification of a menstrual seclusion structure, it does outline the methodology used by one investigator to acknowledge the possible existence of such a building.

Patricia Galloway (1997) adds to the list of attributes a menstrual seclusion structure might embody. Using ethnographic data and oral traditions, Galloway notes that the practice of menstrual seclusion found in indigenous cultures in the southeastern United States may reflect practices of the prehistoric Mississippian culture (ca. CE 800–1500) in the same area. Galloway suggests that Mississippian structures dedicated to women's seclusion would be located at some distance from the main residential area in order to maintain ritual purity. Such structures would likely be positioned near running water for ritual cleansing; and evidence of burned or buried soiled materials might be found within or next to the structures (Galloway 1997). It is exactly these characteristics that define present-day menstrual structures, such as those among the Kalash in Pakistan or the Huaulu of eastern Indonesia (Graziosi 1961; Hoskins 2002; Parkes 1987). Limited evidence for food production would be likely, since it is usually the norm that menstruating women who are secluded are prevented from preparing food for anyone other than themselves. The apparent modern ubiquity of structures dedicated to women's menses seclusion versus the lack of their presence in the archaeological record would seem to suggest that such buildings have either not been found due to their outlying locations or perhaps have been misidentified as simply domestic or perhaps as ritual structures dedicated to some other activity.

A final example comes from Hawaii, where researchers employed ethnographic data to help interpret pre-contact and early contact sites on the Island of Hawaii (Loubser 2009). Previous ethnographic work in the region described a typical *kauhale,* or household complex, which included normal domestic buildings but also other *kapu* structures (translated as "taboo") for avoidance practices. One structure was designated a women's menstrual hut and another was a men's house (*hale mua*), located not far from the main house, where men worked making fishing and farming equipment and where the family's ancestor shrine was kept; women were not allowed in the men's house (see below for further discussion on "men's houses") (Loubser 2009: 6). The menstrual hut (*hale pe'a*) was located quite a distance from the main house and the men's house in order to prevent menstrual "impurity" from affecting the normal daily routine. Women who occupied the menstrual hut were given food by other women of the settlement. While in the hut, women processed *tapa* (bark cloth), so tools associated with this task would be present therein. Ethnographic data suggest that during seclusion women did not consume pork or dog, only shellfish, fish, and non-meat foods. Excavations at over 13 sites, dating between CE 1300 and 1800 offered a range of buildings that fit the descriptions derived from the ethnographic record (Loubser 2009). Archaeologists working at Site 16154 excavated five stone pavements located at the bottom of a steep ridge, away from and invisible to the main *kauhale* household complex (Loubser 2009: 25). There were extensive shellfish remains but little else in the way of domestic items; these structures, based on their size, remote location (possibly near running water), and contents, were identified as *hale pe'a* menstrual seclusion locations. As was the case above, relative isolation, small building size, and the lack of a full complement of domestic goods should be key indicators for any archaeologist who believes menstrual seclusion may have been practiced by the ancient residents of their site.

Men's Structures

Another type of architecture that ensures gendered separation is that of "men's houses," which are also found in a number of cultures, including the Hawaiian *hale mua* above.

Perhaps the best-known examples come from the many cultures that inhabit the island of New Guinea (e.g., Fitz-Patrick and Kimbuna 1983; Herdt 2003; Silverman 2001). These structures are generally found within the village, often near the center, and serve as a meeting place for all initiated men of the village. Though not exclusively, they are often found in cultures with a strong belief in what Mary Douglas (1966) would call "purity and pollution" ideals. Like menstrual structures, men's houses occur when there is a perceived need to separate men from women to preserve men's intrinsic natures, which may be affected by prolonged interaction with women. In cultures with these beliefs, men's houses serve as a sort of "safe house," where men sleep, eat, plan, initiate, and carry out daily tasks. Women live in their own houses, which either they or their husbands build; there they dwell with their children. Husbands come to the house as "visitors" but do not usually stay long, so as to limit the impact of a wife's influence on masculinity. Men take their meals within the men's house, provided by a wife or other household member, which are brought to the door of the house; usually women are strictly forbidden entry into men's houses. Men's houses are found in cultures on most continents (with the possible exception of Australia, where there are places that only men may go, but these are usually not built environments). The characteristics associated with men's houses make them slightly easier to locate and even identify archaeologically than menstrual structures, although ethnographic analogy, as is employed in the Alaskan case study described below, is also a critical resource.

There are a number of characteristics associated with men's houses that render them potentially visible archaeologically. Among Papua New Guinea cultures such as the Sambia, Bundi, and Iatmul, the central "clubhouse" is a large structure usually in the center of the settlement (Bateson 1958; Fitz-Patrick and Kimbuna 1983; Herdt 2003). The material culture in such houses would be distinctly "male" based on ethnographic analogy; weapons and tools abound, as do ritual objects such as ancestral statues and other items displaying elements of traditional mythology and beliefs. Since food is often brought to the clubhouse doorway by a wife or other family member, there is little in the way of cooking materials, suggesting an absence of women on a regular basis.

Such houses are also found among the Shavante of Brazil, but these function more as "bachelor's huts" for unmarried men (Maybury-Lewis 1967: 105–14). After weaning and at the outset of their instructional period, Shavante boys go to live in this hut, traditionally located at the edge of the village but moved near to the mission when Christianity arrived. The boys remain as residents in this hut even after marriage but eventually do take up residence with their wives. The bachelor's hut, however, remains a center of male presence in which women and women's belongings do not intrude.

Mary Ann Larson (1990) used a combination of local ethnographic data and the more general characteristics of men's houses found in worldwide contexts to investigate whether a structure at the Alaskan site of Onion Portage, just inside the Arctic Circle, might be a *kazigi*, or men's house, which functioned as "workshop, male dormitory, ceremonial center, and sweatbath" (1990: 169). The semi-subterranean building at Onion

Portage, dating to 3300–2500 BP, was oval and 5.4 × 7.7 m in size (Larson 1990: 165). Inside the structure were a hearth, lithic debitage, and a few other artifacts. After her thorough examination of the ethnographic database and the Onion Portage building, Larson concluded that the structure was most likely *not* a *kazigi* men's house. Though the structure was of the proper size and placement, the contents did not match the type of items expected in an exclusively male *kazigi*. Absent from the Onion Portage structure were interior benches, oil lamps (necessary for nighttime occupation), ceremonial items, and artifacts representing trade. Larson deduced that the Onion Portage building served as a workshop area with no special ceremonial or symbolic significance. Though again a case of "negative evidence," Larson's study of the Onion Portage site offers a solid methodology for investigating the presence of a men's house in a village setting.

Another example is found among the Kaggaba of Colombia. In this culture, there is a strict division of space at every level, including domestic and religious (Oyuela-Caycedo 1990). The Kaggaba hold strong beliefs in "purity/pollution" that are expressed in a male/female dichotomy, necessitating the regular separation of the sexes. The need to control population in this agriculturally poor area may be one of the root causes of this strong polarity between males and females (Oyuela-Caycedo 1990: 331). The manifestation of this division is quite visible spatially: males do not enter female spaces, and the opposite is also true. Most Kaggaba live on their farmlands and thus are not regularly aggregated in villages. Ethnographic and ethnohistoric data show that there are typically two "dwellings" on a farm, one for the male(s) and one for the females, the latter containing the food processing and cooking paraphernalia and other household goods, while the male dwelling has pots dedicated to the processing of coca leaves, tobacco essence, and cane beer, all of which have a different shape and consistency than vessels used in cooking (Oyuela-Caycedo 1990: 327). When the Kaggaba must travel to the villages, for ceremonial events or for other needs, men reside in the male temple while women pursue domestic activities in the common spaces (generally between buildings).

The ethnographic and ethnohistorical (Spanish Conquest records) data allow archaeologists to better interpret earlier Kaggaba urban and rural settlements. The urban centers served as distribution, trade, and ceremonial nodes, whereas it was in the dispersed villages and farms that people lived the majority of their lives. Villages were laid out so that homes were located near the terraced agricultural fields. In general, two or more dwellings were grouped together in a compound. These had originally been interpreted as single-family homes, perhaps representing kin-related cooperative units; the data just presented allows for a reinterpretation of these structures as separate male and female dwellings for a single-family unit (Oyuela-Caycedo 1990). Thus, the sexual spatial segregation, manifested in separate dwellings, yields a very different economic organization of the "dwellings compound" on terraced farmlands than if these were the houses of two complete family units. Understanding sexual spatial segregation not only informs us about ideological concepts present within a culture but can also help to clarify socioeconomic and other institutional behaviors embedded within a social structure.

Segregation and Seclusion

Segregation and seclusion can also be accomplished by divisions within the family house or compound (e.g., BaHammam 2006). In the last several centuries, the seclusion of women has come to be known as purdah, which literally means "curtain" in Farsi (Papanek 1973); alternatively, it is known in the form of the Ottoman harem, where a sultan's many wives and concubines were secluded from all eyes save those of the sultan and the palace eunuchs (Lewis 2004; Peirce 1993). This type of harem, in which a wealthy man's wives and concubines lived relatively secluded lives together, existed in other cultures found in India, China, and elsewhere (Booth 2010; Ebrey 2003; Grewal 1996; Lal 2005; Pollock 1981). In some modern Muslim and Hindu cultures, the practice of purdah still exists: women of the household have a designated space that is visually separated from other spaces in the domestic setting. The reasons for this type of persistent female segregation (as opposed to the intermittent type, as with a menstrual structure) are manifold, depending on cultural requirements. Hanna Papanek offers one of the most extensive overviews of purdah as it exists in South Asia in both Muslim and Hindu cultures. She describes female segregation as fulfilling two interrelated requirements: to create a separate world for women, and to create "symbolic shelters" (1973: 290). The separate world is related to the sexual division of labor, where women can do their work without interference from the outside world and maintain appropriate social distance from those with whom they should not be interacting—essential non-kin males. The symbolic shelter provides a safe place where women can relax and the rest of household can be certain of their protected status and preservation of their honor (Figure 8.4). The reasons behind the segregation of women in South Asia as reported by Papanek are deeply connected to the practice of the Muslim and Hindu religions, particularly the need to protect women against the dangers of "the tension between the kin unit and the outside world which is seen as a difficult and hostile place. . . . Women become vulnerable when they move outside the home. . . . What is fundamentally implied . . . is that someone needs to be protected, in a given space and time, from forces originating elsewhere" (1973: 315).

In the Qing Dynasty of China (CE 1644–1911), the reasons behind the *xiunu* (seclusion) system included the desire of Manchu rulers to ensure that their offspring had a Manchu ethnic identity, even though, in the early dynasties, wife and concubine selection for the *xiunu* often included women from Mongol or Chinese ethnic groups (Wang 2004). Once ensconced in a Manchu *xiunu*, however, a woman was essentially "Manchu." The other reason behind the *xiunu* system was "to guarantee the Qing emperors and princes the best marriage partners" (Wang 2004: 214), which was

Figure 8.4: Artistic rendering of nomadic tent dwellers (such as might be found in the Middle East) in which the women's area is separated from the public/guest area by a curtain (drawing by Corrina Petit).

accomplished by the careful selection of girls from the "best" families. In imperial China, politics and ethnic purity, rather than religion, drove the need for a system of female seclusion. Ancient texts and other sources indicate that the *harem* system may have existed in ancient Assyrian and Persian cultures for similar political reasons. Seclusion may have also been practiced to ensure a labor force within a family, one produced by the patrilineal line of the household head (Hodder 1984). The mix of reasons behind female seclusion includes the need to "protect" females from unwanted advances by non-kin males, the desire to have exclusive rights over all progeny, and the need to ensure a proper sexual division of labor in the household.

Papanek describes two methods to accomplish *purdah,* or seclusion. One is the covering of the female body: in present-day Muslim and Hindu cultures, a garment known as a *burqa*, which is a full head-to-toe drapery over the female body, with a lattice screen through which women may see out, creates a type of "mobile" seclusion. The other version is the concern of the present chapter: the architectural arrangement that creates women's space within the household compound. Papanek describes houses that have separate entrances for women, sheltered courtyards, and, of course, physical barriers that might consist of walls or curtains, to block the view into the women's spaces (1973:

294). Windows and balconies often have screens so that women may see out but prying eyes may not see in.

There are a number of examples from ethnographic observation that provide clues for identifying architecture meant to incorporate an element of female seclusion. Deborah Pellow's work among the Hausa in western Africa (1999, 2003) illustrates the importance of entryways, courtyards, and the placement of sleeping rooms. Pellow studied houses in Sabon Zongo, on the periphery of Accra in Ghana. The Muslim Hausa members of this community practiced *kulle*, or female seclusion, in the early 20th century, though today the practice is far less common. According to Pellow, *kulle* allowed for the regulation of sexuality and procreation, as well as signaled religious piety and identity; it was also a sign of status in that it proscribed female labor and the ability to seclude household women while still achieving a functioning household. Spatially, *kulle* was accomplished by limiting entry into the walled house compound through a single point that literally "mediated" between public and private space (Pellow 2003: 165). The entry led into a public forecourt area where the household head entertained guests and spent the majority of his time, including taking his meals there. At night, any male guests also slept in this forecourt room. Farther into the house's center was the *shigifa*, "a transitional entryway with staggered doorways to prevent a direct view into the *cikin gida*, the inside section of the home" (Pellow 2003: 166). It was in the *cikin gida* that women essentially lived their lives. Farther toward the back of the house, each wife (the Hausa practice polygyny) would have at least one or usually two rooms that belonged to her and her children. A household could have a number of wives if a father and married sons shared a dwelling. The house belonging to the Sabon Zongo leader was very large, with over 30 rooms in the *cikin gida* side of the house; the other side of the house, which was more public, was far smaller (Pellow 2003: 168). The footprint of this house defined the two sides of the house; to move from the public side to an open court in the female side, one had to pass through a *shigifa* with two doorways and a long hallway. Passage through more doorways was necessary before reaching the private rooms of the women. The contents of the rooms on either side of the compound would likely illustrate the constant presence of women in one part of the home and the more public nature of the space in the other. Access analysis (chapter 3) would offer clear evidence as to the inaccessibility of the women's *cikin gida* areas.

Among scholars of the Classical Greek world, there has been a lively discussion about the level of female seclusion (e.g., Davidson 2011; Goldberg 1999; Jameson 1990a, 1990b; Just 1989; Morris 1999; Nevett 1994, 1999; Walker 1983; Westgate 2007). Ian Morris (1999) suggests that Greek society became more concerned with privacy and possibly began sequestering women from non-kin outsiders during the Greek Archaic age, particularly in the seventh century BCE. In the centuries prior to 750 BCE, Greek houses were single-roomed (oval or apsidal), and all activities, including sleeping, eating and cooking, storage, and craft production, took place there. In such a setting, seclusion of one gender from another was largely impossible. In the century following 750

BCE, rectilinear houses, or *megara*, began to appear, with internal divisions to create individual rooms. Shortly after this development, house compounds with courtyards and high external walls appeared, blocking the casual view inside the household (Morris 1999: 309). The Greek household, or *oikos*, was entered through a narrow access point, which may have let into a space used only by the household head. Morris notes that in the late eighth/early seventh century, a shift from single- to multi-roomed houses, built inside walls and including internal courtyards, was an expensive endeavor and would not have been undertaken without good reason (1999: 310). He concludes that "the great change in central Greek house design in the late eighth and seventh century reveals hardening gender ideologies" in ancient Greek society (Morris 1999: 311). Many scholars feel these ideologies became clearly expressed in the architecture of Classical Greek homes several centuries later.

Greek texts inform archaeologists that Greek houses were composed of at least two areas: the *gunaikon,* which was the women's area, and the *andron* designated specifically for men. One of the first studies (Walker 1983) of fifth- and fourth-century BCE Classical Greek gendered architecture suggested that the *gunaikon* areas were quite secluded from the remainder of the house and functioned much in the way *purdah* does today. However, subsequent studies noted that while the *andron* had been identified archaeologically, the *gunaikon* had not (e.g., Goldberg 1999; Jameson 1990a, 1990b). The *gunaikon* may have been located upstairs in some Greek houses, possibly explaining its absence, but houses in some towns and cities were one-storied and offered no clear evidence of spatial segregation. Lisa Nevett (1994; and see also Goldberg 1999) has offered a very interesting explanation for the spatial differentials between the *andron* and the *gunaikon*. The Classical Greek house consisted of a walled compound into which there was usually only a single entry. This gave way to a courtyard and several rooms, which were the semi-public areas for entertaining guests. These rooms featured couches around the room boundaries, as in the modern *salon* found in a Turkish house. This set of rooms was the *andron*, where males entertained guests, conducted business, and probably took their meals and spent the majority of their time. From this semi-public space, there were no sight lines into the house interior, and to reach inner rooms, several doors and hallways had to be traversed. Nevett (1994) suggests that the *gunaikon* refers not to a select number of "female chambers" at the back of a Greek house but rather to the entire house *other than* the *andron*. In other words, while seclusion of women from non-household members was certainly in place in Classical Greece, the entire house was largely available to them, and only the *andron*, if occupied by non-household members, was off-limits. This would explain why the *gunaikon* is "invisible"—it essentially refers to the rest of the house beyond the *andron* and the entrance (Nevett 1994: 107). In Nevett's analysis, the pathway to identifying gendered segregation in an architectural footprint is not to seek out the areas of seclusion but rather to identify the more public "front" areas (see chapter 3) that are clearly separate, physically and visually, from the remainder of the house.

An example of gendered seclusion in prehistory is offered by Ian Hodder (1984), who focuses on the "longhouses" of Neolithic Europe (fifth and early fourth millennia BCE), which were well over 20 m in length and often trapezoidal in shape. He asserts that the evidence showed these houses were divided into "thirds," with a walled division located several meters inside the doorway, and a second walled division separating the final third of the house from the middle section (1984: 54–57). At the very least, the houses were divided into two rooms, with the smaller one at the front near the door (Figure 8.5). Hearth remains are not always recoverable, but they do seem to have typically been located in the middle and back rooms. Using archaeological reports, Hodder suggests these rooms be labeled "antechamber," "main central room," and back storage area; he goes on to describe the Neolithic European society of this time as "small scale, largely acephalous, although with some degree of differentiation between lineages gradually emerging" (1984: 61). Based on examples from ethnography and archaeological data from Neolithic Europe, Hodder suggests that the longhouses were structured so as to offer seclusion for the women of the household, which was felt essential in this Neolithic age to protect the male lineages and to control

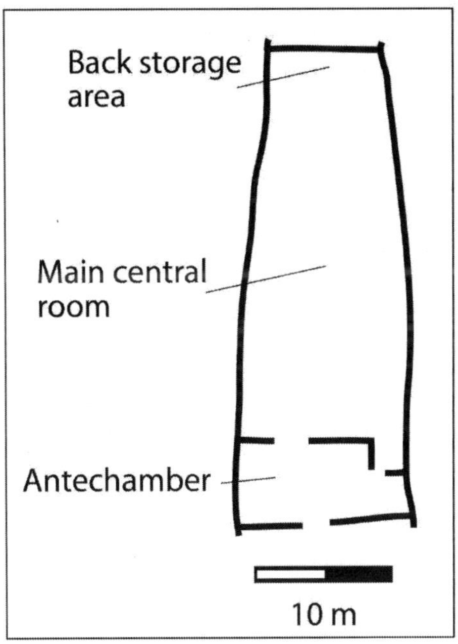

Figure 8.5: Example of a Neolithic European longhouse, showing the spatial divisions that may have allowed for the privacy/seclusion of women in the household (after Hodder 1984: 56, fig. 3.1).

women's reproductive capabilities. Ensuring a strong lineage and producing sufficient offspring to work the land were, in Hodder's assessment, the overriding principles guiding Neolithic European society; he notes that "as the social process of lineage competition built up through time, control of women in the house and settlement, and thus of descent and labour, would have assumed an increased importance, with women as the focal points of reproduction and exchange" (1984: 62). This, then, resulted in domestic structures in which a semi-public space at the front offered the male household members the ability to entertain guests and conduct business while women could remain secluded, and controlled, either in the main central room or even at the back of the house.

These circumstances changed by the late fourth millennium and into the third, when the control of lineage and family became less important and instead the competition for the control of land rights became more prominent. By this time, population had grown and the need to secure sufficient farmlands had, according to Hodder, become far more critical. During this later time, houses decreased in size and complexity, with less evidence for the seclusion of individuals deep inside the house. This is also the age when megalithic chamber tombs came into use, which many identify as a way to demonstrate ownership and control over the land within which they were built. Land, rather than lineage, became the symbolic identity through which European Neolithic peoples negotiated societal position. The seclusion that may have been necessary centuries before became moot, and this resulted in a shift to smaller and more rectilinear houses lacking significant internal divisions. Gendered seclusion apparently became a thing of the distant past.

Cultures that construct separate buildings for their genders do so for good reason, given that such a practice requires materials and energy expenditure. Women who are secluded during their menses are not automatically inferior to the men in the society; in fact, one could argue that their perceived magical powers might even offer an elevated position in society. While having a men's "clubhouse" where important decisions are made does indeed contribute to men's status in a society, it might also enhance women's daily lives; their physical and symbolic separation in such societies may well decrease levels of physical abuse and the placing of limits on women's activities in their own homes; and a more consistent seclusion and segregation of women in their own homes may have a significant impact on their societal position, including their status.

Gender and Status

The spaces people may enter or within which they spend their time can imbue, or at least project, their status, power, and privilege; conversely, those not allowed to enter those spaces, or relegated to work in particular places, may also be slotted into the hierarchical spectrum based on disbarment from some places and consignment to others. Status may derive from political activity, which may be partially negotiated within the domestic sphere as well as in more public venues (e.g., Bowser and Patton 2004 and references therein). Aspects of power and status awarded by the built environment are discussed in chapter 9. This section focuses specifically on theoretical and methodological issues associated with gender, space, and status. Since women's space is most often found inside or near the dwelling, it is there that researchers began attempting to identify gendered status and its relationship to gendered space.

The first widely acknowledged attempt in this area came from Sherry Ortner (1974), whose goal was not to relate gender with status and space but to offer a cultural explanation for the sexual division of labor, in contrast to the pervasive more "biological" arguments described above. Ortner's arguments are similar to the dichotomy described in Bourdieu's Berber House (1973), in that women are associated with certain human concepts and ideals, and men with others. Ortner's title, "Is Female to Male as Nature is to Culture?" encapsulates her argument, which is that universally (more or less), cultures associate women with "nature" and natural things such as childbirth, and men are linked with things that must be learned—"cultural" things, like leadership and warfare. Women's work, such as child care, food preparation, working in and around the house, is in the natural order; in other words, it "comes naturally." For this reason, cultures tend to regard it as less difficult than men's work, which must be learned and requires effort to build the cultural institutions of the society. The universal subordination of women, then, along with the universal sexual division of labor, is explained by human society's belief that women do "natural" and "easier" tasks and men do "cultural" and "harder" tasks, the former in and around the house and the latter usually beyond the household realm. Domestic work, therefore, carries a lower level of status, making the domestic space inferior to other spaces where "cultural" work takes place.

In the same volume in which Ortner's chapter appears, Michelle Rosaldo (1974) offered a supporting theory. Rosaldo considered the dichotomy of public versus private space. She noted that most work carried out by women occurs in or around the household, in private space, while men's work is often out in the open, in public space. The invisibility of women's work inside the home, associated with children and household duties, is, according to Rosaldo, viewed across cultures as secondary and less important. The far more visible work by men—including hunting, warfare, and political actions, all of which affects others and is often done in concert with other societal members (mainly men)—elevates the value of that work. Thus, work that takes place in extra-domestic public space takes on a higher value than work that occurs in domestic, private, space.

While scholars agree that male dominance has been prominent in many cultures, they have argued against the notion that male primacy was ever universal, and many have taken issue with the "culture/nature" dichotomy offered by Ortner (see Comaroff 1987; Lamphere 2001; essays in MacCormack and Strathern 1980; Yanagisako and Collier 1987). Ortner addressed these criticisms in her 1997 book, *Making Gender,* in which she recognized the difficulty of claiming a "universal" male dominance over women if one used only a single criterion, but reaffirmed seeing some type of dominance in all cultures when various *types* of domination, such as social or political power, status, and the limiting of spatial freedoms, are considered. Critics also addressed Rosaldo's concept of domestic/public space and the status associated with the work performed in these two areas. In particular, her notion of work within the household as less important than that performed outside of it was criticized as a particularly Western concept, one that should not be universally applied to non-Western cultures (Lamphere 1974; Reiter [now Rapp] 1975; Yanagisako 1979). Rosaldo herself came to acknowledge this flaw in her argument (1980) but noted, as did others (Comaroff 1987; Rapp 1979) that the domestic/extra-domestic and public/private dichotomy is a valuable concept in assessing gender status.

Thus, while Ortner and Rosaldo's theories were not accepted wholesale, they did lead to a plethora of scholarship on the intersection of space, gender, and status (usually in the context of male domination). Peggy Sanday (1981) weighed in on the debate, suggesting that while male domination was not universal, it was prominent, and she offered extensive investigation into its causes. Regarding the issue of gendered space, she argued that sexual segregation or gendered work was a critical factor in determining gender status within a society. In sexually segregated societies in which men and women do not share activities—that is, where men do men's work and women do women's—Sanday argues that women hold lesser status than their male counterparts. In societies in which there is a high level of integration, in which men help women with work and vice-versa, there are significantly higher levels of gender equality. Daphne Spain (1992, 1993) notes that this can be translated to spatiality; in sexually segregated societies, men do not spend time in the spaces where women do their work. In turn, these spaces where "less important work" takes place become lower-value spaces. This gets back, in part, to Rosaldo's private and public argument. Spain concludes that the greater the level of gender (and spatial) segregation, the lower the status held by females (1993).

A host of ethnographic studies and a significant number of archaeological studies have investigated the multivariate issues that may tie gender status to differentials in spatial perceptions. As noted above, many studies put Rosaldo's argument (i.e., domestic/private = secondary/female status) to the test and found the association wanting. A more productive avenue of investigation regarding space and status turns to the value of one's work within a culture. If work that takes place within the dwelling is considered critical to the overall success of the household, then no matter who performs that work, it is likely that they and the space within which they do it will bear significant status. Also important to determining gender status is access, or the denial of such, to certain places. Case studies above on seclusion and segregation dealt in small part with the impact of these on gender status, but this is addressed more directly here.

A study of gender and changing status over several hundred years was carried out by Patricia Crown and Suzanne Fish (1996) in their examination of pre-Classic and Classic-period (ca. CE 1150–1400) Hohokam sites in Arizona. Their evidentiary database consisted of artifacts identifying labor, domestic architecture, access to ritual spaces, and mortuary data. In particular, these authors were interested in investigating the relative status of women as the Hohokam culture grew in size and complexity over the target centuries. Their methodological approach allowed them to identify growing differentials in women's status by the late Classic period. In pre-Classic Hohokam settlements, people lived in pithouses set in "courtyard groups" in which several houses sat close to one another and doorways led to common courtyard areas where activities took place (Crown and Fish 1996: 806). Women's work, which included food processing and preparation, ceramic and textile production, and child care, was accomplished both inside the houses and in the open courtyards; their work was therefore visible to the community, and they could engage with others on a daily basis. Burial and architectural data do not indicate a significant difference in wealth and status between household members in the pre-Classic period. By the Classic period, there were some substantial changes in Hohokam society. Women's workload in time and energy expenditure had increased significantly, indicated by items associated with food preparation, numbers of textile production tools, and types of pottery produced. It is likely that the production of textiles and ceramics was at the extra-household level, indicating that women's work contributed to the household income (Crown and Fish 1996: 805).

At the same time, open courtyard groups came to an end and, instead, houses were enclosed in walled compounds. Some compounds contained only one or two houses, while others contained multiple houses that had individual walls around them within the larger compound (Crown and Fish 1996: 806). A few courtyard groups built in the pre-Classic period remained unwalled. A second change in domestic residence was that new, larger homes were built atop platform mounds that had, in pre-Classic times, been wholly dedicated to ritual use. The mound-top homes contained both domestic (tools associated with women's work) and ritual items, suggesting that newly emerged elites had moved their homes to the higher locations and were responsible for leading the community in ritual functions (Crown and Fish 1996: 807). Crown and Fish "assume here that any change in domestic architecture that resulted in greater seclusion of women from the community, greater separation of women's work areas from men's work areas, or greater spatial distance between women impacted the relative status of women" (1996: 806). Segregating and secluding women, in their assessment, would have had a significant effect on their access to knowledge, on community visibility and engagement in community activities, and on their interaction with other community members. Alternatively, at least in the larger compounds, segregation may have increased cooperation and loyalty bonds and allowed for some women to engage in part-time task specialization (e.g., ceramic or textile production), thereby increasing household wealth and possibly status.

Crown and Fish conclude that in the Hohokam Classic period, women's status became more differentiated, demonstrated in part by their labor activities and the associated domestic architecture. While women's status may have suffered across the community owing to their increasing invisibility behind compound walls, this may have been partially ameliorated for those who engaged in craft specialization that contributed to household wealth (it is unclear who controlled the distribution of the products of that labor). Women who were engaged in nonspecialized household tasks, now isolated from the larger community, may have occupied the lowest status positions. Furthermore, women who continued to live in unwalled settings had greater access to knowledge, gossip, interaction with community members, and community activities, and were entirely more visible on a daily basis. Finally, women who lived in the larger houses on the platform mounds were clearly members of the elite families and must have derived status from their residential location, possible access to ritual activities, and membership in elite lineages. Mortuary data support the growing differentiation in women's status in Classic Hohokam (Crown and Fish 1996: 808–11).

Christine Hastorf (1991) carried out a similar study on the status of Sausa women after the Inca colonization of the Andes. Hastorf was particularly interested in food processing and spatial distribution, with a special focus on how much work took place inside the house versus in more visible patio areas. In the pre-Inca Sausa Phase II period (CE 1300–1460), Hastorf found a wide variety of plant foods, including potato (the food staple) and maize (often made into beer for ritual purposes), scattered heavily across the patio areas and stored within the houses; also present in the patios was evidence of both ceramic and lithic manufacture (1991: 140–43). In the Phase III Inca period (CE 1460–1532), botanical distribution had changed; greater quantities of maize were discovered, but it was being processed inside the homes and against the house walls near the doorways or hearth. There seems to have been a greater segregation of gendered space in this period, and women's workload seems to have increased: they were producing more maize-based products, including *chichi* beer for ritual and ceremony (Hastorf 1991: 148). Hastorf pairs her analysis with skeletal data: In the Phase II period, isotope analysis suggests that men and women had similar diets, consuming primarily tubers, quinoa, and some maize. However, in the Phase III period, there is an increase in maize consumption, but men are consuming far more than women. Thus, in the Phase III Inca period, women have become more segregated and indeed cramped in their work spaces; they were working harder to produce maize-based products such as *chichi*, but were not in social, economic, or ritual positions that allowed them to consume it, though the men clearly were (Hastorf 1991: 150–51). Skeletal evidence suggests men's nutritional health improved while women's health remained consistent with pre-Inca times. Hastorf concludes that women's status likely declined after Inca colonization of the village and that women's control over the products of their labor, and indeed their use of space, was transferred to men. The more equal distribution of status of the earlier phase became significantly differentiated in the later phase.

Increasing gendered segregation and spatial seclusion of women is at the heart of a third example based on Richard Hingley's (1990) analysis of Iron Age houses in Britain. Hingley notes that artifactual evidence is slim, and the majority of his study rests on architectural evidence alone. He suggests that gendered segregation stretched back into the Late Bronze Age when housing compounds consisted of two round huts, a smaller one for cooking, which he defines as the "female" space, and a larger one for food consumption, which he attributed to males (1990: 128). By the (pre-Roman) Iron Age, the two huts had combined into one large round house, usually with an interior ring of posts which effectively created an inner ring and outer ring of space; a central hearth sat within the inner ring. Taking a page from Bourdieu's Berber House (1973), Hingley described the outer ring as both symbolically and physically dark, dirty, raw, constrained, and private, while the inner ring was light, open, clean, and public (1990: 133). The inner ring, he suggested, was more closely associated with males and the outer one with females. A flaw in this latter argument is, of course, the placement of the hearth, which was located in the center of the inner ring. If food preparation was a task carried out by women, then their presence in the inner ring would have been required on a regular basis. More convincing is Hingley's argument that the Romano-British House of the slightly later Iron Age suggests a change in women's status in Britain. These houses were rectilinear, with entry at one end into one or several rooms, and a central hall; in many houses there were farther rooms at the back. Some larger houses had an "aisle" of rooms along the side (Hingley 1990: 139–40). Hearths in these houses were usually located in the large central room, often toward the back; back and side rooms served as private areas, for storage, or where animals had byres (Figure 8.6). Hingley argues that as Romanization came to Britain, what may have been a tendency toward a public/private separation and some gender segregation became much more standardized and indeed physically enforceable within a rectilinear house. Women were relegated to the more private and lower status back or side aisles, while men enjoyed greater visibility in the more public regions of the home.

The case studies and discussion above suggest there are several critical factors that may help determine whether gendered differentiation in status might be present within a society. First is the front/public and back/private dichotomy. If architectural and artifactual evidence suggests that one gender had particular and consistent access to the more public and visible areas of the home or community, and the other was typically "invisible" in the more private areas, this is often, though not always, a strong indicator of differential status (see Spain 1993). Second is accessibility to important places within the community: are the genders equally welcome into religious and political domains? If one gender is denied access to places where decisions are made and unifying rituals are carried out, then there is likely a differential in status present in the society. Like everything else in archaeology, tracking social status hierarchy or complementarity in an ancient society is challenging at best, but architecture certainly demonstrates that it has a role to play in this endeavor.

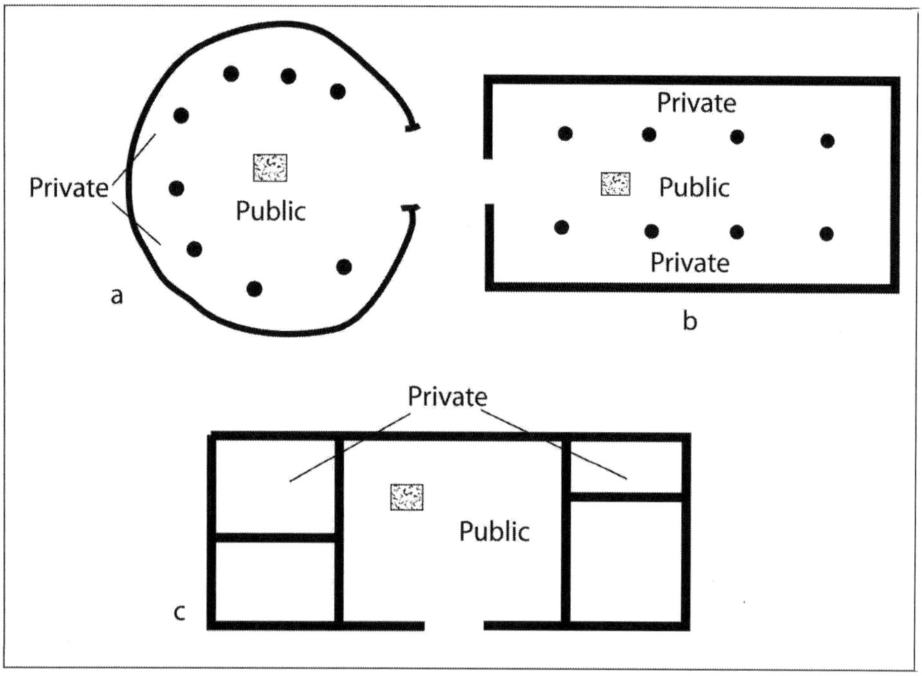

Figure 8.6: Stylized plans of the transition from (a) the British Iron Age round house, with its public/private dichotomy, to (b) the Romano-British rectilinear houses, in which the private zone initially remained in the periphery, until the advent of (c) flanking rooms, which could be physically closed off, allowing for more effective gender segregation (after Hingley 1990: 131, fig. 6.2; 137, fig. 6.3).

Conclusion

The vast field of gender archaeology has only been touched on here, specifically where it intersects directly with architecture and the use of space. As noted numerous times in this chapter and in this entire volume, architecture is often only a shell that emits very little data. The artifactual and ethnographic records are what breathe ancient life back into the shell. Nonetheless, without the walls, doors, and built furniture that frame the open space, the artifacts themselves would be far less forthcoming as data sets. The two together, with the invaluable assistance of ethnographic research, form a vital triad for understanding gender in prehistory.

Section IV

Symbolism and the Built Environment

Chapter 9
Architecture and Power

An entire chapter on the subject of architecture and power might appear to be overkill, as the expression of power through the built environment seems so clearly evident as to require only brief discussion. However, once we delve into how the built environment can be used not only to demonstrate power but also to establish positions of power, control the freedoms and actions of others, and indicate shifts in power, the nuances of the relationship between architecture and power become far more complicated, and interesting.

Addressed here are, first, methodologies for recognizing buildings that are in some way associated with societal notions of power and, second, a review of the concept of "agency," which is a most suitable theoretical model when dealing with expressions of power. The subject of architecture and power is then discussed from four points of view: (1) how architecture can be used to gain and establish power; (2) how it is used to demonstrate power; (3) how the built environment can control the actions, and even the thoughts, of others; and (4) how architecture can be an important indicator of changes in power structures.

Locating Power Structures in the Archaeological Record

Numerous studies are devoted to identifying rank or social stratification in the archaeological record, and many of these employed the assessment of architectural remains (e.g., Ames 2008; Blanton 1994; Carmean 1991; Feinman and Neitzel 1984; Smith 1987;

Archaeology of Domestic Architecture and the Human Use of Space, by Sharon R. Steadman, 221–247.

Trigger 2003; Wason 1994). But what is the nature of the power being expressed? Or perhaps, more specifically, what is power? Archaeology has long been concerned with how to identify social complexity and the expression of power and status (e.g., Bentley and Maschner 2003, 2008; Chapman 2003; Crumley 2001; Diehl 2000a; Trigger 2003). Increasing social complexity involves the development of power strategies that are often manifested materially in adjustments to wealth distribution, the control of craft production, and changes in the distributional patterns of goods across a settlement (Ames 2008; Boone 2000). Also relevant are alterations in the constitution and construction of social networks between the "haves" and the "have-nots," which may be expressed materially and/or ideologically (Bentley 2003; Bourdieu 1977, 1990; Diehl 2000b; Foucault 1980; Mann 1986). Max Weber (1968) describes power as the ability of one, or a few, to influence the actions of others, and Michael Mann notes that there are four interrelated networks of social power: ideological, economic, political, and military (1986); a set of descriptions was later echoed by Eric Wolf (1999). All of these elements of power can be expressed materially and architecturally, making them recoverable in archaeological contexts.

Networks of power expressed through economic, political, and military means are the most readily identifiable archaeologically. Economically, power can be expressed by the possession of decision-making authority over the acquisition, distribution, and exchange of labor and goods and the ability to actually, or seemingly, satisfy societal subsistence needs. Political power can be demonstrated in various ways, including control over the economy but also through the demonstrated ability to control behavior and punish misbehavior in various realms, including civil, religious, and social. Military power might be the easiest to identify, if excavations happen to reveal barracks, weapons stores, evidence of a standing army, and other indicators of a military structure. While not limited to complex societies, such apparati are more commonly found in a state or imperial context. Ideological expressions of power are far harder to identify archaeologically (Ames 2008), but control of religion and ritual activities can often be tracked materially and thus are sometimes recognizable in prehistoric contexts (Diehl 2000b; Mann 1986; Potter 2000); propagandistic expressions of military and political sometimes appear in artistic and architectural media and can be found in the remains of many early states. The next line of inquiry includes the issue of scale; what entity or entities within the community are expressing that power and for what reasons?

In essence, power can reside in a culture's sensibilities, or *habitus* (see below and chapter 5), either in the societal norms that guide behavior or in the individual agent's *decision* to act within or outside of those norms (Bourdieu 1977, 1990). The ability to control people's behavior is only a simplistic definition of power. Foucault cites true power as existent in the very cultural systems within which people live (1980); power in such a scenario is related to knowledge—one who possesses special knowledge and insight *into* the system, or even the ability to manipulate it, also possesses power, whether economic, political, or ideological. Depending on how cultural institutions are arrayed, power wielded within a community can be collected into the hands of individuals, distributed across corporate groups (e.g., kin groups or particular social strata such as the clergy), or managed through institutionalized means. The first of these, individual power, and possibly corporate power, likely involved architectural expressions of that power in the form of more elaborate residences or the ability to control access to important secular and religious areas. Institutionalized power is illustrated in embedded social institutions that effectively manage a population's behavior so that it conforms to underlying societal norms, as described by Foucault (1970, 1977). Buildings such as prisons, schools, and welfare centers can be used as institutional devices not only to guide behavior but to correct it as well. While institutionalized power may well be expressed in the very existence of certain types of buildings, it is far harder to recognize archaeologically, whether that power is exercised by individual or corporate leaders in each generation, or if it is more long-lived and embedded in societal structure. The examples offered in this chapter capture, without doubt, the expression of individualized and also corporate group power; embedded within these, however, may be elements of institutionalized power structures already long existent prior to the erection of the built environment.

Identifying Structures Expressing "Power"

Identifying structures representing power is at once quite easy and incredibly difficult. For instance, discovering a building twice or three times as large as any other in the settlement might mean it functioned as the leader's house or instead it was a communal storage building. Contents in the structure might offer clues but only if the material culture left behind is signatory of the activities inside the building. The only solution, however, is to forge ahead and apply the standard techniques used to archaeologically identify important buildings and elite residences. These would generally include the relative size of the structure(s), the labor invested in its/their construction, the type and importance of the decorative elements, the existence of physical boundaries around the structure(s), and the location.

A building's size within a community, if it can be identified as a domestic structure, would seem to be one good indicator of relative status (Trigger 1990; Wason 1994: 137). A larger house may be desirable, or even necessary, for those of elite status, for several reasons. Size might matter for purposes of "costly signaling" (see below), to alert others as to the status of residents. The size might also relate to practical matters, such as the need for increased storage capability, to house important visitors, or to host public gatherings or more semi-private events such as feasts (Hayden 1995; Hayden and Dietler 2001; Helwing 2003; Steadman 2011). While it is fair to say that "size matters," there is a caveat to this, and it has to do with location. That is, in certain circumstances it might be the location, and not the size, that is the true indicator of status. To use a modern example, the owner of an apartment in Soho in New York City might be just as rich and important as someone living in a mansion in Chicago, Illinois—or even more so. The key here is location: a small, heavily built-up, crowded island (Manhattan) versus the far more widespread and available space of suburban Chicago. Fortunately, in archaeological settings, the anomaly of a Manhattan is somewhat uncommon, and square footage is certainly a more reliable indicator of status in prehistoric, non-state-level settlements.

A second indicator, one that is closely tied to size, is that of labor investment, summarized by Paul Wason, who notes that "energy *will* correlate with rank" (1994: 138; see also Trigger 1990). A larger house of course requires greater labor investment, but so does a well-built house that is identical in size to others of lesser quality in the settlement. For instance, a study of houses in a Mesoamerican community measured the socioeconomic differentiation between householders by the criteria of roofing materials and the existence of fencing (Thomas and Robbins 1985). Houses with better roofs and well-built fences were not necessarily larger, but they exhibited a greater investment of labor and wealth expenditure. A house with thicker walls (for better insulation), higher-quality construction materials, stone versus mud foundations, evidence of repeated plasterings of walls and floors, or any other element of construction that would apparently require greater labor and thus greater cost is a clear expression of the elevated social status or socioeconomic standing of the resident. This was demonstrated in Kenneth Hirth's study (1989) of residence types at Xochicalco (ca. CE 650–900) in central Mexico. Using the criteria of house size, labor investment in house construction, and quality of building materials, Hirth identified a house type he terms "courtyard residences" as most likely belonging to high-status elites in this settlement (1989: 444–47). These houses were the largest, required the most effort to construct, and had finely cut ashlar stone in their walls; the latter was also a construction technique employed in the building of the monumental public structures, further confirming for Hirth the importance of the residents in the courtyard houses.

Related to labor investment is the element of accouterments, or decorative features, that may adorn a house, as compared with those on other houses. Richard Blanton (1994), among others (e.g., Carmean, McAnany, and Sabloff 2011; Duncan 1982; Lyons 2007; Rapoport 1982; Sircar 1987; and, for an excellent ethnographic example, Colloredo-Mansfeld [1994]), has explored the many ways that houses embody—or, more accurately, project—the self-perceived social identity of their occupants. In this way, "the house can also serve as a channel of nonverbal communication that transmits messages from its occupants to others outside the house" (Blanton 1994: 10). Blanton employs the notion of an "indexical mode" by which houses are marked using external decoration and design features, such as wall, facade, and roof decorations, embedded design elements, and forecourts and balconies, to communicate social information to those viewing the house (1994: 120–27). He queries, however, the need to demonstrate status in communities where everyone knows the social standing of every resident; the answer is that visitors to a settlement will not have this embedded knowledge and thus indexical elements are necessary (1994: 142–45).

Another reason to display status on a residence, even to fellow community members who might already know everyone's relative household status, is, according to James Boone (2000), to "advertise" the health and vitality of the residents and thus of the community. Boone asks the same question as Blanton did: Why engage in "costly signaling"?—that is, why invest extra time, energy, and resources on decorative or design elements on a home? Boone argues that costly signaling by elites serves to reassure community members that unexpected crises can be managed; elites can either restrict or provide access to resources in times of danger (depending on what is needed to sustain the community), acquire and distribute necessary goods, and in general, ensure community survival (2000: 87–90). This suggests that embedded in human social evolution is not only the wish to display social status but also to see it displayed. This would explain the ubiquitous representation of social status, in houses and their visible contents, in every type of community, even those in which everyone knows everyone else's status and socioeconomic position down to the last iota. Decorative elements are, therefore, a reliable indicator of social and economic standing in a community, especially when house size is not heavily differentiated.

As outlined in chapter 3, boundary control is a very common method for sending messages regarding status, territorial control, and tolerated levels of community access. Discussion in chapter 3 mainly focused on the housing structure itself with regard to access analysis, profiling front/back studies, and how house residents can regulate access within a house regarding strangers or visitors. Studies show that as socioeconomic differentiation increases in a community, houses belonging to the wealthy create additional access controls, or reorient existing ones, in order to better control both viewing and passage into house interiors from the outside (Foster 1989a, 1989b; Lawrence-Zúñiga 1999; Sanders 1990; Steadman 2000). The same is true of the house itself, or areas controlled by the householders. Power is physically demonstrated when householders control access to important public areas or resources (Ames 2008; Potter 2000). Managing who is allowed to attend important secular or religious events not only demonstrates control over community members but also creates the situation in which those without access attempt to curry favor in order to gain it. Controlling access to important resources not only demonstrates power but can result in greater wealth. A good example of this comes from 10th-century feudal England, in which the manor house, ensconced behind ditches and earthworks, controlled access to the village mill, extracting fees from feudal peasants for its use (Saunders 1990). Human-built physical boundaries (walls, fences, barriers), and the passages through them, are archaeologically identifiable indicators for locating structures whose residents hold significant socioeconomic or political power in a community.

Related to boundary control is the location of structures that may represent power. In the past, when archaeologists wanted to find the palace or main temple in an ancient city, the first place they opened excavations was at the high point inside the city gates. Elite residences are typically in prominent but not easily accessed locations (but see Steadman 2011 for alternatives to this). Houses sited on higher locations, even if artificially elevated by platforms, and then perhaps surrounded by a wall, should be immediately suspect of belonging to residents with higher status in the community (Wason 1994: 139–43, 150). The natural landscape may lend a hand in this. Located on a mountain at an elevation of ca. 3,500 m, the Incan village of Caracas features houses on a terraced mountain slope (Sykes 1989). Not only were the "native lord" residences located at the highest elevation, but they were also the most inaccessible. Location is a significant variable, because the importance of "where" can range quite significantly from one culture to the next: a near-the-market area in one town may be the most important residential area, whereas that same location would be appalling to elites in another culture. It is worth noting that this indicator can work for the reverse situation: identifying low-status houses. In a study of Zoroastrian houses in Iranian settlements, discussed in chapter 5, it was noted that Zoroastrians, who were discriminated against by the Muslim majority, frequently had to locate their residential quarters in undesirable areas, including outside city walls, and were not allowed to occupy houses existing at physically higher elevations than Muslims (Mazumdar and Mazumdar 1997). Location can be yet one more clue to identify residences representing power (or lack thereof) within a settlement.

The above indicators all revolve around the built structure. House contents, however, are often as important as the building itself (Ames 2008; Boone 2000; Netting 1982; Robb 1999a; Steadman 1996, 2000). Residents who have the ability to control labor to the extent that they can construct more elaborate homes also often have preferential access to trade materials and the distribution of important resources (e.g., Costin 1991, 2001; Helms 1992; Hirth 1996; Peregrine 1991; Saitta 1999). Differentiation in house contents is one of the standard reliable indicators of socioeconomic hierarchy in the archaeological investigation of ancient communities. Two examples from Mesoamerica illustrate the usefulness, or lack thereof, in using material culture inside domestic structures as a main indicator of high-ranking residences. A study carried out at Paso de la Amada, in Mexico, compared architecture on Mound 6 and Mound 12, which featured residential structures dating to ca. 1550–1400 BCE (Blake et al. 2006). The material contents of the buildings on the two mounds were relatively consistent, the obsidian, ceramic, and bone items indicating that activities within each were similar. What differentiated the two mounds was the architecture itself. Mound 6 featured far larger buildings and superior construction techniques compared with those on Mound 12 (and other mounds). After reviewing the data, the researchers concluded that "the occupants of the Mound 6 buildings were members of a high-ranking household, perhaps the highest-status household in the community" (Blake et al. 2006: 207). This conclusion rested on the architectural evidence, rather than on the material culture contents in the two mound residences.

Conversely, Julia Hendon (1991) made strong use of material culture contents from residences in Copan Valley, Honduras, to identify elite homes during the period from CE 630 to 1000. The basic residential unit in Copan Valley (and elsewhere) was based on the "patio," which consisted of several structures surrounding an open courtyard typically used for household activities. To identify elite houses, Hendon used the criteria of house size, building material, layout, and decorative elements (1991: 905). Elite residences were built of finely dressed ashlar stones, whereas other, non-elite homes were constructed of wattle and daub; decorative elements such as sculpture or hieroglyphic inscriptions were also indicative of high-status residences (Hendon 1991: 905–6). Hendon used house contents as important additional indicators of elite status; patio houses conforming to high-status architectural criteria also contained large numbers of imported and local "fancy" ceramics, and burials also contained higher-status goods (Hendon 1991: 907–10). The material culture served as a "check" to confirm the architectural criteria employed.

Expressions of Power in the Domestic Sphere

Discerning the meaning represented in monumental public structures might seem the easiest way to go when attempting to find physical "expressions of power" in the archaeological record. However, the case studies offered here primarily illustrate how archaeologists can derive information about societal structures through the examination of residences rather than public monuments, though the latter do appear in discussions below. In many ways, it is the domestic sphere that gives a more holistic insight into the inner workings of a community. While only those in the upper echelons of society can effect the building of monumental public buildings, everyone in a community needs a place to live. The range of living spaces, their location, construction, and their internal and external presentations are essential clues to individual and group behavior within a settlement.

Establishing Social Identity, Attaining and Retaining Status

Architecture and associated material culture are ideal vehicles by which an agent may seek to attain and establish a particular social identity within a community. Depending on the established behavioral codes within the community, the agent may work within those patterns to demonstrate his or her emergent position in society, or may choose to transcend societal norms and forge new behaviors that set the agent apart from the rest (Steadman 2010).

One of the most obvious uses of architecture for establishing a position of power is found in the 16th- and 17th-century CE "age of castles" in Japan (Coaldrake 1996). Japanese civil wars in the earlier 16th century provided the springboard for three strong regional leaders to emerge later in the century: Nobunaga, who established military rule over central Japan, followed by Hideyoshi, who unified Japan politically, and finally Ieyasu, who founded a shogunal dynasty that lasted until 1868 (Coaldrake 1996: 104). Between 1576 and 1639, when these three leaders ruled, castle building was initiated in Japan; prior to this period, monumental architecture of this sort was limited to fortifications rather than to "residences." However, the age of castles allowed a single structure to symbolize the unification of power under one leader.

Nobunaga built Azuchi Castle between 1576 and 1579, just when Japan was emerging from civil war and Nobunaga was determined to sit as the supreme leader. Nobunaga's Azuchi Castle "articulated authority with a universal language of height, technical sophistication, strength and beauty" (Coaldrake 1996: 111). Nobunaga accomplished this in part through the placement of Azuchi Castle, not at the top of a steep hill where fortifications were usually built, but rather on a low, virtually unprotected hill (Coaldrake 1996: 107), thereby symbolizing, through the placement of his castle, his control of the region and his lack of fear of attack by vanquished hostile forces. Several decades later, in the beginning of the 17th century, Ieyasu built the castle keep at Edo to demonstrate the establishment of the emergent Tokugawa shogun (Coaldrake 1996: 132). Though the Edo castle burned down in 1657, it served its purpose as a symbol of the Tokugawa shogunate's unassailable power; it was the tallest castle ever built in Japan, standing nearly 60 m tall and towering above the landscape. Coaldrake summarizes the power of these castles as "representing a separate era in the creation and consolidation of authority in the sixteenth and seventh centuries. . . . Each castle was an expression of a particular moment within a period of rule by control of the built as well as the political environment" (1996: 137). While the discussion of Japanese castles might fit just as well in the section dealing with monumental architecture (below), it well illustrates here how individual agents used the manipulation of "domestic" architecture, through placement, design, and size, to establish and display their newly won authority after the political and military chaos of 16th-century Japan.

The strategy to "build an astonishing residence to express my power" was not limited to Asian contexts. Several studies in Jessica Christie and Patricia Sarro's volume (2006) on the emergence of "palaces" in the Americas profile just this phenomenon. For instance, Sarah Barber and Arthur Joyce (2006: 233–36) trace the evolution of the "Mount 195" elite residence into a "ruler's palace" in the Monte Alban phase (ca. CE 500–800). Typical Monte Alban houses used a standard Mesoamerican layout with rooms arrayed around an enclosed patio; the family tomb was often located in the patio area. While sight lines into patio areas were typically left open, the Mound 195 residence had an "L" shape that not only blocked views of patio activities but also directed foot traffic to specific areas in the residence. Over successive Mount 195 construction phases, a new inner and more private courtyard was built separate from the original one; the original patio, with its family tomb, was elaborately decorated with stucco panels and an altar complex. It had clearly become a semi-public place where Monte Alban residents could come to ritual events celebrating the ruler's family ancestry. Barber and

Joyce note that "the inhabitants of the final residence on Mound 195 were living in a public building: a residential structure that incorporated highly public ceremonial space" (2006: 234). Over the course of a century, an elite residence had become a "palace" in correlation with the consolidation of power by its inhabitants (see Couture 2007 for a similar process in pre-Inca Tiwanaku culture).

The same researchers (Barber and Joyce 2006: 220–23) describe the process of reconstituting and consolidating elite power at the Late Rosario–period occupation (700–500 BCE) at San José Mogote. In the earlier stages of this phase in the Valley of Oaxaca, significant social and political changes took place; the frequent destruction of valley settlements indicates that interpolity conflict was common, and these attacks appear to have broken the confidence commoners had in their leaders to attract protection (through sacrifice) from the supernatural world (Barber and Joyce 2006: 221). Elites and leaders therefore needed to reestablish their prominence, both in the political and religious milieu, to keep commoners from deserting their settlements for the relative safety of the forest. In the later Rosario phase, San José Magote hereditary elites established new residences at "Mound 1," a location previously reserved for public buildings, including temples. Placing their homes among the temples accomplished two goals: first, this more closely associated the elites with cosmological concerns, and, second, it more clearly located their residences as "separate" and more inaccessible than commoner homes (Barber and Joyce 2006: 220). At the same time, elites may have stepped up their sacrificial activities, carrying out human sacrifice more frequently, in order to establish a closer connection with ancestral protectors and thereby assuring commoners of increased protection effected by elite practices. The placement of elaborate tombs within elite compounds furthered the notion of close contact with powerful ancestors; elites could directly connect with ancestral protectors by entering the tombs to communicate with them. Barber and Joyce note (2006: 222) that the restructuring and consolidation of elite religious and political power was "communicated in the architecture and spatial setting of high-status residences. The increasingly enclosed and private setting of elite households, their increasing size and architectural elaboration, the interment of elites in tombs, and the close association of elite residences and public buildings were means by which the identity of nobles" could be established as significantly differentiated from the commoners (see also Joyce and Winter 1996 on this site's elite architecture). At San José Magote, elites who needed to regain religio-political power did so by choosing a residential location adjacent to the temples, as the first step toward a consolidation of control over community residents and further establishing their power at a time of external upheaval and internal uncertainty.

A final example comes from the East African coast (today's Tanzania) during the period of contact and initial colonization processes in the 15th and 16th centuries CE. Prior to these centuries, the culture that became known as the Swahili distinguished themselves from other African cultures by engaging in extensive trade with interior Africa, India, and the Middle East; they also converted to Islam (Fleisher and

LaViolette 2007). Until the 11th and 12th centuries, all houses in this region of Africa were built primarily of mud with palm-leaf thatch roofs, but by the 12th century, the Swahili were building stone houses that were qualitatively different from the standard mud-and-thatch residences (Donley-Reid 1990; Fleisher and LaViolette 2007; Horton 1994; Wynne-Jones 2013). The Swahili stone house involved the architectural elements of extensive labor investment and larger size to signal higher social status (Figure 9.1). Access analysis (chapter 3) helps to shed light on this example: Visitors entered into a foyer requiring passage through additional doors to achieve even the first, most public room in the house; visitors had no line of sight into the house until reaching the first room, and only then into other non-private rooms. Wall niches in these more public rooms displayed items such as porcelain and fine ceramics that Swahili families had acquired through trade; thus, the element of specialized mate-

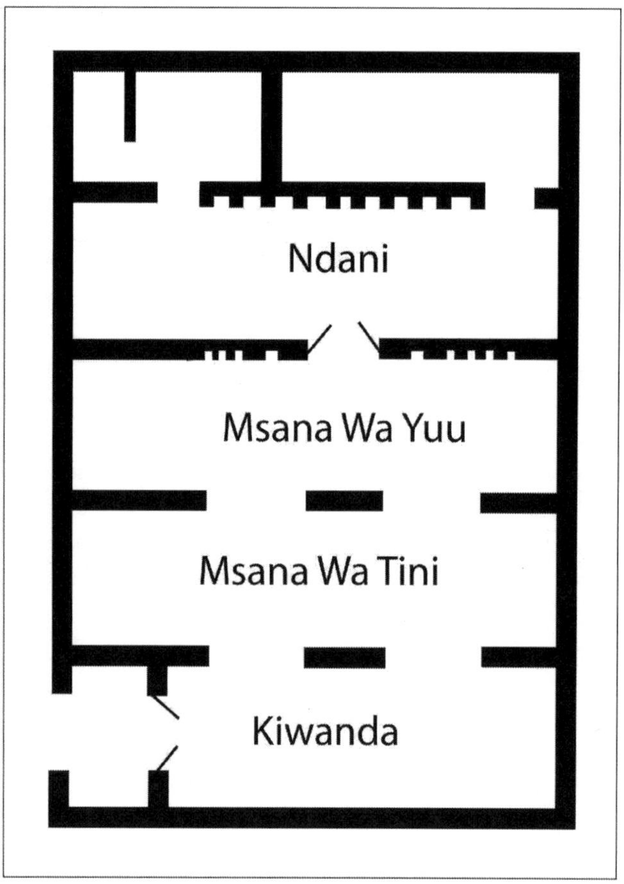

Figure 9.1: Swahili stone house (after Fleisher and LaViolette 2007: 180, fig. 8.2).

rial culture further emphasized their wealth and served as a type of "competition" with other town elites (Fleisher and LaViolette 2007: 187). The private sector of the house, the *ndani*, was both a refuge for women and the ritual space within the house (Donley-Reid 1990; Fleisher and LaViolette 2007); it was toward the back of the house, behind a shuttered doorway. Thus, the "front/back" structure that separates private from public was also operational in the Swahili stone house. The emergence of the stone house on the East African coast is a clear demonstration of elites establishing their Muslim identity and high-ranking social status.

An interesting architectural alteration took place within Swahili stone houses at the time of European arrival. In the 15th and 16th centuries, many coastal towns were abandoned, in part due to the Portuguese arrival and other factors having to do with trade connections with the Middle East and elsewhere. By the 17th century, new Swahili stone houses were being built in an era of extreme competition with European and Arab trade networks (Fleisher and LaViolette 2007: 188). The stone houses were similar to those of previous centuries, though perhaps more heavily fortified. There was one distinct difference inside the houses: the wall niches that had previously been more prominently located in the semi-public rooms were moved into the heavily decorated *ndani*, where only household occupants would typically see the niches and their contents (Fleisher and LaViolette 2007: 191; and see Wynne-Jones 2013). Besides household occupants, the only others who might view the *ndani*, at least the external wall niches and decorative elements, were kin and close friends who attended rituals (births, weddings) inside Swahili stone houses. The relocation of the "wealth indicators" and architectural elaboration served several purposes in later 16th- and 17th-century Swahili homes. First, in an era of extreme competitiveness and somewhat unstable politics, the relocation served to limit the ability of casual visitors, on entering the foyer, to see family wealth and thus perhaps open the household to unwanted hostile attention. Second, the more secure location of these elements served to reassure and reinforce house occupants' belief in their social standing and elite identity in a period of social upheaval (Fleisher and LaViolette 2007: 185–86). Finally, glimpses of these indicators gained by special visitors attending rituals ensured that "knowledge" about the social standing of stone house inhabitants was alive in the community; the relative "invisibility" of the evidence may have served to enhance the standing of Swahili elites among commoners, who could only imagine the riches secured inside the stone boundaries. The Swahili need to reestablish and refortify social standing at a time of political and economic instability was successfully effected through the manipulation of architecture and material contents.

Architecture and Transition: Shifts in Power and Societal Change

Several examples in the previous section have illustrated the circumstance of using architecture as a reaction to, and a reflection of, societal change. The "age of castles" in

16th- to 17th-century Japan occurred in response to the period of civil war and unrest in the region; emerging leaders used the building of the castles to establish their positions of power and to signal a new age of relative peace (Coaldrake 1996). San José Magote residents, during a time of social and political unrest, relocated their residences to areas previously reserved for public, often religious, buildings, to more closely tie their elite status with important cosmological beliefs and practices (Barber and Joyce 2006).

Two other examples clearly illustrate the important role architecture can play in reflecting social change and the recasting of power structures in archaeological settings. In the second century CE, villas in Britain began to add a winged corridor, which closely resembled Roman architecture on the continent (Figure 9.2a–b). While most have interpreted this architectural change as elite emulation of Roman ways, Eleanor Scott (1990) argues that this architectural shift was in response to increasing economic and political tensions during this period (for a similar argument regarding Pompeiian houses, see Grahame 2000). Using access analysis (see chapter 3), Scott argues that for some time, elites in Britain resisted Roman architectural styles, but eventually the addition of winged corridors at the entrance of the villas (leading into courtyards or to public reception areas) were accepted because of their utility in regulating movement into the residence (1990: 149–54). The addition of the winged corridors led visitors to the room in which residents wished to greet guests; prior to the addition of the corridors, guests entered courtyards that opened onto any number of rooms within the villa, both public and private. Scott suggests that this architectural change was in response to several economic and political upheavals taking place in Britain in the second century, including the introduction of the monetary system and a more firmly established Roman bureaucratic system (1990: 164–69). These elicited two responses from elites: the need to establish more boundaries and access controls to private space where monetary and other wealth was kept, and the need to control the movements of increasing numbers of visitors (bureaucrats, politicians, other elites) to the residence. The new winged corridors, as architectural responses to rapid economic and political change, accomplished two goals: to emulate the imperial elites of the continent, but more importantly, to achieve greater controls over personal and private space within the home.

A second example from the Classical period illustrates changing social values and the architectural alterations undertaken to satisfy new elite requirements. Lisa Nevett's survey of ancient Greek houses shows that in the Iron Age settlements of the tenth to eighth centuries BCE, houses were generally built of simple mudbrick, with very little differentiation in size, building materials, or material contents (2007: 365–67). During the eighth to sixth centuries, change in architecture began to signal a movement toward the "ancient Greek city" (Nevett 2007: 368). Though residential buildings continued to be relatively small and built of similar materials, house contents began to illustrate wealth differentiation, with some residents having greater access to prestige goods;

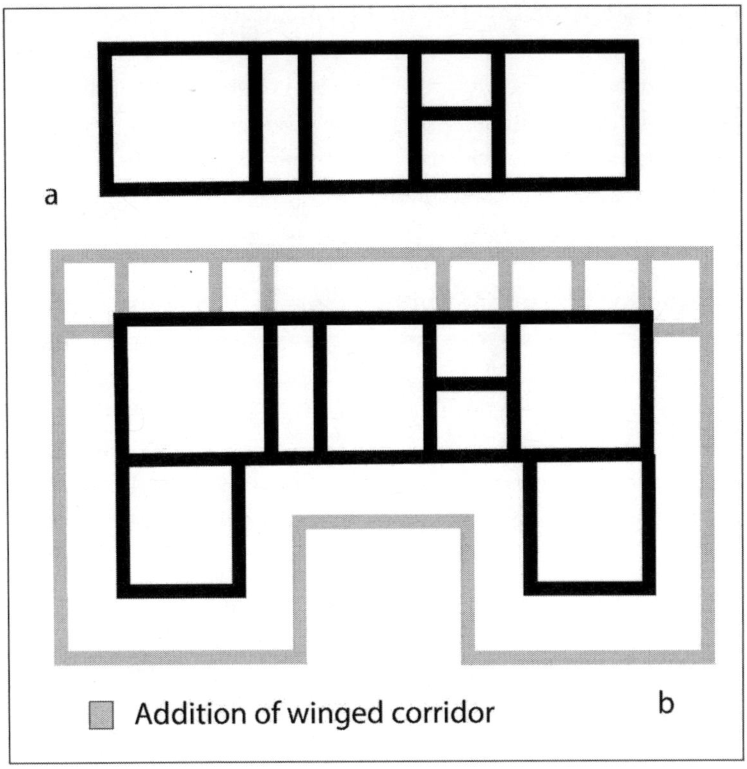

Figure 9.2: Examples of (a) an early villa without a winged-corridor and an open approach via a courtyard; and (b) a Romano-British winged corridor villa that would allow visitors to be guided into one or another room through the corridor (after Scott 1990: 155, fig. 7.5).

differentiation is particularly evident in burials. During the same time period, an increasing number of sanctuary sites and elaborate temples illustrates the ability of members in communities to marshal labor, and to bear the expense, for the building of monumental architecture; by the end of the sixth century, larger houses featuring more specialized rooms became prominent in Greek communities (Nevett 2007: 369–70).

By the fifth and fourth centuries, changes in architecture were extensive and well illustrate alterations in Greek society (Westgate 2007). At communities such as Olynthos (see Cahill 2002 and Nevett 1999), elite houses were built around an internal courtyard and featured 10 or more rooms; decorative features such as mosaic floors and painted plaster columns and walls were introduced (Nevett 2007: 372). These houses were built of finer materials, such as cut ashlar blocks, and doorways led into salons meant for entertaining visitors. A strong "front/back" organization in households was evident by the late fifth century, establishing a private zone closed to outsiders. Nevett attributes this to the emergence of the notion of "Greek citizenry" and the need for

Greek males to be able to document their position as a Greek citizen; this necessitated a need to "protect" Greek women in prominent families so that their marriage and production of children was more controlled (2007: 372–75). Organizing the physical space so that women could remain in back and private rooms while visitors (men) were entertained in the front salons provided a safeguard for the reputation of males through the seclusion of female household members, and legitimized male positions as Greek citizens (see also the discussion on seclusion in chapter 8).

Power beyond the House: The Public Sphere

The sections above have focused mainly on how domestic architecture can be used to attain and retain power. The majority of the following discussion turns to structures built with the public in mind, even though in many cases the public is never allowed inside. The aim of such monumental "public" buildings is to display symbols of power and provide ideological guidance to all who encounter the structure.

The Why of Monumentality

Why do so many cultures erect vast structures on the landscape? Fundamentally, the reason is to send a message to viewers, to signal information (e.g., Figure 9.3). The nature of the information depends on the type of monument, but it is relatively safe to say that in most cases part of the intention is to display the power held by the builders, or at least those who commissioned the construction (e.g., Dovey 1999; Emerson 1997b; Kolb 1994; J. D. Moore 1996a; Pollock 1999; A. T. Smith 2003; Trigger 2003). Kim Dovey makes an important distinction between the meanings of power "over" and power "to" (1999: 9–10; also see Ames 1995). Power "to" denotes empowerment, whether of a few or of many. Dovey notes that the empowerment of some can lead to the oppression of others: "Oppression and liberation are the two sides of the power coin. While the power *to* is the primary form of power, linked to empowerment, one person's empowerment can be another's oppression" (1999: 9). It is the power "over" that this chapter treats, and that monumentality generally is intended to create.

The urge to build monumental structures appears, at least archaeologically, to accompany increasing societal complexity and, in particular, the emergence of strong political leaders (Abrams 1989; Flannery 1998; Peebles and Kus 1977). Such leaders use a variety of means to establish and then maintain their positions of power. Demonstrating their ability to construct a visually impressive structure or monument, and then control the usage of it, is an excellent method of signaling one's command of people and place. Patrick Kirch (1990) offers an example of just this process in his study of the Polynesian colonization of Tonga and Hawaii. After migrating to these two island regions, societies in both places grew in sociopolitical complexity, developing a social hierarchy featuring elites with chiefs at the apex and the remainder population defined

Figure 9.3: Photo of Romania's Palace of Parliament in Bucharest. Nicolae Ceauşescu (who ruled Romania from 1965 to 1989) eradicated roughly one-third of Old Bucharest in order to build this palace, which is larger than the U.S. Pentagon. Ceauşescu intended to impress his own people and visitors with the power, beauty, and opulence of the building (photo by the author).

mainly as commoners; "in Tonga and Hawaii, monumental architecture was utilized by these chiefly elite as symbols through which their dominance was continually reasserted" (Kirch 1990: 207). Separated for 2,000 years, the Tongan and Hawaiian societies developed different styles of monumental architecture, but in both cases the structures illustrated the power of the chiefs. In Tonga, monuments were generally large earthen or stone-filled mounds built across the landscape; these mounds served as the sepulchers of the chiefs or were where important religious rituals took place (Kirch 1990: 209–11). In Hawaii, chiefs built formal temples where the societies' gods were worshipped and where chiefs oversaw important ceremonies associated with cosmology and health (Kirch 1990: 213–17). After arriving and building their societies, each seemingly inevitably moved to the construction of large monuments or edifices; although serving different purposes, the Polynesian monuments in these two island groups imparted the same message: the power over space and people by elites and leaders.

Perhaps the clearest answer to the question of "why monumentality" comes from Bruce Trigger's (1990) seemingly incongruous theory that expending more energy than anyone else demonstrates you have the most power. The key, however, is that the energy being expended is not actually that of the person or group wielding the power but that of those they control. Trigger, like others, notes that monumental architecture is found in nearly all ancient complex societies on every occupied continent, and that these structures, while differently rendered, all serve similar functions, such as defense, royal residences, religious buildings, or tombs; very rarely does the archaeologist come upon the monumental structure dedicated primarily to public use (1990: 119–121). Monumental architecture, in Trigger's view, is a function of "conspicuous consumption," and further it is a symbol of someone's wealth and power because it demonstrates that agent's ability to harness the activities of others (those commandeered to build the monument). He argues that, "[a]t the most elementary and general level, political power is universally perceived as the ability to control energy," and that monumental architecture "constituted the most public material embodiment of the power of upper classes. . . . [I]t was the most enduring statement of power that a ruler could hope to make" (1990: 126, 127). As some of the monuments we study today are thousands of years old, ancient rulers can be satisfied that their gambit for power and recognition was indeed successful.

Public Architecture and the Power to Control

Not all public monuments were meant to control or influence behavior; many, once built, were simply intended to make a strong impression and express a particular ideology to all who viewed them. If one travels to the Anatolian heartland of Turkey, nearly every hill or low mountain sports a tumulus, mounds built by Phrygian kings to mark their tombs. Viewing the tumuli reminded average Phrygians, as they went about their daily tasks, of their past and present leaders and the power of the king, but daily tasks and movement about communities were not restricted or guided by the presence of the tumuli (Figure 9.4). In many other cultures, however, large public monuments or constructions were specifically meant to control movements and behaviors either on a daily basis or at particular points during important ritual or secular events. The message, the ideology, expressed by such structures is directly related to the power of the rulers/elites; to this end, J. Cameron Monroe asserts, "The real potential or architecture as a tool of power may thus rest in its ability to routinize collective perception and experience of the world, the goal of which is to create docile subjects who internalize the agendas of their political masters" (2010: 371).

Archaeologists who wish to determine whether public architecture was meant to exert control over part or all of the community would do well to ask the types of questions Jerry Moore did in his study of ancient Andean structures: "Where is a public building located? . . . How many people could fit inside of it? . . . Were activities associated with the building designed to be hidden or visible? Was access within the building restricted or open?" (1996a: 15). Some of the examples above illustrate the application of such questions to monumental architecture, with the resulting answers indicating that elite power was the intended goal. For instance, building Japanese palaces on low, more accessible hilltops rather than on mountaintops ("Where is the public building located?") symbolized the new leader's control of the region and his certainty that attack on his kingdom was impossible. At San José Magote, the increasing inaccessibility of housing compounds ("Were activities hidden or visible?") was

Figure 9.4: Example of Iron Age (Phrygian-period) tumulus in central Turkey, near the author's site of Çadır Höyük, Yozgat Province (photo by the author).

meant to convince commoners of the stability of elite power and control in a time of political and economic upheaval.

It is in the Americas that the relationship between power and the built environment has been most fully explored (e.g., Ashmore 1989, 2005; Fox 1996; Inomata 2006; Loten 2006; J. D. Moore 1996a). A particular focus has been the elite use of public plazas not only to signal important ideological symbols and messages through public ceremonies but to employ these seemingly open spaces to effectively reaffirm social hierarchies. This is demonstrated by Moore's study of Andean plazas, where open and closed access not only regulated who could attend what ceremonies but simultaneously reinforced social ranking (1996b). As was common in many of the ancient major centers in the Americas, Andean plazas were where important rituals were carried out. Moore notes that in centers such as Cuzco, Inca plazas were enormous, allowing occupancy by much of the common population during important ceremonies like the *Inti Raymi* in which Inca ancestral rulers were celebrated (1996b: 792–93). Access points into the Inca plazas were numerous and permeability was regularized; it was access into the buildings—the shrines and temples—that was denied to all but the royalty, some elites, and the priests (J. D. Moore 1996b: 793). The public ceremonies in the enormous plazas brought all residents together in a shared rite that impressed upon them the power of the state; notions of unity, safety, and economic success provided by the state were ritually and spatially shared with the Inca commoners (J. D. Moore 1996b: 797). The rituals intended to satisfy the needs of the gods, however, were better left to the experts, and these were carried out beyond the presence of any but the most rarified elite individuals.

Similar messages were delivered in a very different setting at Chimu centers such as Chan Chan. Here each ruler built his own palace, and the plazas were incorporated into the palace grounds; courtyards had baffled entrances through which access could be limited and controlled (J. D. Moore 1996b: 794). Plazas were also surrounded by walls, so that any activity taking place within the plaza was invisible to those outside. Moore and others speculate that only the elite classes were allowed into Chimu plazas to witness ceremonies and rituals; the boundaries and limited access to these plazas functioned "as a medium of social control marking significant class distinctions . . . an objectification of a social divide" (J. D. Moore 1996b: 794). Both the Chumu and Inca cultures sought to demonstrate elite status and state power through the use of architecture and plazas but accomplished these through very different methods. The Inca wished to portray solidarity among all the people, restricting them only from the most private of religious ceremonies. These uses of the spatial setting served to inform the people not only of the political stability of the state but also of the intimate relationship between rulers and the cosmological world. At Chimu, solidarity was not intended in the least; the goal was rather for rulers to demonstrate their ultimate authority, and that of the elite classes, over all other social groups. This was accomplished by barring everyone but the most privileged from all important state and religious ceremonies. The Chimu took a "we'll handle it all, don't worry about anything" approach to power and authority, using architecture to convey this message.

Monroe (2010) finds similar strategies employed in the pre-colonial Dahomean culture of West Africa. By the 18th and 19th centuries, Dahomey had grown wealthy and powerful through the Atlantic slave trade. However, this very success had led to political upheaval and occasional usurpation of the throne by challengers to dynastic claimants (Monroe 2010: 373–74). It was essential, therefore, for any leader to demonstrate his power and the stability of the state in order to assuage fears of internal war, which might lead to unrest among the commoners. Architecture was a primary means of conveying a sense of political order and the ultimate authority of the king during these tumultuous centuries. The king's royal palace was the center of political life; a large portion of the palace was set aside for domestic functions, but the rest was divided into areas devoted to political, economic, and ritual activities attended by Dahomey's elite classes (Monroe 2010: 377). A third area associated with the palace was a courtyard just outside the palace gates. Public ceremonies took place here, using the palace as a backdrop, and it was here that non-elites could gather to participate in the festivities. One of the most important of these ceremonies was the *Xwetanu*, meant to honor the arrival of a new king, but the ceremony was also carried out during the king's life. At these ceremonies, great wealth was distributed (by the king himself and by royal officials) to the people, and human sacrifices were performed (Monroe 2010: 374, 377). The *Xwetanu* signaled, in a setting magnified by the monumental palace as backdrop, the king's possession of complete power and authority, even over the very lives of humans, and that the state was unquestionably economically solvent. For attendees at the *Xwetanu*, "Dahomean palaces . . . clearly involved elements of architectural 'shock and awe. . . . [T]he display and distribution of wealth to the masses, the public sacrifice of human captives, and the incorporation of coercive symbols of state authority into the very fabric of these sites collectively served to highlight" the power of the state (Monroe 2010: 378).

Inside the Dahomean kings' palaces, the organization of space was also designed to signal messages—this time, to the officials and elites allowed passage into the structure. A series of courtyards were devoted to activities such as public audiences, dispute resolution, entertainment of high-ranking visitors, and ritual activities, including human sacrifice (Monroe 2010: 379). The most important and restricted activities were carried out in courtyards in the deepest part of the (public) portion of the palace; only the highest officials and elites could gain ingress into these courtyards. The employment of access analysis (see chapter 3) illustrates the increasing number of nodal passages necessary to gain entry into the innermost courtyards (Monroe 2010: 388). Thus, similar to the Inca usage of architecture, the Dahomean kings carried out public ceremonies that welcomed commoners and assured them of the king's authority and the wealth of the state. Inside the palace, strict sociopolitical hierarchical divisions were maintained using semiotic symbols in the form of access, or lack thereof, to various areas within the palace. Lower-ranking elites could proceed only to the most external of the palace courtyards, while those in the "inner circle" gained access to regions deep inside. Messages of individual power, social position, and the state's authority were delivered to commoners and elites alike mainly through the architectural setting of Dahomean palaces.

Monumental architectural symbols of power and authority come in myriad cultures and forms. Obvious examples come first to mind: the Egyptian pyramids, the temples on Athenian acropolis, China's Forbidden City, or perhaps even the Taj Mahal. However, other types of structures, less monumental but just as successful at conveying messages, exist in the archaeological record. The Harappan Great Bath at Mohenjo Daro (Kenoyer 1998; Possehl 2005), set apart from the domestic section of the city, may have signaled the importance of the religious personnel allowed to enter the pool; the long barrow and passage tombs of prehistoric Britain may have touted their owner's power and authority over land and labor (e.g., Hayden 2003); and the strategic hilltop positioning of the Great Zimbabwean king's residence may have provided him ultimate religious authority over his people as he interacted with the great deity believed to dwell in a cave just below the king's residence (Huffman 1996; Steadman 2009).

Architecture and the Transfer of Power

In the same way that architecture can be used to establish or maintain power and authority, it can also indicate a shift in these. An excellent modern example of a shift in power and ideology was the Soviet architectural style that quickly appeared in Russia itself and then in every part of Europe (and elsewhere) that fell under Soviet control in the mid-20th century. Caroline Humphrey (2005: 39) outlines the real and intended impact of this architectural style:

> The relation between early Soviet ideology and infrastructure appears straightforward—yet it has a breathtaking audacity.... [T]he task of Soviet construction was to build material foundations that would mould nothing less than a new society.... After the Revolution, architecture became one of they [*sic*] key arenas of ideology. In the 1920s, it was actually believed that carefully designed living quarters, for example, could eliminate the conditions for individualistic and *meshchanskie* (petty-minded bourgeois) ways of life, and on this basis a new human type would become the norm: Socialist Man and Socialist Woman.

Towering, plainly built "communal-style" buildings, best translated as "dormitories" (*obshchezhitie*), with identical basic facilities in each single room offered each person roughly 4.5 m^2 of living space for as many as 1,300 residents in a single building (Humphrey 2005: 244–47). Such structures began to dot Moscow and Leningrad and later the European cities under Soviet control. Occupants were meant to "work together" and to eschew individualism; they were one with state and party. Humphrey asserts that the Soviet examples demonstrated that "political ideology can take material form," and she goes on to note that "the house built by people for themselves is different from the case of state construction projects in which housing is allocated and the inhabitants are mere passive recipients" (2005: 39). In both domestic and public architecture, the built environment can send messages of power shifts and new ideologies that are meant to be internalized by those living within the new or changing regime, as is demonstrated in the following sections.

The Architectural Imprint of Colonization

The archaeological investigation of colonialism has become a vibrant area of investigation in the last decade or two (Given 2004; Gosden 2004; Lyons and Papadopoulos 2002; Murray 2004; Stein 2005a; Torrence and Clarke 2000). It would seem that architectural styles of the "home country," imposed on a colonized landscape, would be glaring examples illustrating a transfer of power. After all, the Roman imprint on much of the Mediterranean landscape is inescapable, even today. As Susan Alcock points out, it is the Romans who gave us the word, and in many ways perfected the creation of a "colony" (2005: 297). Alcock and others (e.g., Bartel 1980, 1987; Dyson 1985, 2003;

Woolf 1998) use the establishment of the Roman built environment—including roads, but also villas, temples, and architectural features such as winged corridors (discussed above)—to create a rich archaeologically based history of Roman colonization and the changes this brought to both people and landscape.

The colonial process often leads to long-term settlement, and today many colonial structures, and those predating colonial arrival, are buried under more recent urban sprawl or have been bulldozed as sacrificial victims to progress. For instance, Martin Hall notes that Dutch colonies such as "New Amsterdam" (now Manhattan), and another in what is now Recife, in Brazil, are modern urban centers below which only traces of Dutch colonial material culture might remain (Hall 1993: 180). In contrast, the nature of the colonization in southern Africa allows archaeological investigation of the Dutch imprint and the influence exerted on the indigenous population. Outside of the larger centers such as Cape Town, Dutch outposts, either belonging to the Dutch East India Company or to Dutch elites who used them as country estates, still remain (Hall 1993: 182). Buildings, along with associated material culture and, of course, colonial records, reveal the transformation from an open landscape full of roaming cattle herds to that enclosed for "productive" use, including by the African laborers who came to be ensnared in such estates after their traditional livelihoods were no longer viable (e.g., Brink 2004; Mitchell 2001; Schrire 1988, 1995; van Sittert 2002). It is in places such as southern Africa, with relatively uncongested rural landscapes and the existence of a rich historical record, that the architectural imprint of colonization can be more often found.

Architecture can also reflect the process of religious colonization—that is, when a new religion becomes embedded in a culture. Two examples illustrate this phenomenon well, one in West Africa, profiling the arrival of Islam, and the other in Iceland with the arrival of Christianity. Heidi Nast (1996) analyzed the floor plan of the Kano City palace, built ca. CE 1500, after Islam had arrived in the region via clerics and scholars. Kano City is in the northern Hausaland region of Nigeria. Nast employed a methodology using a modified version of both semiotics and access analysis to understand how the use of space had altered within residential settings after the arrival of Islam. She found among the *Maguzawa*, referring to those who do not practice Islam, houses have no gender segregation, and there is no gender-based organization of space outside the home either (1996: 52–53). *Maguzawa* women work in the agricultural fields, go to the markets, and are not barred from any locations where non-kin men might be present. The inference is that this was the gendered social structure of all the peoples of the Kano City region prior to the arrival of Islam. When the king's palace was built in approximately 1500, the internal organization reflected strict attention to gender segregation, and a substantial portion of the palace was devoted to seclusion of the royal wives (Nast 1996: 44, 54–58). The architectural footprint of the palace indicates that principal elements of Muslim attitudes toward gendered segregation (and probably other Islamic-based religious behaviors) had become ensconced in the royal family, possibly in the entire elite class, by the late 15th century.

The arrival of Christianity in Iceland had an impact not only on the architecture but on the landscape as a whole. Norse settlers from Scandinavia first came to previously uninhabited Iceland in the ninth century CE, establishing farmsteads in which all family members resided in the household, generally a single "longhouse" residence (Bolender 2007: 401–2). While Icelandic society was socially hierarchical at this time, with landowners at the pinnacle and servants and slaves in descending order, this was reflected in longhouse living space rather than in residences on the landscape. Farmstead boundaries were marked by the burial of deceased kin; boundaries in pre-Christian beliefs were dangerous places and thus were protected from outside threat or encroachment by the presence of dead ancestors (Bolender 2007: 409). Christianity came to Iceland in the 11th century, and with it came institutionalized hierarchies regarding property ownership that changed housing patterns and boundary identifications. It was at this time that Icelandic "great houses" began to appear on the landscape; the (possibly immigrant) Christian residents appear to have usurped the independent property of original settlers, turning the latter into tenant farmers: "The social and physical landscape of predominately independent houses with individual farmlands was transformed to one of institutionalized inequality among farmsteads while others expanded control to own multiple estates" (Bolender 2007: 413). A socioeconomic hierarchy was established, reflected in the establishment of grand houses and lesser dwellings on smaller plots of land. Another architectural indicator of the new religion was the establishment of churches near the great houses on the large estates. The "fear of borders" was eradicated in the Christian belief system, and the dead were no longer buried under mounds at farmstead boundaries but rather in cemeteries near the churches (Bolender 2007: 415). Instead of ancestral protection, farmstead boundaries were marked by the erection of physical walls. As Bolender notes, "The transformations in the religious and economic relationships among Icelanders were manifest in the landscape" (2007: 413) and in the very structures in which they resided and worshipped.

Internal Shifts in Power: New Leaders, New Ideologies

To a large extent, internal societal changes derived from new ideologies has already been illustrated above. The example from Iceland just discussed shows how the arrival of a new belief system can impact not just the people but their use of space as well. The same can be said of the Kano City palace and its reflection of Islamic principles of gender separation. Finally, the self-consciously "unreligious" Soviet ideology and the massive impact this had on people's housing choices nicely exemplifies how new ideologies adopted within a culture are evident in the built environment. The following case studies portray in stark relief the principles of internal change; in one case, it is the acceptance of a new belief system that allows leaders to radically change the lives, and landscapes, of the people they ruled; and in the other, it is the shift from religious to largely secular rule that results in largely new monumental structures.

One of the most spectacular examples of architecture representing the adoption of a new ideology is the Cambodian landscape that is filled with stone-built temples. By the early centuries CE, both Hinduism and Buddhism were present in Southeast Asia, having traveled with pilgrims and traders from South Asia. At the same time, the first Southeast Asian empire, the Funan, was growing in power (Stark 2004). The Funan, followed by the Kingdom of Chenla in the sixth century CE, had rulers who practiced either the still poorly understood indigenous religions or had converted to Buddhism or Hinduism, as had many of their subjects.

In CE 802, Jayavarman II took up the throne of the Khmer Empire, which stretched across what is today Cambodia to the Gulf of Thailand in the west and Laos in the north. At Jayavarman II's installation ceremony, he instituted a second rite to follow the crowning ceremony making him king of his people: the second ceremony elevated him to the status of a god and he became the representative on earth of the Hindu god Shiva (Higham 1989; Snellgrove 2004). Jayavarman was the first of a string of Khmer kings to become deified rulers, most assuming the representation of Shiva but some choosing Vishnu; in each case, temples to the new god-king had to be erected. Angkor Wat and Angkor Thom, both built in the 12th century CE, are the largest and best known of the Khmer temples (Figure 9.5), which also functioned as mausoleums for the god-kings. In the first four centuries of Khmer rule, hundreds of lavish stone temples were built by direction of the god-king rulers (Stark 2004). Labor was supplied by the Khmer people, who were required to give this service to their god-king. Thousands of stonecutters and stonemasons, architects, artists, and day laborers for every task were removed from their own fields and required to work to construct temples, shrines, canals, and occasionally public works such as hospitals, for the empire. Eventually, this practice took a steep toll on the empire's wealth and aging infrastructure; people were building temples when they should have been assigned to canal repair. The Khmer Empire collapsed in the 15th century, leaving behind a stunning architectural legacy testifying to the impact a new ideology can have within an empire and on its people.

A second example comes from Mesopotamia in the fourth and third millennia BCE and illustrates an ideological shift toward more secular rule, or at least more secular control over the economic sector. In the fourth millennium BCE, southern Mesopotamian cities competed with one another for access to trade routes and resources to feed the needs and desires of growing populations and economies (Algaze 1993, 2008; Pollock 1999; Postgate 1992; Stein 1999). Materials brought back to cities such as Uruk came in raw or partially worked form to be fashioned by city artisans into luxury crafts for elites and utilitarian items for commoners. Farmers and herders provided food for vast populations, bringing in their goods from the countryside on a regular basis. During the second half of the fourth millennium, this complex economic system of farmers and herders, traders, craftmakers, and administrators appears to have been regulated through the temples and their personnel at these Mesopotamian cities (Emberling 2001; Hudson 1999; Matthews 2003; Nissen 1988; Pollock 1999). The apparent absence

Figure 9.5: Photos of Angkor Wat (top) and Angkor Thom (bottom), both temples and mausolea built by Khmer kings (photos by the author).

of substantial secular public buildings, together with the existence of multiple temples where goods were received and redistributed, suggests that rulership of these powerful fourth-millennium southern Mesopotamian city-states was located within the religious realm and handled by those who controlled the temples.

This vast economic system collapsed around the turn of the millennium, followed by a century or two of political and economic instability. In ca. 2900 BCE, a new era called the "Early Dynastic Period" (also known as the "Sumerian civilization") ensued, and southern Mesopotamian cities began to feature spectacular palaces in addition to the temples, both of which dominated city centers. Sumerian kings, whose names are preserved in a historo-mythical document known as the Sumerian King List, now appear to be in charge of important functions within their city-states, including the economy, political relations, and military matters (Nissen 1988; Pollock 1999). While temple priests still wielded significant power, the king had emerged as a major figure in the Sumerian states of the third millennium. Thus, in the fourth millennium BCE, the temples represented the economic and political center of Uruk Mesopotamia; by the late third millennium, the palace represented a vital center of power (perhaps in competition with the temple) in Sumerian city-states.

The Art of Architectural Emulation

Anthropological analyses of cultures impacted by colonialism find that when change is accepted, or at least deemed inevitable, a process of "emulation" often takes place (Spindler 1977). The contacted/conquered culture adopts visual styles symbolic of the more powerful entity in the region, perhaps to acquire favorable treatment from that entity or to assume greater levels of status and power locally through association with it. An excellent example of architecture possibly signaling emulation rather than outright colonization is that found at sites in the later fourth millennium BCE Mesopotamian world. As noted above, the temples appear to have been the physical seat of power in later fourth-millennium Mesopotamian cities such as Uruk. These temples were built in an architectural style known as "niching and buttressing" and were decorated with mosaics formed by using cylindrical wall cones (Forest 1999). Buildings at Uruk were laid out in a distinctive "tripartite" style, with a middle hall and two rows of rooms on each side (Figure 9.6), all built with a particular style of mudbrick known as *Reimchen*. As southern Mesopotamian influence spread northward, these architectural elements began to appear in the north (in settlements in today's Syria and southeastern Turkey).

In some cases, such as at the Syrian site of Habuba Kabira, the public and domestic architecture mimics that of Uruk so perfectly that the site is thought by some to be an Uruk colony (Akkermans and Schwartz 2003: 190–97; Algaze 1993, 2008). In other cases, however, it appears that local elites were emulating Uruk architectural styles. At Tell Brak, also in Syria, a large structure known as the "Eye Temple" was built on a tripartite plan with extensive niching and buttressing, though local architectural styles are also found in the temple complex (Akkermans and Schwartz 2003: 198–200). Brak was a powerful city in its own right in the later fourth millennium, and rather than being an Uruk colony, it seems to have been engaged in productive economic exchange with southern Mesopotamia (Oates et al. 2007). Two other sites in southeastern Turkey offer similar evidence. Arslantepe and Hassek Höyük also built public structures, mainly temples, that featured southern Mesopotamian styles (along with other southern material culture), but their status as Uruk exchange partners rather than as controlled colonies is

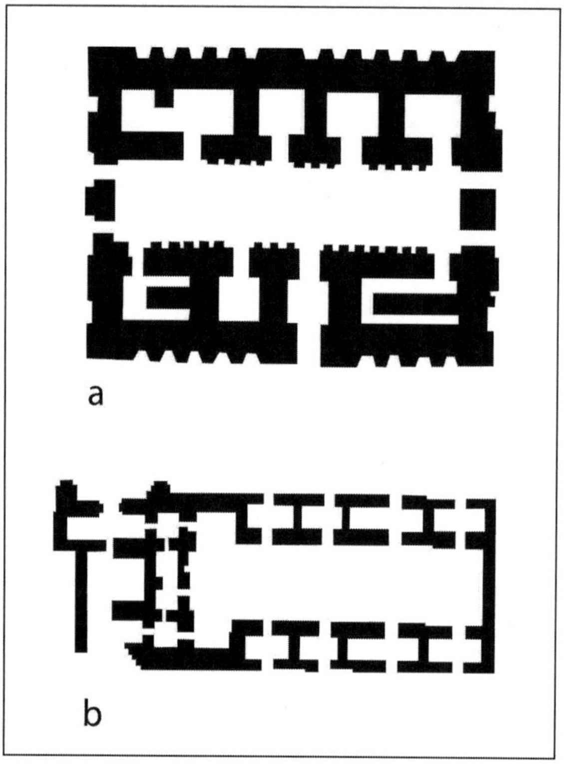

Figure 9.6: Examples of tripartite temples and buildings in southern Mesopotamia that were emulated in other regions. The example depicted in (a) is heavily niched and buttressed.

strongly argued by scholars (Algaze 2008; Frangipane 2001; Helwing 1999; Stein 1999). In general, these architectural characteristics at Syrian and Turkish sites reflect a desire to emulate the power of the southern state, and perhaps to highlight their interaction with it rather than direct control by it (Stein 1999, 2002, 2005b). The emulation of architectural styles commonly known to be associated with the powerful Uruk/southern Mesopotamian state may have lent even more status to local elites, both in their dealings with local populations and also perhaps with emissaries from the south.

A second example of emulation is found in South America during the last quarter of the first millennium CE, when the Wari Empire was at its height. Wari imperial control stretched across many areas of what is today's Peru; in these regions, the Wari established administrative centers in order to effect direct control over the conquered peoples (Jennings and Álvarez 2001). Two sites in Peru's Cotahuasi Valley feature Wari architectural forms that have suggested to many that this valley, like so many others, was under direct Wari administrative control. Justin Jennings and Willy Álvarez argue, however, that it was local elites that built their administrative centers in Wari style "to symbolically link themselves to imperial power" (2001: 144). In other words, the Cotahuasi Valley was never under Wari direct control; instead, local elites emulated the Wari architectural style in order to elevate their own status, and perhaps their level of control, in the valley. Jennings and Álvarez note that, upon close examination, the administrative architecture at the two Cotahuasi sites, Collota and Netahaha, were initially built according to local style but were then "Warified" in outward appearance. While Wari architecture was typically very precise and consistent, architecture at Collota and Netahaha featured rooms of various sizes and a "relative sloppiness" in the building style (Jennings and Álvarez 2001: 153–54). To emulate Wari imperial style, Cotahuasi leaders erected an impressive wall around their previously open administrative centers, which served to physically and visually close them to access by nonelites: "Imposing in form and restrictive in nature, the enclosure was probably a daunting symbol that the power of the new paramount chief was based in something neither personal nor local" (Jennings and Álvarez 2001: 155), though he was most probably indeed a local. Local elites apparently found that emulating, through architecture, Wari imperial power gave them increased influence in their own valley.

Conclusion

This chapter demonstrates that there is quite a bit to say about the intersection of power and architecture. The examples offered above are but a fraction of the studies that document how the placement of a building, the establishment of a wall, the gating of a doorway, or the aggrandizement of a facade can produce feelings of fear, awe, envy, respect, or indignation in those who pass by the structure either every day or in a once-in-a-lifetime visit. An aspect to this subject left unwritten here is resistance to built symbols of power. Like the literature on the archaeology of colonialism, the research on the archaeology of resistance is significant (Ferguson 1991; Liebman and Murphy 2011; Miller, Rowlands, and Tilley 1995; Preucel 2002; Reid et al. 1997; Welk 2012). The archaeological record, including the built environment, can offer quite a nuanced view of the struggle between master and slave, colonizer and colonized, or ruler and subjects.

Chapter 10

The Symbolic and the Sacred: The House and Beyond

The subject of religion and the built environment is very likely in the top three on the list of archaeological investigations of ancient architecture. An equally impressive assemblage of literature is also dedicated to the subject of sacred places on the landscape. Attempting to capture the rich literature concerning the entirety of archaeological thinking on the intersection between humans and their sacred places, be they built or unbuilt, is simply impossible in a single chapter, and perhaps even beyond containment in an entire volume devoted to the subject. Therefore, after an initial discussion, this chapter offers a light brushstroke over the sacred landscape and the methods archaeologists have used to recognize meaningful places. This topic was addressed to some extent in chapter 2; here the focus is not on natural places that might draw one to build one's first house, but on places constructed *after* permanent settlement had commenced.

Following the discussion on landscape, domestic structures are the focus: identifying the ancestral home, finding ritual within the dwelling, and defining methodologies devoted to recognizing the intersection between house and cosmos. The myriad ways that humans embed religiosity into their homes makes archaeological recognition of it hugely challenging. Even more daunting is that not all behavior that appears "ritualistic" is actually religious (Renfrew 1994). Further, the symbolic elements in religious belief are manifold and are sometimes beyond the grasp even of

Archaeology of Domestic Architecture and the Human Use of Space, by Sharon R. Steadman, 249–289.

anthropologists, much less archaeologists (e.g., Fogelin 2007a; Robb 1998; Turner 1967). Nonetheless, archaeologists continue to search the archaeological record for evidence of religious manifestations in the past, often with startling success. Before beginning a discussion on the ritualized landscape or built environment, a brief foray into the subject of human religion is useful. Acknowledging that ancient religion was a near or, more likely, total universality in the past allows archaeologists to devise methodologies that will recognize it in the archaeological record.

Ancient Humans, Ancient Religion

In recent years, topics investigating science and the mind have been explored in the anthropological and archaeological treatment of ancient religion. The field of cognitive archaeology, discussed in chapter 2, plays a critical role in accessing ancient beliefs. This field attempts to discern mental trajectories of ancient peoples and even to predict what human brain functions might produce in terms of behavior in various contexts (Abramiuk 2012; Flannery and Marcus 1998; Mithen 1996; Renfrew 2012). Working from a cognitive approach, scholars have argued that religion emerged among earlier humans as a response to a dangerous, unpredictable, but beautiful environment (Atran 2002; Boyer 2001; de Lumley 2009; Lewis-Williams 2010; Mithen 1996; Rappaport 1999); in essence, religion is hardwired into the human experience (see discussion in Steadman 2009: 21–35). As initial responses to that environment became normalized behavior, they were passed down to succeeding generations, often gaining in number and elaboration depending on the needs of the individual and the community (McCauley and Lawson 2007; Mithen 1997; Rossano 2007; Whitehouse 2000, 2004a, 2004b). Human religious belief and the associated performance of rituals may derive directly from ancient human experience, resulting from the way the human brain functions and thus making religion a human universal (Lewis-Williams 2008; Liénard and Boyer 2006; Rossano 2011, 2013; Whitley 2008; Winkelman 2008).

Discovering religious practice archaeologically is generally as difficult as pinpointing the emergence of religious belief in the human species. What one archaeologist might interpret as a ritual object, space, or building is considered completely secular and utilitarian by another. Nonetheless, there are some circumstances of material culture that generally can be relied upon to be indicative of ritual behavior or sacred space. Richard Blanton attempted to define religiosity in the archaeological and, particularly, the architectural record, terming various types of material culture occurrences as "canonical communication" (1994: 79). Derived from a study that included many cultures, both ethnographic and archaeological, Blanton offers several indicators that should alert a researcher as to the intertwining of religious belief or action within or around a dwelling (1994: 80). Drawing on Blanton, on discussions presented in other studies (Renfrew 1994, 2007a, 2007b; Steadman 2005, 2009; Verhoeven 2002), and on observations of archaeological settings by the author, the following list describes aspects of ritualized or religious behavior that might be recognizable in the architectural record:

- A sacred space within the house, termed by Blanton an "axis mundi," allows residents to achieve interaction with supernatural forces. Persons allowed in the space, which may not be all household members, likely have a higher status, at least in the area of religious practice.
- The location and form of the house, including its layout or orientation, and its treatment at abandonment may suggest the house was designed to align with geomantic concepts present in the culture's belief system, essentially making the house a partial or complete physical representation of the cosmos or at least attractive to supernatural forces that will offer protection and good fortune. An intentional destruction or abandonment of the house may indicate it was "living" along with its inhabitants and that its life cycle had to end for various cosmological reasons.
- Indicators of household ritual and religious belief, in the form of shrines, altars, burials, subfloor deposits, or other material culture can tie the residents to behavior associated with their belief system.
- Constructions, not necessarily structures, built in association with the house, such as earthworks under or near the house, or other features clearly associated with the home but not immediately identifiable as utilitarian, may be indicative of ritual behavior or representative of an ancient cosmological landscape.

These indicators are at the heart of the methodologies discussed below.

Beyond (?) the House

This chapter would not be complete without some discussion of the sacred landscape or, more accurately, religious structures on that landscape. This is a vast topic, however, worthy of a book, or several. Mortuary monuments, for instance, occur on nearly every continent and date to as early as the Neolithic, if not before. As discussed below, the long-barrow tombs of Europe are perhaps meant to represent a permanent *dwelling* for the deceased ancestors; the goods placed in mortuary monuments, in burial mounds in the American South, the Royal Tombs of Ur, the Shang Dynasty tombs, the Egyptian tombs, and others suggest that, in many ways, these final resting places were in fact considered the new "homes" of the dead. It is worth considering, therefore, where a community buried its dead and how that location might have functioned in their cosmology and world view, whether as separate realm or extension of the house. The intention in this short section is to offer a brief overview of a few *types* of constructions that may have been considered a house or extensions of the house. Thus, the odd built "thing" discovered near a prehistoric house might be worth further consideration as to its role within the community's cosmology.

The House as Temple

The discussion here focuses on the spectacular stone monument at Göbekli Tepe in southeastern Turkey, a structure Colin Renfrew describes as "the world's first temple, or first built sanctuary" (2009b: 90). Klaus Schmidt, who excavated the site from 1995 to 2013 (Schmidt 1998, 2002, 2006, 2008), notes that no habitation structures have been found in the vicinity of Göbekli (2010). He identified at least three stratigraphic layers that date to the tenth and ninth millennia BCE. The earliest, Layer III, offers monumental circular enclosures, ca. 10 × 15 m, that comprise concentric walls (Figure 10.1); resting inside these structures are huge T-shaped monoliths and internal pillars that stood as high as 5.5 m (Schmidt 2011). What has caught wide attention is the decoration on the Layer III standing stones. Most commonly depicted are the carved images of animals, including bulls, dogs, birds, a fox, aurochs, gazelle, and others (Schmidt 2011). In addition to the animals, some pillars depict what appear to be human motifs, including arms and hands. It is clear that these huge pillars carried symbolic meaning for their builders. These circular structures were intentionally filled, and at some point, either contemporary with their building or after the infilling, new structures were built in Layer III/II. These are later circular or ovoid structures that are far smaller and seem to be devoid of stone monoliths (Schmidt 2006). The final stratigraphic level, Layer II, features rectangular structures that are smaller, usually ca. 5 × 3 m in size, with nicely constructed stone floors and occasionally including smaller T-shaped pillars that are largely undecorated and reach heights of only about 1.5 m or less. Schmidt and others (e.g., Belfer-Cohen and Goring-Morris 2002, 2005; Watkins 2004b) have argued that the structures at Göbekli were built by the partially or wholly mobile hunter-gatherers of the region as a cult place for ritual activity, including feasting, but that these remarkable structures did not function in any way as habitations.

A different interpretation is offered by Ted Banning (2011b), who draws on a host of data on Neolithic Near Eastern houses and cult activity (e.g., Cauvin 2000; Hodder 2006, 2010; Hodder and Meskell 2010, 2011; Kuijt 2002, 2008b; Simmons 2011; Verhoeven 2002, 2011a; Watkins 1990) to suggest that the Göbekli Tepe structures *did* function as both houses *and* ritual places. Banning argues that peoples of this time and region made virtually no distinction between the natural and symbolic world and that religion and ritual were brought into Near Eastern Neolithic houses in many ways, including through burials, wall decorations, and ritual objects (2011b: 627–29). The very same, Banning suggests, is the case at Göbekli, where residents decorated their house walls with meaningful images testifying to their hunting-gathering past and present lifeways and their emerging sedentary and cultivation-based futures. That the earlier

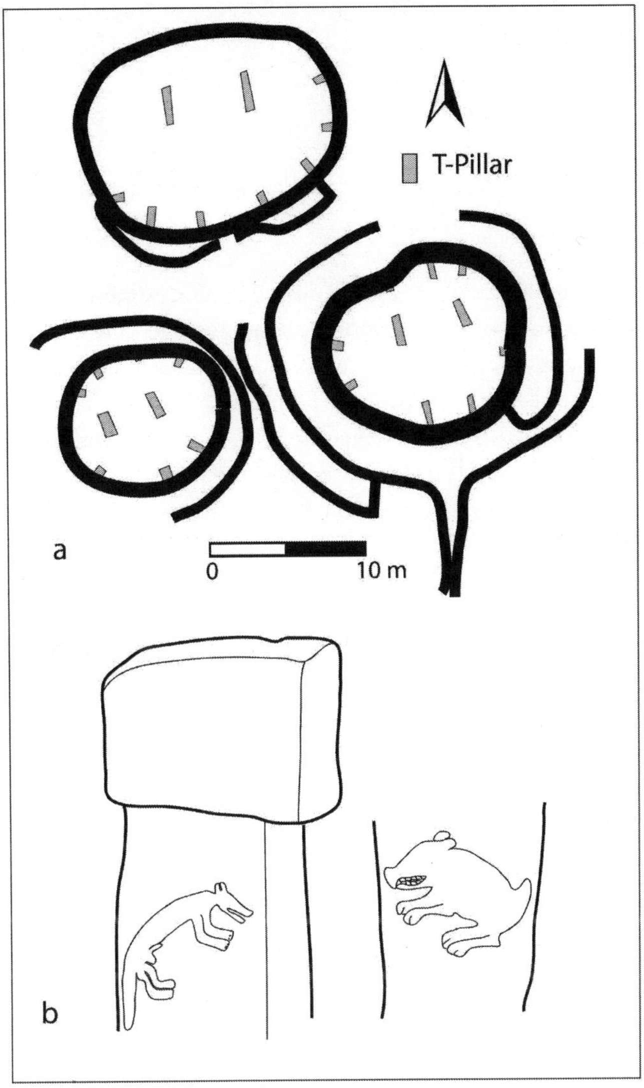

Figure 10.1: (a) Stylized plan of Göbekli Tepe Phase III structures with T-pillars (after Schmidt 2011: 920, fig. 42.4); (b) examples of animals carved on T-pillars (after Schmidt 2011: 924, fig. 42.4; Dietrich et al. 2012: 42).

layer at Göbekli features circular architecture and the later rectangular is not a problem, in Banning's view, given that some of the earliest recognizable architecture in southeastern Turkey and northern Syria is indeed circular, including at sites such as Hallan Çemi, Çayönü, Mureybet, and Jerf al-Ahmar (Cauvin 1977; Rosenberg and

Erim-Özdoğan 2011; Rosenberg and Redding 2000; Schirmer 1990; Stordeur 2000); at Mureybet and Hallan Çemi, "ritual behavior" such as feasting and decoration of the walls is attested. The transition from circular to rectangular domestic structures in the Near East is a well attested change and is discussed in detail in chapter 6. The presence of domestic paraphernalia such as mortars, stone bowls, and other containers suggests habitation was possible; the absence of interior hearths is not, according to Banning, evidence of a non-domestic use of the buildings, as these may have been located in an exterior cooking area.

The Göbekli example serves as a caution regarding immediate assumptions of a "non-domestic" function when a structure appears to have unusual—or, in the case of Göbekli, spectacularly unusual—elements. Perhaps identification is clear when a "temple" sits among unambiguous domestic structures, standing out as startlingly different from the look of any house in an ancient community. More common, perhaps, are cases such as a Harappan house at Mohenjo Daro variously identified as temple, "motel," elite house, and regular house by various archaeologists (McIntosh 2008; Possehl 2002; Ratnagar 2001; Vidale 2010), or the structures at Çatal Höyük identified as "shrines" by Mellaart (1967) but as domestic structures filled with symbolic meaning by Hodder (2006, 2010). Göbekli Tepe offers another type of interpretive conundrum: no contrasting structures. A clear differentiation between domestic and non-domestic in terms of structure size, form, contents, wall decoration, and so forth is simply not present. Given the monumentality and fascinating carvings on the interior, it is not at all surprising that the first and most consistent interpretation is that buildings at the site were entirely dedicated to ritual behavior. The suggestion here, inspired by Banning's exploration of the site, is to pause in such analyses and consider the intersection between domestic and sacred in the prehistoric mind. Might this have yielded a house that is also a temple, a sacred place that also serves as a dwelling?

Houses of the Dead

Charnel houses also exemplify structures that are not strictly "domestic" but perhaps should be considered "residential." Charnel houses today are usually found near churches, used for the storage of skeletal material that has been exposed either accidentally or through intentional removal from a cemetery. In some prehistoric cultures, placement in charnel houses was an important phase in the death process; the charnel house may have been considered the "house of the dead" especially for deceased kin members or ancestors. The Hopewell Mound culture (ca. 200 BCE–CE 500) of the Midwestern United States built charnel houses for their dead. At Seip Mound in southern Ohio, Hopewell people built a three-roomed structure that eventually housed 81 individuals, most cremated but some as simple inhumations (Spielmann 2009). The dead were placed on clay platforms, and, in the case of some inhumations, a log coffin was built around them. Goods, including ceramics and metal items, were often placed with the dead. The final stage was the dismantling of the structure and the creation of a mound over the human remains. There is strong evidence to suggest that feasting activities took place at Hopewell charnel houses, likely associated with the growing reliance on agriculture and the development of sociopolitical complexity (Seeman 1979; Spielmann 2002). Feasting in association with the charnel houses may have served to both recognize the role of the ancestors as well as serve as a redistributive event for food and goods to the community. Evidence suggests that the charnel houses were an important element in Hopewellian cosmological principles (Carr and Case 2006; Pauketat 2013).

Several hundred years later, and to the south (in the Oklahoma region), the Harlan phase charnel houses (ca. CE 1025–1158) demonstrate even more clearly the notion of "houses for the dead." Excavations of several sites have revealed charnel houses that are, in form, like habitation houses; however, they have neither interior hearths nor other normal domestic paraphernalia; their doorways were generally aligned with the winter solstice sunset to the southwest (Kay and Sabo 2006). Human remains were placed in charnel houses to achieve partial or complete decay of the flesh; the remains were then removed and the doorway blocked. The house was destroyed by fire, and a new charnel house was built upon its remains. This ritual process would seem to be an aid to the dead: "[T]he burning of these structures and the resulting column of smoke ascending skyward furthermore may have been identified as an *axis mundi* by which the souls of the deceased were transported to the world of the dead" (Kay and Sabo 2006: 44). The charnel house was the last residence of the dead and their encumbered souls, until the destruction fire and its smoke allowed the souls to separate from their corpora for their final journey.

Charnel houses are also found in the Near East in both Neolithic contexts and at later sites that demonstrate growing socioeconomic and political complexity. At Bronze Age Bab edh-Dhraʿ (ca. 3150–2300 BCE) in Jordan, residents transitioned from burying their dead in shaft tombs in the nearby cemetery to building charnel houses (Schaub 1981; Schaub and Rast 1989). Not long after settling permanently at Bab edh-Dhraʿ, residents built above-ground circular charnel houses capable of containing many more individuals than had the shaft tombs. By the time the town was walled and urbanized, residents were building rectilinear charnel houses, similar to dwellings in the domestic areas of the site. Studies of the skeletal material have demonstrated a genetic relationship, suggesting the charnel houses were dedicated to the burial of particular kinship groups (Bentley 1991). Meredith Chesson (1999) categorizes the houses into "greater" and "lesser" based on their size and the grave goods contents likely deposited when the deceased was interred (Figure 10.2); this dichotomy suggests that socioeconomic differentiation was fairly well developed in urbanized Bab edh-Dhraʿ, which may have affected the elaborateness of rituals associated with deposition of the dead (see also Chesson 2001, 2003, 2007).

Finally, at ninth millennium BCE Abu Hureyra in Syria, the charnel house was located not in a cemetery but in the domestic quarter itself (Moore, Hillman, and Legge

Figure 10.2: Artistic rendering of a mortuary ritual and procession to a charnel house at a site such as Bab edh-Dhra' in Jordan (after Chesson 2007: 332; drawing by Corrina Petit).

2000). A single structure, built much like a house, contained two types of human burials. In one room of the building was a burial pit dug through the plaster floor of the structure. Inside the pit, which was roughly 70 cm deep, were the remains of up to 30 individuals, of which over half were children or adolescents (Moore and Molleson 2000). The deposition of human remains into this pit was secondary, after defleshing had occurred elsewhere; the skulls of some individuals were missing and may have been used in ritual behavior in the community. At the other end of this structure was the charnel room, which contained at least 24 individuals, the vast majority of which were adults. Unlike burials in the pit, these remains were articulated and were likely placed there shortly after death and left to decay in place; skulls were apparently removed at some point and then redeposited. One skull showed evidence of having been wrapped in matting (Moore and Molleson 2000). The excavators of the Abu Hureyra structure have wrestled with the identification of its primary functionality. They note that the pit burial beneath the floor could have taken place before, or while, the house was inhabited as a domestic structure; further, given that the charnel room was at one end, it may have been a built "extension" on a domestic structure. However, "no other house . . . excavated contained such numerous clusters of skeletons. . . . [I]t seems that the dead . . . found there were assembled from other households in that quarter of the village and, therefore, that the building was used for ritual as well as domestic functions" (Moore and Molleson 2000: 283). The dead in the house at Abu Hureyra were likely connected in some fashion, either as a corporate group or through kinship ties; their placement in a "house" likely had powerful symbolic meaning within this very early community.

Enclosures and Foundations

A brief mention of earthen structures that are near to, or sometimes underneath, the house is worthwhile, given that constructing such features takes effort and was likely accomplished for a reason. Sometimes the reason is overtly practical, but in other cases the purpose is less certain, and archaeological speculation as to a ritual or symbolic meaning of earthen structures may be valid. Earthworks *under* houses can be found in many places and time periods. For instance, most ancient Harappan towns and cities in the Indus River Valley civilization (ca. 2500–1800 BCE) were situated on created earthworks, constructed prior to the building of the houses. The larger cities were then surrounded by a mudbrick wall. Archaeologists initially believed that these earthworks were meant to protect residents from the annual floods of the powerful river and its tributaries, but more recent analysis suggests that they may have had more symbolic meanings as well (Kenoyer 1998; McIntosh 2008; see Ross and Steadman forthcoming for discussion).

The creation of a ditch at the fourth-millennium BCE Late Chalcolithic site of Barcın Höyük in northwestern Turkey is worth noting. The ditch, roughly 40 cm deep and 2.5 m wide, surrounded the settlement, and the sedimentary deposit in it suggests that it held water for much of its existence (Gerritsen et al. 2010). It did not extend all the way around the settlement and did not appear to serve as a drainage feature. The excavators explain that "the function of the ditch cannot be determined with certainty but its position in relations to the Late Chalcolithic features suggests that it formed a settlement boundary. Clearly, this would have had a largely symbolic character. For defensive purposes or even to restrict humans and animals to pass across, it would have served poorly" (Gerritsen et al. 2010: 199). The excavators note that other contemporary sites in the region also have such ditches surrounding the community.

In the area of symbolism and earthworks, the two regions of the world that come to mind first are Europe and North America. The Neolithic causewayed enclosures of Central and Western Europe and the British Isles are well known (e.g., Biehl 2007; Bradley 1993, 1998, 2005; Malone 2001; Whittle 1996), and many of them embraced settlements or buildings that may have been domestic in nature. While these gave way over time to the more famous megalithic structures that were almost certainly not domestic, the premegalithic earthworks may have had a close relationship with emerging sedentism and agricultural pursuits in prehistoric Europe. Some of the earliest earthworks in North America are found at the site of Poverty Point in Louisiana (Gibson 2000; Kidder 2012). Beginning around 1800 BCE and lasting for roughly a millennium, residents at this riverside site built a series of semicircular mounds broken into sections, looking something like stadium seating when seen from above (Figure 10.3). Accompanying these linear earthworks were circular mounds resting nearby. Excavations found evidence of post-holes, hearths, and items associated with domestic occupation atop the concentric mounds, suggesting that the Poverty Point dwellings were situated there (see discussion on this site in chapter 5). The mounds at this site were created by the residents toting baskets of earth in what must have been a phenomenal organization of labor. Jon Gibson (1998) discusses the problem of differentiating between "sacred" and "secular" at Poverty Point, given that the mounds themselves would seem to argue for

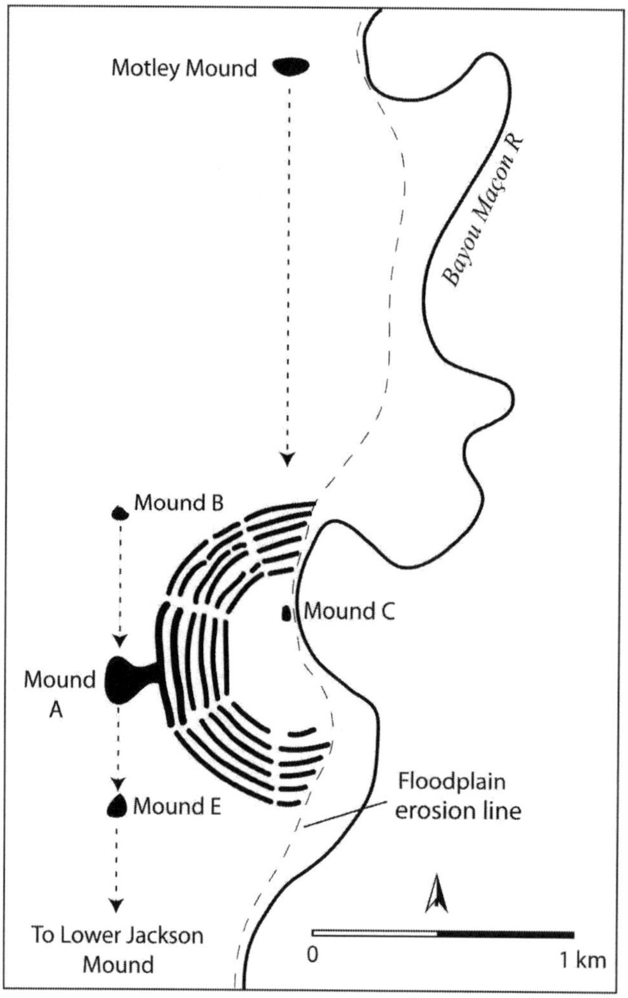

Figure 10.3: Plan of Poverty Point and associated mounds (after Sassaman 2005: 339, fig. 1, and Steadman 2009: 111, fig. 7.2).

sacred but the lack of burials or other "non-ritual" items suggests a more secular function. It is perhaps logical to consider the mounds themselves as the sacred objects, elevating the dwellings in what might have been an important re-creation of Poverty Point cosmology. The earthworks at Poverty Point are only one example of many mounds and enclosures associated with domestic remains in prehistoric North America (e.g., Clark 2004; Mainfort and Sullivan 1998; Milner 2012).

A final example of earthworks associated with dwellings comes from the "Great Houses" built during the main Chacoan period (ca. CE 850–1150) in the American Southwest. Archaeologists have noted that many of the Chaco great houses are surrounded by intentionally built mounds, platforms, or terraces; earlier in the 20th century, it was believed that they were simply middens and trash dumps, but further investigation suggests they had ritual significance (Lekson 1986; Stein and Lekson 1992; Toll 2001). These earthen structures may have been created through the ritual deposition of food remains, ceramic vessels, and other items following the completion of a ceremony. Construction materials in the mounds (Wills 2001) suggest that at least some of the ceremonies may have involved building and renewing the great houses. Even outside of the Chaco Canyon center, Chaco-era great houses had mounded earth, termed "berms," surrounding the structures. At Bluff Great House in Utah, located on the outer reaches of the Chaco cultural area (Cameron 2002, 2009; Cameron and Geib 2007), four separate linear berms surround the great house but do not include the great kiva (ritual structure) that stands outside the enclosed space. The berms are of varying lengths (roughly 10–20 m long and 2 m or more in height) and have spaces between them to allow access to the house. The berms show the same type of episodic deposition of ceramics and food remains as were found at Chaco Canyon sites (Toll 2001). Great house mounds seem to have been intentionally created to commemorate important ceremonies that took place in association with the domestic structure.

The discussion in this section falls woefully short of a complete survey of the many types of constructions that might be considered "extensions" of the sacred or ritualized house. This brief glimpse serves mainly to show how non-architectural or seemingly non-domestic constructions may have contributed to cosmological and ritual representation and practice in the domestic realm.

Rituals and Sacred Spaces in the Dwelling

As has been noted (e.g., Fogelin 2007a, 2007b; Marcus 2007; Renfrew 1994; Rowan 2012; Steadman 2009; Verhoeven 2011b; Whitley 2005), identifying ritual behavior in the archaeological record is a daunting task. Though it might seem easy to separate the ritual objects from the utilitarian ones in a house or to identify the sacred furniture versus the sitting and sleeping places, rarely is it that straightforward. To quote from a study on this subject: "Ritual behavior is easier to identify archaeologically than are myths, since ritual practices are more likely to leave behind material culture (e.g., altars, offering bowls, burned animals bones).... However, the old cliché in archaeology, 'if you can't identify the artifact, it must be a ritual item,' is both a truism and a trap" (Steadman 2009: 39). The "offering bowl" may do double duty as a serving bowl, burned animal bones may just be a clumsy hand that dropped a shank into the fire, and who knows what an altar might look like (the section below exemplifies the wide variety). Nonetheless, identifying ritual in an archaeological setting is a time-honored undertaking and is often accomplished with some success. Rather than offer a series of case studies, this short section provides some suggestions about what to look for or, perhaps more accurately, what you might be looking at in the archaeological record.

Foundation Deposits

Years ago while working at a site in southeastern Turkey, I excavated over a dozen walls that represented multiple building phases. Under the corners of several of these walls was a small pit containing a caprid horn and another small animal bone. I immediately knew I was looking at a foundation deposit, probably laid prior to the building of that set of walls. Again, at my current site of Çadır Höyük, the supervisor in one of the prehistoric trenches found an intentional deposit after removing a significant Early Bronze wall; the deposit consisted of some small bones and river-rounded pebbles placed in a shallow pit directly under the wall. Nerissa Russell has written extensively on the practice of foundation deposits that involve the placement of animal remains (Russell 2012a, 2012b; Russell and Meece 2006). In a survey of such deposits in both the Near East and Europe, she finds that placement under thresholds is quite common (Russell 2012a). In many cases, the animal remains may have come from a feast that commemorated the construction of the new home.

At Neolithic Çatal Höyük on the central Anatolian plateau, the most common deposit placed under house floors or walls, prior to construction, comes from cattle, primarily scapula and horns (Moses 2012; Russell 2012a). The importance of the cow at this site is well documented from the appearance of bovine imagery inside the structures, including heads molded in the walls and horns built into walls and benches (see below). Foundation rituals may have also involved the burial of neonates and infants (Whitehouse and Hodder 2010). Also present at Çatal Höyük are what Russell and colleagues term "commemorative deposits," which are placed below house floors *after* occupation of the house (Russell, Martin, and Twiss 2009; and see Nakamura 2010). In addition to animal bones, these commemorative deposits also included flint and obsidian, shells, ground stone segments, or pot sherds. Rather than marking the original construction of the house, these deposits may have served as memorials for special events that occurred after the occupants took up residence.

Various types of foundation deposits are found in a variety of prehistoric European settings (Bradley 1990; Brück 2011; Souvatzi 2008; Souvatzi and Hadji 2012). Discussed in more detail below are the infant burials at Neolithic Balkan sites such as Lepenski

Vir, where evidence suggests that these were placed prior to the building of the house. Similarly, neonate burials were found under slightly later LBK (*Linearbandkeramik*) houses in Central Europe and under Iron Age houses in England (Bradley 2005: 51–54; Cunliffe 1993; Hill 1995), perhaps representing a beginning, or end, to the house. Foundation deposits seem to have been very common during the pre-Roman and Roman periods in Europe. For instance, animal parts, including skulls or partially articulated skeletons of horses or dogs, were often deposited prior to the building of Roman-period Danish farmhouses (Groot 2009); and animals were sacrificed and buried under floors of Celtic houses in Spain (Alfayé 2007; González-Ruibal 2006). In addition to animals, the placement of small ceramic vessels at the base of post-holes or in wall foundations was also common in Iron Age and Roman-period houses in the Netherlands and Scandinavia (Gerritsen 2003; Groot 2009). The variety of objects that might be considered sacred and worthy of deposit is discussed by Richard Bradley (1990), though Fokke Gerritsen (2003) warns that not all votive deposits are detectable; many may have simply consisted of burned plant or other organic material offerings, appearing as nothing more than a smudge beneath a wall foundation or under a doorway.

Such foundation or post-occupancy deposits are not limited to the Middle East and Europe. Hendon discusses a number of deposits—or "caches," as she terms them—placed under a variety of locations in Mesoamerican sites, including patios, houses, ballcourts, and ceremonial places (2000, 2010). Contents in these caches may include human burials or parts of the skeleton, animal remains, shells, ceramics, and other items. Joseph Kovacik (1999) describes the discovery of carnivore and raptor bones beneath Chaco Canyon structures nearly 1,500 years ago as "structured," or intentional, deposits associated with memories of foundation and experience. As noted above, it is more than likely that only a fraction of actual foundation deposits or votive offerings have actually been identified, given that the act of deposition may have been largely ephemeral (see Hukantaival 2007 for discussion). A close look under doorways, wall corners, hearths, and other critical nodes in a house may yield a surprising find when looking for ritual in and for the house.

The purpose and meaning of foundation or commemorative deposits are likely as varied as their contents (as discussed by Brück 1999). To divine such, one must have a long archaeological acquaintance with the ancient culture practicing the act, and delve into the fields of cognitive archaeology and the interpretation of symbols (e.g., Osborne 2004; Renfrew 1994; Robb 1998; and see references above). That these deposits were meant to protect the house and its occupants in some fashion is likely; the intention to bring good luck, happiness, fertility, and long life is also a safe inference. Identifying the meaning of individual buried objects is more difficult. While cattle were of great symbolic importance at Çatal Höyük, what they represented for residents of that town is still largely beyond the grasp of its excavators. Foundation deposits are endlessly fascinating but also perpetually frustrating, in that they seem to point so clearly to ritual activity and symbolic thought but defy precise interpretation.

Specialized Rooms and Spaces

How can one know that a certain room or particular space within a house was considered sacred or was set aside for special ceremonies? The best advice that can be offered here is to look for both the absence *and* presence of certain objects. The *presence* of certain objects is easy to cover here because, for the most part, the reader's attention can be directed to other portions of this chapter, including the discussion on altars and objects that immediately follows, or the longer exploration of "The Ancestral House" just beyond. When objects or furniture that are distinctly "non-domestic" occur in a particular space inside a house, and when this is a pattern repeated in other domestic structures within the community, then it is ordinarily safe to claim "ritual activity" in a report. For instance, at Neolithic Dikili Tash in Greece, a single-roomed house featured a bucranium attached to a wall, with several vessels resting below that held stone and bone tools (Souvatzi 2008: 194). Nearby was a fully outfitted food production and cooking area. This setting, Souvatzi notes, "serves to emphasise the importance of the household not only as an economic, but also as a ritual unit" (2008: 195); she goes on to note that bucrania and cattle skulls are common occurrences in Neolithic houses across Europe and the Middle East.

Figurines can serve as unambiguous indicators of ritual activity; special vessels, animal (or human) bones, whether burned or not, objects with no identifiable utilitarian purpose, and a host of other items might certainly speak to a "sacred space" within the house. The complication arises when the "sacred space" does double duty as a "domestic space" after the ritual activity is completed. Examples of this can be found in the following discussion and in the exploration of "house societies" in chapter 6. However, caution is advised when using objects to assign ritual to locations. A decade ago, excavations at my site turned up an unusual object dating to the Byzantine period of the first millennium CE; crosses and other apparently religious objects had been discovered in the same location. This object was a beautiful rounded marble piece in the shape of an egg. Recently, at a conference on Byzantine archaeology, I showed a picture of this object; afterward, a specialist on textile production told me it was precisely the type of "sock darning device" she had seen at other Byzantine sites, though far finer than most. So, was my marble egg-shaped object a utilitarian textile object, likely for an elite residence, or a sacred object, or both?

It is possible that the *absence* of objects is just as telling, if not more so, of sacred space within a house. The absence in this case refers to utilitarian objects, evidence of activity and work spaces in a particular room. As has been seen throughout this volume, prehistoric houses, even in small communities, are rarely large and spacious. Economy of labor usually plays an important role in the building and maintenance of a house, and space is generally allotted based on need: the number of people inhabiting it, and the types of activities that must be accomplished. Exceptions occur, such as the LBK longhouses discussed in more detail below; but, in general, "extra space" is not the norm in the typical prehistoric house. Thus, a room, or particular space within a house, that is free of any domestic paraphernalia is notable. It is perhaps there that the ancestor or spirits dwell. Possibly, the ritual objects (altar? offerings?) that rested there during occupancy, constructed of organic materials, are absent hundreds or thousands of years later. At ancient Titriş Höyük, Yoko Nishimura (2012) found that in many houses, a rather large room was generally devoid of objects associated with tasks or other daily activities. Further investigation revealed that such rooms often contained cist tombs or pot burials. Residents at ancient Titriş intentionally built an "ancestral" or mortuary room, meant for no other purpose. Though "empty spaces" are rarely described in excavation reports, if a domestic area is recognized as suspiciously "empty," a search for clues as to the non-domestic actions that may have taken place there can commence.

Altars, Objects, and Ritual Places

Closely related to the foregoing is the identification of specific places in the home that do double duty; that is, they serve both sacred and functional purposes within the house. Archaeological interpretation of such places tends to categorize them as either domestic or sometimes ritual. Rather, such places may have been *primarily* sacred, and thus every activity that took place there, domestic or not, was imbued with specialized meaning for the inhabitants of that house (see discussions in Hinde 1998; Mithen 1998; and Renfrew 2007a, 2007b). The description of the intersection between ritual and domestic place within the house could go on for pages, given the ubiquity of these in the archaeological record; however, a few representative examples should suffice.

Rarely do archaeologists find the wall of prehistoric houses still standing. Reconstructing what the walls looked like when standing can be challenging: Were there windows? Was it decorated? Did it have something hanging from it? The bucrania that once protruded from the Dikili Tash walls, mentioned above, and those still preserved at the Neolithic site of Çatal Höyük remind us that sacred places within a home may be above our heads. At Çatal Höyük, the bucrania, which do not occur in every house, are typically found either on east or west walls and rarely in the southern reaches of the structure (Hodder 2006: 137–38). Subfloor burials were generally found near north or east walls, suggesting that the more northerly half of the house may have been considered the more sacred area. Three small clay zoomorphic objects found on the floor of a structure at another Neolithic Greek site had flat bases and were hollow. It is likely that they were either once affixed to the wall or were hung from some part of the architecture, possibly suspended above the heads of the inhabitants (Souvatzi 2008: 195). The lesson here, then, is "look up." What rests on the ground in the archaeological setting might once have decorated a wall or may have hung from the ceiling, making either that particular space, or perhaps the entire house, a sacred place with everyday activities ritualized.

The hearth is a very likely candidate for a location of ritual activity within the home. Hodder, who sees the hearth as central to the notion of *domus,* or home, in prehistoric Europe and the Middle East, notes that in some houses in Neolithic southeastern Europe, the domed hearth so resembles the house structure that it has been mistaken by excavators as a house model rather than a cooking installation (1990: 57–59). Further, ceramic house models, considered to be ritual objects, frequently occur in Neolithic southeastern European contexts and often contain a representation of the hearth within them. In a recent study, Michael Press (2011) discusses the problems of identifying "cult" behavior in domestic contexts. While tempting to do so, Press cautions against automatically identifying the presence of objects such as figurines with cult practice (see Nelson 2014 for extensive discussion). Nonetheless, Press notes that the ubiquity of figurines located under doorways and at hearths in ancient Near Eastern contexts is more than likely an indicator of ritual behavior or of sacred space within the dwelling (see also Hitchcock 2011). Robert Hall (1997) offers numerous examples of the importance of the hearth in ancient (and present-day) Native American societies. For instance, the hearth of a Skiri Pawnee village house (ca. CE 1800) is placed at the center of the structure. Nearby is another square pit that is considered a hearth by the Skiri Pawnee but is not used as such; rather, it represents the hearth of heaven where the elders sit (Hall 1997: 97). Similarly, an ethnographic study of Circumpolar peoples demonstrates the antiquity of a sacred hearth in this region (Anderson, Wishart, and Vaté 2013). In many African cultures, the hearth serves as the "heart" of the house, and beyond the house, the metalworking furnace carried ritual significance (Insoll 2013; Prussin 1996; Schmidt and Mapunda 1997). It is not surprising to find hearths at the center of ritual activity. It is the bright warm place in what was, quite often, a dim and dank interior inside a prehistoric house. The hearth is worth a close look when considering whether ritual activity took place inside the dwelling.

Finally, a brief mention here of altars in the household usefully precedes the next section, in which a variety of altars associated with ancestor veneration are discussed. Altars, or non-domestic ritual installations within houses, are simultaneously easy and incredibly difficult to identify. They seem easy to spot, as they do not conform to the archaeologist's modern notion of necessary furniture or domestic accouterment; they are difficult to classify for the same reason. What seems an unusual installation in a house, taking up precious space (and which therefore must have functioned in a religious or ritual arena), may have been a completely ordinary piece of furniture. An excellent example of this comes from the site of Qermez Dere in northern Iraq, which dates to the second half of the ninth millennium BCE, excavated by Trevor Watkins (Watkins 1990, 2004a; Watkins, Dobney, and Nesbitt 1995). Several oval semi-subterranean houses were inhabited at this site. The interiors were nicely plastered and very clean, as the residents deposited their trash away from the houses in a different area of the settlement. Houses had centrally located hearths, and standing not far from them were pillars made of clay and plaster (Figure 10.4), often associated with a stone slab

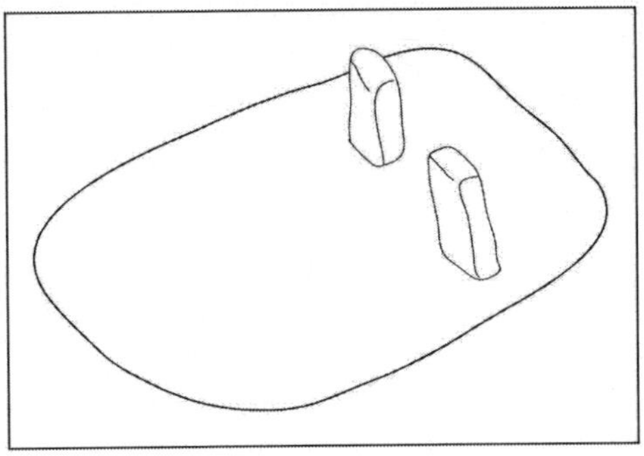

Figure 10.4: Sketch of interior of Qermez Dere house with stone pillars (after Watkins 2004a: 100, fig. 9.1).

(Watkins 1990, 2004a). Less than 2 m in height, the pillars appear to have had roughly flattened tops; they were of insufficient height to support the roofing of the structures (but see Biçakçi 2003). Watkins avoids calling these installations "shrines" or "altars" but fully admits that these installations likely served a non-utilitarian function in the house.

Another illustrative example is the "lustration slabs" found in later second-millennium BCE houses at el-Amarna in Egypt (Spence 2007). These are usually set in limestone mortar, placed on an incline, and have a raised edge leading to a smaller slab at the front set slightly lower than the main one; they are usually located in the central room within the house. The interpretation of these items has an interesting history. Kate Spence (2007: 287) notes that the original excavators in the late 19th and early 20th centuries identified them as stands for water jars or as stone trays. Over the course of the next century, suggestions of washing trays or bathroom installations were made; Spence (2007: 288) asserts that the location of these slabs in the central room of the house argues against their identification as part of a bathroom. This placement, together with their significant size within the room (as large as 2.5 × 1.5 m), and their bright white color, which contrasted with the mudbrick furniture in the house, all point to the likelihood that the slabs served a cultic role in the house (Spence 2004, 2007; and see Stevens 2006). The Amarna stone slabs are a fine example of how objects might straddle the fence between "simply utilitarian" and "central cult place" within the household. It would be fruitless here to attempt to describe what altars inside the house would "look like." The simple suggestion to regard every type of constructed or emplaced item within the house with a critical eye will suffice. The Amarna stones may have been both washing places and lustration slabs; the Qermez Dere pillars may have been both altars and stands for household items. The following section offers a more detailed discussion of the dazzling variety of altars and shrines that appear in houses, demonstrating the ubiquity of their presence and the difficulty of their interpretation.

The Ancestral House

The topic of ancestors was raised in chapter 2 primarily in the context of where people might first choose to place their (semi-)permanent residences. If ancestors were thought to have resided in a particular landscape, then settling near them, or even among them, would have influenced residential location choice. Ancestors would be expected to take care of their descendants, protect property, perhaps maintain health, and even bring prosperity. There is, of course, no universal architectural "type" associated with household ancestor veneration. Therefore, there are few reliable archaeological indicators for tracking the presence of ancestors in residences. Other than place longevity, only two recommended indicators can be noted here: burials within (under) homes and the presence of ancestral shrines.

Longevity of place can have myriad explanations well beyond that of ancestral homes. Archaeologists working in southeastern Europe and the Middle East have long wondered at the existence of mounds (more commonly known as *höyük* in Turkish, *tepe* in Farsi, *tell* in Arabic) created by the continuous occupation of the same place over centuries and millennia and resulting in a human-generated mounds of occupational detritus. Explanations for why people in these regions and others remained in place can range from the location being strategic (e.g., defensible, on a trade route, or intentionally not on arable land), to a sense of landownership, to, of course, the idea that one's ancestors live in just that place and thus remaining there is critical to success and perhaps even survival (Steadman 2005). The presence of burials or material remains that may be interpreted as shrines are much stronger indicators that kinship ties and ancestor veneration are an integral part of the architectural location and placement of a household within a community.

Household Shrines to the Ancestors

Ancestor veneration is probably as old as religion itself. If one accepts that spirits inhabit the universe, a natural extension might be to believe that a deceased relative's spirit will continue to look after the living, or need care-taking in the netherworld, just as she or he did in life. Household-based ancestor veneration can be found in any society, but it is particularly common in cultures practicing unilineal descent (particularly those with patrilineal kinship) that cede property through inheritance (Michaelson and Goldschmidt 1976). Recognition and care-taking of the ancestors not only solidifies family ties through frequent ritual activity but is a public acknowledgment that the living have the right to the inheritance (including land, house, or other property) passed down by deceased elders. Though ancestral rituals might include prayers alone, it is more common for some sort of shrine to exist in or near the home or on the lands (Michaelson and Goldschmidt 1976).

When excavating a house featuring a portable or built shrine, the first inference may be that the culture practiced ancestor veneration, but this may not be wholly accurate.

For instance, in many Hindu houses in India, there is a shrine room built as part of the architectural footprint of the structure (Figure 10.5). This small room is where the household altar, dedicated to the residents' favorite Hindu gods, is constructed, and it is here that daily prayers and offerings are made to those gods and goddesses. A similar situation is found in Southeast Asia, in the countries of Thailand, Laos, and Cambodia. Here people erect a "spirit house" outside of their own homes, and occasionally inside houses or businesses. These are miniature houses resting on platforms that are considered houses for the spirits. Here they can be appeased (and cajoled into refraining from causing trouble) through the provision of a pleasant place to live and the giving of frequent offerings (Figure 10.6). In these cases, shrines found inside or just outside houses are not recognizing ancestors, but in many other cases they are. When excavating a house, the problem is identifying which shrines belong to a culture that practiced ancestor veneration versus non-kin spirit worship and appeasement.

Ethnographic Examples

A good place to start is with ethnographic examples: Suzanne Blier's study of the Batammaliba culture of Togo and Benin in West Africa offers some interesting insights into methods of ancestor veneration. Each Batammaliba house recognizes and provides a resting place for elder ancestors from lineages of both the husband and wife (Blier 1987: 152–53). Each ancestor (spatially differentiated by sex and by lineage affiliation) has a *liboloni*, or clay oblong platform, built into the house's architecture, usually along a wall or pillar and always facing west. Each evening, the deceased elders' souls return to their *liboloni* on the last rays of the setting sun, to be safe through the night and provide safety to their descendants (Blier 1987: 151–52). The placement of the *liboloni* along walls and pillars, notes Blier, is symbolic of the "supportive role" they provide to their living descendants (1987: 154). A further indicator that ancestor veneration is critical to the Batammaliba is the presence of a "tombstone" in the center of each house. Upon the death of the household (male) elder, the tombstone is removed and taken to the cemetery to serve as his tomb closure: "The prominent place of this tombstone within the house underscores the critical bond made between the living and the dead . . . alluding to the importance of each elder's death for family continuity," as that elder will then protect the living from the supernatural realm (Blier 1987: 154). Were Batammaliba houses to become archaeological sites, the *liboloni* might not be immediately recognizable as an item representing ancestor veneration. The tombstones found both within the center of the houses and in the cemeteries might well signal to the archaeologist the importance ancestors played in Batammaliba culture.

It is exceedingly common to find an ancestor altar (*butsudan*) in Japanese households, usually consisting of pictures or representations of the deceased, flowers, candles, and various types of offerings (Kawano 2005). Altars may be inside a cabinet or set upon a piece of furniture such as a table; thus, unlike in Batammaliba homes, Japanese altars are not built into the architectural footprint of the house but instead are

Figure 10.5: A Hindu house in South India with (above) a built-in altar room, and (on facing page) with an altar inside dedicated to Hindu gods (photos by the author).

Figure 10.5, continued.

Figure 10.6: Example of a spirit house in Cambodia (photo by the author).

separate entities. In fact, not every Japanese household has a *butsudan*. In some cases, cramped conditions make such a use of space impossible, and in others the branch of the family may not yet have had elders pass away (Roehmer 2012). Most Japanese households with *butsudan* carry out rites quite frequently during the week; ritual activities include the lighting of candles and the offering of dedications, including food and flowers, all often accompanied by prayers and drum music (Roehmer 2012). Ancestor veneration in Japan is an extremely ancient practice; patrilineal ancestors are most often represented at the altars, but other members of the family may also be recognized. Ancestral veneration in Japan "helps sustain the household by identifying a family's social status, origins, or (perhaps most frequently) by simply acknowledging one's predecessors" (Roehmer 2012: 34); veneration also provides comfort for the souls of the ancestors, allows them to remain connected to family (Kawano 2005), and ensures the well-being of family, both alive and deceased.

Archaeology and Household Shrines

While there are certainly numerous examples of living cultures that practice ancestor veneration, finding archaeological examples is quite challenging. This may stem from a variety of issues, the first being that altars in ancient homes may have been built of organic materials, and likewise, the activities and ritual offerings (e.g., food, plants) may have left no visible trace. Even recognizing the presence of a built-in altar can be difficult. A wall niche, or a bench, built as part of the architectural footprint might well be interpreted as furniture rather than as a place for religious activity. Finally, as will be shown in the Roman example below, a normal part of the home, such as the hearth, or perhaps a doorway, might be considered the "home" of the ancestors, and the ritual activities that might have occurred there are hidden by the altar's dual utilitarian nature.

In ancient Rome, many households had a *Lar familiaris* ("protector of the family") associated with the hearth and thought to represent the ancestor (usually paternal) who founded the house (Waites 1920; Hillner 2003). *Lares familiares* are known through two sources, textual references and archaeological material remains. Texts inform us that boys and girls made ritual offerings (of childhood toys and symbols) to the *Lar familiaris* to ensure growth into adulthood (Rives 2007: 118–19). In some households, ritual activities to the *Lar* took place at the hearth. But in many, as attested by archaeological excavation at sites such as Pompeii and Herculaneum, there is an actual shrine, generally in the form of a wall painting placed above or near the hearth. However, even with both textual and archaeological evidence, there is still much to be learned about the Roman "hearth spirits" of the *Lares*. For instance, a *lararium* at Pompeii displaying three human figures above a snake eating from a bowl of fruit will have two different interpretations as to which is the *Lar*; one scholar identifies the "crested and bearded snake" as the figure "used to represent the *Lar familiaris*" (Rüpke 2007: 97), while another scholar suggests it is the two figures flanking the central human above the snake (Rives 2007: 120).

Patrick Kirch used the ethnographic record as a major source to support his belief that a particular ceramic style found in houses of Lapita cultures living on southwest Pacific islands between 1,500 and 3,000 years ago represented ancestor veneration. "Lapita" refers to Austronesian-language speakers who, approximately 4,000 years ago, set sail from their Melanesian island homelands (e.g., New Guinea and the Bismarck Archipelago) to colonize islands in the Micronesian and Polynesian areas of the Pacific (Kirch 1997). At a site on the island of Mussau in the Bismarck Archipelago (northwest of New Guinea), Kirch excavated decorated ceramics featuring human faces, found in the remains of stilt-houses that once stood over shallow waters (Kirch 1997: 118–41). The ceramics with human faces were not utilitarian but rather were pedestaled bowls and cylinders that were "best suited for display or serving but not for storage or cooking" (Kirch 1997: 140). To interpret the meaning of these elaborately decorated anthropomorphic vessels and their presence in domestic structures, Kirch turned to the ethnographic record. Roxana Waterson's study of houses in Indonesia and beyond (1990) offers examples of indigenous (Lapita-descendant) cultures displaying carved images (on planks and wooden statues) of ancestors inside the house; Kirch noted that there were distinct parallels in the representative artistry found on the Lapita anthropomorphic ceramics and the present-day ancestral images (Kirch 1997: 144).

Another example comes from Lio houses on the island of Flores in Indonesia. Villages in this culture contain several types of "houses": those people live in, those that once housed people but have now become ceremonial, and those that are intentionally constructed as a type of temple (Howell 1995). Over time, the ceremonial houses have come to look more like the temples, but they still have a domestic cast to them; in these ceremonial houses, a sacred area at the back has wooden panels carved with images of the ancestors or at least body representations such as breasts (Howell 1995: 159). Ritual offerings to the ancestors are made at this shrine.

Finding Ancestor Veneration Archaeologically

Ancestor veneration is exceedingly common in present-day societies (Steadman, Palmer, and Tilley 1996) and thus surely was in the past. However, archaeologists are justly cautioned that "there are too many ancestors in contemporary archaeological interpretation, and they are being asked to do too much" (Whitley 2002: 119; and see Insoll 2011). Add to this the preceding discussion on non-ancestral shrines such as those in Hindu homes, and one might well complain that ancestors, though ubiquitous, can be quite archaeologically elusive.

As noted above, longevity of place is a first point for consideration. Why would residents remain, generation after generation, in the same house or at least rebuild in exactly the same place, even if it becomes inconvenient to stay there? Religion is a powerful motivator, and the belief that one's ancestors inhabit just that place might be a fairly accurate explanation for long inhabitation of the same locale (Steadman 2005). If a community features houses with furniture (movable or built-in) that appears to have been dedicated to ritual use, then the first but not the *only* inference an archaeologist should make is that ancestor veneration may have been present in the household and society. Even identifying ritual behavior on or around the furniture can be challenging; burned offerings (archaeobotanical analyses can be exceedingly helpful here), non-utilitarian artifacts, and unusual decorations are key indicators (Renfrew 1994; Steadman 2009; Verhoeven 2011b; Whitley 2005). A lack of such furniture in homes does not necessarily negate an interpretation of ancient ancestor veneration in the society; "young" Japanese households that have not yet experienced the death of an elder will not have an altar set up in the home. The associated artifactual assemblage might provide vital clues; carvings of human visages on the furniture on or other objects (such as the Lapita ceramics) could be indicators. It would be particularly helpful if such images varied from household to household, perhaps portraying the visages of actual ancestors—though identifying which image represents the ancestor might be challenging; witness the confusion over whether snake or human represents the Roman *Lar* above. In truth, identifying a house dedicated to or protected by the ancestors can be confounding and often impossible. One factor that assists tremendously in this effort, however, is the presence of burials in or near the home.

Houses, Burials, and Ancestors

When ancestors are part of the architectural footprint, identifying their veneration becomes a more realistic archaeological goal. The Neolithic site of Khok Phanom Di (ca. 2000–1500 BCE) in present-day Thailand was discussed in chapter 2 as an example of why a previously mobile population might have chosen to settle a particular place: because the ancestors both literally and figuratively inhabited the land. Settling roughly 4,000 years ago near a sheltered estuary, residents deposited 11 cultural layers and burials representing up to 17 generations of occupation (Higham et al. 1992). The dead were buried in clusters, which have been interpreted as family groups; houses stood above the burials, suggesting that living family members occupied the house resting atop the burial of deceased family members. Environmental conditions limited the recovery of much of the above-ground community (Higham 2002a); had it survived, archaeologists would not have been surprised at evidence of household rituals venerating the dead buried beneath.

Burial below house floors is quite common in the prehistoric Near East. A series of Pre-Pottery Neolithic A and B sites (ca. 9700–6200 BCE) in the Levant offer fairly convincing evidence of ancestor veneration, possibly associated with the advent of agricultural cultivation (Goring-Morris and Belfer-Cohen 2002; Kuijt 2000b, 2000c; Parker Pearson 2000; Verhoeven 2002; Watkins 2006, 2012). Some of the most famous examples of burials under the floors, accompanied by ancestor veneration activities, come from the sites of Jericho in Palestine and 'Ain Ghazal in Jordan (Kenyon 1957; Rollefson and Simmons 1987; Rollefson, Simmons, and Kafafi 1992). At both sites, burials were placed under the floors of houses, and in some cases the skulls were removed; skulls were then specially treated, often plastered to re-create the model of a head, and kept in the home. Similar situations have been discovered at a variety of other Neolithic Levantine sites dating to this period (Bar-Yosef 1998; Cauvin 2000; Kuijt 2002; Kuijt and Chesson 2005; Stordeur 2003a, 2003b, Verhoeven 2011a; Watkins 2004b), and this behavior is also seen as far afield as in the Balkan Neolithic (Naumov 2007). The burial of the dead beneath the floor, together with the specialized treatment of the skull, which may have once rested at an altar within the house, is perhaps the closest archaeological equivalent to actual present-day informants describing their ancestor veneration rituals. Architectural features that are clearly "altars" are not typically found in these Levantine contexts. There are other examples that do combine burial and architectural footprint.

Alexis Mantha (2009) has offered an insightful study of ancestor veneration and architectural remains found at sites in the Rapayán Valley in the central Andes (ca. CE 1000–1450). Mantha identified three types of architectural structures: multistoried buildings, *chullpas* (small, non-residential, rectangular structures containing human bone), and small quadrangular residential structures. The multistoried buildings ranged up to 15 m high, with open plazas in front of them. These structures held quantities of human bone and remnants of ceramics and textiles, leading Mantha (and others) to conclude that these buildings had a mortuary function; mummies of ancestors interred in these buildings may have been at the center of ancestor veneration ceremonies held in the plazas (Mantha 2009: 164–67). The *chullpas*, which were quite numerous, also seem to have functioned as scenes of mortuary ritual and interment of mummies. Mantha's excavation of the quadrangular residential structures at Rapayán revealed they were two- to four-roomed, encompassing between 30 and 33 m^2 in area. Standard in these houses were cavities in the wall dividing front from back rooms; the cavities were sealed save for a small window. Mantha interprets these cavities as household mortuary chambers for the placement of mummified (embalmed) ancestors, the windows offering residents a point of access through which they could make offerings to the dead (Mantha 2009: 167). At Rapayán, therefore, all structures, both ceremonial and domestic, seem to have had some function related to ancestor veneration.

There is too much variation in the nature of household shrines dedicated to ancestors and too many contexts of ancestral burials or display in archaeologically investigated homes than can be summarized here. As stated at other points in this volume, often it is best to rely on the standard "you know it when you see it" formula. Finding ritual and religion in an ancient site is best undertaken by those who know the culture well and who can recognize when something seems beyond the mundane, the utilitarian, and the "secular norm." While it is difficult enough to confidently identify a household altar or declare that a subfloor burial is evidence of ancestor veneration, as we will see in the following section, perhaps the most challenging interpretive arena is where the physical structure of the house is partially or wholly representative of an entire belief system.

The House as Embodiment of Cosmos and Ritual Landscape

Bourdieu's Berber house has been referenced numerous times in this book. It is *the* example of the "symbolic house," particularly regarding "opposites" in Berber culture, including dark and light, wet and dry, male and female (Bourdieu 1977). In some cultures, it is the bones of the house itself that represents the sacred cosmos (see Wason 2010 for discussion). This may be expressed in the position or layout of the house, or in the shape of it, or built into the very architecture. Examples of this have been seen in previous chapters. For instance, in the chapter 5 discussion of first houses, Shafer (1995) argues that the shift from pithouses in the Mimbres culture of the American Southwest to above-ground pueblo-style dwellings reflects a shift in Mimbres cosmology. The rooftop doorway, the deeply dug hearth, and the four corners of the dwelling mimic the horizontally layered cosmos and the vertical shape of the universe. Numerous examples of religious belief built into the dwellings within a "house society" are found in chapter 6. The ubiquity of the "four-roomed house" in the Iron Age Levant, a focus of discussion on households in chapter 7, leads many scholars to speculate on whether the structure of the house itself had religious meaning in the ancient Levantine world; Faozi Ujam (2006) argues that the ubiquitous "courtyard house" of the modern Middle East traces its roots back to ancient Mesopotamia and symbolic representations of the divine. Finally, Trevor Watkins suggests that "architecture exploded in the early Neolithic of southwest Asia as a novel and powerful system of symbolic representation, the scaffolding of a pre-literate mode of external symbolic storage" (2004b: 5; and see Watkins 2006, 2009), a concept explored below in the discussion of Neolithic architecture. The following examples illustrate well the notion of an ancient cosmology captured in the physical architecture of the house.

Lessons from the Ethnographic Record

Following the now recognized standard procedure in this book, it is best to start with an ethnographic example. The maloca longhouses built by the Tukanoans of Amazonian Colombia have been well described by Stephen Hugh-Jones (1993, 1995) and were discussed in chapter 6. His study has formed the basis of several other discussions on the subject of "house as cosmos" (e.g., Århem 1998; Goldman 2004; Lewis-Williams and Pearce 2005; Steadman 2005). Maloca houses are communal, measuring as much as 30 m long × 12 m wide × 10 m high; they can house up to 30 people who are kin-related, primarily brothers and their wives and children (Hugh-Jones 1993). The maloca houses the entire community, and a neighboring maloca community may be a couple of hours distant by foot. The roofs of the maloca, built of palm thatch, are A-framed, with the sides reaching almost to the ground (see Figure 6.5); wooden columns running down the center of the structure and pillars on the sides support the roof. One end of the structure, the "back" is apsidal, and it is here that the women's entrance and area, including the kitchen, are situated; this area is screened off from the frontal areas of the maloca. The front of the house, with the men's entrance centered in the wall, is squared. Entering through the men's doorway, one comes to the men's area and the public visitor's area to the side. On the sides, near the back, are the living quarters. On the outside of the house, by the men's entrance, there are paintings of human figures and geometrical designs; inside, a box containing feathered ornaments hangs from the ceiling (Hugh-Jones 1993). The performance of rituals, which often includes dance, takes place in the center of the maloca. The entire longhouse, according to Hugh-Jones, "replicates and models the structure of the cosmos" (1995: 233).

The creation myth represented by the *maloca* includes a female deity who dwelled in a house made of feathers; within the house, five "thunders" were created, one at each corner and the final one suspended from the ceiling (Hugh-Jones 1993). The fifth suspended thunder was responsible for the creation of the first males and females, who then traveled by canoe along a river, occasionally landing on the river shore to perform dances. Upon reaching their final destination (the Tukanoan homeland), these initial humans were complete and they became the ancestors of all the peoples in the region (Hugh-Jones 1993). Hugh-Jones describes the universe as represented in the house: "[I]ts floor is the earth and its posts are the mountains supporting the roof or sky above" (1995: 233). Further, the center of the *maloca* is considered to be a symbolic river, such as that traveled by the initial people. During rituals, the river represents that journey and the emergence of Tukanoan peoples. The box that hangs from the center and the four architectural points of the *maloca* recall the five thunders, the fifth being the most important, as it is this one that gave birth to the initial people. In an overall sense, the house symbolizes the female womb, as it was this shape that covered the original female deity: "Not surprisingly, the maloca itself is sometimes spoken about as a woman: the rounded rear of the house is her head, the front entrance is her vagina, and the cavernous interior is her womb" (Hugh Jones 1993: 102). The house symbolizes the birth of the Tukanoans in their initial form and the journey they undertook to become fully human.

Translating Cosmology from the Ancient American Built Environment

Turning to the archaeological record but continuing to depend on ethnographic data, an example emerges from the American South. The Mississippian culture (ca. CE 750–1500) began as a collection of scattered agricultural settlements. These settlements featured rectangular homes arrayed around central courtyards; four-cornered storage pits were available for communal access (Mehrer 1995). By ca. 950–1000, the population and communities had grown, with larger structures that were either rectangular or circular in shape and featuring both external and internal storage. Some towns built ceremonial mounds near open areas for public ceremonies; others featured a single household that was much larger and had significant open areas near it that may have been used to host public ceremonies or events (Mehrer 1995). By 1050, "temple towns," the largest of which was Cahokia, had emerged. Cahokia, famous for its central "Monks Mound," also has well over 100 mounds, many of which contain burials or support buildings, a massive central plaza, and wooden henge structures. Monks Mound, the central plaza, and many of the central structures were surrounded by a wooden palisade. The mounds at Cahokia take three shapes. The most common are the platform mounds, rectangular and flat-topped. Fewer in number and often associated with the platform mounds are the conical mounds, roughly circular and mounded, which generally hold burials. Finally, at least eight "ridge-topped" mounds are arrayed at the outer boundaries of the settlement or at important intersecting points within it; the ridge-topped mounds likely delineated important spatial nodes at Cahokia (Fowler 1997; Young and Fowler 2000). Besides marking settlement limits, the ridge mounds are placed within the settlement so that lines drawn between them intersect at other major mounds at Cahokia (including the famous Mound 72 featuring many burials) and with Monks Mound, forming east–west and north–south lines.

A number of scholars suggest that intrinsic to the Mississippian belief system was the quadrilateral cosmos, divided into an upper layer (representing, in some views, "life") and the lower, earth layer (the oppositional "death"), which was divided by an east–west axis that served to center and negotiate between the two (Brown 1976; Emerson and Pauketat 2008; Fowler 1999; Hall 1997; Pauketat and Alt 2003; Young and Fowler 2000); the east–west axis and the north and south halves then create a four-cornered, dual-layered, universe. A second prominent theme is that of "duality" played out not just in the two layers and the northern and southern halves, but in other ways, as in the physical manifestation of rectangular and circular, perhaps representing the summer and winter seasons (Emerson 1989; Fowler 1999; Hall 1997). These beliefs are mapped out in Mississippian settlements, including at Cahokia, in the physical setting of buildings, mounds, and plazas. Monks Mound is surrounded by four rectangular plazas oriented to the four cardinal directions. This central mound itself is rectangular at its base, mimicking the settlement (and cosmic) layout (Figure 10.7). Arrayed around the central mound were rectangular mounds, often paired with conical mounds, representing the duality just mentioned. In some cases, rectangular mounds formed the basis for circular structures, capturing the duality in layout and emplacement of a dwelling (Emerson 1997a, 1997b; Kelly 1997). The elevated residences, atop the mounds, suggest these residents inhabited the upper ("life") layer of the cosmological universe, and those living on the ground, more regularly found in the outlying communities, were closer to or perhaps even representative of the lower earth ("death"). This lower layer may not have been a negative realm, but rather the one associated with agricultural productivity and renewal of fertility.

The emplacement of buildings, plazas, and spaces, designed to represent these concepts of duality and quadrilateralness, are also found in outlying Mississippian culture sites that likely served as countryside religious centers (Emerson, Alt, and Pauketat 2008). Further evidence that renewal, perhaps associated with fertility, was a critical element in Mississippian belief is the frequent resurfacing of mounds at Cahokia and some of the outlying centers. Structures on the mounds were dismantled, and a new layer of earth, sometimes embedded with pebbles or other earth treated with pigments, was spread over the mound's surface; following this, a new structure was built (Emerson,

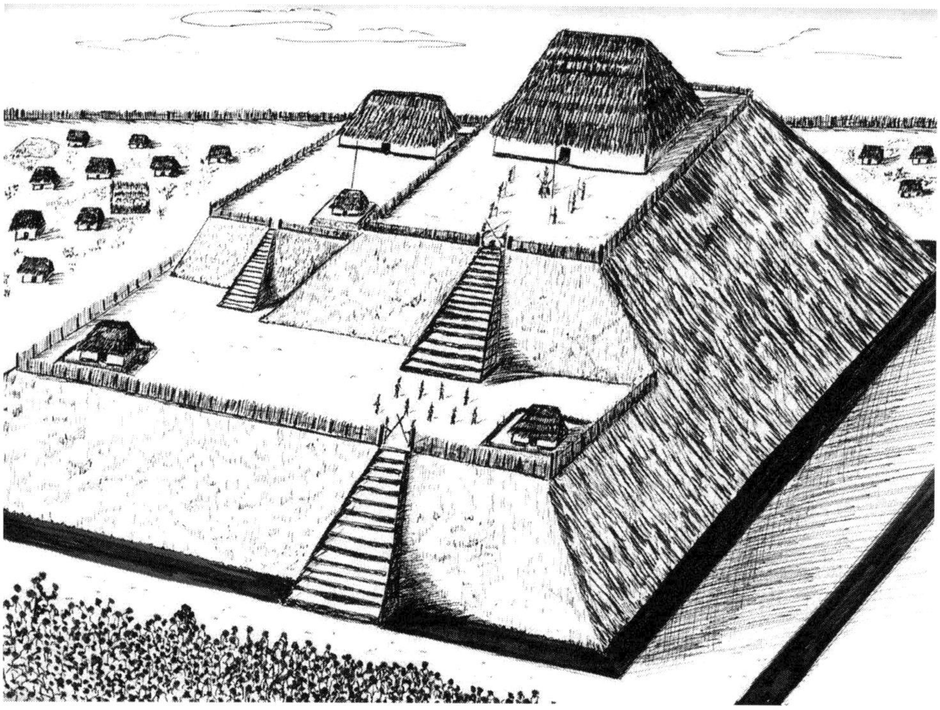

Figure 10.7: Artistic rendering of Monk's Mound at Cahokia (drawing by Mary Jean Hughes).

Alt, and Pauketat 2008; Pauketat and Alt 2003; Young and Fowler 2000). The discussion here has not delved into the far more complicated issues of the growth of social complexity in the Mississippian culture and the possible imposition of this cosmology upon outlying communities by Cahokian elites concerned about control and the regular production of subsistence goods (e.g., Emerson 1997a, 1997b; Emerson, Alt, and Pauketat 2008; Pauketat 1994, 2000, 2004; and see Ross and Steadman forthcoming). Whether imposed, freely accepted, or transmitted through a deep history, the dualistic quadrilateral cosmology is represented in the very layout, distribution, and positioning of Mississippian public buildings and houses. Even absent the ethnographic clues derived from Native American religion, the mounds and buildings of differing shapes and positioning would have provided clues to archaeologists that a system larger than just agricultural production guided housing form and placement. House and community in the Mississippian culture may have been, as it was to more recent Native American cultures, "a recreation of the world and the cosmos. Each community saw itself as a map of the universe" (Young and Fowler 2000: 266).

Cosmology and Early Dwellings in the Neolithic Near East

Neolithic Çatal Höyük in central Anatolia has long captured the interest of archaeologists. James Mellaart's excavations (1967) revealed rooms with wall paintings and built-in decorated furniture that all but shouted "ritual." Benches with bull's horns protruding from them, wall decorations with the same bucrania or other animal imagery, and human skulls resting on the floor were all more than sufficient for Mellaart to identify these rooms as seventh-millennium BCE "shrines." Ian Hodder's more recent excavations have suggested that these were instead living spaces perhaps with specialized interiors (1996a, 1996b, 1999; Hodder and Cessford 2004; Hodder and Matthews 1998; and see Düring 2005, 2007). The site's architecture captured the interest of David Lewis-Williams (2004; Lewis-Williams and Pearce 2005), who sees both vertical and horizontal layering in the Çatal architecture. Domestic architecture at Çatal Höyük is tightly packed; some structures are agglutinated, and others have individual walls. Ground-level doorways were not the norm. Rather, entrance into homes was through rooftop openings into which descended a wooden ladder (Figure 10.8). Dwellings often had internal partitions creating several rooms. Open courtyards are distributed

Figure 10.8: Artistic rendering of life at Çatal Höyük, showing rooftop openings, internal partitioning, and tightly packed living quarters (drawing by Corrina Petit).

throughout the housing area, serving to some extent as work areas but also as refuse dump areas. Most houses contained a hearth, storage bins, and built-in furniture such as benches or platforms (Hodder 1999). Many structures contained evidence of domestic production activities such as flint-knapping and bone-working.

Lewis-Williams suggests that the rooftops may have represented an upper layer in a Neolithic Anatolian tiered cosmology, and the ladder extending through rooftop openings allowed descent into the middle layer. Because there are few windows to the outside and the rooftop openings are limited, the interior of Çatal houses were dimly lit, rather cavelike in Lewis-Williams's estimation (2004; Lewis-Williams and Pearce 2005: 105). Ladders were not the only representation of the vertical layering; many rooms had partial "columns" or jutting buttresses standing floor to ceiling. These, according to Lewis-Williams, were interior reminders of a vertical universe. Finally, the burial of the dead beneath floors might have represented the lowest layer of the cosmos.

In addition to the verticality, a multilayered cosmos was also represented on the horizontal plane. Passage between rooms and dwellings within the Çatal Höyük neighborhoods was accomplished through small holes, rather than full doorways, cut into the walls separating rooms. Such openings forced inhabitants to duck or even almost crawl between rooms, again mimicking cavelike behavior (Lewis-Williams 2004). Possibly, this method of transitioning from room to room was meant to resemble passage from one horizontal plane to the next. Another type of evidence Lewis-Williams uses to establish the notion of permeable horizontal layers is that of Çatal's wall decorations. As noted above, some walls portray animals, usually bovines but sometimes other creatures (humans among them), molded so that they jut beyond the walls into the interior space. The goal of such wall decorations may be to remind the house inhabitants that the animal world (or a spirit world comprising avatars of familiars or humans) exists just beyond the walls (see discussion in Hodder 2006: 195–98).

A final element at Çatal Höyük that may suggest an intertwining of house and cosmology is the ubiquitous use of red paint within the rooms (for a discussion of Neolithic building materials and use of colors, see Clarke 2012 and Love 2013). The color red, found in nearly all the rooms, on walls, benches, niches, and other features, including floors and platforms under which burials were laid, appears to be of some importance. Derived from red ocher, red paint is found in Chalcolithic-period buildings at Çatal Höyük (Erdoğu and Ulubey 2011). Lewis-Williams notes that the red paint is often found in the lower areas of the walls, and Hodder (2006) concurs with this analysis. Hodder agrees that red paint likely represented an important spiritual/cosmological ideology and suggests that perhaps it was used to interact with, or calm, the spirits living among the residents, perhaps just beyond the walls (2006: 196). Lewis-Williams summarizes his theories in the following: "[T]he walls of Çatalhöyük structures were ritually important. They were . . . thought of as a permeable interface between people in the structure and therefore already in a lower level of the cosmos and a spirit world that lay behind the walls" (2004: 38). There can be no denying that the architecture at this ancient site is indeed fascinating and doubtless was imbued with deep meaning for its inhabitants.

Life, Death, and Belief in Prehistoric European Houses

In Neolithic houses in the southeastern European Balkans, archaeologists have discovered ceramic anthropomorphized house models in which the house forms the lower or middle portion of a human body. Several other factors, associated with the building and destruction of houses, have led numerous scholars to suggest that for people living in the sixth and fifth millennia BCE of southeastern Europe, houses were not just dwellings but had a life cycle that ran parallel to the that of the family inhabiting the structure (Bailey 1990, 2000; Bradley 2005; Burdo et al. 2013; Naumov 2010, 2013; Tringham 1991a, 2005). Building the house was its birth, dwelling within it constituted its life, and upon abandonment, or perhaps at the death of the family lineage, the house was "killed" (Burdo et al. 2013; Gheorghiu 2007; Nauman 2013; Tringham 1991a, 2005). In many cases but not all, houses were then rebuilt on precisely the same place where its predecessor had stood (Bailey 1990, 1996). This might suggest a connection to *that* place, where the family or lineage had deep ancestral and symbolic ties (Steadman 2005; and see above). But it is rare to find archaeological clues to the circumstance that ancient inhabitants envisioned their home as an extension of themselves. They cooked, slept, stored, and worked within its walls, leaving behind the traces typical only of domestic activities. Occasionally, houses may have been decorated with symbols and images that would alert an excavator to the presence of symbolic meaning, but more often than not, such decorations were either lost to time or never present in the first place. An important clue may have been the intentional destruction of the house: not a conflagration that destroyed neighbors or the entire settlement, but a careful razing of a particular structure. Such delicate clues—the rebuilding in a particular location, the single artifactual indicator of a ceramic anthropomorphic "house," and the razing of some structures—are all that were needed for a robust literature to develop on the house as a symbolic embodiment in the southeast European Neolithic.

Remaining in prehistoric Europe, an examination of the Neolithic longhouses and later long-barrow tombs presents many of the same elements discussed above. European longhouses emerged in the mid-sixth millennium BCE in Germany and surrounding regions, and over the course of more than 500 years, the house style spread across central, western, and northwestern Europe (Whittle 1996). First associated with the Linear Pottery Culture (Linearbandkeramik in German), these houses are variously referred to as "longhouses" or "LBK houses." Their rapid spread was traditionally attributed to population migrations from the east westward, carrying with them the practice of agricultural production (e.g., Ammerman and Cavalli-Sforza 1984; Dennell 1984). More recent discussions have suggested that ideologies rather than people may have spread behaviors and knowledge (Amkreutz 2013; Last 1996; Pechtl

2009; Whittle 2003, 2009; see discussion in Milisauskas 2011). LBK longhouses were rectangular and later trapezoidal, ranging in size from 10 to 46 m in length and were up to 7 m wide; they were built of wooden timbers with doors in one end (Bickle 2013; Whittle 1996, 2003). Though most LBK houses were likely single-storied, some may have had lofts or functional second stories. Houses appear to have been inhabited for several decades but were abandoned before they became too dilapidated to live in. Three rows of posts were typical (Figure 10.9), necessary for the gabled roof support. Longhouses were built in the same orientation within the community and were separated by some meters; some may have been built in "pairs," perhaps representing a social unit (Bickle 2013).

The internal structure of the longhouses was based on a tripartite model. The middle portion was the human living area, and it was here that most refuse from cooking and working was found (usually off to one side of the structure); the "back" end may have served as a storage area and the front end as a byre (Bradley 2001; Hodder 1990;

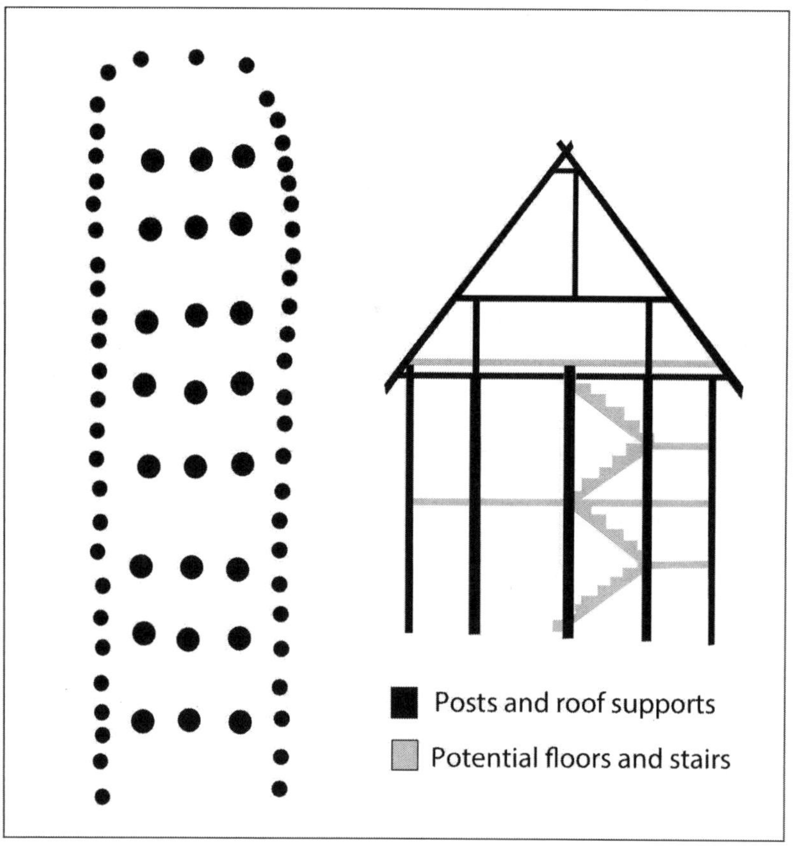

Figure 10.9: Stylized plan of a Neolithic European LBK house with a section of the front showing potential upper floors.

Whittle 1996). Though quite large, LBK structures were apparently not meant to house multiple families or even large numbers of people. Archaeologists have noted that far more hands were required to build the structures than would eventually dwell within each (Bickle 2013; Coudart 1998; Startin 1978; Whittle 1996, 2003).

A number of scholars (e.g., Bickle 2013; Borić 2008; Bradley 2001; Hodder 1990; Jones 2005; Pyzel 2013) have suggested that the collective evidence associated with LBK houses describes a "life cycle" of the house: a birth, a life (perhaps the length of a human generation), and a death, which is represented by abandonment and the construction of a new house, usually next door and very occasionally partially overlapping the "origin" house. The association of house with inhabitants suggests, as described above, that the LBK longhouse was considered a physical extension of the family or social group that dwelled within it. The house, like the people, lived its life from birth (building) to death, a life cycle that coincided with that of the head of household who commissioned the building of the structure in the first place (or perhaps a descendant, if more than one generation lived in the house). At the death of the human, so too was the house put to death. Rather than setting it afire, however, LBK people appear to have abandoned the house and built another close by, leaving the remains of the original house to decay and collapse, perhaps like the ancestors buried near the settlement.

According to Hodder, Bradley, and others (Bradley 1993, 1998, 2002; Hodder 1990, 1994; Last 2013; Midgley 2005), the final stage of the LBK longhouse took place later and in more western regions: the longhouse transformed into the long-barrow tomb, creating an ancestral burial house. By the mid-fifth millennium BCE, long rectangular or trapezoidal cairns or long barrows began to appear in central Western Europe and spread westward; their resemblance to LBK longhouses is notable. Archaeologists suggest that the longhouse became embedded in the cosmologies of Neolithic European cultures as a type of "ideal" house, one necessary for the housing of the ancestors in perpetuity.

A Perfect Storm: Lepenski Vir

The final case study in this chapter, and in fact in this book, brings together all the elements of "the symbolic and the sacred" discussed here: a sacred landscape, ritual in the house, and the house as cosmos. The site is Lepenski Vir in the Iron Gates (Danube Gorges) region of the Danube River (Radovanović 1996; Srejović 1972). Residents at sites such as Lepenski Vir, Vlasac, and Padina practiced a hunting-and-gathering subsistence, possibly engaging in some beginning stages of cultivation. In the late eighth or early seventh millennium BCE, inhabitants at these sites built semi-subterranean trapezoidal structures along the river, usually with well-constructed limestone floors. Evidence suggests the following characteristics were common at most Iron Gates sites, but preservation at Lepenski Vir offers the best data on ancient European beliefs in this region.

Lepenski Vir houses had stone foundations and post-holes for wooden beams that created a slanted-wall superstructure which leaned inward to create the roofing; main posts supporting the central roofing beam were secured with large flat stones surrounding their bases (Srejović 1972: 52–61). Many of the houses had a "patio" of flat stones at the entrance. The walls of the houses were formed by the surrounding earth, and the upper skeleton of the house was covered by organic materials, possibly including skins. The houses were built in an "upstream" and "downstream" arrangement, with the wider end of the trapezoidal structure featuring the doorway and facing the river. The houses at Lepenski Vir were individual, and most held a rectangular stone hearth set into the limestone floor in the center and frontal area of the structure. The original excavator identified five building phases at Lepenski Vir, but more recent investigation suggests there may have been fewer (Bonsall 2008; Bonsall et al. 2008; Borić 2002). Regardless of the earliest settlement and abandonment (currently in flux) dates, Lepenski Vir was inhabited for nearly a millennium. Residents of these sites hunted deer, pig, and other wild animals and gathered the wild plants of the region. They also exploited the riverine resources, with fish constituting a major part of their diet.

The landscape surrounding Lepenski Vir and the other Mesolithic sites in the Iron Gates region is quite dramatic. Resting just above a large horseshoe bend in the Danube, Lepenski Vir is named for the whirlpool in the river that was slowly but steadily eating away at the site nestled next to the riverbank. Upstream and downstream, the river winds through dramatic hills and mountains (Figure 10.10), and directly across the river from Lepenski Vir, a massive stone cliff, roughly trapezoidal in shape, rises into the sky "like a giant sentinel of the prehistoric settlement" (Srejović 1972: 18). Nature's dramatic beauty, and its power, evidenced by the whirlpool and towering mountains and stone cliffs, must have created a powerful landscape for the Lepenski Vir residents. Their consistency of place for nearly a millennium suggests they remained in their settlement for reasons beyond its easy accessibility to the river.

Evidence for ritual in the Lepenski Vir homes, and ancestors associated with them, is manifold. Regarding the performance of ritual within the house, this discussion begins with perhaps the most "prosaic" of the evidence, the internal hearths. Hearths were generally quite elaborately built, elliptical or rectangular in shape and set into the floor. Initially, hearths were surrounded by large stone slabs set flush into the floor; these may have been functional, serving as work surfaces or tables (Srejović 1972: 69–70). They circled the hearth to meet the stone paving at the doorway, the latter often set in a fan or trapezoidal shape (Figure 10.11). However, somewhat later, these flagstones were replaced by enigmatic A-shaped stone features surrounding the hearths. Made of red stone plaquettes, the point of the "A" rested near or against the hearth, with the open end pointing away. The excavator suggested that possibly these were leg stands for a wooden superstructure over the hearth, but both he and others recognize that their placement is not symmetrical and that it is equally or perhaps more likely that these had a more symbolic than functional purpose (Borić 2008; Radovanović 1996: 133; Srejović 1972: 71). A further indicator of the symbolic nature of the "A" features and the hearths is the presence of human bones built into the hearth structure, discussed in more detail below.

Figure 10.10: Photo of the Iron Gates (photo by the author).

Figure 10.11: Artistic reconstruction of the houses at Neolithic Lepenski Vir. Note the hearth inside the home (Srejović 1972: 55, fig. 9; 63, fig. 12; drawing by Corrina Petit).

Another set of finds includes animal bones that may not have been deposited solely through discardment. Animal bones were also deposited in burials, discussed below, and are part of the evidence suggesting that animal-based ritual may have occurred at Lepenski Vir. Perhaps even more notable is the occurrence of red deer antlers and skulls, dog mandibles, and a wild boar carcass inside the Lepenski Vir houses, not buried, but on the floors (Dimitrijević 2008), possibly once resting on wooden or other organic supports. Some of these may have been placed in the houses when they were being abandoned.

"Altars," so named by the excavator, and statues appeared at Lepenski Vir not long after the site was settled; more recently, the altars were identified as "mortars" (Borić 2005, 2008). These stone features were quarried from a red Permian sandstone outcrop not far from the site (Radovanović 1996: 140); the excavator notes that residents consistently obtained their altars/mortars and statues from this particular place despite the fact that the boulder-strewn landscape around the site provides much closer raw materials (Srejović 1972: 80). The altars/mortars and statues were hammered into rounded or egg-shaped forms. They typically rested at the inner end of the hearth, closer to the back of the structure, though some were also near the front (closer to the doorway) of the hearth. Altars/mortars had a cup-like hole dug out of their center; some were undecorated. but a number either had designs carved upon them or were shaped into the form of animal heads (such as a deer) or into a fish shape. Undecorated "altars" appear to predate those featuring designs or zoomorphic representation. The statues are even more remarkable. These are rounded boulders, larger than the "altars," and may be undecorated, carved with designs, or represent human-like or animal faces and bodies (Figure 10.12). Some of the anthropomorphic sculptures depict female genitalia and what appear to be breasts; others feature only a face that sometimes appears distinctly "fish-like." The carved designs on the statues are often identical to those on the altars. Many of these sculptures once stood upright on stone pavings at the back of the hearth, occasionally accompanied by a stone "altar."

Upward of 80 burials were recovered at Lepenski Vir. The majority of these were infants or children under the age of three, buried under the Lepenski Vir house floors, behind the hearth near the back of the house, or sometimes at a back corner. Evidence suggests that some of the infant burials took place prior to the construction of the house; in many of the houses with neonate burials, adult human skeletal parts were located either in the hearth or in another subfloor interment (Radovanović 2000; Srejović 1972: 118; Stefanović and Borić 2008). Somewhat older children and adults were buried under the house floors, but the majority of adults were buried *between* the houses or at the back of the community (away from the river), usually in supine positions and parallel to the river; burials inside the house often had sculptures placed above where the skulls rested (Radovanović 1996, 2000). The burials of adults and older juveniles were sometimes accompanied by animal bones: partially or wholly articulated dogs and the scapula or skull of red deer were the most common (Dimitrijević 2008; Radovanović 1996).

Figure 10.12: Lepenski Vir statues (possibly resembling fish) found in houses (drawing by Rebecca Jennison).

Adult human skeletal parts found inside the houses were often associated with the hearth. Female mandibles were sometimes built into the hearth structure, and other bones, including clavicles, scapula, femurs, and ribs, were also recovered, perhaps removed from burials located between the houses (Radovanović 2000). The sequence of burial placement—newborns and infants buried prior to the building of the house, burials of older children and young adults within the house, and the placement of adult skeletal parts above ground at a later date—has led some to suggest that this process both establishes membership in the house and "opens" and "closes" the house, perhaps demarcating the beginning and end of an ancestral line (Bailey 2000: 150–52; Chapman 2000: 200–201; Radovanović 1997; Srejović 1972: 119). Some equate the burials and associated ritual artifacts in the Lepenski Vir houses with death (Hodder 1990: 20–52; Stefanović and Borić 2008); it can be argued that residents must have recognized that death was always present, especially in the "wilds" outside the house. By recognizing death through burial, they achieved a sort of "taming" of the fear of death, or perhaps the infants, in particular, served as a protection against it.

Finally, elements of the house itself suggest that the building was also an important entity in Lepenski Vir belief. The shape and orientation of the houses are notable: not rectangular or oval, but trapezoidal, with the wide end facing the river and the massive stone cliff across the river. The creation of the substantial house floors bears mention here. First, the stone foundations, posts and stone supports, and stone slabs for the hearth, were put in place. Then red limestone marl was mixed with sand, water, and lime mortar to create a paste which was then laid over the previously placed building materials, laid thinly over upwardly protruding areas such as stone foundations and as much as 25 cm thick in other areas. The flooring was then smoothed and left to dry. Some house floors had the addition of red or white polished stones as decoration (Srejović 1972: 54). The construction of these floors was so solid that some eight millennia later, when excavated, they remained hard-packed and provided a clearly visible layout of the ancient Lepenski Vir houses.

How might archaeologists interpret the extensive symbolism represented by the setting, houses, and contents at Lepenski Vir and its neighboring sites? A number of attempts to make sense of the Lepenski Vir cosmology have been offered over the decades (e.g., Bailey 2000; Borić 2007; Borić and Stefanović 2004; Chapman 2000; Hodder 1994; Radovanović 1996, 1997; Steadman 2009). Some relationship likely exists between the intentionally ubiquitous presence of animal remains and cosmology. Given that the inhabitants of the site depended on hunting of red deer, and that dogs may have assisted in hunting, this correlation is not a far stretch. Likewise, fish imagery on the statues would seem to fit with ritual behavior associated with ensuring a bountiful harvest of fish on a continual basis. That examples of the statuary evoke a "human-fish" element (and the fish aspects look surprisingly like the beluga sturgeon native to the river) suggests to some that the combination was not accidental. The statuary may have represented the need for a "rebirth" of the fish in their migratory cycle and the rebirth of humans as they benefit from the process, or, even more symbolically, the merging of fish and ancestor after human death, creating a supernatural being that not only looks after descendants but ensures subsistence success in the settlement (Borić 2005; Radovanović 1997). The designs found on altars and sculptures (the interpretation of which is at present unfathomable) may have had deep symbolic meaning, perhaps pertaining to Lepenski Vir cosmology and world view, or to kinship groups, or to both. Such designs within the house may have been meant to promote long life, health, fertility, or a host of other desired states and outcomes. Already mentioned is the possibility that the Lepenski Vir houses had a "life cycle" much as did their inhabitants. That the houses became the home of the ancestors marked by the placement, perhaps, of their bones, and were thus "closed" when the ancestor died, is suggested by the building of new houses next to, but not usually over, the original house. Finally, the houses in their trapezoidal form, with openings to the river, may have literally "embodied" elements of the cosmology. Perhaps facing the river, and the stone cliff, represented life, rebirth, continuation; the red floors could perhaps be reminiscent of life blood (or, perhaps, blood represented death). If the people of Lepenski Vir believed in a multilayered universe, as many in other cultures do, one might suggest that the solid floors were built to separate the living from the dead, especially those under the house floors. Perhaps only the ancestors, placed *outside* the houses, could be trusted to protect and ensure the family line.

Conclusion

In many ways, the preceding chapter was the most challenging to construct because religious belief and ritual practice are such individualized cultural institutions. What is an altar in one house is a table in another; the burial of an infant under the floor of one house gives deep symbolic meaning to the structure, when in another it is simply the cultural norm, emblematic of nothing more than expediency. In addition to being one of the most difficult chapters to write, it is also one of the longest! Be assured, it could have been double or triple its present length and still have failed to cover even a fraction of the archaeological examples of ritualized behavior and belief found in the house and household. Nonetheless, the examples and cases studies cited offer at least a broad framework of how ritual and religious belief are often represented in the archaeological record, at least with regard to the house itself. With luck, potentially deeper meanings of the odd and unusual—or, at least, the slightly less mundane—recently discovered in a site somewhere in the world will resonate with the archaeologist who has chanced to read this chapter.

Postscript
Shingles on a Rooftop

If the first chapter offered an introduction to this volume, a foundation to this edifice, the chapters that followed constituted the body of the house. This final word presents nothing that can be considered relevant to the types of questions and subjects pursued in those chapters. Rather, it reflects this author's thoughts about what has been accomplished and, more importantly, left unfinished. Roofs are made of many materials. Today's wooden, slate, or composite shingles were yesterday's thatch or matting, wooden poles or branches, skin or packed mud. If each topic covered in this volume were equal to a single shingle, a branch, or piece of thatch, I fear the residents of that house would find a woefully incomplete roof over their dwelling. That is to say, there is so much more to cover, explore, and investigate. The ancient built environment is multivarious in its manifestations and meanings, and these are likely forever beyond the total ken of archaeologists. Rather than view this as a hopeless situation, it should serve as a challenge. What new methodologies can be developed to continue to reveal what was denoted by the builders of ancient dwellings?

Writing this book was joyful and humbling. What I did not know and still certainly have yet to learn about the archaeology of architecture was, and is, daunting, to say the least. The excellent work of so many of the scholars cited in this book, and of others for which there simply was not space, is enlightening and gratifying, as it serves to illustrate that while there is still so much to discover, with skilled and careful work, new ways to understand the past will certainly come to light.

Archaeology of Domestic Architecture and the Human Use of Space, by Sharon R. Steadman, 291–292.

The acknowledgments at the beginning of this volume recognize friends, family, and colleagues who have helped and supported this work from its outset. Actually, all of the scholars who produced the case studies discussed in the body of this volume should be listed right alongside those few who are in fact cited there. I acknowledge careful excavations undertaken by these many archaeologists, their attention to detail, and their bravery in sometimes offering significant interpretive leaps in order to understand the essence, both physical and symbolic, of the home or structure presented to them in the archaeological record. The ongoing work of these and new generations of archaeologists will continue to build shingles on the rooftop.

REFERENCES

Abramiuk, Marc

2012 *The Foundations of Cognitive Archaeology*. Boston: MIT Press.

Abrams, Elliott

1989 Architecture and Energy: An Evolutionary Perspective. In *Archaeological Method and Theory*, Vol. 1, edited by M. B. Schiffer, pp. 47–87. Tucson: University of Arizona Press.

Adams, Robert McC.

1965 *Land behind Baghdad: A History of Settlement in the Diyala Plains*. Chicago: University of Chicago Press.

1981 *Heartland of Cities: Surveys of Ancient Settlement and Land Use on the Central Floodplain of the Euphrates*. Chicago: University of Chicago Press.

Adams, Ron L.

2007 Maintaining Cohesion in House Societies of West Sumba, Indonesia. In *The Durable House: House Society in Models in Archaeology*, edited by R. A. Beck, Jr., pp. 344–62. Center for Archaeological Investigations, Occasional Paper No. 35. Carbondale: Southern Illinois University.

Adovasio, J. M., Olga Soffer, and Jake Page

2007 The Fashioning of Women. In *Gender in Cross-Cultural Perspective*, 5th ed., edited by C. B. Brettell and C. F. Sargent, pp. 65–83. Upper Saddle River: Pearson/Prentice-Hall.

Ahrentzen, Sherry

2003 The Space between the Studs: Feminism and Architecture. *Signs: Journal of Women in Culture and Society* 29.1: 179–206.

Archaeology of Domestic Architecture and the Human Use of Space, by Sharon R. Steadman, 293–375.

Akkermans, Peter M. M. G., and Glenn M. Schwartz
2003 *The Archaeology of Syria: From Complex Hunter-Gatherers to Early Urban Societies (ca. 16,000–300 BC)*. Cambridge: Cambridge University Press.

Alcock, Susan E.
2005 Roman Colonies in the Eastern Empire: A Tale of Four Cities. In *The Archaeology of Colonial Encounters*, edited by G. Stein, pp. 297–329. Santa Fe: School of American Research Press.

Aldenderfer, Mark
1993a (ed.) *Domestic Architecture, Ethnicity and Complementarity in the South-Central Andes*. Iowa City: University of Iowa Press.
1993b Ritual, Hierarchy, and Change in Foraging Societies. *Journal of Anthropological Archaeology* 12: 1–40.

Aldenderfer, Mark S., and Herbert D. G. Maschner (eds.)
1996 *Anthropology, Space, and Geographic Information Systems*. Oxford: Oxford University Press.

Aldenderfer, Mark S., and Charles Stanish
1993 Domestic Architecture, Household Archaeology, and the Past in the South Central Andes. In *Domestic Architecture, Ethnicity and Complementarity in the South-Central Andes*, edited by M. S. Aldenderfer, pp. 1–12. Iowa City: University of Iowa Press.

Alfayé, Silvia
2007 Contexts of Cults in *Hispania Celtica*. In *Cult in Context: Reconsidering Ritual in Archaeology*, edited by D. A. Barrowclough and C. Malone, pp. 313–20. Oxford: Oxbow.

Algaze, Guillermo
1993 *The Uruk World System. The Dynamics of Expansion of Early Mesopotamian Civilization*. Chicago: University of Chicago Press.
2008 *Ancient Mesopotamia at the Dawn of Civilization: The Evolution of an Urban Landscape*. Chicago: University of Chicago Press.

Allen, Michael J., and Julie Gardiner
2002 A Sense of Time. Cultural Markers in the Mesolithic of Southern England? In *The Inscribed Landscape: Marking and Making Place*, edited by B. David and M. Wilson, pp. 139–53. Honolulu: University of Hawaii Press.

Allen, Kathleen M. S., Stanton W. Green, and Ezra B. W. Zubrow (eds.)
1990 *Interpreting Space: GIS and Archaeology*. New York: Taylor and Francis.

Allison, Penelope M.
1999a Introduction. In *The Archaeology of Household Activities*, edited by P. M. Allison, pp. 1–18. London: Routledge.
1999b (ed.) *The Archaeology of Household Activities*. London: Routledge.
1999c Labels for Ladles: Interpreting the Material Culture of Roman Households. In *The Archaeology of Household Activities*, edited by P. M. Allison, pp. 57–77. London: Routledge.

Altman, Irwin
1975 *The Environment and Social Behavior. Privacy, Personal Space, Territory*. Monterey, CA: Brooks/Cole.

Ames, Kenneth M.

1995 Chiefly Power and Household Production on the Northwest Coast. In *Foundations of Social Inequality*, edited by T. D. Price and G. M. Feinman, pp. 155–87. New York: Plenum Press.

2008 The Archaeology of Rank. In the *Handbook of Archaeological Theories*, edited by R. A. Bentley, H. D. G. Maschner, and C. Chippendale, pp. 487–511. Lanham, MD: AltaMira Press.

Amiran, Ruth, and Omit Ilan

1996 *Early Arad II: The Chalcolithic and Early Bronze IB Settlements and Early Bronze II City: Architecture and Planning. Sixth to Eighteenth Seasons of Excavations, 1971–1978, 1980–1984.* Jerusalem: Israel Exploration Society.

Amkreutz, Luc

2013 Home Is When You Build It. Characteristics of Building and Occupation in the Lower Rhine Area Wetlands (5500–2500 cal BC). In *Tracking the Neolithic House in Europe: Sedentism, Architecture, and Practice*, edited by D. Hofmann and J. Smyth, pp. 229–59. New York: Springer.

Ammerman, Albert J., and Luigi L. Cavalli-Sforza.

1984 *The Neolithic Transition and the Genetics of Populations in Europe*. Princeton: Princeton University Press.

Anderson, David G., Robert P. Wishart, and Virginie Vaté (eds.)

2013 *About the Hearth: Perspectives on the Home, Hearth and Household in the Circumpolar North*. New York: Berghahn Books

Andrews, Peter A.

1981 The Turkmen Tent. *Halı* 4.2: 108–17.

1986 Felt Tents in Anatolia. *Sosyal Antropoloji ve Etnoloji Dergisi* 4: 33–63.

1997 *Nomad Tent Types in the Middle East*, Parts I and II. Wiesbaden: Ludwig Reichert Verlag.

Ansari-Renani, Hamid R., Barbara Rischkowsky, Joaquin P. Mueller, Seyed M. S. Momen, and Sepehr Moradi

2013 Nomadic Pastoralism in Southern Iran. *Pastoralism: Research, Policy and Practice* 3: 11: 1–25.

Anschuetz, K. F., R. H. Wilshusen, and C. L. Scheick

2001 An Archaeology of Landscapes: Perspectives and Directions. *Journal of Archaeological Research* 9: 157–211.

Anyon, Roger, and S. A. LeBlanc

1984 *The Galaz Ruin: A Prehistoric Mimbres Village in Southwestern New Mexico*. Albuquerque: University of New Mexico Press.

Arbuckle, Benjamin

2009 Chalcolithic Caprines, Dark Age Dairy, and Byzantine Beef: A First Look at Animal Exploitation at Middle and Late Holocene Çadır Höyük, North Central Turkey. *Anatolica* 35: 179–224.

Archer, Margaret S.

2000 *Being Human: The Problem of Agency*. Cambridge: Cambridge University Press.

Ardener, Shirley (ed.)

1993 *Women and Space: Ground Rules and Social Maps*. Rev. ed. Oxford: Berg.

Århem, Kaj

1998 Powers of Place: Landscape, Territory and Local Belonging in Northwest Amazonia. In *Locality and Belonging*, edited by N. Lovell, pp. 75–98. London: Routledge.

Arnold, Bettina, and Nancy L. Wicker (eds.)

2001 *Gender and the Archaeology of Death*. Lanham, MD: AltaMira Press.

Arnold, Jeanne E.

1992 Complex Hunter-Gatherer-Fishers of Prehistoric California: Chiefs, Specialists, and Maritime Adaptations of the Channel Islands. *American Antiquity* 57.1: 60–84.

1996a The Archaeology of Complex Hunter-Gatherers. *Journal of Archaeological Method and Theory* 3.2: 77–126.

1996b (ed.) *Emergent Complexity: The Evolution of Intermediate Societies*. Ann Arbor: International Monographs in Prehistory.

1996c Organizational Transformations: Power and Labor among Complex Hunter-Gatherers and Other Intermediate Societies. In *Emergent Complexity: The Evolution of Intermediate Societies*, edited by J. E. Arnold, pp. 59–73. Archaeological Series 9. Ann Arbor: International Monographs in Prehistory.

2000 Revisiting Power, Labor Rights, and Kinship: Archaeology and Social Theory. In *Social Theory in Archaeology*, edited by M. B. Schiffer, pp. 14–30. Salt Lake City: University of Utah Press.

2001 (ed.) *The Origins of a Pacific Coast Chiefdom: The Chumash of the Channel Islands*. Salt Lake City: University of Utah Press.

2004 (ed.) *Foundations of Chumash Complexity*. Perspectives in California Archaeology, Vol. 7. Los Angeles: Cotsen Institution of Archaeology.

2006 Households on the Pacific Coast: The Northwest Coast and California in Comparative Perspectives. In *Household Archaeology on the Northwest Coast*, edited by E. A. Sobel, D. A. Trieu Gahr, and K. M, Ames, pp. 270–85. Ann Arbor: International Monographs in Prehistory.

Arnold, Jeanne E., Roget H. Colten, and Scott Pletka

1997 Contexts of Cultural Change in Insular California. *American Antiquity* 62.2: 300–318.

Ashcraft, Norman, and Albert E. Scheflen

1976 *People Space. The Making and Breaking of Human Boundaries*. Garden City, NJ: Anchor Press/Doubleday.

Ashmore, Wendy

1989 Construction and Cosmology: Politics and Ideology in Lowland Maya Settlement Patterns. In *Word and Image in Maya Culture: Explorations in Language, Writing, and Representation*, edited by W. F. Hanks and D. S. Rice, pp. 272–86. Salt Lake City: University of Utah Press.

2000 "Decisions and Dispositions": Socializing Spatial Archaeology. *American Anthropologist* New Series, 104.4: 1172–83.

2005 The Idea of a Maya Town. In *Structure and Meaning in Human Settlements*, edited by T. Atkin and J. Rykwert, pp. 35–54. Pennsylvania: University of Pennsylvania Museum of Archaeology and Anthropology.

2006 Gender and Landscapes. In *Handbook of Gender in Archaeology*, edited by S. M. Nelson, pp. 199–218. Lanham, MD: AltaMira Press.

Ashmore, Wendy, and A. Bernard Knapp (eds.)
1999 *Archaeologies of Landscape: Contemporary Perspectives.* Oxford: Blackwell.
Ashmore, Wendy, and Richard R. Wilk
1988 Household and Community in the Mesoamerican Past. In *Household and Community in the Mesoamerican Past,* edited by R. R. Wilk and W. Ashmore, pp. 1–27. Albuquerque: University of New Mexico Press.
Aston, Michael, and Trevor Rowley
1974 *Landscape Archaeology: An Introduction to Fieldwork Techniques on Post-Roman Landscapes.* Newton Abbot, UK: David and Charles.
Atkin, Tony, and Carol H. Krinsky
1996 Cultural Identity in Modern Native American Architecture: A Case Study. *Journal of Architectural Education* 49.4: 237–45.
Atran, Scott
2002 *In Gods We Trust: The Evolutionary Landscape of Religion.* New York: Oxford University Press.
Ault, Bradley A., and Lisa C. Nevett
1999 Digging Houses: Archaeologies of Classical and Hellenistic Greek Domestic Assemblages. In *The Archaeology of Household Activities,* edited by P. M. Allison, pp. 43–56. London: Routledge.
Bafna, Sonit
2003 Space Syntax: A Brief Introduction to Its Logic and Analytical Techniques. *Environment and Behavior* 25: 17–29.
BaHammam, Omar S.
2006 The Role of Privacy in the Design of the Saudi Arabian Courtyard House. In *Courtyard Housing: Past, Present and Future,* edited by B. Edwards, M. Sibley, M. Hakmi, and P. Land, pp. 77–82. New York: Taylor & Francis.
Bailey, Douglass W.
1990 The Living House: Signifying Continuity. In *The Social Archaeology of Houses,* edited by R. Samson, pp. 17–48. Edinburgh: Edinburgh University Press.
1996 The Life, Times and Works of House 59, Tell Ovcharovo, Bulgaria. In *Neolithic Houses in North-West Europe and Beyond,* edited by T. Darvill and J. Thomas, pp. 142–56. Oxford: Oxbow.
2000 *Balkan Prehistory: Exclusion, Incorporation and Identity.* London: Routledge.
Bandy, Matthew S.
2004 Fissioning, Scalar Stress, and Social Evolution in Early Village Societies. *American Anthropologist* 106.2: 322–33.
2010 Population Growth, Village Fissioning, and Alternative Early Village Trajectories. In *Becoming Villagers: Comparing Early Village Societies,* edited by M. S. Bandy and J. R. Fox, pp. 19–36. Tucson: University of Arizona Press.
Bandy, Matthew S., and Jake R. Fox (eds.)
2010 *Becoming Villagers: Comparing Early Village Societies.* Tucson: University of Arizona Press.
Banning, E. B.
1993 Where the Wild Stones Have Been Gathered Aside: Pastoralist Campsites in Wadi Ziqlâb, Jordan. *Biblical Archaeologist* 56.4: 212–27.

1995 Herders . . . or Homesteaders? A Neolithic Farm in Wadi Ziqlâb, Jordan. *Biblical Archaeologist* 58: 1–13.

1996 Houses, Compounds and Mansions in the Prehistoric Near East. In *People Who Lived in Big Houses: Archaeological Perspectives on Large Domestic Structures*, edited by G. Coupland and E. B. Banning, pp. 165–85. Madison, WI: Prehistory Press.

1997 Spatial Perspectives on Early Urban Development in Mesopotamia. In *Urbanism in Antiquity: From Mesopotamia to Crete*, edited by W. E. Aufrecht, N. A. Mirau, and S. W. Gauley, pp. 17–34. Sheffield: Sheffield Academic Press.

2002 Spatial and Architectural Aspects of Neolithization. In *Material Culture and Mental Spheres: Rezeption archaologischer Denkrichtungen in der Vorderasiatischen Altertumskunde*, edited by A. Hausleiter, S. Kerner, and B. Müller-Neuhof, pp. 307–12. Münster: Ugarit-Verlag.

2003 Housing Neolithic Farmers. *Near Eastern Archaeology* 66.1–2: 4–21.

2011a Houses, Households, and Changing Society in the Late Neolithic and Chalcolithic of the Southern Levant. *Paléorient* 36.1: 49–87.

2011b So Fair a House: Göbekli Tepe and the Identification of Temples in the Pre-Pottery Neolithic of the Near East. *Current Anthropology* 52.5: 619–60.

Banning, E. B., and Brian F. Byrd

1987 Houses and the Changing Residential Unit: Domestic Architecture at PPNB 'Ain Ghazal, Jordan. *Proceedings of the Prehistoric Society* 53: 309–25.

Banning, E. B., and Ilse Köhler-Rollefson

1983 Ethnoarchaeological Survey in the Beidha Area, Southern Jordan. *Annual of the Department of Antiquities of Jordan* 27: 375–83.

1992 Ethnographic Lessons for the Pastoral Past: Camp Locations and Material Remains near Beidha, Southern Jordan. In *Pastoralism in the Levant: Archaeological Materials in Anthropological Perspectives*, edited by O. Bar-Yosef and A. Khazanov, pp. 181–204. Monographs in World Archaeology, No. 10. Madison, WI: Prehistory Press.

Barber, Elizabeth W.

1994 *Women's Work: The First 20,000 Years.* New York: W.W. Norton and Co.

Barber, Sarah B., and Arthur A. Joyce

2006 When Is a House a Palace? Elite Residences in the Valley of Oaxaca. In *Palaces and Power in the Americas: From Peru to the Northwest Coast*, edited by J. J. Christie and P. J. Sarro, pp. 211–55. Austin: University of Texas Press.

Bard, Kathryn A.

2008 Royal Cities and Cult Centers, Administrative Towns, and Workmen's Settlements in Ancient Egypt. In *The Ancient City: New Perspectives on Urbanism in the Old and New World*, edited by J. Marcus and J. A. Sabloff, pp. 165–82. Santa Fe: School for Advanced Research Press.

Barfield, Thomas J.

1993 *The Nomadic Alternative.* Englewood Cliffs, NJ: Prentice-Hall.

Barile, Kerri S., and Jamie C. Brandon (eds.)

2004 *Household Chores and Household Choices: Theorizing the Domestic Sphere in Historical Archaeology*. Tuscaloosa: University of Alabama Press.

Barkai, Ran, and Roy Liran

2008 Midsummer Sunset at Neolithic Jericho. *Time and Mind: The Journal of Archaeology, Consciousness and Culture* 1.3: 273–84.

Barker, Graeme
2009 *The Agricultural Revolution in Prehistory: Why did Foragers Become Farmers?* Oxford: Oxford University Press.

Barnes, Gina
1999 Buddhist Landscapes of East Asia. In *Archaeologies of Landscape: Contemporary Perspectives*, edited by W. Ashmore and A. B. Knapp, pp. 101–23. Oxford: Blackwell.

Barrett, John C.
1999 The Mythical Landscapes of the British Iron Age. In *Archaeologies of Landscape: Contemporary Perspectives*, edited by W. Ashmore and A. B. Knapp, pp. 253–65. Oxford: Blackwell.
2001 Agency, the Duality of Structure, and the Problem of the Archaeological Record. In *Archaeological Theory Today*, edited by I. Hodder, pp. 141–64. Cambridge: Polity Press.

Barrett, John C., Richard Bradley, and Martin Green (eds.)
1991 *Landscape, Monuments, and Society: The Prehistory of Cranborne Chase.* Cambridge: Cambridge University Press.

Bartel, Brad
1980 Colonialism and Cultural Responses: Problems Related to Roman Provincial Analysis. *World Archaeology* 12.1: 11–26.
1987 Acculturation and Ethnicity in Roman Moesia Superior. In *Centre and Periphery. Comparative Studies in Archaeology*, edited by T. C. Champion, pp. 173–85. London: Unwin Hyman.

Barth, Frederik
1961 *Nomads of South Persia: The Basseri Tribe of the Khamseh Confederacy.* Boston: Little, Brown, and Company.

Bar-Yosef, Ofer
1984 Seasonality among Neolithic Hunter-Gatherers in Southern Sinai. In *Animals and Archaeology: Early Herders and Their Flocks*, edited by J. Clutton-Brock and C. Grigson, pp. 145–61. BAR International Series 202. Oxford: BAR International.
1986 The Walls of Jericho: An Alternative Interpretation. *Current Anthropology* 27: 157–62.
1998 The Natufian Culture in the Levant, Threshold to the Origins of Agriculture. *Evolutionary Anthropology* 6: 159–77.
2001 From Sedentary Foragers to Village Hierarchies: The Emergence of Social Institutions. In *The Origin of Human Social Institutions*, edited by W. G. Runciman, pp. 1–38. Oxford: Oxford University Press.
2002 Natufian: A Complex Society of Foragers. In *Beyond Foraging and Collecting: Evolutionary Change in Hunter-Gatherer Settlement Systems*, edited by B. Fitzhugh and J. Habu, pp. 91–149. New York: Kluwer Academic/Plenum.
2008 Farming, Herding, and the Transformation of Human Landscapes in Southwestern Asia. In *Handbook of Landscape Archaeology*, edited by B. David and J. Thomas, pp. 315–27. Walnut Creek, CA: Left Coast Press, Inc.

Bar-Yosef, Ofer, and Anna Belfer-Cohen
1991 From Sedentary Hunter-Gatherers to Territorial Farmers in the Levant. In *Between Bands and States*, edited by S. A. Gregg, pp. 181–202. Center for Archaeological Investigations Occasional Paper 9. Carbondale: Southern Illinois University.

Basso, Keith H.

1996a *Wisdom Sits in Places: Landscape and Language among the Western Apache.* Albuquerque: University of New Mexico Press.

1996b Wisdom Sits in Places: Notes on a Western Apache Landscape. In *Senses of Place,* edited by S. Feld and K. H. Basso, pp. 53–90. Santa Fe: School of American Research Press.

Bateson, Gregory

1958 *Naven: The Culture of the Iatmul People of New Guinea as Revealed through a Study of the 'Naven' Ceremonial.* 2nd ed. Stanford: Stanford University Press.

Bauer, Alexander A.

2002 Is What You See All You Get? Recognizing Meaning in Archaeology. *Journal of Social Archaeology* 2.1: 37–52.

Bawden, Garth

1982 Community Organization Reflected by the Household: A Study of Pre-Columbian Social Dynamics. *Journal of Field Archaeology* 9.2: 165–81.

1990 Domestic Space and Social Structure in Pre-Columbian Northern Peru. In *Domestic Architecture and the Use of Space: An Interdisciplinary Cross-Cultural Study,* edited by S. Kent, pp. 153–71. Cambridge: Cambridge University Press.

Baydar, Gülsüm

2004 The Cultural Burden of Architecture. *Journal of Architectural Education* 57.4: 19–27.

Beck, Robin A., Jr.

2007a (ed.) *The Durable House: House Society Models in Archaeology.* Center for Archaeological Investigations Occasional Paper No. 35. Carbondale: Southern Illinois University Press.

2007b The Durable House: Material, Metaphor, and Structure. In *The Durable House: House Society in Models in Archaeology,* edited by R. A. Beck, Jr., pp. 3–24. Center for Archaeological Investigations, Occasional Paper No. 35. Carbondale: Southern Illinois University.

Beit-Arieh, Itzhak

1981 A Pattern of Settlement in Southern Sinai and Southern Canaan in the Third Millennium B.C. *Bulletin of the American Schools of Oriental Research* 263: 27–54.

Belfer-Cohen, Anna

1991 The Natufian in the Levant. *Annual Review of Anthropology* 20: 167–86.

Belfer-Cohen, Anna, and Ofer Bar-Yosef

1989 The Origins of Sedentism and Farming Communities in the Levant. *Journal of World Prehistory* 40: 447–98.

2000 Early Sedentism in the Near East: A Bumpy Ride to Village Life. In *Life in Neolithic Farming Communities: Social Organization, Identity, and Differentiation,* edited by I. Kuijt, pp. 19–37. New York: Kluwer Academic/Plenum.

Belfer-Cohen, Anna, and A. Nigel Goring-Morris

2002 Recent Developments in Near Eastern Neolithic Research. *Paléorient* 28: 143–48.

2005 Which Way to Look? Conceptual Frameworks for Understanding Neolithic Processes. *Neo-Lithics* 2/05: 22–24.

2011 The Origins of Agriculture: New Data, New Ideas. *Current Anthropology* 54.S4: S209–20.

Bender, Barbara (ed.)
1995 *Landscape: Politics and Perspectives*. Oxford: Berg.

Bender, Donald
1967 A Redefinement of the Concept of Household: Families Coresidence and Domestic Functions. *American Anthropologist* 69.5: 493–504.

Bensa, Alban, and Isabelle Leblic
2000 *En pays kanak: Ethnologie, linguistique, archéologie, histoire de la Nouvelle-Calédonie*. Paris: Éditions de la Maison des sciences de l'homme.

Bentley, Gillian R.
1991 A Bioarchaeological Reconstruction of the Social and Kinship Systems at Early Bronze Age Bab edh-Dhra', Jordan. In *Between Bands and States*, edited by S. A. Gregg, pp. 5–34. Carbondale: Southern Illinois University Press.

Bentley, R. Alexander
2003 An Introduction to Complex Systems. In *Complex Systems and Archaeology*, edited by R. A. Bentley and H. D. G. Maschner, pp. 9–26. Salt Lake City: University of Utah.

Bentley, R. Alexander, and Herbert D. G. Maschner
2003 (eds.) *Complex Systems and Archaeology*. Salt Lake City: University of Utah Press.
2008 Complexity Theory. In *Handbook of Archaeological Theories*, edited by R. A. Bentley, H. D. G. Maschner, and C. Chippendale, pp. 245–70. Lanham, MD: AltaMira Press.

Bergengren, Charles
1994 From Lovers to Murderers: The Etiquette of Entry and the Social Implications of House Form. *Winterthur Portfolio* 29.1: 43–72.

Bernbeck, Reinhard
2008 An Archaeology of Multisited Communities. In *The Archaeology of Mobility: Old World and New World Nomadism*, edited by H. Barnard and W. Wendrich, pp. 43–77. Los Angeles: Cotsen Institute of Archaeology, UCLA.

Bettinger, Robert L.
1991 *Hunter-Gatherers: Archaeological and Evolutionary Theory*. New York: Plenum Press.

Betts, Alison
1982 Prehistoric Sites of Qa'a Mejalla, Eastern Jordan. *Levant* 14: 1–14.

Bianchi, Giovanna
2012 Building, Inhabiting and Perceiving Private Houses in Early Medieval Italy. *Arqueología de la arquitectura* 9: 195–212.

Biçakçı, Erhan
2003 Observations on the Early Pre-Pottery Neolithic Architecture in the Near East. 1. New Building Materials and Construction Techniques. In *From Village to Cities: Early Villages in the Near East*, edited by M. Özdoğan, H. Hauptmann, and N. Başgelen, pp. 385–413. Istanbul: Arkeoloji ve Sanat Yayınları.

Bickle, Penny
2013 Of Time and the House: The Early Neolithic Communities of the Paris Basin and Their Domestic Architecture. In *Tracking the Neolithic House in Europe: Sedentism, Architecture, and Practice*, edited by D. Hofmann and J. Smyth, pp. 151–81. New York: Springer.

Biehl, Peter F.
2007 Enclosing Places: A Contextual Approach to Cult and Religion in Neolithic Central Europe. In *Cult in Context: Reconsidering Ritual in Archaeology*, edited by D. A. Barrowclough and C. Malone, pp. 173–82. Oxford: Oxbow.
Bille, Mikkel, and Tim Flohr Sørensen (eds.)
2015 *Assembling Architecture: Archaeology, Affect, and the Performance of Building Spaces*. London: Routledge.
Binford, Lewis R.
1978a Dimensional Analysis of Behavior and Site Structure: Learning from an Eskimo Hunting Stand. *American Antiquity* 43: 330–61.
1978b *Nunamiut Ethnoarchaeology*. New York: Academic Press.
1980 Willow Smoke and Dogs' Tails: Hunter-Gatherer Settlement Systems and Archaeological Site Formation. *American Antiquity* 45.1: 4–20.
1982 The Archaeology of Place. *Journal of Anthropological Archaeology* 1: 5–31.
1990 Mobility, Housing and Environment: A Comparative Study. *Journal of Anthropological Research* 46.2: 119–52.
Birch, Jennifer (ed.)
2013 *From Prehistoric Villages to Cities: Settlement Aggregation and Community Transformation*. New York: Routledge.
Bird, C. F. M.
1993 Woman the Tool Maker: Evidence for Women's Use and Manufacture of Flaked Stone-Tools in Australia and New Guinea. In *Women in Archaeology: A Feminist Critique*, edited by H. du Cros and L. Smith, pp. 22–30. Canberra: Australian National University.
Bird-David, Nurit
1992a Beyond "The Original Affluent Society." *Current Anthropology* 33.1: 25–47.
1992b Beyond "The Hunting and Gathering Mode of Subsistence": Culture-Sensitive Observations on the Nayaka and Other Modern Hunter-Gatherers. *Man*, New Series 27.1: 19–44.
Birdwell-Pheasant, Donna, and Denise Lawrence-Zúñiga
1999 Introduction: Houses and Families in Europe. In *House Life. Space, Place and Family in Europe*, edited by D. Birdwell-Pheasant and D. Lawrence-Zúñiga, pp. 1–35. Oxford: Berg.
Blake, Emma
2006 The Residence of Power at Paso de la Amada, Mexico. In *Palaces and Power in the Americas: From Peru to the Northwest Coast,* edited by J. J. Christie and P. J. Sarro, pp. 191–210. Austin: University of Texas Press.
Blake, Michael, Richard G. Lesure, Warren D. Hill, Luis Barba, and John E. Clark
2007 Space, Spatiality, and Archaeology. In *A Companion to Social Archaeology*, edited by L. Meskell and R. W. Preucel, pp. 230–53. Oxford: Blackwell.
Blankholm, Hans P.
1991 *Intrasite Spatial Analysis in Theory and Practice*. Aarhus: Aarhus University Press.
Blanton, Richard E.
1978 *Monte Alban: Settlement Patterns at the Ancient Zapotec Capital*. New York: Academic Press.
1994 *Houses and Households: A Comparative Study*. New York: Plenum Press.

Blier, Suzanne P.
1987 *The Anatomy of Architecture: Ontology and Metaphor in Batammaliba Architectural Expression*. Chicago: University of Chicago Press.

Boast, Robin, and Eugenia Yiannouli
1986 Creating Space. *Archaeological Review from Cambridge* 5: 136–205.

Bocquet-Appel, Jean-Pierre (ed.)
2008 *Recent Advances in Palaeodemography: Data, Techniques, Patterns*. Dordrecht: Springer.

Bogucki, Peter
1999 *The Origins of Human Society*. Oxford: Blackwell.

Bolender, Douglas J.
2007 House, Land, and Labor in a Frontier Landscape: The Norse Colonization of Iceland. In *The Durable House. House Society Models in Archaeology*, edited by R. A. Beck, Jr., pp. 400–421. Center for Archaeological Investigations, Occasional Paper No. 35. Carbondale: Southern Illinois University.

Bolger, Diane
2003 *Gender in Ancient Cyprus: Narratives of Social Change on a Mediterranean Island.* Walnut Creek, CA: AltaMira Press.
2008 (ed.) *Gender through Time in the Ancient Near East*. Lanham, MD: AltaMira Press.

Bonanno, A., T. Gouder, C. Malone, and S. Stoddart
1990 Monuments in an Island Society: The Maltese Context. *World Archaeology* 22.2 190–205.

Bonsall, Clive
2008 The Mesolithic of the Iron Gates. In *Mesolithic Europe*, edited by G. Bailey and P. Spikins, pp. 238–79. Cambridge: Cambridge University Press.

Bonsall, Clive, Ivana Radovanović, Mirjana Roksandic, Gordon Cook, Thomas Higham, and Catriona Pickard
2008 Dating Burial Practices and Architecture at Lepenski Vir. In *The Iron Gates in Prehistory: New Perspectives*, edited by C. Bonsall, V. Boroneanţ, and I. Radovanović, pp. 175–204. BAR International Series 1893. Oxford: Archaeopress.

Boone, James L.
2000 Status Signaling, Social Power, and Lineage Survival. In *Hierarchies in Action. Cui Bono?*, edited by M. W. Diehl, pp. 84–110. Center for Archaeological Investigations, Occasional Paper No. 27. Carbondale: Southern Illinois University.

Booth, Marilyn
2010 *Harem Histories: Envisioning Places and Living Spaces*. Durham, NC: Duke University Press.

Borić, Dušan
2002 The Lepenski Vir Conundrum: Reinterpretation of the Mesolithic and Neolithic Sequences in the Danube Gorges. *Antiquity* 76.294: 1026–39.
2005 Body Metamorphosis and Animality: Volatile Bodies and Boulder Artworks from Lepenski Vir. *Cambridge Archaeological Journal* 15: 35–69.
2007 The House between Grand Narrative and Microhistory: A House Society in the Balkans. In *The Durable House: House Society Models in Archaeology*, edited by R. A. Beck, Jr., pp. 97–129. Center for Archaeological Investigations, Occasional Paper No. 35. Carbondale: Southern Illinois University.

2008 First Households and "House Societies" in European Prehistory. In *Prehistoric Europe: Theory and Practice*, edited by A. Jones, pp. 109–42. Oxford: Wiley-Blackwell.

Borić, Dušan, and Sofija Stefanović

2004 Birth and Death: Infant Burials from Vlasac and Lepenski Vir. *Antiquity* 78.301: 526–46.

Boserup, Ester

1970 *Women's Role in Economic Development*. London: Allen and Unwin.

Boulay, Sébastien

2007 The Role of Architecture in Society: Structuring of the Family Unit among Moorish Pastoral Nomads of Mauritania. *Nomadic Peoples* 11.1:49–67.

Bourdieu, Pierre

1973 The Berber House of the World Reversed. In *Rules and Meanings*, edited by M. Douglas, pp. 98–110. London: Harmondsworth/Penguin.

1977 *Outline of a Theory of Practice*. Cambridge: Cambridge University Press.

1990 *The Logic of Practice*. Palo Alto, CA: Stanford University Press.

Boyd, Brian

2006 On "Sedentism" in the Later Epipalaeolithic (Natufian) Levant. *World Archaeology* 38.2: 164–78.

Boyer, Pascal

2001 *Religion Explained: The Evolutionary Origins of Religious Thought*. New York: Basic Books.

Bowser, Brenda J., and John Q. Patton

2004 Domestic Spaces as Public Places: An Ethnoarchaeological Case Study of Houses, Gender, and Politics in the Ecuadorian Amazon. *Journal of Archaeological Method and Theory* 11.2: 157–81.

Bradley, John J.

2008 When a Stone Tool Is a Dingo: Country and Relatedness in Australian Aboriginal Notions of Landscape. In *Handbook of Landscape Archaeology*, edited by B. David and J. Thomas, pp. 633–37. Walnut Creek, CA: Left Coast Press, Inc.

Bradley, Richard

1990 *The Passage of Arms: An Archaeological Analysis of Prehistoric Hoards and Votive Deposits*. Cambridge: Cambridge University Press.

1993 *Altering the Earth: The Origins of Monuments in Britain and Continental Europe*. Society of Antiquaries of Scotland Monograph Series No. 8. Edinburgh: Society of Antiquaries of Scotland.

1998 *The Significance of Monuments*. London: Routledge.

2001 Orientations and Origins: A Symbolic Dimension to the Long House in Neolithic Europe. *Antiquity* 75.287: 50–58.

2002 *The Past in Prehistoric Societies*. London: Routledge.

2005 *Ritual and Domestic Life in Prehistoric Europe*. London: Routledge.

Brady, James E., and Wendy Ashmore

1999 Mountains, Caves, Water: Ideational Landscapes of the Ancient Maya. In *Archaeologies of Landscape*, edited by W. Ashmore and A. B. Knapp, pp. 124–45. Oxford: Blackwell.

Brandt, Steven A., and Kathryn Weedman

2002 Woman the Toolmaker. *Archaeology* 55.5: 50–53.

Brentano, Franz

1995 *Psychology from an Empirical Standpoint.* Trans. by A. C. Rancurello, D. B. Terrell, and L. L. McAlister. London: Routledge.

Brink, Yvonne

2004 The Transformation of Indigenous Societies in the South-western Cape during the Rule of the Dutch East India Company, 1652–1795. In *The Archaeology of Contact Settler Societies*, edited by T. Murray, pp. 91–108. Cambridge: Cambridge University Press.

Briz, Ivan, Débora Zurro, Myrian Álvarez, and Assumpció Vila

2013 The Integrity of Social Space: Hunter-Gatherers at the End of the World. In *The Archaeology of Household*, edited by M. Madella, G. Kovács, B. Kulcsarne-Berzsenyi, and I. Briz, pp. 23–44. Oxford: Oxbow Books.

Brody, Aaron J.

2011 The Archaeology of the Extended Family: A Household Compound from Iron II Tell En-Naṣbeh. In *Household Archaeology in Ancient Israel and Beyond*, edited by A. Yasur-Landau, J. R. Ebeling and L. B. Mazow, pp. 237–54. Leiden: Brill.

Brooks, Alison, and John Yellen

1987 The Preservation of Activity Areas in the Archaeological Record: Ethnoarchaeological and Archaeological Work in Northwest Ngamiland, Botswana. In *Method and Theory for Activity Area Research: An Ethnoarchaeological Approach*, edited by S. Kent, pp. 63–106. New York: Columbia University Press.

Browman, David L.

2008 Pastoral Nomadism in the Central Andes: A Historic Retrospective Example. In *The Archaeology of Mobility: Old World and New World Nomadism*, edited by H. Barnard and W. Wendrich, pp. 160–73. Los Angeles: Cotsen Institute of Archaeology, UCLA.

Brown, James A.

1976 The Southern Cult Reconsidered. *Midcontinental Journal of Archaeology* 1: 115–35.

Brown, Judith

1970 A Note on the Division of Labor by Sex. *American Anthropologist* 72.5: 1073–78.

Brück, Joanna

1999 What's in a Settlement? Domestic Practice and Residential Mobility in Early Bronze Age Southern England. In *Making Places in the Prehistoric World: Themes in Settlement Archaeology*, edited by J. Brück and M. Goodman, pp. 52–75. London: Routledge.

2011 Fire, Earth, Water: An Elemental Cosmography of the European Bronze Age. In *The Oxford Handbook of the Archaeology of Ritual and Religion*, edited by T. Insoll, pp. 387–404. Oxford: Oxford University Press.

Brück, Joanna, and Melissa Goodman (eds.)

1999 *Making Places in the Prehistoric World: Themes in Settlement Archaeology*. London: Routledge.

Brusasco, Paolo

2007 *The Archaeology of Verbal and Nonverbal Meaning: Mesopotamian Domestic Architecture and Its Textual Dimension*. BAR International Series 1631. Oxford: Archaeopress.

Brumbach, Hetty Jo, and Robert Jarvenpa
1997 Ethnoarchaeology of Subsistence Space and Gender: A Subarctic Dene Case. *American Antiquity* 62: 414–36.
2007 Gender Dynamics in Hunter-Gatherer Society: Archaeological Methods and Perspectives. In *Identity and Subsistence: Gender Strategies for Archaeology*, edited by S. M. Nelson, pp. 169–201. Lanham, MD: Roman & Littlefield Publishers, Inc.
Brumfiel, Elizabeth M.
1991 Weaving and Cooking: Women's Production in Aztec Mexico. In *Engendering Archaeology: Women in Prehistory*, edited by J. M. Gero and M. W. Conkey, pp. 224–51. Oxford: Blackwell.
Brumfiel, Elizabeth M., and Timothy K. Earle (eds.)
1987 *Specialization, Exchange, and Complex Societies: Unraveling the Threads of the Past and the Present*. Cambridge: Cambridge University Press.
Brumfiel, Elizabeth M., and Cynthia Robin
2008 Gender, Households, and Society: An Introduction. In *Gender, Households, and Society*, edited by C. Robin and E. M. Brumfiel, pp. 1–16. Archaeological Papers of the American Anthropological Association, No. 18. Malden, MA: Blackwell.
Buckley, Thomas, and Alma Gottlieb (eds.)
1988 *Blood Magic: The Anthropology of Menstruation*. Berkeley: University of California Press.
Buikstra, Jane E., and Douglas K. Charles
1999 Centering the Ancestors: Cemeteries, Mounds, and Sacred Landscapes of the Ancient North American Midcontinent. In *Archaeologies of Landscape: Contemporary Perspectives*, edited by W. Ashmore and A. B. Knapp, pp. 201–28. Oxford: Blackwell.
Burch, Ernest S., Jr., and Linda J. Ellanna (eds.)
1994 *Key Issues in Hunter-Gatherer Research*. Oxford: Berg.
Burdo, Natalia, Mikhail Videiko, John Chapman, and Bisserka Gaydarska
2013 Houses in the Archaeology of the Tripillia-Cucuteni Groups. In *Tracking the Neolithic House in Europe: Sedentism, Architecture, and Practice*, edited by D. Hofmann and J. Smyth, pp. 95–115. New York: Springer.
Burger, Richard L., and Robert M. Rosenswig (eds.)
2012 *Early New World Monumentality*. Gainesville: University Press of Florida.
Burton, Michael L., and Douglas R. White
1984 Sexual Division of Labor in Agriculture. *American Anthropologist* 86: 568–83.
Butzer, Karl W.
1964 *Environment and Archaeology: An Ecological Approach to Prehistory*. Chicago: Aldine.
1982 *Archaeology as Human Ecology: Method and Theory for a Contextual Approach*. Cambridge: Cambridge University Press.
Byrd, Brian F.
1994 Public and Private, Domestic and Corporate: The Emergence of the Southwest Asian Village. *American Antiquity* 59.4: 639–66.
1995 *The Neolithic Village of Beidha: Architecture, Occupation History and Spatial Organization*. Jutland Archaeological Society Publications, Vol. 23.2. Åarhus: Åarhus University Press.

2000 Households in Transition: Neolithic Social Organization within Southwest Asia. In *Life in Neolithic Farming Communities: Social Organization, Identity, and Differentiation*, edited by I. Kuijt, pp. 63–97. New York: Kluwer Academic/Plenum.

2005 Reassessing the Emergence of Village Life in the Near East. *Journal of Archaeological Research* 13.3: 231–90.

Byrd, Brian F., and Edward B. Banning

1988 Southern Levantine Pier Houses: Intersite Architectural Patterning during the Pre-Pottery Neolithic B. *Paléorient* 14.1: 65–72.

Cahill, Nicholas D.

2002 *Household and City Organization at Olynthus*. New Haven, CT: Yale University Press.

Cameron, Catherine M.

2002 Sacred Earthen Architecture in the Northern Southwest: The Bluff Great House Berm. *American Antiquity* 67.4: 677–95.

2009 *Chaco and After in the Northern San Juan: Excavations at the Bluff Great House*. Tucson: University of Arizona Press.

Cameron, Catherine M., and Andrew I. Duff

2008 History and Process in Village Formation: Context and Contrasts from the Northern Southwest. *American Antiquity* 73.1: 29–57.

Cameron, Catherine M., and Phil R. Geib

2007 Earthen Architecture at the Bluff Great House Site in SE Utah. *Journal of Field Archaeology* 32.4: 339–52.

Canuto, Marcello A., and Jason Yaeger (eds.)

2000 *The Archaeology of Communities: A New World Perspective*. London: Routledge.

Carballo, David M.

2011 Advances in the Household Archaeology of Highland Mesoamerica. *Journal of Archaeological Research* 19.2: 133–89.

Carmean, Kelli

1991 Architectural Labor Investment and Social Stratification at Sayil, Yucatan, Mexico. *Latin American Antiquity* 2.2: 151–165.

Carmean, Kelli, Patricia McAnany, and Jeremy Sabloff

2011 People Who Lived in Stone Houses: Local Knowledge and Social Difference in the Classic Maya Puuc Region of Yucatán, Mexico. *Latin American Antiquity* 22.2: 143–58.

Carmichael, David L.

1994 Places of Power: Mescalero Apache Sacred Sites and Sensitive Areas. In *Sacred Sites, Sacred Places*, edited by D. L. Carmichael, J. Hubert, B. Reeves, and A. Schanche, pp. 89–98. London: Routledge.

Carmichael, David L., Jane Hubert, Brian Reeves, and Audhild Schanche (eds.)

1994 *Sacred Sites, Sacred Places*. London: Routledge.

Carr, Christopher, and D. Troy Case

2006 *Gathering Hopewell: Society, Ritual, and Ritual Interaction*. New York: Springer.

Carsten, Jane

2003 *After Kinship*. Cambridge: Cambridge University Press.

Carsten, Janet, and Stephen Hugh-Jones (eds.)

1995 *About the House: Lévi-Strauss and Beyond*. Cambridge: Cambridge University Press.

Carter, Anthony T.
1984 Household Histories. In *Households: Comparative and Historical Studies of the Domestic Group*, edited by R. McC. Netting, R. R. Wilk, and E. J. Arnould, pp. 44–83. Berkeley: University of California Press.

Casella, Eleanor Conlin, and Chris Fowler (eds.)
2005 *The Archaeology of Plural and Changing Identities: Beyond Identification*. New York: Kluwer Academic/Plenum.

Casey, Edward S.
1996 How to Get from Space to Place in a Fairly Short Stretch of Time. In *Senses of Place*, edited by S. Feld and K. H. Basso, pp. 13–51. Santa Fe: School of American Research.
2008 *Place* in Landscape Archaeology: A Western Philosophical Prelude. In *Handbook of Landscape Archaeology*, edited by B. David and J. Thomas, pp. 44–50. Walnut Creek, CA: Left Coast Press, Inc.

Casselberry, Samuel E.
1974 Further Refinement of Formulae for Determining Population from Floor Area. *World Archaeology* 6.1: 117–22.

Castro Gessner, A. Gabriela
2010 Shared Painting: The Practice of Decorating Late Neolithic Pottery in Northern Mesopotamia. In *Agency and Identity in the Ancient Near East: New Paths Forward*, edited by S. R. Steadman and J. C. Ross, pp. 99–116. London: Equinox.

Cattin, Marie-Isabelle
2010 Comparing Social Organizations of Magdalenian Hunter-Gatherers. In *The Magdalenian Household: Unraveling Domesticity*, edited by E. Zubrow, F. Audouze, and J. G. Enloe, pp. 213–21. Albany: State University of New York Press.

Cauvin, Jacques
1977 Les fouilles de Mureybet (1971–1974) et leur signification pour les origines de la sédentarisation au Proche-Orient. *Annual of the American Schools of Oriental Research* 44: 19–48.
2000 *The Birth of the Gods and the Origins of Agriculture*. Cambridge: Cambridge University Press.

Çevik, Ayla
1995 Social Meanings of Household Spaces: A Modern Material Culture Study in an Anatolian Village. *Archaeological Dialogues* 2.1: 39–56.

Chamberlain, Andrew
2006 *Demography in Archaeology*. Cambridge: Cambridge University Press.
2009 Archaeological Demography. *Human Biology* 81.2–3: 275–86.

Chandler, Daniel
2007 *Semiotics: The Basics*. 2nd ed. London: Routledge.

Chang, Claudia, and Perry A. Tourtellotte
1993 Ethnoarchaeological Survey of Pastoral Transhumance Sites in the Grevena Region, Greece. *Journal of Field Archaeology* 20.3: 249–64.

Chang, Kwang-chih
1968 *Settlement Archaeology*. Palo Alto, CA: National Press Books.

Chapdelaine, Claude
1993 The Sedentarization of the Prehistoric Iroquoians: A Slow or Rapid Transformation? *Journal of Anthropological Archaeology* 12: 173–209.

2012 Overview of the St. Lawrence Archaic through Woodland. In *The Oxford Handbook of North American Archaeology*, edited by T. R. Pauketat, pp. 249–61. New York: Oxford University Press.

Chapman, Henry

2006 *Landscape Archaeology and GIS*. Stroud: Tempus.

Chapman, John

2000 *Fragmentation in Archaeology: People, Places and Broken Objects in the Prehistory of Southeastern Europe*. London: Routledge.

Chapman, Robert

2003 *Archaeologies of Complexity*. New York: Routledge.

Chase, Sabrina M.

1991 Polygyny, Architecture and Meaning. In *The Archaeology of Gender: Proceedings of the Twenty-Second Annual Conference of the Archaeological Association of the University of Calgary*, edited by D. Walde and N. D. Willows, pp. 150–58. Calgary: University of Calgary.

Chatters, James C., and William C. Prentiss

2005 A Darwinian Macro-Evolutionary Perspective on the Development of Hunter-Gatherer Systems in Northwestern North America. *World Archaeology* 37.1: 46–65.

Chesson, Meredith S.

1999 Libraries of the Dead: Early Bronze Age Charnel Houses and Social Identity at Urban Bab edh-Dhraʿ, Jordan. *Journal of Anthropological Archaeology* 18: 137–64.

2001 Embodied Memories of Place and People: Death and Society in an Early Urban Community. *Archaeological Papers of the American Anthropological Association* 10.1: 100–113.

2003 Households, Houses, Neighborhoods and Corporate Villages: Modeling the Early Bronze Age as a House Society. *Journal of Mediterranean Archaeology* 16: 79–102.

2007 House, Town, Field, and Wadi: Economic, Political and Social Landscapes in Early Bronze Age Walled Communities of the Southern Levant. In *The Durable House: Architecture, Ancestors and Origins*, edited by R. A. Beck, Jr., pp. 317–43. Center for Archaeological Investigations, Occasional Paper No. 35. Carbondale: Southern Illinois University.

2012 Homemaking in the Early Bronze Age. In *New Perspectives on Household Archaeology*, edited by B. J. Parker and C. P. Foster, pp. 45–79. Winona Lake, IN: Eisenbrauns.

Chesson, Meredith S., and Nathan Goodale

2014 Population Aggregation, Residential Storage and Socioeconomic Inequality at Early Bronze Age Numayra, Jordan. *Journal of Anthropological Archaeology* 35: 117–34.

Childe, V. Gordon

1950 The Urban Revolution. *Town Planning Review* 21: 3–17.

Chippendale, Christopher

1992 Grammars of Archaeological Design. In *Representations in Archaeology*, edited by J.-C. Gardin and C. S. Peebles, pp. 251–76. Bloomington: Indiana University Press.

Christie, Jessica Joyce, and Patricia Joan Sarro (eds.)

2006 *Palaces and Power in the Americas: From Peru to the Northwest Coast*. Austin: University of Texas Press.

Cieraad, Irene (ed.)
1999 *At Home: An Anthropology of Domestic Space*. Syracuse: Syracuse University Press.
Ciolek, T. Matthew
1978 Spatial Arrangements in Social Encounters: An Attempt at Taxonomy. *Man-Environment Systems* 8.2: 52–59.
Ciolek-Torrello, Richard
1996 Domestic Group Composition and Platform Mounds in Two Non-riverine Hohokam Communities. In *People Who Lived in Big Houses: Archaeological Perspectives on Large Domestic Structures*, edited by G. Coupland and E. B. Banning, pp. 47–69. Monographs in World Archaeology, No. 27. Madison, WI: Prehistory Press.
Claassen, Cheryl P.
1991 Gender, Shellfishing, and the Shell Mound Archaic. In *Engendering Archaeology: Women and Prehistory*, edited by J. M. Gero and M. W. Conkey, pp. 276–300. Oxford: Blackwell.
Claassen, Cheryl, and Rosemary A. Joyce (eds.)
1997 *Women in Prehistory: North America and Mesoamerica*. Philadelphia: University of Pennsylvania Press.
Clark, Bonnie J.
2005 Lived Ethnicity: Archaeology and Identity in Mexicano America. *World Archaeology* 37.3: 440–52.
Clark, John E.
2004 Surrounding the Sacred: Geometry and Design of Early Mound Groups as Meaning and Function. In *Signs of Power: The Rise of Cultural Complexity in the Southeast*, edited by J. L. Gibson and P. J. Carr, pp. 162–213. Tuscaloosa: University of Alabama Press.
Clark, John E., and Michael Blake
1996 The Power of Prestige: Competitive Generosity and the Emergence of Rank Societies in Lowland Mesoamerica. In *Contemporary Archaeology in Theory*, edited by R. W. Preucel and I. Hodder, pp. 258–81. Oxford: Blackwell.
Clark, John E., Jon L. Gibson, and James Zeidler
2010 First Towns in the Americas: Searching for Agriculture, Population Growth, and Other Enabling Conditions. In *Becoming Villagers: Comparing Early Village Societies*, edited by M. S. Bandy and J. R. Fox, pp. 205–45. Tucson: University of Arizona Press.
Clarke, David L.
1972 A Provisional Model of an Iron Age Society and Its Settlement System. In *Models in Archaeology*, edited by D. L. Clarke, pp. 801–69. London: Methuen.
1977 *Spatial Archaeology*. London: Academic Press.
Clarke, David S.
1987 *Principles of Semiotic*. London: Routledge.
Clarke, Joanne
2012 Decorating the Neolithic: An Evaluation of the Use of Plaster in the Enhancement of Daily Life in the Middle Pre-Pottery Neolithic B of the Southern Levant. *Cambridge Archaeological Journal* 22.2: 177–86.

Coaldrake, William H.
1996 *Architecture and Authority in Japan*. London: Routledge.

Cochrane, Ethan E., and Andrew Gardner
2011 *Evolutionary and Interpretive Archaeologies: A Dialogue*. Walnut Creek, CA: Left Coast Press, Inc.

Cole, Donald P.
1975 *Nomads of the Nomads: The Al Murrah Bedouin of the Empty Quarter*. Chicago: Aldine Publishing.

Colloredo-Mansfeld, Rudolf
1994 Architectural Conspicuous Consumption and Economic Change in the Andes. *American Anthropologist* 96.4: 845–65.

Colson, Elizabeth
1997 Places of Power and Shrines of the Land. *Paideuma* 43: 47–57.

Comaroff, John L.
1987 *Sui Genderis*: Feminism, Kinship Theory, and Structural 'Domains'. In *Gender and Kinship: Essays Toward a Unified Analysis*, edited by J. F. Collier and S. J. Yanagisako, pp. 53–85. Stanford: Stanford University Press.

Conkey, Margaret W.
1991 Contexts of Action, Contexts for Power: Material Culture and Gender in the Magdalenian. In *Engendering Archaeology: Women and Prehistory*, edited by J. M. Gero and M. W. Conkey, pp. 57–92. Oxford: Blackwell.

Conkey, Margaret J., and Janet Spector
1984 Archaeology and the Study of Gender. In *Advances in Archaeological Method and Theory*, Vol. 7, edited by M. B. Schiffer, pp. 10–38. New York: Academic Press.

Cook, Sherburne F.
1972 *Prehistoric Demography*. Reading, MA: Addison-Wesley.

Cook, Sherburne F., and Robert F. Heizer
1968 Relationships among Houses, Settlement Areas, and Population in Aboriginal California. In *Settlement Archaeology*, edited by K. C. Chang, pp. 79–115. Palo Alto, CA: National Press Books.

Cooper, Lisa
2006 *Early Urbanism on the Syrian Euphrates*. New York: Routledge.

Corbett, Ray
2004 Chumash Bone Whistles: The Development of Ceremonial Integration in Chumash Society. In *Foundations of Chumash Complexity*, edited by J.E. Arnold, pp. 65–73. Perspectives in California Archaeology, Vol. 7. Los Angeles: Cotsen Institution of Archaeology.

Costin, Christine L.
1991 Craft Specialization: Issues in Defining, Documenting, and Explaining the Organization of Production. *Archaeological Method and Theory* 3: 1–56.
1993 Textiles, Women, and Political Economy in Late Prehispanic Peru. *Research in Economic Anthropology* 14: 3–28.
1996 Exploring the Relationship between Gender and Craft in Complex Societies: Methodological and Theoretical Issues of Gender Attribution. In *Gender and Archaeology*, edited by R. P. Wright, pp. 111–40. Philadelphia: University of Pennsylvania Press.

2001 Craft Production Systems. In *Archaeology at the Millennium: A Sourcebook*, edited by G. M. Feinman and T. D. Price, pp. 273–327. New York: Kluwer Academic/Plenum.

Coudart, Anick
1998 *Architecture et société néolithique: l'unité et la variance de la maison Danubienne.* Paris: Éditions de la Maison des sciences de l'homme.

Coupland, Gary
1996 The Evolution of Multi-Family Households on the Northwest Coast of North America. In *People Who Lived in Big Houses: Archaeological Perspectives on Large Domestic Structures*, edited by G. Coupland and E. B. Banning, pp. 121–30. Monographs in World Archaeology, No. 27. Madison, WI: Prehistory Press.
2013 Household Archaeology of Complex Hunter-Gatherers on the North-West Coast of North America. In *The Archaeology of Household*, edited by M. Madella, G. Kovács, B. Kulcsarne-Berzsenyi, and I. Briz, pp. 45–66. Oxford: Oxbow Books.

Coupland, Gary, and E. B. Banning
1996 *People Who Lived in Big Houses: Archaeological Perspectives on Large Domestic Structures.* Monographs in World Archaeology, No. 27. Madison, WI: Prehistory Press.

Couture, Nicole C.
2007 The Production and Representation of Status in a Tiwanaku Royal House. In *The Durable House: House Society Models in Archaeology*, edited by R. A. Beck, Jr., pp. 422–45. Occasional Paper No. 35. Carbondale: Southern Illinois University.

Cowan, Gregory
2002 Nomadology in Architecture: Ephemerality, Movement and Collaboration. M.A. thesis, University of Adelaide.

Cowgill, George L.
2004 Origins and Development of Urbanism: Archaeological Perspectives. *Annual Review of Anthropology* 33: 525–49.
2007 The Urban Organization of Teotihuacan, Mexico. In *Settlement and Society: Essays Dedicated to Robert McCormick Adams*, edited by E. C. Stone, pp. 261–95. Los Angeles: Cotsen Institute of Archaeology, UCLA.
2008 An Update on Teotihuacan. *Antiquity* 82: 962–75.

Crabtree, Pam
2006 Women, Gender, and Pastoralism. In *Handbook of Gender in Archaeology*, edited by S. M. Nelson, pp. 571–92. Lanham, MD: Rowman & Littlefield Publishers.

Crane, Tim
1998 Intentionality as the Mark of the Mental. *Current Issues in Philosophy of Mind.* Royal Institute of Philosophy Supplement 43, edited by A. O'Hear, pp. 229–51. Cambridge: Cambridge University Press.

Crawford, Gary W., and David G. Smith
1996 Migration in Prehistory: Princess Point and the Northern Iroquoian Case. *American Antiquity* 61.4: 782–90.

Creel, Darrell, and Roger Anyon
2003 New Interpretations of Mimbres Public Architecture and Space: Implications for Cultural Change. *American Antiquity* 68.1: 67–92.

Creese, John L.
2009 Post Molds and Preconceptions: New Observations about Iroquoian Longhouse Architecture. *Northeast Anthropology* 77–78: 47–69.
Cribb, Roger
1991 *Nomads in Archaeology*. Cambridge: Cambridge University Press.
Crown, Patricia L.
1985 Morphology and Function of Hohokam Small Structures. *Kiva* 50.4: 75–94.
2000 (ed.) *Women and Men in the Prehispanic Southwest: Labor, Power, and Prestige*. Santa Fe: School of American Research Press.
Crown, Patricia L., and Suzanne K. Fish
1996 Gender and Status in the Hohokam Pre-Classic to Classic Transition. *American Anthropologist* 98.4: 803–17.
Crown, Patricia L., and W. James Judge (eds.)
1991 *Chaco and Hohokam. Prehistoric Regional Systems in the American Southwest*. Santa Fe: School of American Research Press.
Crown, Patricia L., and Timothy A. Kohler
1994 Community Dynamics, Site Structure, and Aggregation in the Northern Río Grande. In *The Ancient Southwestern Community: Models and Methods for the Study of Prehistoric Social Organization*, edited by W. H. Wills and R. D. Leonard, pp. 103–17. Albuquerque: University of New Mexico Press.
Crumley, Carole L.
1995 Heterarchy and the Analysis of Complex Societies. In *Heterarchy and the Analysis of Complex Societies*, edited by R. Ehrenreich, C. Crumley, and J. Levy, pp. 1–5. Archaeological Papers of the American Anthropological Association, No. 6. Washington, DC: American Anthropological Association.
1999 Sacred Landscapes: Constructed and Conceptualized. In *Archaeologies of Landscape: Contemporary Perspectives*, edited by W. Ashmore and A. B. Knapp, pp. 269–76. Oxford: Blackwell.
2001 Communication, Holism, and the Evolution of Socio-Political Complexity. In *From Leaders to Rulers*, edited by J. Haas, pp. 19–33. New York: Kluwer Academic/Plenum.
Cunliffe, Barry W.
1993 *Fertility, Propitiation and the Gods in the British Iron Age*. Amsterdam: Stichting Nederlands Museum voor Anthropologie en Prahistorie.
Curet, L. Antonio
1998 New Formulae for Estimating Prehistoric Populations for Lowland South America and the Caribbean. *Antiquity* 72.276: 359–75.
Cutting, Marion
2003 The Use of Spatial Analysis to Study Prehistoric Settlement Architecture. *Oxford Journal of Archaeology* 22.1: 1–21.
2006a More Than One Way to Study a Building: Approaches to Prehistoric Household and Settlement Space. *Oxford Journal of Archaeology* 25.3: 225–46.
2006b Traditional Architecture and Social Organisation: The Agglomerated Buildings of Aşıklı Höyük and Çatalhöyük in Neolithic Central Anatolia. In *Domesticating Space: Construction, Community, and Cosmology in the Late Prehistoric Near East*, edited by E.B. Banning and M. Chazan, pp. 91–101. Studies in Early Near Eastern Production, Subsistence, and Environment 6. Berlin: Ex oriente.

Dahlberg, Frances
1981 *Woman the Gatherer*. New Haven, CT: Yale University Press.
Daker, Naoras
1984 Contribution à l'étude de l'évolution de l'habitat Bédouin en Syrie. In *Nomades et sédentaires: perspectives ethnoarchéologiques*, edited by O. Aurenche, pp. 51–79. Paris: Éditions Recherche sur les Civilisations.
D'Altroy, Terence N.
1992 *Provincial Power in the Inka Empire*. Washington, DC: Smithsonian Institution Press.
D'Altroy, Terence, and Christine Hastorf (eds.)
2001 *Empire and Domestic Economy*. New York: Kluwer Academic.
David, Bruno
2002 *Landscapes, Rock-Art and the Dreaming. An Archaeology of Preunderstanding*. London: Leicester University Press.
2004 Intentionality, Agency and an Archaeology of Choice. *Cambridge Archaeological Journal* 14.1: 67–71.
David, Bruno, and Julian Thomas
2008a (eds.) *Handbook of Landscape Archaeology*. Walnut Creek, CA: Left Coast Press, Inc.
2008b Landscape Archaeology: Introduction. In *Handbook of Landscape Archaeology*, edited by B. David and J. Thomas, pp. 27–43. Walnut Creek, CA: Left Coast Press, Inc.
David, Bruno, and Meredith Wilson (eds.)
2002 *Inscribed Landscapes: Marking and Making Place*. Honolulu: University of Hawai'i Press.
Davidson, James
2011 Bodymaps: Sexing Space and Zoning Gender in Ancient Athens. *Gender and History* 23.3: 597–614.
Davidson, Janet
1984 *The Prehistory of New Zealand*. Auckland: Longman Paul.
Davis, Whitney
1992 The Deconstruction of Intentionality in Archaeology. *Antiquity* 66: 334–47.
Deaver, Sherri
1989 Space, Worldview and Architectural Form. In *Households and Communities. Proceedings of the Twenty-first Annual Conference of the Archaeological Association of the University of Calgary*, edited by S. MacEachern, D. J. W. Archer, and R. D. Garvin, pp. 243–55. Calgary: University of Calgary.
de Beaune, Sophie A., Frederick L. Coolidge, and Thomas Wynn (eds.)
2009 *Cognitive Archaeology and Human Evolution*. Cambridge: Cambridge University Press.
Deetz, James
1977 *In Small Things Forgotten: The Archaeology of Early American Life*. New York: Doubleday.
1982 Households: A Structural Key to Archaeological Explanation. *American Behavioral Scientist* 25: 717–24.
1996 *In Small Things Forgotten: An Archaeology of Early American Life*. New York: Anchor Books.

Delaney, Carol
1991 *The Seed and the Soil. Gender and Cosmology in Turkish Village Society*. Berkeley: University of California Press.

de Lumley, Henry
2009 The Emergence of Symbolic Thought: The Principal Steps of Hominisation Leading Towards Greater Complexity. In *Becoming Human: Innovation in Prehistoric Material and Spiritual Culture*, edited by C. Renfrew and I. Morley, pp. 10–26. Cambridge: Cambridge University Press.

Dennell, Robin W.
1984 The Expansion of Exogenous-Based Economies across Europe: The Balkans and Central Europe. In *Exploring the Limits: Frontiers and Boundaries in Prehistory*, edited by S. P. De Atley and F. J. Findlow, pp. 93–116. BAR International Series, Vol. 233. Oxford: British Archaeological Reports.

De Roche, C. D.
1983 Population Estimates from Settlement Area and Number of Residences. *Journal of Field Archaeology* 10.2: 187–92.

Díaz-Andreu, Margarita, Sam Lucy, Stasa Babić, and David N. Edwards (eds.)
2005 *The Archaeology of Identity. Approaches to Gender, Age, Status, Ethnicity and Religion*. London: Routledge.

Diehl, Michael W.
1996 The Intensity of Maize Processing and Production in Upland Mogollon Pithouse Villages A.D. 200–1000. *American Antiquity* 61.1: 102–15.
1997 Changes in Architecture and Land Use Strategies in the American Southwest: Upland Mogollon Pithouse Dwellers, A.C. 200–1000. *Journal of Field Archaeology* 24.2: 179–94.
2000a (ed.) *Hierarchies in Action. Cui Bono?* Carbondale: Southern Illinois University.
2000b Some Thoughts on the Study of Hierarchies. In *Hierarchies in Action. Cui Bono?*, edited by M. W. Diehl, pp. 11–29. Carbondale: Southern Illinois University.

Dietrich, Oliver, Çiğdem Köksal-Schmidt, Jens Notroff, Klaus Schmidt, and Cihat Kürkçüoğlu
2012 Göbekli Tepe: A Stone Age Ritual Center in Southeastern Turkey. *Actual Archaeology* 2: 33–51.

Dimitrijević, Vesna
2008 Lepenski Vir Animal Bones: What Was Left in the Houses? In *The Iron Gates in Prehistory: New Perspectives*, edited by C. Bonsall, V. Boroneanţ, and I. Radovanović, pp. 117–30. BAR International Series 1893. Oxford: Archaeopress.

Divale, William T.
1977 Living Floor Area and Marital Residence: A Replication. *Behavior Science Research* 12: 109–15.

Dobres, Marcia-Anne
2000 *Technology and Social Agency: Outlining a Practice Framework for Archaeology*. London: Blackwell.

Dobres, Marcia-Anne, and John E. Robb (eds.)
2000 *Agency in Archaeology*. London: Routledge.

Dohm, Karen M.

1990 Effect of Population Nucleation on House Size for Pueblos in the American Southwest. *Journal of Anthropological Archaeology* 9: 201–39.

1996 Rooftop Zuni: Extending Household Territory beyond Apartment Walls. In *People Who Lived in Big Houses: Archaeological Perspectives on Large Domestic Structures*, edited by G. Coupland and E. B. Banning, pp. 89–105. Monographs in World Archaeology No. 27. Madison, WI: Prehistory Press.

Donley-Reid, Linda W.

1990 A Structuring Structure: The Swahili House. In *Domestic Architecture and the Use of Space*, edited by S. Kent, pp. 114–26. Cambridge: Cambridge University Press.

Dornan, Jennifer L.

2002 Agency and Archaeology: Past, Present and Future Directions. *Journal of Archaeological Method and Theory* 9.4: 303–29.

Douglas, Mary

1966 *Purity and Danger: An Analysis of the Concepts of Pollution and Taboo*. London: Routledge.

Dovey, Kim

1999 *Framing Places. Mediating Power in Built Form*. London: Routledge.

Dowson, Thomas A.

2006 Archaeologists, Feminists and Queers: Sexual Politics in the Construction of the Past. In *Feminist Anthropology: Perspectives on Our Past, Present, and Future*, edited by P. L. Geller and M. K. Stockett. Philadelphia: University of Pennsylvania Press.

Drake, Michael

1974 *Historical Demography: Problems and Projects*. Bletchley, England: Open University Press.

Duffy, Paul R., William A. Parkinson, Attila Guycha, and Richard W. Yerkes

2013 Coming Together, Falling Apart: A Multiscalar Approach to Prehistoric Aggregation and Interaction on the Great Hungarian Plain. In *From Prehistoric Villages to Cities: Settlement Aggregation and Community Transformation*, edited by J. Birch, pp. 44–62. New York: Routledge.

Duke, Philip

1991 Recognizing Gender in Plains Hunting Groups: Is it Possible or Even Necessary? In *The Archaeology of Gender: Proceedings of the Twenty-Second Annual Conference of the Archaeological Association of the University of Calgary*, edited by D. Walde and N. D. Willows, pp. 280–83. Calgary: University of Calgary.

Duncan, James S. (ed.)

1982 *Housing and Identity: Cross-Cultural Perspectives*. New York: Holmes and Meier.

Düring, Bleda S.

2005 Building Continuity in the Central Anatolian Neolithic: Exploring the Meaning of Buildings at Aşıklı Höyük and Çatalhöyük. *Journal of Mediterranean Archaeology* 18.1: 3–29.

2006 *Constructing Communities: Clustered Neighbourhood Settlements of the Central Anatolian Neolithic ca. 8500–5500 cal BC*. Leiden: Nederlands Instituut voor Het Nabije Oosten.

2007 The Articulation of Houses at Neolithic Çatalhöyük, Turkey. In *The Durable House: House Society Models in Archaeology*, edited by R.A. Beck, Jr., pp. 130–53. Center for Archaeological Investigations, Occasional Paper No. 35. Carbondale: Southern Illinois University.

Düring, Bleda S., and Arkadiusz Marciniak

2006 Households and Communities in the Central Anatolian Neolithic. *Archaeological Dialogues* 12.2: 165–87.

Durning, M. L., and Richard Wrigley (eds.)

2000 *Gender and Architecture*. New York: Wiley.

Dyson, Stephen L.

1985 *The Creation of the Roman Frontier*. Princeton, NJ: Princeton University Press.

2003 *The Roman Countryside*. London: Duckworth.

Dyson-Hudson, Rada, and Neville Dyson-Hudson

1980 Nomadic Pastoralism. *Annual Review of Anthropology* 9: 15–61.

Earle, Timothy K.

1997 *How Chiefs Come to Power: The Political Economy in Prehistory*. Stanford, CA: Stanford University Press.

2001 Exchange and Social Stratification in the Andes: The Xauxa Case. In *Empire and Domestic Economy*, edited by T. N. D'Altroy and C. A. Hastorf, pp. 297–324 New York: Kluwer/Plenum.

Ebrey, Patricia B.

2003 *Woman and the Family in Chinese History*. London: Routledge.

Eco, Umberto

1976 *A Theory of Semiotics*. Bloomington: Indiana University Press.

1980 Function and Sign: The Semiotics of Architecture. In *Signs, Symbols, and Architecture*, edited by G. Broadbent, R. Bunt, and C. Jencks, pp. 11–69. New York: Wiley and Sons.

1986 *Semiotics and the Philosophy of Language*. Bloomington: Indiana University Press.

Edney, Julian J.

1974 Human Territoriality. *Psychological Bulletin* 81.12: 959–75.

Edwards, Phillip C.

1989 Problems of Recognizing Earliest Sedentism: The Natufian Example. *Journal of Mediterranean Archaeology* 2.1: 5–48.

Eerkens, Jelmer W.

2004 Privatization, Small-Seed Intensification, and the Origins of Pottery in the Western Great Basin. *American Antiquity* 69.4: 653–70.

2009 Privatization of Resources and the Evolution of Prehistoric Leadership Strategies. In *The Evolution of Leadership: Transitions in Decision making from Small-Scale to Middle-Range Societies*, edited by K. J. Vaughn, J. W. Eerkens, and J. Kantner, pp. 73–94. Santa Fe: School for Advanced Research Press.

Eerkens, Jelmer W., and Amy M. Spurling

2008 Obsidian Acquisition and Exchange Networks: A Diachronic Perspective on Households in the Owens Valley. *Journal of California and Great Basin Anthropology* 28.2: 111–26.

Eighmy, Jeffrey L.

1981 The Archaeological Significance of Counting Houses: Ethnoarchaeological Evidence. In *Modern Material Culture. The Archaeology of Us*, edited by R. A. Gould and M. B. Schiffer, pp. 225–33. New York: Academic Press.

Ekvall, Robert B.
1968 *Fields on the Hoof: Nexus of Tibetan Nomadic Pastoralism*. New York: Holt, Rinehart and Winston.

Ember, Carol R.
1983 The Relative Decline in Women's Contribution to Agriculture with Intensification. *American Anthropologist* 85: 285–304.

Ember, Melvin
1973 An Archaeological Indicator of Matrilocal versus Patrilocal Residence. *American Antiquity* 38: 177–82.

Emberling, Geoff
1997 Ethnicity in Complex Societies: Archaeological Perspectives. *Journal of Archaeological Research* 5: 295–344.
2001 Political Control in an Early State: The Eye Temple and the Uruk Expansion in Northern Mesopotamia. In *Of Pots and Plans: Papers on the Archaeology and History of Mesopotamia and Syria Presented to David Oates in Honour of His 75th Birthday*, edited by L. al-Gailana, J. Curtis, H. Martin, A. McMahon, J. Oates, and J. Reade, pp. 82–90. Charleston, SC: Nabu.

Emerson, Thomas E.
1989 Water, Serpents, and the Underworld: An Exploration into Cahokian Symbolism. In *The Southeastern Ceremonial Complex: Artifacts and Analysis*, edited by P. Galloway, pp. 45–92. Lincoln: University of Nebraska Press.
1997a Cahokian Elite Ideology and the Mississippian Cosmos. In *Cahokia Domination and Ideology in the Mississippian World*, edited by T. R. Pauketat and T. E. Emerson, pp. 190–228. Lincoln: University of Nebraska.
1997b *Cahokia and the Archaeology of Power*. Tuscaloosa: University of Alabama Press.

Emerson, Thomas E., Susan M. Alt, and Timothy R. Pauketat
2008 Locating American Indian Religion at Cahokia and Beyond. In *Religion, Archaeology, and the Material World*, edited by L. Fogelin, pp. 216–36. Center for Archaeological Investigations Occasional Paper, No. 36. Carbondale: Southern Illinois University Press.

Emerson, Thomas E., and Timothy R. Pauketat
2008 Historical-Processual Archaeology and Culture Making: Unpacking the Southern Cult and Mississippian Religion. In *Belief in the Past: Theoretical Approaches to the Archaeology of Religion*, edited by D. S. Whitley and K. Hays-Gilpin, pp. 167–88. Walnut Creek, CA: Left Coast Press, Inc.

Erdoğu, Burcin, and Aydin Ulubey
2011 Colour Symbolism in the Prehistoric Architecture of Central Anatolia and Raman Spectroscopic Investigation of Red Ochre in Chalcolithic Çatalhöyük. *Oxford Journal of Archaeology* 30.1: 1–11.

Escalera, Jordi E., and Ignacio C. Conte
2013 Domestic Space: Analysis of the Activities of a Hunter-Gatherer Social Unit at the Southern End of the American Continent. In *The Archaeology of Household*, edited by M. Madella, G. Kovács, B. Kulcsarne-Berzsenyi, and I. Briz, pp. 67–85. Oxford: Oxbow Books.

Esin, Ufuk
1996 Aşıklı Ten Thousand Years Ago, A Habitation Model from Central Anatolia. In *Housing and Settlement in Anatolia: A Historical Perspective*, edited by Y. Sey, pp. 31–42. Istanbul: Türkiye Ekonomik ve Toplumsal Tarih Vakfı.

Esin, Ufuk, and Savas Harmankaya
1999 Aşıklı. In *The Neolithic of Turkey*, edited by M. Özdoğan and N. Başgelen, pp. 115–32. Istanbul: Arkeoloji ve Sanat Yayınları.

Fairclough, Graham
1992 Meaningful Constructions--Spatial and Functional Analysis of Medieval Buildings. *Antiquity* 66: 348–66.

Feinman, Gary M.
2000a Corporate/Network: New Perspectives on Models of Political Action and the Puebloan Southwest. In *Social Theory in Archaeology*, edited by M. B. Schiffer, pp. 31–51. Salt Lake City: University of Utah Press.
2000b Dual-Processual Theory and Social Formations in the Southwest. In *Alternative Leadership Strategies in the Prehispanic Southwest*, edited by B. J. Mills, pp. 207–24. Tucson: University of Arizona.
2001 Mesoamerican Political Complexity: The Corporate–Network Dimension. In *From Leaders to Rulers*, edited by J. Haas, pp. 151–75. New York: Kluwer Academic/Plenum.

Feinman, Gary M., Kent G. Lightfoot, and Steadman Upham
2000 Political Hierarchies and Organizational Strategies in the Puebloan Southwest. *American Antiquity* 65.3: 449–70.

Feinman, Gary, and Jill Neitzel
1984 Too Many Types: An Overview of Sedentary Prestate Societies in the Americas. In *Advances in Archaeological Method and Theory*, Vol. 7, edited by M. B. Schiffer, pp. 39–102. New York: Academic Press.

Feld, Steven, and Keith H. Basso (eds.)
1996 *Senses of Place*. Santa Fe: School of American Research Press.

Feldman, Marian H.
2010 Object Agency? Spatial Perspective, Social Relations, and the Stele of Hammurabi. In *Agency and Identity in the Ancient Near East: New Paths Forward*, edited by S. R. Steadman and J. C. Ross, pp. 148–65. London: Equinox.

Ferguson, Leland
1991 Struggling with Pots in Colonial South Carolina. In *The Archaeology of Inequality*, edited by R. H. McGuire and R. Paynter, pp. 28–39. Oxford: Blackwell.

Finlayson, Bill, and Graeme M. Warren
2010 *Changing Natures: Hunter-Gatherers, First Farmers and the Modern World*. London: Duckworth.

Fish, Suzanne K., and Paul R. Fish
1994 Prehistoric Desert Farmers of the Southwest. *Annual Review of Anthropology* 23: 83–108.

Fish, Suzanne K., and Stephen A. Kowalewski (eds.)
1990 *The Archaeology of Regions: A Case for Full-Coverage Survey*. Washington, DC: Smithsonian Institution Press.

Fisher, Kevin D.
2009 Placing Social Interaction: An Integrative Approach to Analyzing Past Built Environments. *Journal of Anthropological Archaeology* 28: 439–57.

Fitzhugh, Ben
2003 *The Evolution of Complex Hunter-Gatherers: Archaeological Evidence from the North Pacific*. New York: Kluwer Academic/Plenum.

Fitzhugh, Ben, and Junko Habu (eds.)
2002 *Beyond Foraging and Collecting: Evolutionary Change in Hunter-Gatherer Settlement Systems*. New York: Kluwer Academic/Plenum.

Fitz-Patrick, David G., and John Kimbuna
1983 *Bundi: The Culture of a Papua New Guinea People*. Nerang, Queensland.: Ryebuck Publications.

Flannery, Kent V.
1972 The Origin of the Village as a Settlement Type in Mesoamerica and the Near East: A Comparative Study. In *Man, Settlement, and Urbanism*, edited by P. Ucko, R. Tringham, and G. Dimbleby, pp. 25–53. London: Duckworth.
1976 (ed.) *The Early Mesoamerican Village*. New York: Academic Press.
1998 The Ground Plans of Archaic States. In *Archaic States*, edited by G. M. Feinman and J. Marcus, pp. 15–57. Santa Fe: School of American Research Press.
1999 Process and Agency in Early State Formation. *Cambridge Archaeological Journal* 9.1: 3–21.
2002 The Origins of the Village Revisited: From Nuclear to Extended Households. *American Antiquity* 67.3: 417–34.

Flannery, Kent V., and Joyce Marcus
1998 Cognitive Archaeology. *Cambridge Archaeological Journal* 3: 260–70.

Flannery, Kent V., and Marcus C. Winter
1976 Analyzing Household Activities. In *The Early Mesoamerican Village*, edited by K. V. Flannery, pp. 34–44. New York: Academic Press.

Fleisher, Jeffrey B., and Adria LaViolette
2007 The Changing Power of Swahili Houses, Fourteenth to Nineteenth Centuries A.D. In *The Durable House: House Society Models in Archaeology*, edited by R. A. Beck, Jr., pp. 175–97. Center for Archaeological Investigations, Occasional Paper No. 35. Carbondale: Southern Illinois University.

Fletcher, Roland J.
1981 Space and Community Behavior: Spatial Order in Settlements. In *Universals of Human Thought*, edited by B. Lloyd and J. Gay, pp. 97–128. Cambridge: Cambridge University Press.
1984 Identifying Spatial Disorder: A Case Study of a Mongol Fort. In *Intrasite Spatial Analysis in Archaeology*, edited by H. J. Hietala, pp. 196–223. Cambridge: Cambridge University Press.

Fogelin, Lars
2007a The Archaeology of Religious Ritual. *Annual Review of Anthropology* 36: 55–71.
2007b Finding Ritual: Calibrating the Evidence. In *The Archaeology of Ritual*, edited by E. Kyriakidis, pp. 9–22. Los Angeles: Cotsen Institute of Archaeology, UCLA.
2008 (ed.) *Religion, Archaeology, and the Material World*. Center for Archaeological Investigations Occasional Paper No. 36. Carbondale: Southern Illinois University.

Forest, Jean-Daniel
1999 *Les premiers temples de Mésopotamie*. BAR International Series 765. Oxford: BAR International.

Foster, Catherine P.
2012 The Uruk Phenomenon: A View from the Household. In *New Perspectives on Household Archaeology*, edited by B. J. Parker and C. P. Foster, pp. 437–72. Winona Lake, IN: Eisenbrauns.

Foster, Sally M.
1989a Analysis of Spatial Patterns in Buildings (Access Analysis) as an Insight into Social Structure: Examples from the Scottish Atlantic Iron Age. *Antiquity* 63: 40–50.
1989b Transformations in Social Space: The Iron Age of Orkney and Caithness. *Scottish Archaeological Review* 6: 34–55.

Foucault, Michel
1970 *The Order of Things: An Archaeology of the Human Sciences*. New York: Vintage.
1977 *Discipline and Punish: The Birth of the Prison*. New York: Pantheon.
1980 *Power/Knowledge: Selected Interviews and Other Writings 1972–1977*. Edited by C. Gordon. New York: Pantheon.

Fowler, Chris
2004 *The Archaeology of Personhood: An Anthropological Approach*. London: Routledge.

Fowler, Melvin L.
1997 *The Cahokia Atlas: A Historical Atlas of Cahokia Archaeology*. Rev. ed. Urbana-Champaign: University of Illinois.
1999 Who Were These People? In *The Mound 72 Area: Dedicated and Sacred Space in Early Cahokia*, edited by M. L. Fowler, J. C. Rose, B. Vander Leest, and S. R. Ahler, pp. 183–89. Springfield: Illinois State Museum.

Fox, John G.
1996 Playing with Power. Ballcourts and Political Ritual in Southern Mesoamerica. *Current Anthropology* 37.3: 483–509.

Frachetti, Michael D.
2008 Variability and Dynamic Landscapes of Mobile Pastoralism in Ethnography and Prehistory. In *The Archaeology of Mobility: Old World and New World Nomadism*, edited by H. Barnard and W. Wendrich, pp. 366–96. Los Angeles: Cotsen Institute of Archaeology, UCLA.

Frachetti, Michael D., Norbert Benecke, Alexei N. Mar'yashev, and Paula N. Doumani
2010 Eurasian Pastoralists and Their Shifting Regional Interactions at the Steppe Margin: Settlement History at Mukri, Kazakhstan. *World Archaeology* 42.4: 622–46.

Frachetti, Michael D., and Alexei N. Mar'yashev
2007 Long-Term Occupation and Seasonal Settlement of Eastern Eurasian Pastoralists at Begash, Kazakhstan. *Journal of Field Archaeology* 32.3: 221–42.

Frangipane, Marcella
2001 Centralization Processes in Greater Mesopotamia: Uruk Expansion as the Climax of Systemic Interactions among Areas of the Greater Mesopotamian Region. In *Uruk Mesopotamia and Its Neighbors: Cross-Cultural Interactions in the Era of State Formation*, edited by M. S. Rothman, pp. 307–47. Santa Fe: School of American Research Press.

Frankel, David, and Jennifer M. Webb
2012 Household Continuity and Transformation in a Prehistoric Cypriot Village. In *New Perspectives on Household Archaeology*, edited by B. J. Parker and C. P. Foster, pp. 473–500. Winona Lake, IN: Eisenbrauns.
Friedl, Ernestine
1975 *Women and Men: An Anthropologist's View*. New York: Holt, Rinehart, and Winston.
Frink, Lisa, and Kathryn Weedman (eds.)
2005 *Gender and Hide Production*. Lanham, MD: AltaMira Press.
Fullagar, Richard, and Lesley Head
1999 Exploring the Prehistory of Hunter-Gatherer Attachments to Place: An Example from the Keep River Area, Northern Territory, Australia. In *The Archaeology and Anthropology of Landscape: Shaping Your Landscape*, edited by P. J. Ucko and R. Layton, pp. 322–35. London: Routledge.
Furhold, Martin, Marin Hinz, and Doris Mischka (eds.)
2012 *As Time Goes By? Monumentality, Landscapes and the Temporal Perspective*. Bonn: Verlag Dr. Rudolf Habelt GmbH.
Gadot, Yuval
2011 Houses and Households in Settlements along the Yarkon River, Israel, during the Iron Age I: Society, Economy, and Identity. In *Household Archaeology in Ancient Israel and Beyond*, edited by A. Yasur-Landau, J. R. Ebeling, and L. B. Mazow, pp. 155–81. Leiden: Brill.
Gallivan, Martin
2002 Measuring Sedentariness and Settlement Population: Accumulations Research in the Middle Atlantic Region. *American Antiquity* 67.3: 535–57.
Galloway, Patricia
1997 Where Have All the Menstrual Huts Gone? The Invisibility of Menstrual Seclusion in the Late Prehistoric Southeast. In *Women in Prehistory: North America and Mesoamerica*, edited by C. Claasen and R. A. Joyce, pp. 47–62. Philadelphia: University of Pennsylvania Press.
Galvin, Kathleen A.
2009 Transitions: Pastoralists Living with Change. *Annual Review of Anthropology* 38: 185–98.
Gardin, Jean-Claude
1992 Semiotic Trends in Archaeology. In *Representations in Archaeology*, edited by J.-C. Gardin and C. S. Peebles, pp. 87–104. Bloomington: Indiana University Press.
Gardin, Jean-Claude, and Christopher S. Peebles (eds.)
1992 *Representations in Archaeology*. Bloomington: Indiana University Press.
Gardner, Andrew
2004 (ed.) *Agency Uncovered: Archaeological Perspectives on Social Agency, Power, and Being Human*. London: UCL Press.
2008 Agency. In the *Handbook of Archaeological Theories*, edited by R. A. Bentley, H. D. G. Maschner, and C. Chippendale, pp. 95–108. Lanham, MD: AltaMira Press.
Garfinkel, Yosef
2006 The Social Organization at Neolithic Sha'ar Hagolan: The Nuclear Family, the Extended Family and the Community. In *Domesticating Space: Construction, Community, and Cosmology in the Late Prehistoric Near East*, edited by E. B. Banning and M. Chazen, pp. 103–11. Berlin: Ex oriente.

Gates St-Pierre, Christian
2004 The Middle Woodland Ancestors of the St. Lawrence Iroquoians. In *A Passion for the Past: Papers in Honour of James F. Pendergast*, edited by J. V. Wright and J.-L. Pilon, pp. 395–417. Mercury Series, Archaeology Paper 164. Gatineau: Canadian Museum of Civilization.

Gates St-Pierre, Christian, and Claude Chapdelaine
2013 After Hopewell in Southern Québec. *Archaeology of Eastern North America* 41: 69–89.

Gell, Alfred
1998 *Art and Agency: An Anthropological Theory*. Oxford: Oxford University Press.

Geneste, Jean-Michel, Jean-Christophe Castel, and Jean-Pierre Chadelle
2008 From Physical to Social Landscapes: Multidimensional Approaches to the Archaeology of Social Place in the European Upper Palaeolithic. In *Handbook of Landscape Archaeology*, edited by B. David and J. Thomas, pp. 228–36. Walnut Creek, CA: Left Coast Press, Inc.

Gero, Joan M.
1991 Genderlithics: Women's Roles in Stone Tool Production. In *Engendering Archaeology: Women and Prehistory*, edited by J. M. Gero and M. W. Conkey, pp. 163–94. Oxford: Blackwell.

Gero, Joan M., and Margaret W. Conkey (eds.)
1991 *Engendering Archaeology: Women and Prehistory*. Oxford: Blackwell.

Gero, Joan M., and C. Scatollin
2001 Beyond Complementarity and Heterarchy: New Definitions for Archaeological Gender Relations. In *In Pursuit of Gender: Worldwide Archaeological Approaches*, edited by S. M. Nelson and M. Rosen-Ayalon, pp. 155–71. Walnut Creek, CA: AltaMira Press.

Gerritsen, Fokke A.
2003 *Local Identities: Landscape and Community in the Late Prehistoric Meuse-Demer-Scheldt Region*. Amsterdam: Amsterdam University Press.

Gerritsen, Fokke, Rana Özbal, Laurens Thissen, Hadi Özbal, and Alfred Galik
2010 The Late Chalcolithic Settlement of Barcın Höyük. *Anatolica* 36: 197–225.

Gheorghiu, Dragos
2007 A Fire Cult in South European Chalcolithic Traditions? On the Relationship between Ritual Contexts and the Instrumentality of Fire. In *Cult in Context: Reconsidering Ritual in Archaeology*, edited by D. A. Barrowclough and C. Malone, pp. 269–84. Oxford: Oxbow.

Gibson, Jon L.
1998 Broken Circles, Owl Monsters, and Black Earth Midden: Separating Sacred and Secular at Poverty Point. In *Ancient Earthen Enclosures of the Eastern Woodlands*, edited by R. C. Mainfort, Jr., and L. P. Sullivan, pp. 17–30. Gainesville: University Press of Florida.
2000 *The Ancient Mounds of Poverty Point: Place of Rings*. Gainesville: University Press of Florida.

Giddens, Anthony
1979 *Central Problems in Social Theory: Action, Structure, and Contradiction in Social Analysis*. Berkeley: University of California Press.
1984 *The Constitution of Society: Outline of the Theory of Structuration*. Berkeley: University of California Press.

Gieryn, Thomas F.
2002 What Buildings Do. *Theory and Society* 31: 35–74.
Gifford-Gonzalez, Diane
1991 Bones Are Not Enough: Analogues, Knowledge, and Interpretive Strategies in Zooarchaeology. *Journal of Anthropological Archaeology* 10: 215–54.
1998 Gender and Early Pastoralists in East Africa. In *Gender in African Prehistory*, edited by S. Kent, pp.115–37. Walnut Creek, CA: Sage Publications.
Gilboa, Ayelet, Ilan Sharon, and Jeffrey R. Zorn
2014 An Iron Age I Canaanite/Phoenician Courtyard House at Tel Dor: A Comparative Architectural and Functional Analysis. *Bulletin of the American Schools of Oriental Research* 372: 39–80.
Gilchrist, Roberta
1999 *Gender and Archaeology: Contesting the Past.* London: Routledge.
Gillespie, Dair L., and Ann Leffler
1983 Theories of Nonverbal Behavior: A Critical Review of Proxemics Research. *Sociological Theory* 1: 120–54.
Gillespie, Susan D.
2000 Lévi-Strauss: *Maison and Société à Maisons.* In *Beyond Kinship: Social and Material Reproduction in House Societies*, edited by R. A. Joyce and S. D. Gillespie, pp. 22–52. Philadelphia: University of Pennsylvania Press.
2001 Personhood, Agency, and Mortuary Ritual: A Case Study from the Ancient Maya. *Journal of Anthropological Archaeology* 20: 73–112.
2007 When Is a House? In *The Durable House: House Society Models in Archaeology*, edited by R. A. Beck, jr., pp. 25–50. Center for Archaeological Investigations, Occasional Paper No. 35. Carbondale: Southern Illinois University Press.
Gilman, Patricia A.
1987 Architecture as Artifact: Pit Structures and Pueblos in the American Southwest. *American Antiquity* 52.3: 538–64.
Gilmore, Kevin P.
2005 These Boots Were Made for Walking: Moccasin Production, Gender, and the Late Prehistoric Hideworking Sequence on the High Plains of Colorado. In *Gender and Hide Production*, edited by L. Frink and K. Weedman, pp. 13–36. Lanham, MD: AltaMira Press.
Given, Michael
2004 *The Archaeology of the Colonized.* London: Routledge.
Glassie, Henry
1975 *Folk Housing in Middle Virginia: A Structural Analysis of Historic Artifacts.* Knoxville: University of Tennessee Press.
2000 *Vernacular Architecture.* Bloomington: Indiana University Press.
Goldberg, Marilyn Y.
1999 Spatial and Behavioral Negotiation in Classical Athenian City Houses. In *The Archaeology of Household Activities*, edited by P. M. Allison, pp. 142–61. London: Routledge.
Goldman, Irving
2004 *Cubeo Heh Newa Religious Thought: Metaphysics of a Northwestern Amazonian People.* Edited by P. J. Wilson. New York: Columbia University Press.

Goldstein, Melvyn C., and Cynthia M. Beall
1990 *Nomads of Western Tibet: The Survival of a Way of Life*. Berkeley: University of California Press.

González-Ruibal, Alfredo
2006 House Societies vs. Kinship-based Societies: An Archaeological Case from Iron Age Europe. *Journal of Anthropological Archaeology* 25: 144–73.

Goody, Jack
1972 The Evolution of the Family. In *Household and Family in Past Time*, edited by P. Laslett and R. Wall, pp. 103–24. Cambridge: Cambridge University Press.

Goring-Morris, A. Nigel
1993 From Foraging to Herding in the Negev and Sinai: The Early to Late Neolithic Transition. *Paléorient* 19.1: 65–89.
2000 The Quick and the Dead: The Social Context of Aceramic Neolithic Mortuary Practices as Seen from Kfar HaHoresh. In *Life in Neolithic Farming Communities: Social Organization, Identity, and Differentiation*, edited by I. Kuijt, pp. 103–36. New York: Kluwer Academic/ Plenum.

Goring-Morris, A. Nigel, and Anna Belfer-Cohen
2002 Symbolic Behaviour from the Epipalaeolithic and Early Neolithic of the Near East: Preliminary Observations on Continuity and Change. In *Magic Practices and Ritual in the Near Eastern Neolithic*, edited by H. G. K. Gebel, B. D. Hermansen, and C. H. Jensen, pp. 67–79. Berlin: Ex oriente.
2010 "Great Expectations," or the Inevitable Collapse of the Early Neolithic in the Near East. In *Becoming Villagers: Comparing Early Village Societies*, edited by M. S. Bandy and J. R. Fox, pp. 62–77. Tucson: University of Arizona Press.
2011 Neolithization Processes in the Levant: The Outer Envelope. *Current Anthropology* 52.S4: S195–S208.
2013 Houses and Households: A Near Eastern Perspective. In *Tracking the Neolithic House in Europe: Sedentism, Architecture and Practice*, edited by D. Hofmann and J. Smyth, pp. 19–44. New York: Springer.

Gosden, Chris
2004 *Archaeology and Colonialism: Cultural Contact from 5000 B.C. to the Present*. Cambridge: Cambridge University Press.

Gottlieb, Alma
2009 From Pollution to Love Magic: The New Anthropology of Menstruation. In *Gender in Cross-Cultural Perspective*, 5th ed. edited by C. B. Brettell and C. F. Sargent, pp. 264–75. Upper Saddle River, NJ: Pearson Publications.

Gould, Richard
1980 *Living Archaeology*. Cambridge: Cambridge University Press.

Gould, Richard A., and John E. Yellen
1987 Man the Hunted: Determinants of Household Spacing in Desert and Tropical Foraging Societies. *Journal of Anthropological Archaeology* 6: 77–103.

Grahame, Mark
2000 *Reading Space: Social Interaction and Identity in the Houses of Roman Pompeii. A Syntactical Approach to the Analysis and Interpretation of Built Space*. BAR International Series 886. Oxford: Archaeopress.

Graves-Brown, Paul, Sian Jones, and Clive Gamble (eds.)
1996 *Cultural Identity and Archaeology: The Construction of European Communities.* London: Routledge.
Graziosi, Paolo
1961 The Wooden Statue of Dezalik, A Kalash Divinity, Chitral, Pakistan. *Man* 61: 149–51.
Greenberg, Rafi
2002 *Early Urbanizations in the Levant: A Regional Narrative.* London: Leicester University.
Greenfield, Haskel J.
2010 The Secondary Products Revolution: The Past, the Present, and the Future. *World Archaeology* 42.1: 29–54.
Greverus, Ina-Maria
1976 Human Territoriality as an Object of Research in Cultural Anthropology. In *The Mutual Interaction of People and Their Built Environment*, edited by A. Rapoport, pp. 145–57. The Hague: Mouton Publishers.
Grewal, Inderpal
1996 *Harem: Nation, Gender, Empire, and the Cultures of Travel.* Durham, NC: Duke University Press.
Groot, Maaike
2009 Searching for Patterns among Special Animal Deposits in the Dutch River Area during the Roman Period. *Journal of Archaeology in the Low Countries* 1–2: 49–81.
Grum, Anders
1995 Rendille Habitation. In *African Nomadic Architecture: Space, Place and Gender*, edited by L. Prussin, pp. 150–69. Washington, DC: Smithsonian University Press.
Guengerich, Anna
2014 The Architect's Signature: The Social Production of a Residential Landscape at Monte Viudo, Chachapoyas, Peru. *Journal of Anthropological Archaeology* 34: 1–16.
Gumerman, G. J. (ed.)
1991 *Exploring the Hohokam: Prehistoric Desert Peoples of the American Southwest.* Amerind Foundation New World Studies No. 1, edited by A. I. Woosley. Albuquerque: University of New Mexico Press.
Habu, Junko
2008 Growth and Decline in Complex Hunter-Gatherer Societies: A Case Study from the Jomon Period Sannai Maruyama Site, Japan. *Antiquity* 82: 571–84.
Hall, Edward T.
1959 *The Silent Language.* Garden City,NJ: Doubleday.
1963 A System for the Notation of Proxemic Behavior. *American Anthropologist* 65.5: 1003–26.
1966 *The Hidden Dimension.* Garden City,NJ: Doubleday.
1968 Proxemics. *Current Anthropology* 9.2/3: 83–108.
1974 *Handbook for Proxemic Research.* Washington, DC: Society for the Anthropology of Visual Communication.
Hall, Martin
1993 The Archaeology of Colonial Settlement in Southern Africa. *Annual Review of Anthropology* 22: 177–200.

Hall, Robert L.
1997 *An Archaeology of the Soul: North American Indian Belief and Ritual.* Urbana: University of Illinois Press.

Hamann, Byron
1997 Weaving and the Iconography of Prestige: The Royal Gender Symbolism of Lord 5 Flower's/Lady 4 Rabbit's Family. In *Women in Prehistory: North America and Mesoamerica*, edited by C. Claassen and R. A. Joyce, pp. 153–72. Philadelphia: University of Pennsylvania Press.

Hamilton, Sue, Ruth D. Whitehouse, and Katherine I. Wright (eds.)
2007 *Archaeology and Women: Ancient and Modern Issues.* Walnut Creek, CA: Left Coast Press, Inc.

Hammel, E. A.
1980 Household Structure in Fourteenth-Century Macedonia. *Journal of Family History* 5: 242–73.
1984 On the *** of Studying Household Form and Function. In *Households: Comparative and Historical Studies of the Domestic Group*, edited by R. McC. Netting, R. R. Wilk, E.J. Arnould, pp. 29–43. Berkeley: University of California Press.

Hammer, Emily
2014 Local Landscape Organization of Mobile Pastoralists in Southeastern Turkey. *Journal of Anthropological Archaeology* 35: 269–88.

Hanson, Julianne
1998 *Decoding Homes and Houses.* Cambridge: Cambridge University Press.

Hardin, James W.
2011 Understanding Houses, Households, and the Levantine Archaeological Record. In *Household Archaeology in Ancient Israel and Beyond*, edited by A. Yasur-Landau, J. R. Ebeling, and L. B. Mazow, pp. 9–25. Leiden: Brill.
2012 Household Archaeology in the Southern Levant: An Example from Iron Age Tell Halif. In *New Perspectives on Household Archaeology*, edited by B. J. Parker and C. P. Foster, pp. 519–56. Winona Lake, IN: Eisenbrauns.

Harmanşah, Ömür
2013 *Cities and the Shaping of Memory in the Ancient Near East.* Cambridge: Cambridge University Press.

Hart, John P., Lisa M. Anderson, and Robert S. Feranec
2011 Additional Evidence for CAL. Seventh-Century A.D. Maize Consumption at the Kipp Island Site, New York. In *Current Research in New York Archaeology A.D. 700–1300*, edited by C. B. Rieth and J. P. Hart, pp. 27–40. Albany: New York State Museum.

Hart, John P., and Bernard K. Means
2002 Maize and Villages: A Summary and Critical Assessment of Current Northeast Early Late Prehistoric Evidence. In *Northeast Subsistence-Settlement Change: A.D. 700–1300*, edited by J. P. Hart and C. B. Rieth, pp. 345–58. Albany: University of the State of New York.

Hassan, Fekri A.
1981 *Demographic Archaeology.* New York: Academic Press.

Hastorf, Christine A.
1991 Gender, Space, and Food in Prehistory. In *Engendering Archaeology: Women and Prehistory*, edited by J. M. Gero and M. W. Conkey, pp. 132–59. Cambridge: Basil Blackwell.
Haury, Emil W.
1976 *The Hohokam: Desert Farmers and Craftsmen: Excavations at Snaketown, 1964–1965.* Tucson: University of Arizona Press.
Hayden, Brian
1982 Comment on Testart: "The Significance of Food Storage among Hunter-Gatherers." *Current Anthropology* 23.5: 531.
1994 Competition, Labor, and Complex Hunter-Gatherers. In *Key Issues in Hunter-Gatherer Research*, edited by E. S. Burch, Jr. and L. J. Ellanna, pp. 223–40. Oxford: Berg.
1995 Pathways to Power: Principles for Creating Socioeconomic Inequalities. In *Foundations of Social Inequality*, edited by T. D. Price and G. M. Feinman, pp. 15–86. New York: Plenum.
2000a (ed.) *The Ancient Past of Keatley Creek: Taphonomy*, Vol. I. Burnaby, BC: Archaeology Press of Simon Fraser University.
2000b (ed.) *The Ancient Past of Keatley Creek: Socioeconomy*, Vol. II. Burnaby, BC: Archaeology Press of Simon Fraser University.
2001 Richman, Poorman, Beggarman, Chief: The Dynamics of Social Inequality. In *Archaeology at the Millennium: A Sourcebook*, edited by G. Feinman and T. D. Price, pp. 213–68. New York: Kluwer Academic.
2003 *A Prehistory of Religion: Shamans, Sorcerers, and Saints.* Washington, DC: Smithsonian Institution Press.
2005 The Emergence of Large Villages and Large Residential Corporate Group Structures among Complex Hunter-Gatherers at Keatley Creek. *American Antiquity* 70: 169–74.
Hayden, Brian, and Ron Adams
2004 Ritual Structures in Transegalitarian Communities. In *Complex Hunter-Gatherers: Evolution and Organization of Prehistoric Communities on the Plateau of Northwestern North America*, edited by W. Prentiss and I. Kuijt, pp. 84–102. Salt Lake City: University of Utah Press.
Hayden, Brian, and Aubrey Cannon
1982 The Corporate Group as an Archaeological Unit. *Journal of Anthropological Archaeology* 1: 132–58.
Hayden, Brian, and Michael Dietler (eds.)
2001 *Feasts: Archaeological and Ethnographic Perspectives on Food, Politics, and Power.* Washington, DC: Smithsonian Institution Press.
Hays-Gilpin, Kelley, and David S. Whitley (eds.)
1998 *Reader in Gender Archaeology.* London: Routledge.
Head, Lesley
1993 Unearthing Prehistoric Cultural Landscapes: A View from Australia. *Transactions of the Institute of British Geographers* 18: 481–99.
Healan, Dan M.
1977 Architectural Implications of Daily Life in Ancient Tollan, Hidalgo, Mexico. *World Archaeology* 9.2: 140–56.

Hegmon, Michelle, Scott G. Ortman, and Jeannette L. Mobley-Tanaka

2000 Women, Men, and the Organization of Space. In *Women and Men in the Prehispanic Southwest: Labor, Power, and Prestige*, edited by P. L. Crown, pp. 43–90. Santa Fe: School of American Research Press.

Heidegger, Martin

2008 Building, Dwelling, Thinking. In *Basic Writings: Martin Heidegger*, edited by D. F. Krell, pp. 347–63. London: Routledge.

Helms, Mary W.

1992 Long-Distance Contacts, Elite Aspirations, and the Age of Discovery in Cosmological Context. In *Resources, Power, and Interregional Interaction*, edited by E. M. Schortman and P. A Urban, pp. 157–74. New York: Plenum.

1998 *Access to Origins: Affines, Ancestors, and Aristocrats*. Austin: University of Texas Press.

Helwing, Barbara

1999 Cultural Interaction at Hassek Höyük, Turkey. New Evidence from Pottery Analysis. *Paléorient* 25.1: 91–99

2003 Feasts as a Social Dynamic in Prehistoric Western Asia—Three Case Studies from Syria and Anatolia. *Paléorient* 29.2: 63–85.

Hendon, Julia A.

1991 Status and Power in Classic Maya Society: An Archaeological Study. *American Anthropologist* 93.4: 894–918.

1996 Archaeological Approaches to the Organization of Domestic Labor: Household Practices and Domestic Relations. *Annual Review of Anthropology* 25: 45–61.

1997 Women's Work, Women's Space, and Women's Status among the Classic-Period Maya Elite of the Copan Valley, Honduras. In *Women in Prehistory: North America and Mesoamerica*, edited by C. Claassen and R. A. Joyce, pp. 33–46. Philadelphia: University of Pennsylvania Press.

2000 Having and Holding: Storage, Memory, Knowledge, and Social Relations. *American Anthropologist* 102.1: 42–53.

2002 Social Relations and Collective Identities: Household and Community in Ancient Mesoamerica. In *The Dynamics of Power*, edited by M. O'Donovan, pp. 273–300. Center for Archaeological Investigations, Occasional Paper No. 30. Carbondale: Southern Illinois University.

2006 The Engendered Household. In *Handbook of Gender in Archaeology*, edited by S. M. Nelson, pp. 171–98. Lanham, MD: AltaMira Press.

2007 Living and Working at Home: The Social Archaeology of Household Production and Social Relations. In *A Companion to Social Archaeology*, edited by L. Meskell and R. W. Preucel, pp. 272–86. Oxford: Blackwell.

2010 *Houses in a Landscape: Memory and Everyday Life in Mesoamerica*. Durham, NC: Duke University Press.

Henley, Nancy M.

1973 Power, Sex, and Nonverbal Communication. *Berkeley Journal of Sociology* 18: 1–26.

Henry, Donald O.

1989 *From Foraging to Agriculture: The Levant at the End of the Ice Age*. Philadelphia: University of Pennsylvania.

1991 Foraging, Sedentism, and Adaptive Vigor in the Natufian: Rethinking the Linkages. In *Perspectives on the Past: Theoretical Biases in Mediterranean Hunter-Gatherer Research*, edited by G. A. Clark, pp. 353–70. Philadelphia: University of Pennsylvania Press.

Herdt, Gilbert H.

2003 *Secrecy and Cultural Reality: Utopian Ideology of the New Guinea Men's House*. Ann Arbor: University of Michigan Press.

Hiatt, Lester R., and Rhys Jones

1988 Aboriginal Conceptions of the Workings of Nature. In *Australian Science in the Making*, edited by R. W. Home, pp. 1–22. Cambridge: Cambridge University Press.

Hietala, Harold (ed.)

1984 *Intrasite Spatial Analysis in Archaeology.* Cambridge: Cambridge University Press.

Higgs, Eric S.

1975 *Paleoeconomy*. New York: Cambridge University Press.

Higham, Charles

1989 *The Archaeology of Mainland Southeast Asia. From 10,000 B.C. to the Fall of Angkor.* Cambridge: Cambridge University Press.

2002a *Early Cultures of Mainland Southeast Asia*. Chicago: Art Media Resources.

2002b Women in the Prehistory of Mainland Southeast Asia. In *In Pursuit of Gender: Worldwide Archaeological Approaches*, edited by S. M. Nelson and M. Rosen-Ayalon, pp. 207–24. Walnut Creek, CA: AltaMira Press.

2004 Mainland Southeast Asia from the Neolithic to the Iron Age. In *Southeast Asia from Prehistory to History*, edited by I. Glover and P. Bellwood, pp. 41–67. London: RoutledgeCurzon.

Higham, Charles, Rachanie Bannanurag, Grame Mason, and Nancy Tayles

1992 Human Biology, Environment and Ritual at Khok Phanom Di. *World Archaeology* 24.1: 35–54.

Hildebrand, Elisabeth A., and Katherine M. Grillo

2012 Early Herders and Monumental Sites in Eastern Africa: Dating and Interpretation. *Antiquity* 86: 338–52.

Hill, J. D.

1995 *Ritual and Rubbish in the Iron Age of Wessex: A Study on the Formation of a Specific Archaeological Record*. BAR British Series 242. Oxford: British Archaeological Reports.

Hill, James N.

1994 Prehistoric Cognition and the Science of Archaeology. In *The Ancient Mind: Elements of Cognitive Archaeology*, edited by E. B. Zubrow, pp. 83–92. Cambridge: Cambridge University Press.

Hillier, Bill, and Julienne Hanson

1984 *The Social Logic of Space*. Cambridge: Cambridge University Press.

Hillier, Bill, Julianne Hanson, and H. Graham

1987 Ideas Are in Things: An Application of the Space Syntax Method to Discovering House Genotypes. *Environment and Planning B: Planning and Design* 14: 363–85.

Hillier, Bill, Adrian Leaman, P. Stansall, and M. Bedford

1976 Space Syntax. *Environment and Planning B* 3: 147–185.

Hillner, Julia
2003 Domus, Family, and Inheritance: The Senatorial Family House in Late Antique Rome. *Journal of Roman Studies* 93: 129–45.
Hinde, Robert A.
1998 Mind and Artefact: A Dialectical Perspective. In *Cognition and Material Culture: The Archaeology of Symbolic Storage*, edited by C. Renfrew and C. Scarre, pp. 175–79. Cambridge: McDonald Institute for Archaeological Research.
Hingley, Richard
1990 Domestic Organisation and Gender Relations in Iron Age and Romano-British Households. In *The Social Archaeology of Houses*, edited by R. Samson, pp. 125–47. Edinburgh: Edinburgh University Press.
Hirth, Kenneth G.
1989 Domestic Architecture and Social Rank in a Mesoamerican Urban Center. In *Households and Communities. Proceedings of the Twenty-First Annual Conference of the Archaeological Association of the University of Calgary*, edited by S. MacEachern, D. J. W. Archer and R.D. Garvin, pp. 441–49. Calgary: University of Calgary.
1996 Political Economy and Archaeology: Perspectives on Exchange and Production. *Journal of Archaeological Research* 4.3: 203–39.
Hitchcock, Louise A.
2011 Cult Corners in the Aegean and the Levant. In *Household Archaeology in Ancient Israel and Beyond*, edited by A. Yasur-Landau, J. R. Ebeling and L. B. Mazow, pp. 321–45. Leiden: Brill.
Hodder, Ian
1982 (ed.) *Symbolic and Structural Archaeology*. Cambridge: Cambridge University Press.
1984 Burials, Houses, Women and Men in the European Neolithic. In *Ideology, Power and Prehistory*, edited by D. Miller and C. Tilley, pp. 51–68. Cambridge: Cambridge University Press.
1986 *Reading the Past: Current Approaches to Interpretation in Archaeology*. Cambridge: Cambridge University Press.
1990 *The Domestication of Europe*. Oxford: Basil Blackwell.
1992 *Theory and Practice in Archaeology*. London: Routledge.
1994 Architecture and Meaning: The Example of Neolithic Houses and Tombs. In *Architecture and Order: Approaches to Social Space*, edited by M. Parker Pearson and C. Richards, pp. 73–86. London: Routledge.
1996a (ed.) *On the Surface: Çatalhöyük 1993–95*. BIAA Monograph No. 22. Cambridge: McDonald Institute for Archaeological Research.
1996b Çatalhöyük: 9000 Year Old Housing and Settlement in Central Anatolia. In *Housing and Settlement in Anatolia: A Historical perspective*, edited by Y. Sey, pp. 43–48. Istanbul: Tarih Vakfı Yayınları.
1999 Renewed Work at Çatalhöyük. In *Neolithic in Turkey: The Cradle of Civilization*, edited by M. Özdoğan and N. Başgelen, pp. 159–64. Istanbul: Arkeoloji ve Sanat Yayınları.
2006 *The Leopard's Tale: Revealing the Mysteries of Çatalhöyük*. London: Thames & Hudson.

2010 (ed.) *Religion in the Emergence of Civilization: Çatalhöyük as a Case Study*. Cambridge: Cambridge University Press.

2012 *Entangled: An Archaeology of the Relationships between Humans and Things*. West Sussex: Wiley-Blackwell.

Hodder, Ian, and Craig Cessford

2004 Daily Practice and Social Memory at Çatalhöyük. *American Antiquity* 69.1: 17–40.

Hodder, Ian, and Roger Matthews

1998 Çatalhöyük: The 1990s Seasons. In *Ancient Anatolia: Fifty Years' Work by the British Institute of Archaeology at Ankara*, edited by R. Matthews, pp. 43–51. Ankara: British Institute of Archaeology.

Hodder, Ian, and Lynn Meskell

2010 The Symbolism of Çatalhöyük in Its Regional Context. In *Religion in the Emergence of Civilization: Çatalhöyük as a Case Study*, edited by I. Hodder, pp. 32–72. Cambridge: Cambridge University Press.

2011 A "Curious and Sometimes a Trifle Macabre Artistry": Some Aspects of Symbolism in Neolithic Turkey. *Current Anthropology* 52.2: 235–63.

Hodder, Ian, and Clive Orton

1976 *Spatial Analysis in Archaeology*. Cambridge: Cambridge University Press.

Hodgson, Dorothy L. (ed.)

2000 *Rethinking Pastoralism in Africa: Gender, Culture and the Myth of the Patriarchal Pastoralist*. Oxford: James Currey.

Hoffman, Brian W.

1999 Agayadan Village: Household Archaeology on Unimak Island, Alaska. *Journal of Field Archaeology* 26.2: 147–61.

Hofmann, Daniela, and Jessica Smyth (eds.)

2013 *Tracking the Neolithic House in Europe: Sedentism, Architecture and Practice*. New York: Springer.

Hollimon, Sandra E.

2004 The Role of Ritual Specialization in the Evolution of Prehistoric Chumash Complexity. In *Foundations of Chumash Complexity*, edited by J. E. Arnold, pp. 53–63. Perspectives in California Archaeology, Vol. 7. Los Angeles: Cotsen Institute of Archaeology, UCLA.

Holter, Uta

1995 Mahria Tents: The Woman's Domain. In *African Nomadic Architecture: Space, Place and Gender*, edited by L. Prussin, pp. 124–49. Washington, DC: Smithsonian Institution Press.

Hopkins, Liza

2003 *Archaeology at the North East Anatolian Frontier, VI. An Ethnoarchaeological Study of Sos Höyük and Yiğittaşı Village*. Ancient Near Eastern Studies, Supplement 11. Louvain: Peeters Press.

Horne, Lee

1994 *Village Spaces: Settlement and Society in Northeastern Iran*. Washington, DC: Smithsonian Institution Press.

Horton, Mark

1994 Swahili Architecture, Space and Social Structure. In *Architecture and Order. Approaches to Social Space*, edited by M. Parker Pearson and C. Richards, pp. 147–69. London: Routledge.

Hoskins, Janet
2002 The Menstrual Hut and the Witch's Lair in Two Eastern Indonesian Societies. *Ethnology* 41.4: 317–34.
Howell, Nancy
1986 Demographic Anthropology. *Annual Review of Anthropology* 15: 219–46.
Howell, Signe
1995 The Lio House: Building, Category, Idea, Value. In *About the House: Lévi-Strauss and Beyond*, edited by J. Carsten and S. Hugh-Jones, pp. 149–69. Cambridge: Cambridge University Press.
Huckell, Bruce B.
1996 The Archaic Prehistory of the North American Southwest. *Journal of World Prehistory* 10.3: 305–73.
Hudson, Michael
1999 From Sacred Enclosure to Temple to City. In *Urbanization and Land Ownership in the Ancient Near East*, edited by M. Hudson and B. Levine, pp. 117–64. Boston: Peabody Museum of Archaeology.
Huffman, Thomas N.
1996 *Snakes and Crocodiles: Power and Symbolism in Ancient Zimbabwe*. Johannesburg: Witwatersrand University.
Hugh-Jones, Stephen
1993 Clear Descent or Ambiguous Houses: A Re-Examination of Tukanoan Social Organization. *L'Homme* 33.128–28: 95–120.
1995 Inside-Out and Back-to-Front: The Androgynous House in Northwest Amazonia. In *About the House: Lévi-Strauss and Beyond*, edited by J. Carsten and S. Hugh-Jones, pp. 226–52. Cambridge: Cambridge University Press.
Hukantaival, Sonja
2007 Hare's Feet under a Hearth: Discussing "Ritual" Deposits in Buildings. In *Hortus Novus: Fresh Approaches to Medieval Archaeology in Finland*, edited by V. Immonen, M. Lempiäinen, and U. Rosendahl, pp. 66–75. Archaeologia Medii Aevi Finlandiae XIV. Turku: Suomen Keskiajan Arkeologian Seura.
Humphrey, Caroline
2005 Ideology in Infrastructure: Architecture and Soviet Imagination. *Journal of the Royal Anthropological Institute* 11.1: 39–58.
Hurtado, A. Magdalena, Kim Hill, Ines Hurtado, and Hillard Kaplan
1992 Tradeoffs between Female Food Acquisition and Child Care among Hiwi and Ache Foragers. *Human Nature* 3.3: 185–216.
Hutson, Scott
2010 *Dwelling, Identity, and the Maya: Relational Archaeology at Chunchucmil*. Lanham, MD: AltaMira Press.
Ingold, Tim
1982 Comment on Testart: "The Significance of Food Storage among Hunter-Gatherers." *Current Anthropology* 23.5: 531–32.
1983 The Significance of Storage in Hunting Societies. *Man*, New Series 18.3: 553–71.
1993 The Temporality of the Landscape. *World Archaeology*, 25: 152–74.
2007 (ed.) *The Archaeology of Identities: A Reader*. London: Routledge.
2013 *Making: Anthropology, Archaeology, Art and Architecture*. London: Routledge.

Inomata, Takeshi
2006 Plazas, Performers, and Spectators: Political Theaters of the Classic Maya. *Current Anthropology* 47.5: 805–42.

Insoll, Timothy
2004 *Archaeology, Ritual, Religion*. London: Routledge.
2011 Ancestor Cults. In *The Oxford Handbook of the Archaeology of Ritual and Religion*, edited by T. Insoll, pp. 1043–58. Oxford: Oxford University Press.
2013 The Archaeology of Ritual and Religions in Africa. In *The Oxford Handbook of African Archaeology*, edited by P. Mitchell and P. Lane, pp. 163–75. Oxford: Oxford University Press.

Isaac, Glynn
1989 *The Archaeology of Human Origins*. Cambridge: Cambridge University Press.

Jackson, Michael
1995 *At Home in the World*. Durham, NC: Duke University Press.

Jameson, Michael H.
1990a Private Space and the Greek City. In *The Greek City from Homer to Alexander*, edited by O. Murray and S. Price, pp. 171–95. Oxford: Clarendon.
1990b Domestic Space in the Greek City-State. In *Domestic Architecture and the Use of Space*, edited by S. Kent, pp. 92–113. Cambridge: Cambridge University Press.

Janusek, John W.
2004 Household and City in Tiwanaku. In *Andean Archaeology*, edited by H. Silverman, pp. 183–207. Madden, MA: Blackwell.

Janzen, Jorg
1986 *Nomads in the Sultanate of Oman*. Boulder, CO: Westview Press.

Jarno, Roland
1984 Tente et maison: Le jeu anuel de la sédentarisation a Qdeir (Syrie). In *Nomades et sédentaires: perspectives ethnoarchéologiques*, edited by O. Aurenche, pp. 191–229. Paris: Éditions Recherche sur les Civilisations.

Jarvenpa, Robert, and Hetty Jo Brumbach
1999 The Gendered Nature of Living and Storage Space in the Canadian Subarctic. In *From the Ground Up: Beyond Gender Theory in Archaeology*, edited by N. L. Wicker, and B. Arnold, pp. 107–23. BAR International Series 812. Oxford: Archaeopress.
2006 (eds.) *Circumpolar Lives and Livelihood: A Comparative Ethnoarchaeology of Gender and Subsistence*. Lincoln: University of Nebraska Press.

Jennings, Justin, and Willy Y. Álvarez
2001 Architecture, Local Elites, and Imperial Entanglements: The Wari Empire and the Cotahuasi Valley of Peru. *Journal of Field Archaeology* 29.1–2: 143–59.

Joachim, Michael A.
1988 Optimal Foraging and the Division of Labor. *American Anthropologist* 90: 130–36.

Joffee, Alex H.
1993 *Settlement and Society in the Early Bronze Age I and II, Southern Levant: Complementarity and Contradiction in a Small-Scale Complex Society*. Sheffield: Sheffield Academic Press.

Johnson, Allen W., and Timothy Earle
1987 *The Evolution of Human Societies: From Foraging Group to Agrarian State*. Stanford, CA: Stanford University Press.

Johnson, Gary A.
1977 Aspects of Regional Analysis in Archaeology. *Annual Review of Anthropology* 6: 479–508.

Jones, Andrew
2005 Lives in Fragments? Personhood and the European Neolithic. *Journal of Social Archaeology* 5: 193–224.

Jones, Rhys
1991 Landscapes of the Mind: Aboriginal Perceptions of the Natural World. In *The Humanities and the Australian Environment*, edited by D. J. Mulvaney, pp. 21–48. Canberra: Australian Academy of Humanities.

Jones, Siân
1997 *The Archaeology of Ethnicity: Constructing Identities in the Past and Present*. London: Routledge.
2008 Ethnicity: Theoretical Approaches, Methodological Implications. In *Handbook of Archaeological Theories*, edited by R. A. Bentley, H. D. G. Maschner, and C. Chippendale, pp. 321–32. Lanham, MD: AltaMira Press.

Jordan, Peter
2008 Hunters and Gatherers. In *Handbook of Archaeological Theories*, edited by R. A. Bentley, H. D. G. Maschner, and C. Chippindale, pp. 447–65. Lanham, MD: AltaMira Press.

Joyce, Arthur A., and Marcus Winter
1996 Ideology, Power, and Urban Society in Pre-Hispanic Oaxaca. *Current Anthropology* 37: 33–86.

Joyce, Rosemary A.
2005 Archaeology of the Body. *Annual Review of Anthropology* 34: 139–58.

Joyce, Rosemary A., and Susan D. Gillespie (eds.)
2000 *Beyond Kinship: Social and Material Reproduction in House Societies*. Philadelphia: University of Pennsylvania Press.

Just, Roger
1989 *Women in Athenian Law and Life*. London: Routledge.

Kafafi, Zeidan A.
2006 Domestic Activities at the Neolithic Site, ʽAin Ghazal. In *Domesticating Space: Construction, Community, and Cosmology in the Late Prehistoric Near East*, edited by E. B. Banning and M. Chazan, pp. 81–89. Studies in Early Near Eastern Production, Subsistence, and Environment 6. Berlin: Ex oriente.

Kahn, Jennifer G.
2007 Power and Precedence in Ancient House Societies: A Case Study from the Society Island Chiefdoms. In *The Durable House: House Society in Models in Archaeology*, edited by R. A. Beck, Jr., pp. 198–223. Center for Archaeological Investigations, Occasional Paper No. 35. Carbondale: Southern Illinois University.

Kane, Susan (ed.)
2003 *The Politics of Archaeology and Identity in a Global Context*. Boston: Archaeological Institute of America.

Kantner, John
2004 *Ancient Puebloan Southwest*. Cambridge: Cambridge University Press.
2008 The Archaeology of Regions: From Discrete Analytical Toolkit to Ubiquitous Spatial Perspective. *Journal of Archaeological Research* 16: 37–81.

Kapuches, Mima

1987 The Auda Site: An Early Pickering Iroquois Component in Southeastern Ontario. *Archaeology of Eastern North America* 15: 155–75.

1990 The Spatial Dynamics of Ontario Iroquoian Longhouses. *American Antiquity* 55.1: 49–67.

Kawano, Satsuki

2005 *Ritual Practice in Modern Japan: Ordering Place, People, and Action*. Honolulu: University of Hawaii Press.

Kay, Marvin, and George Sabo III

2006 Mortuary Ritual and Winter Solstice Imagery of the Harlan-Style Charnel House. *Southeastern Archaeology* 25.1: 29–47.

Keeley, Lawrence H.

2010 The Probable Sexual Division of Labor in Magdalenian Hide Work: Ethnological Evidence. In *The Magdalenian Household: Unraveling Domesticity*, edited by E. Zubrow, F. Audouze, and J. G. Enloe, pp. 227–34. Albany: State University of New York Press.

Keith, Kathryn

2003 The Spatial Patterns of Everyday Life in Old Babylonian Neighborhoods. In *The Social Construction of Ancient Cities*, edited by M. L. Smith, pp. 36–80. Washington, DC: Smithsonian Institution Press.

Kelly, John E.

1997 Stirling-Phase Sociopolitical Activity at East St. Louis and Cahokia. In *Cahokia: Domination and Ideology in the Mississippian World*, edited by T. R. Pauketat and T. E. Emerson, pp. 141–66. Lincoln: University of Nebraska Press.

Kelly, Robert L.

1995 *The Foraging Spectrum: Diversity in Hunter-Gatherer Lifeways*. Washington, DC: Smithsonian Institution Press.

Kemp, Barry J.

1989 *Ancient Egypt: Anatomy of a Civilization*. London: Routledge.

Kenoyer, Jonathon M.

1998 *Ancient Cities of the Indus Valley Civilization*. Karachi: Oxford University.

Kent, Susan

1984 *Analyzing Activity Areas: An Ethnoarchaeological Study of the Use of Space*. Albuquerque: University of New Mexico Press.

1987a Understanding the Use of Space: An Ethnoarchaeological Approach. In *Method and Theory for Activity Area Research: An Ethnoarchaeological Approach*, edited by S. Kent, pp. 1–62. New York: Columbia University Press.

1987b (ed.) *Method and Theory for Activity Area Research: An Ethnoarchaeological Approach*. New York: Columbia University Press.

1990 A Cross-Cultural Study of Segmentation, Architecture, and the Use of Space. In *Domestic Architecture and the Use of Space*, edited by S. Kent, pp. 127–52. Cambridge: Cambridge University Press.

1991a The Relationship between Mobility Strategies and Site Structure. In *The Interpretation of Spatial Patterning*, edited by E. M. Kroll and T. D. Price, pp. 33–59. New York: Plenum Publishing.

1991b (ed.) *Cultural Diversity among Twentieth-Century Foragers*. Cambridge: Cambridge University Press.

1991c Partitioning Space: Cross-Cultural Factors Influencing Domestic Spatial Segmentation. *Environment and Behavior* 23: 438–473.

1992 Studying Variability in the Archaeological Record: An Ethnoarchaeological Model for Distinguishing Mobility Patterns. *American Antiquity* 57.4: 635–60.

1998a Invisible Gender—Invisible Foragers: Hunter-Gatherer Spatial Patterning and the Southern African Archaeological Record. In *Gender in African Prehistory*, edited by S. Kent, pp. 39–67. Walnut Creek, CA: AltaMira Press.

1998b (ed.) *Gender in African Prehistory*. Walnut Creek, CA: AltaMira Press.

1999 The Archaeological Visibility of Storage: Delineating Storage from Trash Areas. *American Antiquity* 64.1: 79–94.

Kenyon, Kathleen

1957 *Digging Up Jericho*. London: Benn.

Khazanov, Anatoly M., and Günther Schlee (eds.)

2012 *Who Owns the Stock? Collective and Multiple Forms of Property in Animals*. New York: Berghahn Books.

Khazanov, Anatoly M., and André Wink (eds.)

2001 *Nomads in the Sedentary World*. New York: Routledge.

Kidder, Tristram R.

2012 Poverty Point. In *The Oxford Handbook of North American Archaeology*, edited by T. R. Pauketat, pp. 460–69. Oxford: Oxford University Press.

Kinahan, John

1996 The Archaeology of Social Rank among Eighteenth-Century Nomadic Pastoralists in Southern Namibia. *African Archaeological Review* 13.4: 225–45.

Kirch, Patrick V.

1990 Monumental Architecture and Power in Polynesian Chiefdoms: A Comparison of Tonga and Hawaii. *World Archaeology* 22.2: 206–22.

1997 *The Lapita Peoples: Ancestors of the Oceanic World*. Cambridge: Blackwell.

Kirkbride, Diana

1966 Five Seasons at the Prepottery Neolithic Village of Beidha in Jordan. *Palestine Exploration Quarterly* 98: 5–61.

Knapp, A. Bernard

1997 *The Archaeology of Late Bronze Age Cypriot Society: The Study of Settlement, Survey and Landscape*. Glasgow: University of Glasgow.

Kohler, Timothy A., Matt P. Gaude, Jean-Pierre Bocquet-Appel, and Brian M. Kemp

2008 The Neolithic Demographic Transition in the U.S. Southwest. *American Antiquity* 73.4: 645–69.

Kohler, Timothy A., and Mark D. Varien

2010 A Scale Model of Seven Hundred Years of Farming Settlements in Southwestern Colorado. In *Becoming Villagers: Comparing Early Village Societies*, edited by M. S. Bandy and J. R. Fox, pp. 37–61. Tucson: University of Arizona Press.

Kolb, Michael J.

1994 Monumentality and the Rise of Religious Authority in Precontact Hawai'i. *Current Anthropology* 35.5: 521–47.

Kolb, Charles C.

1985 Demographic Estimates in Archaeology: Contributions from Ethnoarchaeology on Mesoamerican Peasants. *Current Anthropology* 26.5: 581–99.

Kostof, Spiro

1991 *The City Shaped: Urban Patterns and Meanings through History*. Boston: Little, Brown and Co.

1992 *The City Assembled: The Elements of Urban Form Through History*. Boston: Little, Brown and Co.

Kovacik, Joseph J.

1999 Memory and Pueblo Space. In *Making Places in the Prehistoric World: Themes in Settlement Archaeology*, edited by J. Brück and M. Goodman, pp. 160–77. London: Routledge.

2002 Radical Agency, Households, and Communities: Networks of Power. In *The Dynamics of Power*, edited by M. O'Donovan, pp. 51–65. Carbondale: Southern Illinois University.

Kozlowski, Stefan K.

2006 The Hunter-Gatherer "Villages" of the PPNA/EPPNB. In *Domesticating Space: Construction, Community, and Cosmology in the Late Prehistoric Near East*, edited by E. B. Banning and M. Chazan, pp. 43–51. Studies in Early Near Eastern Production, Subsistence, and Environment 6. Berlin: Ex oriente.

Krader, Lawrence

1963 *Social Organization of the Mongol-Turkic Pastoral Nomads*. The Hague: Mouton.

Kramer, Carol

1977 Pots and Peoples. In *Mountains and Lowlands: Essays in the Archaeology of Greater Mesopotamia*, edited by L. Levine and T. C. Young, Jr., pp. 91–112. Bibliotheca Mesopotamica 7. Malibu: Undena.

1983 Spatial Organization in Contemporary Southwest Asian Villages and Archaeological Sampling. In *The Hilly Flanks. Essays on the Prehistory of Southwestern Asia Presented to Robert J. Braidwood*, pp. 347–68. Studies in Ancient Oriental Civilization, No. 36. Chicago: Oriental Institute, University of Chicago.

Kroll, Ellen M., and T. Douglas Price (eds.)

1991 *The Interpretation of Archaeological Spatial Patterning*. New York: Plenum Press.

Kuijt, Ian

2000a (ed.) *Life in Neolithic Farming Communities: Social Organization, Identity, and Differentiation*. New York: Plenum.

2000b Keeping the Peace: Ritual, Skull Caching, and Community Integration in the Levantine Neolithic. In *Life in Neolithic Farming Communities: Social Organization, Identity, and Differentiation*, edited by I. Kuijt, pp. 137–64. New York: Kluwer Academic/Plenum.

2000c People and Space in Early Agricultural Villages: Exploring Daily Lives, Community Size, and Architecture in the Late Pre-Pottery Neolithic. *Journal of Anthropological Archaeology* 19: 75–102.

2002 Reflections on Ritual and the Transmission of Authority in the Pre-Pottery Neolithic of the Southern Levant. In *Magic Practices and Ritual in the Near Eastern Neolithic*, edited by H. G. K. Gebel, B. D. Hermansen, and C. H. Jensen, pp. 81–90. Berlin: Ex oriente.

2008a Demography and Storage Systems during the Southern Levantine Neolithic Demographic Transition. In *The Neolithic Demographic Transition and Its Consequences*, edited by J.-P. Bocquet-Appel and O. Bar-Yosef, pp. 287–313. London: Springer.

2008b The Regeneration of Life. Neolithic Structures of Symbolic Remembering and Forgetting. *Current Anthropology* 49.2: 171–97.

Kuijt, Ian, and Meredith S. Chesson

2000 People and Space in Early Agricultural Villages: Exploring Daily Lives, Community Size, and Architecture in the Late Pre-Pottery Neolithic. *Journal of Anthropological Archaeology* 19: 75–102.

2005 Lumps of Clay and Pieces of Stone: Ambiguity, Bodies, and Identity as Portrayed in Neolithic Figurines. In *Archaeologies of the Middle East: Critical Perspectives*, edited by S. Pollock and R. Bernbeck, pp. 152–83. Oxford: Blackwell.

Kuijt, Ian, and Nathan Goodale

2009 Daily Practice and the Organization of Space at the Dawn of Agriculture: A Case Study from the Near East. *American Antiquity* 74.3: 403–22.

Kulakoğlu, Fikri

2010 Kültepe Kanesh Karum: The Earliest International Trade Center in Anatolia. In *Anatolia's Prologue: Kultepe Kanish Karum*, edited by F. Kulakoğlu, pp. 40–50. Kayseri: Kayseri Metropolitan Municipality.

2011 Kultepe-Kaneš: A Second Millennium B.C.E. Trading Center on the Central Plateau. In *The Oxford Handbook of Ancient Anatolia (10,000–323 BCE)*, edited by S. R. Steadman and G. McMahon, pp. 1012–30. Oxford: Oxford University Press.

Kuwanwisiwma, Leigh J., and T. J. Ferguson

2009 Hopitutskwa and Ang Kuktota. The Role of Archaeological Sites in Defining Hopi Cultural Landscapes. In *The Archaeology of Meaningful Places*, edited by B. J. Bowser and M. Nieves Zedeño, pp. 90–106. Salt Lake City: University of Utah Press.

Kvamme, Kenneth L.

1999 *Archeo-geophysical Surveys at Effigy Mounds National Monument, Iowa*. Fayetteville: University of Arkansas.

Lal, Ruby

2005 *Domesticity and Power in the Early Mughal World*. Cambridge: Cambridge University Press.

Lamphere, Louise

1974 Strategies, Cooperation, and Conflict among Women in Domestic Groups. In *Women, Culture, and Society*, edited by M. Z. Rosaldo and L. Lamphere, pp. 97–112. Stanford, CA: Stanford University Press.

2001 The Domestic Sphere of Women and the Public World of Men: The Strengths and Limitations of an Anthropological Dichotomy. In *Gender in Cross-Cultural Perspective*, edited by C. B. Brettell and C. F. Sargent, 3rd ed., pp. 100–109. Upper Saddle River, NJ: Prentice-Hall.

Larson, Mary Ann

1990 Determining the Function of a "Men's House." In *The Archaeology of Gender: Proceedings of the Twenty-Second Annual Conference of the Archaeological Association of the University of Calgary*, edited by D. Walde and N. D. Willows, pp. 165–75. Calgary: University of Calgary.

Laslett, Peter

1972 Introduction: The History of the Family. In *Household and Family in Past Time*, edited by P. Laslett and R. Wall, pp. 1–89. Cambridge: Cambridge University Press.

Last, Jonathan

1996 Neolithic Houses—A Central European Perspective. In *Neolithic Houses in Northwest Europe and Beyond*, edited by T. Darvill and J. Thomas, pp. 27–40. Oxford: Oxbow Press.

2013 The End of the Longhouse. In *Tracking the Neolithic House in Europe: Sedentism, Architecture, and Practice*, edited by D. Hofmann and J. Smyth, pp. 261–82. New York: Springer.

Lau, George F.

2010 House Forms and Recuay Culture: Residential Compounds at Yayno (Ancash, Peru), a Fortified Hilltop Town, AD 400–800. *Journal of Anthropological Archaeology* 29: 327–51.

Lavin, Marjorie Woods

1981 Boundaries in the Built Environment: Concepts and Examples. *Man-Environment Systems* 11: 195–206.

Lawrence, Denise L., and Setha M. Low

1990 The Built Environment and Spatial Form. *Annual Review of Anthropology* 19: 453–505.

Lawrence, Roderick J.

1984 Transition Spaces and Dwelling Design. *Journal of Architectural and Planning Research* 1: 261–71.

1990 Public Collective and Private Space: A Study of Urban Housing in Switzerland. In *Domestic Architecture and the Use of Space: An Interdisciplinary Cross-Cultural Study*, edited by S. Kent, pp. 73–91. Cambridge: Cambridge University Press.

Lawrence, Susan

1999 Towards a Feminist Archaeology of Households: Gender and Household Structure on the Australian Goldfields. In *The Archaeology of Household Activities*, edited by P. M. Allison, pp. 121–41. London: Routledge.

Lawrence-Zúñiga, Denise

1999 Suburbanizing Rural Lifestyles through House Form in Southern Portugal. In *House Life: Space, Place and Family in Europe*, edited by D. Birdwell-Pheasant and D. Lawrence-Zúñiga, pp. 157–75. Oxford: Berg.

Layton, Robert

1999 The Alawa Totemic Landscape: Ecology, Religion and Politics. In *The Archaeology and Anthropology of Landscape: Shaping Your Landscape*, edited by P. J. Ucko and R. Layton, pp. 219–39. London: Routledge.

2003 Art and Agency: A Reassessment. *Journal of the Royal Anthropological Institute* 9.3: 447–63.

Layton, Robert, Robert Foley, and Elizabeth Williams

1991 The Transition between Hunting and Gathering and the Specialized Husbandry of Resources: A Socio-ecological Approach. *Current Anthropology* 32.3: 255–74.

Lea, Vanessa

1995 The Houses of the Mẽbengokre (Kayapó) of Central Brazil—A New Door to Their Social Organization. In *About the House: Lévi-Strauss and Beyond*, edited by J. Carsten and S. Hugh-Jones, pp. 206–25. Cambridge: Cambridge University Press.

Leach, Edmund

1976 *Culture and Communication. The Logic by Which Symbols Are Connected.* Cambridge: Cambridge University Press.

1978 Does Space Syntax Really "Constitute the Social"? In *Social Organisation and Settlement: Contributions from Anthropology*, edited by D. Green, C. Haselgrove, and C. Spriggs, pp. 385–401. BAR International Series 471. Oxford: British Archaeological Reports.

Leacock, Eleanor

1978 Women's Status in Egalitarian Society: Implications for Social Evolution. *Current Anthropology* 19.2: 247–75.

Leacock, Eleanor, and Richard Lee (eds.)

1982 *Politics and History in Band Societies*. Cambridge: Cambridge University Press.

LeBlanc, Steven

1971 An Addition to Naroll's Suggested Floor Area and Settlement Population Relationship. *American Antiquity* 36.2: 210–11.

Lee, Georgia

2002 *Wahi Pana*: Legendary Places on Hawai'i Island. In *The Inscribed Landscape: Marking and Making Place*, edited by B. David and M. Wilson, pp. 79–92. Honolulu: University of Hawaii Press.

Lee, Richard

1981 What Hunters Do for a Living, or How to Make Out on Scarce Resources. In *Man the Hunter*, edited by R. B. Lee and I. de Vore, pp. 30–48. Chicago: Aldine.

1982 Politics, Sexual and Non-Sexual, in an Egalitarian Society. In *Politics and History in Band Societies*, edited by E. Leacock and R. Lee, pp. 37–59. Cambridge: Cambridge University Press.

Lee, Richard B., and Irven de Vore (eds.)

1968 *Man the Hunter*. Chicago: Aldine.

Lee, Yun Kuen

2007 Centripetal Settlement and Segmentary Social Formation of the Banpo Tradition. *Journal of Anthropological Archaeology* 26: 630–75.

Leffler, Ann, Dair L. Gillespie, and Joseph C. Conaty

1982 The Effects of Status Differentiation on Nonverbal Behavior. *Social Psychology Quarterly* 45.3: 153–61.

Lehner, Mark

2002 The Pyramid Age Settlement of the Southern Mount at Giza. *Journal of the American Research Center in Egypt* 39: 27–74.

Lekson, Stephen H.

1986 *Great Pueblo Architecture of Chaco Canyon*. Albuquerque: University of New Mexico Press.

2007 *The Architecture of Chaco Canyon, New Mexico*. Salt Lake City: University of Utah Press.

LeMoine, Genevieve

2003 Women of the House: Gender, Architecture, and Ideology in Dorset Prehistory. *Arctic Anthropology* 40.1: 121–38.

Leone, Mark P.

1973 Archaeology as the Science of Technology: Mormon Town Plans and Fences. In *Research and Theory in Current Archaeology*, edited by C. L. Redman, pp. 125–50. New York: Wiley.

1979 *Roots of Modern Mormonism*. Cambridge: Harvard University Press.

Lévi-Strauss, Claude

1963 *Structural Anthropology*. Harmondsworth: Penguin.

1979 *Le voie des masques*. Paris: Plon.

1982 *The Way of the Masks*. Translated by S. Modelski. Seattle: University of Washington Press.

1987 *Anthropology and Myth: Lectures 1951–1982*. Translated by R. Willis. Oxford: Blackwell.

Lewis, Reina

2004 *Rethinking Orientalism: Women, Travel, and the Ottoman Harem*. New Brunswick, NJ: Rutgers University Press.

Lewis-Williams, David

2002 *The Mind in the Cave*. London: Thames and Hudson.

2004 Constructing a Cosmos: Architecture, Power and Domestication at Çatalhöyük. *Journal of Social Archaeology* 4.1: 28–59.

2008 Religion and Archaeology: An Analytical, Materialist Account. In *Belief in the Past: Theoretical Approaches to the Archaeology of Religion*, edited by D. S. Whitley and K. Hays-Gilpin, pp. 23–43. Walnut Creek, CA: Left Coast Press, Inc.

2010 *Conceiving God: The Cognitive Origin and Evolution of Religion*. London: Thames & Hudson.

Lewis-Williams, David, and David Pearce

2005 *Inside the Neolithic Mind*. London: Thames & Hudson.

Liebman, Matthew, and Melissa S. Murphy (eds.)

2011 *Enduring Conquests: Rethinking the Archaeology of Resistance to Spanish Colonialism in the Americas*. Santa Fe: School of Advanced Research Press.

Liénard, Pierre, and Pascal Boyer

2006 Whence Collective Rituals? A Cultural Selection Model of Ritualized Behavior. *American Anthropologist* 108.4: 814–27.

Lightfoot, Kent G.

1980 Mormon Sociopolitical Development in Northern Arizona, 1876–1906: Implications for a Model of Prehistoric Change. *Ethnohistory* 27.3: 197–223.

Lightfoot, Kent G., and Antoinette Martinez

1995 Frontiers and Boundaries in Archaeological Perspective. *Annual Review of Anthropology* 24: 471–92.

Liran, Roy, and Ran Barkai

2011 Casting a Shadow on Neolithic Jericho. *Antiquity* 85.327 (online).

Lock, Gary R. (ed.)

2000 *Beyond the Map: Archaeology and Spatial Technologies*. Amsterdam: IOS Press.

Lock, Gary R., and Zoran Stančič (eds.)

1995 *Archaeology and Geographical Information Systems*. London: Taylor & Francis.

Löfgren, Orvar

1974 Family and Household among Scandinavian Peasants: An Exploratory Essay. *Ethnologica Scandinavia* 74: 1–52.

Loten, H. Stanley

2006 The Machine in the Ceremonial Centre. In *Space and Spatial Analysis in Archaeology*, edited by E. C. Robertson, J. D. Seibert, D. C. Fernandez, and M. U. Zender, pp. 115–22. Alberta: University of Calgary.

Loubser, Johannes H. N.
2009 The Archaeology of a Fishing Community in Hawai'i as seen within an Ethnographically Informed Context. *Southern African Humanities* 21: 1–40.

Love, Serena
2013 Architecture as Material Culture: Building Form and Materiality in the Pre-Pottery Neolithic of Anatolia and Levant. *Journal of Anthropological Archaeology* 32: 746–58.

Low, Setha M., and Denise Lawrence-Zúñiga (eds.)
2003 *The Anthropology of Space and Place*. Oxford: Blackwell.

Lowell, Julie C.
1990 Reflections of Sex Roles in the Archaeological Record: Insights from Hopi and Zuni Ethnographic Data. In *The Archaeology of Gender: Proceedings of the Twenty-Second Annual Conference of the Archaeological Association of the University of Calgary*, edited by D. Walde and N. D. Willows, pp. 452–61. Calgary: University of Calgary.

Lyons, Claire L., and John K. Papadopoulos (eds.)
2002 *The Archaeology of Colonialism*. Los Angeles: Getty Research Institute.

Lyons, Diane E.
2007 Building Power in Rural Hinterlands: An Ethnoarchaeological Study of Vernacular Architecture in Tigray, Ethiopia. *Journal of Archaeological Method and Theory* 14.2: 179–207.
2009 How I Built My House: An Ethnoarchaeological Study of Gendered Technical Practice in Tigray, Ethiopia. *Ethnoarchaeology* 1.2: 137–61.

MacCormack, Carol, and Marilyn Strathern (eds.)
1980 *Nature, Culture and Gender*. Cambridge: Cambridge University Press.

Macdonald, Charles
1987 *De la hutte au palais: sociétés à maison en Asie du Sud-Est insulaire*. Paris: Centre national de la recherche scientifique.

MacEachern, Scott, David J. W. Archer, and Richard D. Garvin (eds.)
1989 *Households and Communities: Proceedings of the Twenty-First Annual Conference of the Archaeological Association of the University of Calgary*. Calgary: University of Calgary.

Madella, M., G. Kovács, B. Kulcsarne-Berzsenyi, and I. Briz i Godino (eds.)
2013 *The Archaeology of Household*. Oxford: Oxbow Books.

Mainfort, Robert C., and Lynne P. Sullivan (eds.)
1998 *Ancient Earthen Enclosures of the Eastern Woodlands*. Gainesville: University Press of Florida.

Malone, Caroline
2001 *Neolithic Britain and Ireland*. Stroud: Tempus.

Mann, Michael
1986 *The Sources of Social Power*, Vol.1: *A History of Power from the Beginning to A.D. 1760*. Cambridge: Cambridge University Press.

Mantha, Alexis
2009 Territoriality, Social Boundaries and Ancestor Veneration in the Central Andes of Peru. *Journal of Anthropological Archaeology* 28: 158–76.

Marciniak, Arkadiusz
2011 The Secondary Products Revolution: Empirical Evidence and Its Current Zooarchaeological Critique. *Journal of World Prehistory* 24: 117–30.

Marcus, Joyce

2007 Rethinking Ritual. In *The Archaeology of Ritual*, edited by E. Kyriakidis, pp. 43–76. Los Angeles: Cotsen Institute of Archaeology, UCLA.

Marcus, Joyce, and Jeremy A. Sabloff

2008a (eds.) *The Ancient City: New Perspectives on Urbanism in the Old and New World.* Santa Fe: School for Advanced Research Press.

2008b Introduction. In *The Ancient City: New Perspectives on Urbanism in the Old and New World*, edited by J. Marcus and J. A. Sabloff, pp. 3–26. Santa Fe: School for Advanced Research Press.

Marsden, Donald J.

1976 The Qashqā'i Nomadic Pastoralists of Fars Province. In *The Qashqā'I of Iran*, edited by Whitworth Art Gallery, pp. 9–18. Manchester: Manchester University Press.

Marshall, Fiona

2000 The Origins of Domesticated Animals in Eastern Africa. In *The Origins and Development of African Livestock: Archaeology, Genetics, Linguistics and Ethnography*, edited by K. C. McDonald and R. M. Blench, pp. 191–221. London: University College London Press.

Marshall, Yvonne

1985 Who Made the Lapita Pots? A Case Study in Gender Archaeology. *Journal of the Polynesian Society* 94: 205–33.

Martin, M. Kay, and Barbara Voorhies

1975 *Female of the Species*. New York: Columbia University Press.

Massey, Doreen

1994 *Space, Place and Gender*. Minneapolis: University of Minnesota.

Matson, Richard G.

1996 Households as Economic Organization: A Comparison between Large Houses on the Northwest Coast and in the Southwest. In *People Who Lived in Big Houses: Archaeological Perspectives on Large Domestic Structures*, edited by G. Coupland and E. B. Banning, pp. 107–19. Monographs in World Archaeology, No. 27. Madison, WI: Prehistory Press.

Matthews, Roger

2003 *The Archaeology of Mesopotamia: Theories and Approaches*. London: Routledge.

Maybury-Lewis, David

1967 *Akwẽ-Shavante Society*. Oxford: Clarendon Press.

Mazumdar, Sanjoy, and Shmpa Mazumdar

1997 Intergroup Social Relations and Architecture: Vernacular Architecture and Issues of Status, Power, and Conflict. *Environment and Behavior* 29.3: 374–421.

McCafferty, Sharisse D., and Geoffrey G. McCafferty

1998 Spinning and Weaving as Female Gender Identity in Post-Classic Mexico. In *Reader in Gender Archaeology*, edited by K. Hays-Gilpin and D. S. Whitley, pp. 213–30. London: Routledge.

McCall, John C.

1999 Structure, Agency, and the Locus of the Social: Why Poststructural Theory Is Good for Archaeology. In *Material Symbols: Culture and Economy in Prehistory*, edited by J. E. Robb, pp. 16–20. Center for Archaeological Investigations, Occasional Paper No. 26. Carbondale: Southern Illinois University.

McCauley, Robert N., and E. Thomas Lawson
2007 Cognition, Religious Ritual, and Archaeology. In *The Archaeology of Ritual*, edited by E. Kyriakidis, pp. 209–54. Los Angeles: Cotsen Institute of Archaeology, UCLA.
McGuire, Randall H., and Michael B. Schiffer
1983 A Theory of Architectural Design. *Journal of Anthropological Archaeology* 2: 277–303.
McIntosh, Jane R.
2008 *The Ancient Indus Valley: New Perspectives*. Santa Barbara: ABC/Clio.
McKinnon, Susan
1983 Hierarchy, Alliance and Exchange in the Tanimbar Islands. Ph.D. thesis, University of Chicago.
1991 *From a Shattered Sun: Hierarchy, Gender and Alliance in the Tanimbar Islands*. Madison: University of Wisconsin Press.
1995 Houses and Hierarchies: The View from a South Moluccan Society. In *About the House: Lévi-Strauss and Beyond*, edited by J. Carsten and S. Hugh-Jones, pp. 170–88. Cambridge: Cambridge University Press.
2000 The Tanimbarese *Tavu*: The Ideology of Growth and the Material Configurations of Houses and Hierarchy in an Indonesian Society. In *Beyond Kinship: Social and Material Reproduction in House Societies*, edited by R. A. Joyce and S. D. Gillespie, pp. 161–76. Philadelphia: University of Pennsylvania Press.
McMahon, Gregory
2010 Agency, Identity, and the Hittite State. In *Agency and Identity in the Ancient Near East: New Paths Forward*, edited by S. R. Steadman and J. C. Ross, pp. 181–89. London: Equinox.
Mehrer, Mark W.
1995 *Cahokia's Countryside: Household Archaeology, Settlement Patterns, and Social Power*. DeKalb: Northern Illinois University.
Mellaart, James
1967 *Çatal Hüyük, a Neolithic Town in Anatolia*. New York: McGraw-Hill.
Menze, Björn H., Jason A. Ur, and Andrew G. Sherratt
2006 Detection of Ancient Settlement Mounds: Archaeological Survey Based on the SRTM Terrain Model. *Photogrammetric Engineering and Remote Sensing* 72: 321–27.
Meskell, Lynn
1999 *Archaeologies of Social Life: Age, Sex, Class Etc. in Ancient Egypt*. Oxford: Blackwell.
2001 Archaeologies of Identity. In *Archaeological Theory Today*, edited by I. Hodder, pp. 187–213. Cambridge: Polity Press.
2002 The Intersections of Identity and Politics in Archaeology. *Annual Review of Anthropology* 31: 279–301.
Meskell, Lynn, and Robert W. Preucel (eds.)
2007 *A Companion to Social Archaeology*. Oxford: Blackwell.
Michaelson, Evalyn J., and Walter Goldschmidt
1976 Family and Land in Peasant Ritual. *American Ethnologist* 3.1: 87–96.
Midgley, Magdalena
2005 *Monumental Cemeteries of Prehistoric Europe*. Stroud: Tempus.

Miller, Daniel, Michael Rowlands, and Chris Tilley (eds.)
1995 *Domination and Resistance*. Boston: Unwin Hyman.

Millon, René
1976 Social Relations in Ancient Teotihuacan. In *The Valley of Mexico: Studies in Pre-Hispanic Ecology and Society*, edited by E. R. Wolf, pp. 205–48. Albuquerque: University of New Mexico.

Milisauskas, Sarunas (ed.)
2011 *European Prehistory: A Survey*. 2nd ed. New York: Springer.

Milner, George R.
2012 Mound-Building Societies of the Southern Midwest and Southeast. In *The Oxford Handbook of North American Archaeology*, edited by T. R. Pauketat, pp. 437–46. Oxford: Oxford University Press.

Mitchell, Laura J.
2001 Traces in the Landscape: Hunters, Herders and Farmers on the Cedarberg Frontier, South Africa, 1725–95. *Journal of African History* 43: 431–50.

Mitchell, Peter
2002 *The Archaeology of Southern Africa*. Cambridge: Cambridge University Press.

Mithen, Steven
1996 *The Prehistory of the Mind*. London: Thames & Hudson.
1997 Cognitive Archaeology, Evolutionary Psychology and Cultural Transmission, with Particular Reference to Religious Ideas. *Archaeological Papers of the American Anthropological Association* 7.1: 67–74.
1998 The Supernatural Beings of Prehistory and the External Storage of Religious Ideas. In *Cognition and Material Culture: The Archaeology of Symbolic Storage*, edited by C. Renfrew and C. Scarre, pp. 97–106. Cambridge: McDonald Institute for Archaeological Research.

Molleson, Theya
1994 The Eloquent Bones of Abu Hureyra. *Scientific American* 271.2: 60–65.
2007 Bones of Work at the Origins of Labour. In *Archaeology and Women: Ancient and Modern Issues*, edited by S. Hamilton, R. D. Whitehouse, and K. I. Wright, pp. 185–97. Walnut Creek, CA: Left Coast Press, Inc.

Monroe, J. Cameron
2010 Power by Design: Architecture and Politics in Precolonial Dahomey. *Journal of Social Archaeology* 10.3: 367–97.

Montgomery, Rita E.
1974 A Cross-Cultural Study of Menstruation, Menstrual Taboos, and Related Social Variables. *Ethos* 2.2: 137–70.

Moore, A. M. T., G. C. Hillman, and A. J. Legge
2000 *Village on the Euphrates: From Foraging to Farming at Abu Hureyra*. Oxford: Oxford University Press.

Moore, A. M. T., and T. I. Molleson
2000 Disposal of the Dead. In *From Foraging to Farming at Abu Hureyra*, edited by A. M. T. Moore, G. C. Hillman, and A. J. Legge, pp. 277–299. Oxford: Oxford University Press.

Moore, Henrietta
1996 *Space, Text, and Gender: An Anthropological Study of the Marakwet of Kenya.* New York: Guilford Press.

Moore, Jerry D.
1996a *Architecture and Power in the Ancient Andes: The Archaeology of Public Buildings.* Cambridge: Cambridge University Press.
1996b The Archaeology of Plazas and the Proxemics of Ritual: Three Andean Traditions. *American Anthropologist* 98.4: 789–802.
2003 Archaeology in Search of Architecture. In *Theory and Practice in Mediterranean Archaeology: Old World and New World Perspectives. An Advanced Seminar in Honor of Lloyd Cotsen*, edited by J. K. Papadopoulos and R. M. Levanthal, pp. 235–66. Los Angeles: Cotsen Institute of Archaeology, UCLA.
2005 *Cultural Landscapes in the Ancient Andes: Archaeologies of Place.* Gainesville: University Press of Florida.
2006 The San Quintín–El Rosario Region. In *The Prehistory of Baja California: Advances in the Archaeology of the Forgotten Peninsula*, edited by D. Laylander and J. Moore, pp. 179–95. Gainesville: University Press of Florida.
2012 *The Prehistory of Home.* Berkeley: University of California Press.

Morgan, Christopher
2012 Modeling Modes of Hunter-Gatherer Food Storage. *American Antiquity* 77.4: 714–36.

Morin, Eugène
2001 Early Late Woodland Social Interaction in the St. Lawrence River Valley. *Archaeology of Eastern North America* 29: 65–100.

Morin, Jesse
2010 Ritual Architecture in Prehistoric Complex Hunter-Gatherer Communities: A Potential Example from Keatley Creek, on the Canadian Plateau. *American Antiquity* 75.3: 599–625.

Morris, Ian
1999 Archaeology and Gender Ideologies in Early Archaic Greece. *Transactions of the American Philological Association* 317: 305–17.

Moses, Sharon
2012 Sociopolitical Implications of Neolithic Foundations Deposits and the Possibility of Child Sacrifice: A Case Study at Çatalhöyük, Turkey. In *Sacred Killing: The Archaeology of Sacrifice in the Ancient Near East*, edited by A. M. Porter and G. M. Schwartz, pp. 57–77. Winona Lake, IN: Eisenbrauns.

Mueller, James W.
1975 *Sampling in Archaeology.* Tucson: University of Arizona Press.

Murdock, George P.
1949 *Social Structure.* New York: Macmillan.

Murdock, George P., and Caterina Provost
1973 Factors in the Division of Labor by Sex: A Cross-Cultural Analysis. *Ethnology* 12: 203–25.

Murray, Tim (ed.)
2004 *The Archaeology of Contact Settler Societies.* Cambridge: Cambridge University Press.

Myers, Fred R.
1988 Critical Trends in the Study of Hunter-Gatherers. *Annual Review of Anthropology* 17: 261–82.
Na'amneh, Mahmoud, Mohammed Shunnaq, and Aysegul Tasbasi
2008 The Modern Sociocultural Significance of the Jordanian Bedouin Tent. *Nomadic Peoples* 12.1: 149–63.
Nadal, D.
2003 The Ohalo II Brush Huts and the Dwelling Structures of the Natufian and PPNA Sites in the Jordan Valley. *Archaeology, Ethnology and Anthropology of Eurasia* 13.1: 34–48.
Nadal, D., and I. Hershkovitz
1991 New Subsistence Data and Human Remains from the Earliest Levantine Epipalaeolithic. *Current Anthropology* 32.5: 631–35.
Nadal, David, Ehud Weiss, Orit Simchoni, Alexander Tsatskin, Avinoam Danin, and Mordechai Kislev
2004 Stone Age Hut in Israel Yields World's Oldest Evidence of Bedding. *Proceedings of the National Academy of Sciences* 101.17: 6821–26.
Naess, Marius W., Dondrup Lhagyal, Drolma Yangzom, Per Mathiesen, Joseph L. Fox, and Bård J. Bårdsen
2004 Nomadic Pastoralism in the Aru Basin of Tibet's Chang Tang. *Rangifer* 15: 39–46.
Nakamura, Carolyn
2010 Magical Deposits at Çatalhöyük: A Matter of Time and Place? In *Religion in the Emergence of Civilization: Çatalhöyük as a Case Study*, edited by I. Hodder, pp. 300–331. Cambridge: Cambridge University Press.
Nakhai, Beth A.
2001 *Archaeology and the Religions of Canaan and Israel.* Atlanta: American Schools of Oriental Research.
2011 Varieties of Religious Expression in the Domestic Setting. In *Household Archaeology in Ancient Israel and Beyond*, edited by A. Yasur-Landau, J. R. Ebeling, and L.B. Mazow, pp. 347–60. Leiden: Brill.
Naroll, Raoul
1962 Floor Area and Settlement Population. *American Antiquity* 27.4: 587–89.
Nash, Donna J.
2009 Household Archaeology in the Andes. *Journal of Archaeological Research* 17: 205–61.
Nash, Ronald J.
1997 Archetypal Landscapes and the Interpretation of Meaning. *Cambridge Archaeological Journal* 7.1: 57–69.
Nast, Heidi J.
1996 Islam, Gender, and Slavery in West Africa circa 1500: A Spatial Archaeology of the Kano Palace, Northern Nigeria. *Annals of the Association of American Geographers* 86.1: 44–77.
Naumov, Goce
2007 Housing the Dead: Burials inside Houses and Vessels in the Neolithic Balkans. In *Cult in Context: Reconsidering Ritual in Archaeology*, edited by D. A. Barrowclough and C. Malone, pp. 257–68. Oxford: Oxbow.

2010 Neolithic Anthropocentrism: Imagery Principles and Symbolic Manifestation of Corporeality in the Balkans. *Documenta Praehistorica* 37: 227–38.

2013 Embodied Houses: The Social and Symbolic Agency of Neolithic Architecture in the Republic of Macedonia. In *Tracking the Neolithic House in Europe: Sedentism, Architecture and Practice*, edited by D. Hofmann and J. Smyth, pp. 65–94. New York: Springer.

Naveh, Danny

2003 PPNA Jericho: A Socio-Political Perspective. *Cambridge Archaeological Journal* 13.1: 83–96.

Nelson, Margaret, Donna Glowacki, and Annette Smith

2002 The Impact of Women on Household Economies: A Maya Case Study. In *In Pursuit of Gender: Worldwide Archaeological Approaches*, edited by S. M. Nelson and M. Rosen-Ayalon, pp. 125–54. Walnut Creek, CA: AltaMira Press.

Nelson, Sarah M.

2004 *Gender in Archaeology: Analyzing Power and Prestige*. 2nd ed. Walnut Creek. CA: AltaMira Press.

2006 (ed.) *Handbook of Gender in Archaeology*. Lanham, MD: AltaMira Press.

2007 (ed.) *Women in Antiquity: Theoretical Approaches to Gender and Archaeology*. Lanham, MD: AltaMira Press.

2014 *Shamans, Queens, and Figurines: The Development of Gender Archaeology*. Walnut Creek: Left Coast Press, Inc.

Nelson, Sarah M., and Myriam Rosen-Ayalon (eds.)

2002 *In Pursuit of Gender: Worldwide Archaeological Approaches*. Walnut Creek, CA: AltaMira Press.

Netting, Robert M.

1982 Some Home Truths on Household Size and Wealth. *American Behavioral Scientist* 25: 641–62.

Netting, Robert McC., Richard R. Wilk, and Eric J. Arnould (eds.)

1984 *Households: Comparative and Historical Studies of the Domestic Group*. Berkeley: University of California Press.

Nevett, Lisa

1994 Separation or Seclusion? Towards an Archaeological Approach to Investigating Women in the Greek Household in the Fifth to Third Centuries BC. In *Architecture and Order: Approaches to Social Space*, edited by M. Parker Pearson and C. Richards, pp. 98–112. London: Routledge.

1999 *House and Society in the Ancient Greek World*. Cambridge: Cambridge University Press.

2007 Domestic Architecture and Household Wealth: The Case of Ancient Greece. In *The Durable House: House Society Models in Archaeology*, edited by R. A. Beck, Jr., pp. 365–79. Center for Archaeological Investigations, Occasional Paper No. 35. Carbondale: Southern Illinois University.

2010 *Domestic Space in Classical Antiquity*. Cambridge: Cambridge University Press.

Nielsen, Axel E.

2009 Pastoralism and the Non-Pastoral World in the Late Pre-Columbian History of the Southern Andes (1000–1535). *Nomadic Peoples* 13.2: 17–35.

Nishimura, Yoko

2007 The North Mesopotamian Neighborhood: Domestic Activities and Household Space at Titriş Höyük. *Near Eastern Archaeology* 70.1: 53–56.

2012 The Life of the Majority: A Reconstruction of Household Activities and Residential Neighborhoods at the Late-Third-Millennium Urban Settlement at Titriş Höyük in Northern Mesopotamia. In *New Perspectives on Household Archaeology*, edited by B. J. Parker and C. P. Foster, pp. 347–72. Winona Lake, IN: Eisenbrauns.

Nissen, Hans J.

1988 *The Early History of the Ancient near East 9000–2000 B.C.* Chicago: Chicago University Press.

Oates, Joan, August McMahon, Philip Karsgaard, Salam al-Quntar, and Jason Ur

2007 Early Mesopotamian Urbanism: A View from the North. *Antiquity* 81.313: 585–600.

Oetelaar, Gerald A.

1993 Identifying Site Structure in the Archaeological Record: An Illinois Mississippian Example. *American Antiquity* 58.4: 662–87.

O'Gorman, Jodie A.

2010 Exploring the Longhouse Community in Tribal Society. *American Antiquity* 75.3: 571–97.

Oliver, Paul

1987 *Dwellings: The House across the World.* Austin: University of Texas Press.

Olsen, Bjønar

1998 Saqqaq Housing and Settlement in Southern Disko Bay, West Greenland. *Acta Borealia: A Nordic Journal of Circumpolar Societies* 15.2: 81–128.

Orhun, D., B. Hillier, and J. Hanson

1995 Spatial Types in Traditional Turkish Homes. *Environment and Planning B: Planning and Design* 22: 475–98.

Ortner, Sherry B.

1974 Is Female to Male as Nature Is to Culture? In *Women, Culture, and Society*, edited by M. Z. Rosaldo and L. Lamphere, pp. 67–87. Stanford, CA: Stanford University Press.

1997 *Making Gender: The Politics and Erotics of Culture*. Boston: Beacon Press.

Ortner, Sherry B., and Harriet Whitehead (eds.)

1981 *Sexual Meanings*. Cambridge: Cambridge University Press.

Osborne, James F.

2014 *Approaching Monumentality in Archaeology*. Albany: State University of New York Press.

Osborne, Robin

2004 Hoards, Votives, offerings: The Archaeology of the Dedicated Object. *World Archaeology* 36.1: 1–10.

Oswald, Dana Beth

1987 The Organization of Space in Residential Buildings: Cross-Cultural Perspective. In *Method and Theory for Activity Area Research: An Ethnoarchaeological Approach*, edited by S. Kent, pp. 295–344. New York: Cambridge University Press.

Owen, Linda R.
2000 Lithic Functional Analysis as a Means of Studying Gender and Material Culture in Prehistory. In *Gender and Material Culture in Archaeological Perspective*, edited by M. Donald and L. Hurcombe, pp. 185–205. London: MacMillan Press.

Oyuela-Caycedo, Augusto
1990 Ideology and Structure of Gender Spaces: The Case of the Kaggaba Indians. In *The Archaeology of Gender: Proceedings of the Twenty-Second Annual Conference of the Archaeological Association of the University of Calgary*, edited by D. Walde and N. D. Willows, pp. 327–35. Calgary: University of Calgary.

Özbal, Rana
2012 The Challenge of Identifying Households at Tell Kurdu (Turkey). In *New Perspectives on Household Archaeology*, edited by B. J. Parker and C. P. Foster, pp. 321–46. Winona Lake, IN: Eisenbrauns.

Özbaşaran, Mihriban
1998 The Heart of a House: The Hearth. Aşıklı Höyük, A Pre-pottery Neolithic Site in Central Anatolia. In *Light on Top of the Black Hill: Studies Presented to Halet Çambel*, edited by G. Arsebük, M. J. Mellink, and W. Schirmer, pp. 555–66. Istanbul: EGE Yayınlarım.

Özgenel, Lale
2007 Public Use and Privacy in Late Antique Houses in Asia Minor: The Architecture of Spatial Control. In *Housing in Late Antiquity, From Palaces to Shops*, edited by L. Lavan, L. Özgenel, and A. Sarantis, pp. 239–81. Leiden: Brill.

Özgüç, Tahsin
2005 *Kültepe*. Istanbul: Yapi Kredi Yayınları.

Paige, Karen E., and Jeffrey M. Paige
1981 *The Politics of Reproductive Ritual*. Berkeley: University of California Press.

Paine, Richard R. (ed.)
1997 *Integrating Archaeological Demography: Multidisciplinary Approaches to Prehistoric Population*. Center for Archaeological Investigations, Occasional Paper 24. Carbondale: Southern Illinois University.

Papagianni, Dimitra, Robert Layton, and Herbert Maschner (eds.)
2008 *Time and Change: Archaeological and Anthropological Perspectives on the Long-Term in Hunter-Gatherer Societies*. Oxford: Oxbow.

Papanek, Hanna
1973 Separate Worlds and Symbolic Shelter. *Comparative Studies in Society and History* 15.3: 289–325.

Papineau, David
1987 *Reality and Representation*. Oxford: Blackwell.

Parker, Bradley J., and Catherine Foster (eds.)
2012 *New Perspectives on Household Archaeology*. Winona Lake, IN: Eisenbrauns.

Parker Pearson, Michael
2000 *The Archaeology of Death and Burial*. College Station: Texas A&M University Press.

Parker Pearson, Michael, Ramilsonina, and Retsihisatse
1999 Ancestors, Forests and Ancient Settlements: Tandroy Readings of the Archaeological Past. In *The Archaeology and Anthropology of Landscape: Shaping Your Landscape*, edited by P. J. Ucko and R. Layton, pp. 397–410. London: Routledge.

Parker Pearson, Michael, and Colin Richards (eds.)

1994 *Architecture and Order: Approaches to Social Space*. London: Routledge.

Parkes, Peter

1987 Livestock Symbolism and Pastoral Ideology among the Kafirs of the Hindu Kush. *Man* 22.4: 637–60.

Parkington, John

2002 Men, Women, and Eland: Hunting and Gender among the San of Southern Africa. In *In Pursuit of Gender: Worldwide Archaeological Approaches*, edited by S. M. Nelson and M. Rosen-Ayalon, pp. 93–117. Walnut Creek, CA: AltaMira Press.

Parsons, Jeffrey R.

1972 Archaeological Settlement Patterns. *Annual Review of Anthropology* 1: 127–50.

Pasternak, Burton, Carol R. Ember, and Melvin Ember

1976 On the Conditions Favoring Extended Family Households. *Journal of Anthropological Research* 32.2: 109–23.

Pauketat, Timothy R.

1994 *The Ascent of Chiefs: Cahokia and Mississippian Politics in Native North America*. Tuscaloosa: University of Alabama Press.

2000 The Tragedy of the Commoners. In *Agency in Archaeology*, edited by M.-A. Dobres and J. E. Robb, pp. 113–29. London: Routledge.

2004 *Ancient Cahokia and the Mississippians*. Cambridge: Cambridge University Press.

2013 *An Archaeology of the Cosmos: Rethinking Agency and Religion in Ancient America*. New York: Routledge.

Pauketat, Timothy R., and Susan M. Alt

2003 Mounds, Memory, and Contested Mississippian History. In *Archaeologies of Memory*, edited by R. Van Dyke and S. Alcock, pp. 149–79. Oxford: Blackwell.

Paz, Sarit

2012 Changing Households at the Rise of Urbanism: The EB I–II Transition at Tel Bet Yerah. In *New Perspectives on Household Archaeology*, edited by B. J. Parker and C. P. Foster, pp. 407–34. Winona Lake, IN: Eisenbrauns.

Pechtl, Joachim

2009 A Monumental Prestige Patchwork. In *Creating Communities: New Advances in Central European Neolithic Research*, edited by D. Hofmann and P. Bickle, pp. 186–201. Oxford: Oxbow.

Peebles, Christopher, and Susan Kus

1977 Some Archaeological Correlates of Ranked Society. *American Antiquity* 42: 421–48.

Peirce, Leslie P.

1993 *The Imperial Harem: Women and Sovereignty in the Ottoman Empire*. Oxford: Oxford University Press.

Pellow, Deborah

1999 The Power of Space in the Evolution of an Accra Zongo. In *Theorizing New Urban Anthropology Reader*, edited by S. Low, pp. 277–314. Highland Park, NJ: Rutgers University Press.

2003 The Architecture of Female Seclusion in West Africa. In *The Anthropology of Space and Place: Locating Culture*, edited by S. M. Low and D. Lawrence-Zúñiga, pp. 160–83. Oxford: Blackwell.

Pendergast, James F.
1975 An In-Situ Hypothesis to Explain the Origin of the St. Lawrence Iroquoians. *Ontario Archaeology* 25: 47–51.
Pennock, J. Roland, and John W. Chapman (eds.)
1971 *Privacy*. Nomos XIII. New York: Atherton Press.
Peregrine, Peter
1991 Some Political Aspects of Craft Specialization. *World Archaeology* 23: 1–11.
Peterson, Jane
2002 *Sexual Revolutions: Gender and Labor at the Dawn of Agriculture*. Walnut Creek, CA: AltaMira Press.
Peterson, Christian E., and Gideon Shelach
2012 Jiangzhai: Social and Economic Organization of a Middle Neolithic Chinese Village. *Journal of Anthropological Archaeology* 31: 265–301.
Philip, Graham
2001 The Early Bronze I–III Ages. In *The Archaeology of Jordan*, edited by B. MacDonald, R. Adams, and P. Bienkowski, pp. 163–232. Sheffield: Sheffield Academic Press.
Plimpton, C. L., and F. A. Hassan
1987 Social Space: A Determinant of House Architecture. *Environment and Planning B: Planning and Design* 14: 439–49.
Pluckhahn, Thomas J.
2010 Household Archaeology in the Southeastern United States: History, Trends, and Challenges. *Journal of Archaeological Research* 18.4: 331–85.
Polat, Fecri
2013 *Doğu Anadolu Yayla Kültürü ve Yayla Mimiarisi*: *Etnoarkeolojik Bir Bakiş*. Istanbul: Arkeoloji ve Sanat Yayinlari.
Pollock, Nancy Lee
1981. Women on the Inside: Divisions of Space in Imperial China. *Heresies* II 3.3: 34–37.
Pollock, Susan
1999 *Ancient Mesopotamia*. Cambridge: Cambridge University Press.
2003 Feasts, Funerals, and Fast Food in Early Mesopotamian States. In *The Archaeology and Politics of Food and Feasting in Early States and Empires*, edited by T. L. Bray, pp. 17–38. New York: Kluwer Academic/Plenum.
Porteous, J. Douglas
1977 *Environment and Behavior: Planning and Everyday Urban Life*. Reading, MA: Addison-Wesley.
Porter, Anne
2010 Considering Power and Intent in Third-Millennium BCE Mesopotamia. In *Agency and Identity in the Ancient Near East: New Paths Forward*, edited by S. R. Steadman and J. C. Ross, pp. 166–80. London: Equinox.
2012 *Mobile Pastoralism and the Formation of Near Eastern Civilizations: Weaving Together Society*. Cambridge: Cambridge University Press.
Portnoy, Alice W.
1981 A Microarchaeological View of Human Settlement Space and Function. In *Modern Material Culture: The Archaeology of Us*, edited by R. A. Gould and M. B. Schiffer, pp. 213–224. New York: Academic Press.

Possehl, Gregory
2002 *The Indus Civilization: A Contemporary Perspective.* Walnut Creek, CA: AltaMira Press.
2005 Mohenjo-Daro: The Symbolic Landscape of an Ancient City. In *Structure and Meaning in Human Settlements,* edited by T. Atkin and J. Rykwert, pp. 67–83. Philadelphia: University of Pennsylvania Museum of Archaeology and Anthropology.
Postgate, J. N.
1992 *Early Mesopotamia: Society and Economy at the Dawn of History.* London: Routledge.
Potter, James M.
2000 Ritual, Power, and Social Differentiation in Small-Scale Societies. In *Hierarchies in Action. Cui Bono?,* edited by M. W. Diehl, pp. 295–316. Occasional Papers No. 27. Carbondale: Southern Illinois University.
Powers, Marla N.
1980 Menstruation and Reproduction: An Oglala Case. *Signs* 6.1: 54–65.
Pred, Allen
1990 *Making Histories and Constructing Human Geographies.* Boulder, CO: Westview.
Prentiss, Anna Marie, Natasha Lyons, Lucille E. Harris, Melisse R. P. Burns, and Terrence M. Godin
2007 The Emergence of Status Inequality in Intermediate Scale Societies: A Demographic and Socio-Economic History of the Keatley Creek Site, British Columbia. *Journal of Anthropological Archaeology* 26: 299–327.
Prentiss, William C., and Ian Kuijt (eds.)
2004 *Complex Hunter-Gatherers: Evolution and Organization of Prehistoric Communities on the Plateau of Northwestern North America.* Salt Lake City: University of Utah Press.
Press, Michael
2011 A Problem of Definition: "Cultic" and "Domestic" Contexts in Iron Age Philistia. In *Household Archaeology in Ancient Israel and Beyond,* edited by A. Yasur-Landau, J. Ebeling, and L. Mazow, pp. 361–89. Leiden: Brill.
Preucel, Robert W.
2000 Making Pueblo Communities: Architectural Discourse at Kotyiti, New Mexico. In *The Archaeology of Communities. A New World Perspective,* edited by M. A. Canuto and J. Yaeger, pp. 58–77. London: Routledge.
2002 *Archaeologies of the Pueblo Revolt: Identity, Meaning, and the Renewal in the Pueblo World.* Albuquerque: University of New Mexico Press.
2006 *Archaeological Semiotics.* Oxford: Blackwell.
Preziosi, Donald
1979 *The Semiotics of the Built Environment: An Introduction to Architectonic Analysis.* Bloomington: Indiana University Press.
1983 *Minoan Architectural Design, Formation and Signification.* New York: Mouton.
Price, Neil (ed.)
2001 *The Archaeology of Shamanism.* London: Routledge.
Price, T. Douglas, and James A. Brown (eds.)
1985 *Prehistoric Hunter-Gatherers: The Emergence of Cultural Complexity.* Orlando, FL: Academic Press.

Price, T. Douglas, and Gary M. Feinman (eds.)
1995 *Foundations of Social Inequality*. New York: Plenum.
Price-Beggerly, Patricia
1981 Don't Fence Me In. In *Modern Material Culture: The Archaeology of Us*, edited by R. A. Gould and M. B. Schiffer, pp. 127–35. New York: Academic Press.
Prussin, Labelle
1974 An Introduction to Indigenous African Architecture. *Journal of the Society of Architectural Historians* 33.3: 182–205.
1995 *African Nomadic Architecture: Space, Place and Gender*. Washington, DC: Smithsonian Institution Press.
1996 When Nomads Settle: Changing Technologies of Building and Transport and the Production of Architectural Form among the Gabra, the Rendille, and the Somalis. In *African Material Culture*, edited by M. J. Arnoldi, C. M. Geary, and K. L. Hardin, pp. 73–102. Bloomington: Indiana University Press.
Purdue, Theda
1998 *Cherokee Women: Gender and Culture Change*. Lincoln: University of Nebraska.
Pyzel, Joanna
2013 Change and Continuity in the Danubian Longhouses of Lowland Poland. In *Tracking the Neolithic House in Europe: Sedentism, Architecture, and Practice*, edited by D. Hofmann and J. Smyth, pp. 183–96. New York: Springer.
Radovanović, Ivana
1996 *The Iron Gates Mesolithic*. International Monographs in Prehistory Archaeological Series 11. Ann Arbor: International Monographs in Prehistory.
1997 The Culture of Lepenski Vir: A Contribution to the Interpretation of Its Ideological Aspects. In *Antidoron Dragoslavo Srejovici Completis LXV Annis ad Amicis, Collegis, Discipulis Oblatum*, pp. 85–93. Belgrade: Centar za Arheološka Istraživanja, Filozofski Fakultet.
2000 Houses and Burials at Lepenski Vir. *European Journal of Archaeology* 3.3: 330–49.
Rapoport, Amos
1969 *House Form and Culture*. Upper Saddle River, NJ: Prentice-Hall.
1976 (ed.) *The Mutual Interaction of People and the Built Environment*. The Hague: Mouton.
1980 Vernacular Architecture and the Cultural Determinants of Form. In *Buildings and Society: Essays on the Social Development of the Built Environment*, edited by A. D. King, pp. 283–305. London: Routledge.
1982 *The Meaning of the Built Environment: A Nonverbal Communication Approach*. Beverly Hills: Sage.
1988 Levels of Meaning in the Built Environment. In *Cross-Cultural Perspectives in Nonverbal Communication*, edited by F. Poyatos, pp. 317–336. Toronto: C.J. Hogrefe.
1990 Systems of Activities and Systems of Settings. In *Domestic Architecture and the Use of Space*, edited by S. Kent, pp. 9–20. Cambridge: Cambridge University Press.
2005 *Culture, Architecture, and Design*. Chicago: Locke Science Publications.
2006 Archaeology and Environment-Behavior Studies. *Archaeological Papers of the American Anthropological Association* 16.1: 59–70.
2008 Environment-Behavior Studies: Past, Present, and Future. *Journal of Architectural and Planning Research* 25.4: 276–81.

Rapp, Reyna
1979 Examining Family History: Household and Family. *Feminist Studies* 5: 175–81.
Rappaport, Roy
1999 *Ritual and Religion in the Making of Humanity.* Cambridge: Cambridge University Press.
Rasmussen, Susan
2001 Pastoral Nomadism and Gender: Status and Prestige, Economic Contribution, and Division of Labor among the Tuareg of Niger. In *Gender in Cross-Cultural Perspective*, 3rd ed., edited by C. B. Brettell and C. E. Sargent, pp. 280–93. Upper Saddle, NJ: Prentice-Hall.
Ratnagar, Shereen
2001 *Understanding Harappa: Civilization in the Greater Indus Valley.* New Delhi: Tulika.
Read, Dwight W., and Steven A. LeBlanc
1978 Descriptive Statements, Covering Laws, and Theories in Archaeology. *Current Anthropology* 19.2: 307–35.
Regev, Eyal
2011 Royal Ideology in the Hasmonaean Palaces in Jericho. *Bulletin of the American Schools of Oriental Research* 363: 45–72.
Reid, Andrew, Paul Lane, Alinah Segobye, Lowe Borjeson, Nonofo Mathibidi, and Princess Sekgarametso
1997 Tswana Architecture and Responses to Colonialism. *World Archaeology* 28.3: 370–92.
Reinhardt, Gregory A.
2002 Puzzling Out Gender-Specific "Sides" to a Prehistoric House in Barrow, Alaska. In *Many Faces of Gender: Roses and Relationships through Time in Indigenous Northern Communities*, edited by L. Frink, R. S. Shepard, and G. A. Reinhardt, pp. 121–50. Boulder: University Press of Colorado.
Reiter, Rayna
1975 Men and Women in the South of France: Public and Private Domains. In *Toward an Anthropology of Women*, edited by R. R. Reiter, pp. 252–82. New York: Monthly Review Press.
Renfrew, Colin
1982 *Toward an Archaeology of Mind.* Cambridge: Cambridge University Press.
1994 The Archaeology of Religion. In *The Ancient Mind: Elements of Cognitive Archaeology*, edited by C. Renfrew and E. B. W. Zubrow, pp. 47–54. Cambridge: Cambridge University Press.
2001 Commodification and Institution in Group-Oriented and Individualizing Societies. In *The Origin of Human Social Institutions*, edited by W. G. Runciman, pp. 93–117 Oxford: Oxford University Press.
2007a Ritual and Cult in Malta and Beyond: Traditions of Interpretation. In *Cult in Context*, edited by D. Barrowclough and C. Malone, pp. 8–13. Oxford: Oxbow.
2007b The Archaeology of Ritual, of Cult, and of Religion. In *The Archaeology of Ritual*, edited by E. Kyriakidis, pp. 109–22. Los Angeles: Cotsen Institute of Archaeology, UCLA.
2009a Demography and Archaeology. *Human Biology* 81.2–3: 381–84.

2009b Situating the Creative Explosion: Universal or Local? In *Becoming Human: Innovation in Prehistoric Material and Spiritual Culture*, edited by C. Renfrew and I. Morley, pp. 74–92. Cambridge: Cambridge University Press.

2012 Towards a Cognitive Archaeology: Material Engagement and the Early Development of Society. In *Archaeological Theory Today*, 2nd ed., edited by I. Hodder, pp. 124–45. Cambridge: Polity Press.

Renfrew, Colin, Christopher D. Firth, and Lambros Malafouris (eds.)

2009 *The Sapient Mind: Archaeology Meets Neuroscience*. Oxford: Oxford University Press.

Renfrew, Colin, and John F. Cherry (eds.)

1986 *Peer Polity Interaction and Socio-Political Change*. Cambridge: Cambridge University Press.

Renfrew, Colin, and Ezra B. W. Zubrow (eds.)

1994 *The Ancient Mind: Elements of Cognitive Archaeology*. Cambridge: Cambridge University Press.

Rives, James B.

2007 *Religion in the Roman Empire*. Oxford: Blackwell.

Robb, John E.

1998 The Archaeology of Symbols. *Annual Review of Anthropology* 27: 329–46.

1999a Secret Agents: Culture, Economy, and Social Reproduction. In *Material Symbols: Culture and Economy in Prehistory*, edited by J. E. Robb, pp. 3–15. Carbondale: Southern Illinois University Press.

1999b (ed.) *Material Symbols: Culture and Economy in Prehistory*. Center for Archaeological Investigations, Occasional Paper No. 26. Carbondale: Southern Illinois University Press.

Robertson, Elizabeth C., Jeffrey D. Seibert, Deepika C. Fernandez, and Marc U. Zender (eds.)

2006 *Space and Spatial Analysis in Archaeology*. Alberta: University of Calgary Press.

Robin, Cynthia

2003 New Directions in Classic Maya Household Archaeology. *Journal of Archaeological Research* 11.4: 307–56.

Rocek, Thomas R.

1995 Sedentarization and Agricultural Dependence: Perspectives from the Pithouse-to-Pueblo Transition in the American Southwest. *American Antiquity* 60.2: 218–39.

1998 Pithouses and Pueblos on Two Continents: Interpretations of Sedentism and Mobility in the Southwestern United States and Southwest Asia. In *Seasonality and Sedentism: Archaeological Perspectives from Old and New World Sites*, edited by T. R. Rocek and O. Bar-Yosef, pp. 199–216. Peabody Museum Bulletin 6. Cambridge: Harvard University.

Rodning, Christopher B.

2009 Mounds, Myths, and Cherokee Townhouses in Southwestern North Carolina. *American Antiquity* 74.4: 627–63.

Roehmer, Michael K.

2012 Thinking of Ancestors (and Others) at Japanese Household Altars. *Journal of Ritual Studies* 26.1: 33–45.

Rogers, J. Daniel
1995 The Archaeological Analysis of Domestic Organization. In *Mississippian Communities and Households*, edited by J. D. Rogers and B. D. Smith, pp. 7–31. Tuscaloosa: University of Alabama Press.
Rogers, J. Daniel, and Bruce D. Smith (eds.)
1995 *Mississippian Communities and Households*. Tuscaloosa: University of Alabama Press.
Rollefson, Gary O.
1986 Neolithic 'Ain Ghazal (Jordan): Ritual and Ceremony II. *Paléorient* 12.1: 45–52.
1997 Changes in Architecture and Social Organization at 'Ain Ghazal. In *The Prehistory of Jordan II*, edited by H. G. Gebel, Z. A. Kafafi, and G. O. Rollefson, pp. 287–307. Berlin: Ex oriente.
Rollefson, Gary O., and Alan H. Simmons
1987 The Life and Death of 'Ain Ghazal. *Archaeology* 40.6: 38–45.
Rollefson, Gary O., Halan H. Simmons, and Zeidan Kafafi
1992 Neolithic Cultures at 'Ain Ghazal, Jordan. *Journal of Field Archaeology* 19: 443–71.
Rosaldo, Michelle Z.
1974 Women, Culture, and Society: A Theoretical Overview. In *Women, Culture, and Society*, edited by M. Z. Rosaldo and L. Lamphere, pp. 17–42. Stanford, CA: Stanford University Press.
1980 The Use and Abuse of Anthropology: Reflections on Feminism and Cross-Cultural Understanding. *Signs: Journal of Women in Culture and Society* 5.3: 389–417.
Rosaldo, Michelle Z., and Louise Lamphere (eds.)
1974 *Women, Culture, and Society*. Stanford, CA: Stanford University Press.
Rosenberg, Michael
1998 Cheating at Musical Chairs: Territoriality and Sedentism in an Evolutionary Context. *Current Anthropology* 39.5: 653–81.
Rosenberg, Michael, and Aslı Erim-Özdoğan
2011 The Neolithic in Southeastern Anatolia. In *The Oxford Handbook of Ancient Anatolia*, edited by S. R. Steadman and G. McMahon, pp. 125–49. Oxford: Oxford University Press.
Rosenberg, Michael, and Robert W. Redding
2000 Hallan Çemi and Early Village Organization in Eastern Anatolia. In *Life in Neolithic Farming Communities: Social Organization, Identity, and Differentiation*, edited by I. Kuijt, pp. 39–61. New York: Kluwer Academic/Plenum.
Ross, Jennifer C.
2010 The Scribal Artifact: Technological Innovation in the Uruk Period. In *Agency and Identity in the Ancient Near East: New Paths Forward*, edited by S. R. Steadman and J. C. Ross, pp. 80–98. London: Equinox.
Ross, Jennifer C., and Sharon R. Steadman
2010 Agency and Identity in the Ancient Near East: New Paths Forward. In *Agency and Identity in the Ancient Near East: New Paths Forward*, edited by S. R. Steadman and J. C. Ross, pp. 1–10. London: Equinox.
forthcoming *Ancient Complex Societies: An Archaeology of Civilization*. Walnut Creek, CA: Left Coast Press, Inc.

Rossano, Matt J.
2007 Supernaturalizing Social Life: Religion and the Evolution of Human Cooperation. *Human Nature* 18: 272–94.
2011 Setting Our Own Terms: How We Used Ritual to Become Human. In *Neuroscience, Consciousness and Spirituality*, edited by H. Walach, S. Schmidt, and W. B. Jonas, pp. 39–56. New York: Springer.
2013 *Mortal Rituals*. New York: Columbia University Press.

Rossignol, Jacqueline, and LuAnn Wandsnider (eds.)
1992 *Space, Time, and Archaeological Landscapes*. New York: Plenum Press.

Roth, Barbara J. (ed.)
2010 *Engendering Households in the Prehistoric Southwest*. Tucson: University of Arizona Press.

Routledge, Bruce
2013 Household Archaeology in the Levant. *Bulletin of the American Schools of Oriental Research* 370: 207–19.

Rowan, Yorke M.
2012 Beyond Belief: The Archaeology of Religion and Ritual. *Archaeological Papers of the American Anthropological Association* 21.1: 1–10.

Rowlands, Michael
1994 The Politics of Identity in Archaeology. In *Social Construction of the Past: Representation as Power*, edited by G. C. Bond and A. Gilliam, pp. 129–143. London: Routledge.

Rowlands, Michael, Mogens Larsen, and Kristian Kristiansen (eds.)
1987 *Centre and Periphery in the Ancient World*. Cambridge: Cambridge University Press.

Rowley-Conwy, Peter
1991 Time, Change and the Archaeology of Hunter-Gatherers: How Original Is the "Original Affluent Society"? In *Hunter-Gatherers: An Interdisciplinary Perspective*, edited by C. Panter-Brick, R. H. Layton, and P. Rowley-Conwy, pp. 39–72. Cambridge: Cambridge University Press.

Rowton, Michael
1973 Urban Autonomy in a Nomadic Environment. *Journal of Near Eastern Studies* 32.2: 201–15.
1974 Enclosed Nomadism. *Journal of the Economic and Social History of the Orient* 17: 1–30.

Rüpke, Jörg
2007 *Religion of the Romans*. Cambridge: Polity.

Russell, Lynette
2004 Drinking from the Penholder: Intentionality and Archaeological Theory. *Cambridge Archaeological Journal* 14.1: 64–67.
2005 "Either, or, Neither Nor": Resisting the Production of Gender, Race and Class Dichotomies in the Pre-Colonial Period. In *The Archaeology of Plural and Changing Identities: Beyond Identification*, edited by E. C. Casella and C. Fowler, pp. 33–53. New York: Kluwer Academic/Plenum.

Russell, Nerissa
2012a *Social Zooarchaeology: Humans and Animals in Prehistory*. New York: Cambridge.

2012b Hunting Sacrifice at Neolithic Çatalhöyük. In *Sacred Killing: The Archaeology of Sacrifice in the Ancient Near East*, edited by A. M. Porter and G. M. Schwartz, pp. 79–95. Winona Lake, IN: Eisenbrauns.

Russell, Nerissa, and Amy Bogaard

2010 Subsistence Actions at Çatalhöyük. In *Agency and Identity in the Ancient Near East: New Paths Forward*, edited by S. R. Steadman and J. C. Ross, pp. 63–79. London: Equinox.

Russell, Nerissa, Louise Martin, and Katheryn C. Twiss

2009 Building Memories: Commemorative Deposits at Çatalhöyük. *Anthropozoologica* 44.1: 103–25.

Russell, Nerissa, and Stephanie Meece

2006 Animal Representations and Animal Remains at Çatalhöyük. In *Çatalhöyük Perspectives: Reports from the 1995–99 Seasons*, edited by I. Hodder, pp. 209–30. Cambridge: McDonald Institute for Archaeological Research.

Sack, Robert D.

1986 *Human Territoriality: Its Theory and History*. Cambridge: Cambridge University Press.

Sadr, Karim

1998 The First Herders at the Cape of Good Hope. *African Archaeological Review* 15: 101–32.

2003 The Neolithic of Southern Africa. *Journal of African History* 44: 195–209.

2008 Invisible Herders? The Archaeology of Khoekhoe Pastoralists. *Southern African Humanities* 20: 179–203.

Sahlins, Marshall

1972 *Stone Age Economics*. London: Tavistock.

Saidel, Benjamin A.

1993 Round House or Square? Architectural Form and Socio-Economic Organization in the PPNB. *Journal of Mediterranean Archaeology* 6: 65–108

Saitta, Dean J.

1999 Prestige, Agency, and Change in Middle-Range Societies. In *Material Symbols: Culture and Economy in Prehistory*, edited by J. E. Robb, pp. 135–49. Center for Archaeological Investigations, Occasional Paper No. 26. Carbondale: Southern Illinois University.

Salisbury, Roderick B., and Dustin Keeler (eds.)

2007 *Space—Archaeology's Final Frontier? An Intercontinental Approach*. Newcastle: Cambridge Scholars Publishing.

Salzman, Philip C.

1967 Political Organization among Nomadic Peoples. *Proceedings of the American Philosophical Society* 111.2: 115–31.

Samson, Ross (ed.)

1990 *The Social Archaeology of Houses*. Edinburgh: Edinburgh University Press.

Sanday, Peggy R.

1981 *Female Power and Male Dominance: On the Origins of Sexual Inequality*. Cambridge: Cambridge University Press.

Sanders, Donald

1990 Behavioral Conventions and Archaeology: Methods for the Analysis of Ancient Architecture. In *Domestic Architecture and the Use of Space*, edited by S. Kent, pp. 43–72. Cambridge: Cambridge University Press.

Sanders, William T., Jeffrey R. Parsons, and Robert S. Santley

1979 *The Basin of Mexico: Ecological Patterns and the Evolution of a Civilization*. New York: Academic Press.

Sanderson, Stephen K.

1999 *Social Transformations: A General Theory of Historical Development*. Lanham, MD: Rowman and Littlefield Publishers.

Santley, Robert S., and Kenneth Hirth (eds.)

1993 *Prehispanic Domestic Units in Western Mesoamerica: Studies of the Household, Compound, and Residence*. Boca Raton: CRC Press.

Sassaman, Kenneth E.

1992 Lithic Technology and the Hunter-Gatherer Sexual Division of Labor. *North American Archaeologist* 13: 249–62.

1998 Lithic Technology and the Hunter-Gatherer Sexual Division of Labor. In *Reader in Gender Archaeology*, edited by K. Hays-Gilpin and D. S. Whitley, pp. 159–71. Oxford: Routledge.

2004 Complex Hunter-Gatherers in Evolution and History: A North American Perspective. *Journal of Archaeological Research* 12.3: 227–80.

2005 Poverty Point as Structure, Event, Process. *Journal of Archaeological Method and Theory* 12.4: 335–63.

Saunders, Nicholas J.

1994 At the Mouth of the Obsidian Cave: Deity and Place in Aztec Religion. In *Sacred Sites, Sacred Places*, edited by D. L. Carmichael, J. Hubert, B. Reeves and A. Schanche, pp. 172–83. London: Routledge.

Saunders, Tom

1990 The Feudal Construction of Space: Power and Domination in the Nucleated Village. In *The Social Archaeology of Houses*, edited by R. Samson, pp. 181–96. Edinburgh: Edinburgh University Press.

Scarre, Chris

2008 Shrines of the Land and Places of Power: Religion and the Transition to Farming in Western Europe. In *Belief in the Past: Theoretical Approaches to the Archaeology of Religion*, edited by D. S. Whitley and K. Hays-Gilpin, pp. 209–26. Walnut Creek, CA: Left Coast Press, Inc.

Scarry, John F.

1995 Apalachee Homesteads: The Basal Social and Economic Units of a Mississippian Chiefdom. In *Mississippian Communities and Households*, edited by J. D. Rogers and B. D. Smith, pp. 201–23. Tuscaloosa: University of Alabama Press.

Scarry, John F., and Bonnie G. McEwan

1995 Domestic Architecture in Apalachee Province: Apalachee and Spanish Residential Styles in the Late Prehistoric and Early Historic Period Southeast. *American Antiquity* 60.3: 482–95.

Schachner, Gregson
2010 Corporate Group Formation and Differentiation in Early Puebloan Villages of the American Southwest. *American Antiquity* 75.3: 473–96.
Schacht, Robert
1981 Estimating Past Population Trends. *Annual Review of Anthropology* 10: 119–40.
Schaub, R. Thomas
1981 Patterns of Burial at Bab edh-Dhraʿ. *Annual of the American Schools of Oriental Research* 46: 45–68.
Schaub, R. Thomas, and Walter E. Rast
1989 *Bab edh-Dhraʿ, Excavations in the Cemetery Directed by Paul W. Lapp (1965–1967).* Winona Lake, IN: Eisenbrauns.
Scheflen, Albert E., and Norman Ashcraft
1976 *Human Territories: How We Behave in Space-Time.* Englewood Cliffs, NJ: Prentice-Hall.
Schefold, Reimar, Gaudenz Domenig, and Peter J. M. Nas (eds.)
2003 *Indonesian Houses: Tradition and Transformation in Vernacular Architecture.* Leiden: Kitlv Press.
Schirmer, Wulf
1990 Some Aspects of Building at the "Aceramic-Neolithic" Settlement of Cayonu Tepesi. *World Archaeology* 12.3: 363–87.
Schlanger, Nathan
1994 Mindful Technology: Unleashing the *chaîne opératoire* for an Archaeology of Mind. In *The Ancient Mind: Elements of Cognitive Archaeology*, edited by C. Renfrew and E. B. W. Zubrow, pp. 143–51. Cambridge: Cambridge University Press.
Schlanger, Sarah H.
1988 Patterns of Population Movement and Long-Term Population Growth in Southwestern Colorado. *American Antiquity* 53.4: 773–93.
Schlegel, Alice
1972 *Male Dominance and Female Autonomy: Domestic Authority in Matrilineal Societies.* New Haven, CT: Human Relations Area Files.
Schloen, J. David
2001 *The House of the Father as Fact and Symbol: Patrimonialism in Ugarit and the Ancient Near East.* Winona Lake, IN: Eisenbrauns.
Schmidt, Klaus
1998 Beyond Daily Bread: Evidence of Early Neolithic Ritual from Göbekli Tepe. *Neo-Lithics* 2/98: 1–5.
2002 The 2002 Excavations at Göbekli Tepe (Southeastern Turkey): Impressions from an Enigmatic Site. *Neo-Lithics* 2/02: 8–13.
2006 *Sie Bauten die ersten Tempel: das rätselhafte Heiligtum der Steinzeitjäger.* Munich: Deutscher Taschenbuch.
2008 Die zähnefletschenden Raubtiere des Göbekli Tepe. In *Fundstellen: Gesammelte Schriften zur Archäologie und Geschichte Altvorderasiens ad honorem Hartmut Kühne*, edited by D. Bonatz, R. M. Czichon, and F. J. Kreppner, pp. 61–69. Wiesbaden: Harrassowitz.
2010 Göbekli Tepe—The Stone Age Sanctuaries. New Results of Ongoing Excavations with a Special Focus on Sculptures and High Reliefs. *Documenta Praehistorica* 37: 239–56.

2011 Göbekli Tepe: A Neolithic Site in Southeastern Anatolia. In *The Oxford Handbook of Ancient Anatolia*, edited by S. R. Steadman and G. McMahon, pp. 917–33. Oxford: Oxford University Press.

Schmidt, Peter R., and Bertram B. Mapunda
1997 Ideology and the Archaeological Record in Africa: Interpreting Symbolism in Iron Smelting Technology. *Journal of Anthropological Archaeology* 16: 73–102.

Schoenauer, Norbert
2000 *6,000 Years of Housing*. Rev. ed. New York: W. W. Norton and Co.

Schreiber, Katharina J., and Keith W. Kintigh
1996 A Test of the Relationship between Site Size and Population. *American Antiquity* 61.3: 573–79.

Schrire, Carmel
1988 The Historical Archaeology of the Impact of Colonialism in 17th-Century South Africa. *Antiquity* 62: 214–25.
1995 *Digging through Darkness: Chronicles of an Archaeologist*. Charlottesville: University of Virginia Press.

Scott, Eleanor
1990 Romano-British Villas and the Social Construction of Space. In *The Social Archaeology of Houses*, edited by R. Samson, pp. 149–72. Edinburgh: University of Edinburgh.

Searle, John
1983 *Intentionality*. Cambridge: Cambridge University Press.

Seeman, Mark F.
1979 Feasting with the Dead: Ohio Hopewell Charnel House Ritual as a Context for Redistribution. In *Hopewell Archaeology: The Chillicothe Conference*, edited by D. Brose and N. Greber, pp. 39–46. Kent, OH: Kent State University Press.

Sellet, Frédéric
1993 *Chaîne Opératoire:* The Concept and Its Applications. *Lithic Technology* 18: 106–12.

Sept, Jeanne M.
1992 Was There No Place Like Home? A New Perspective on Early Hominid Archaeological Sites from the Mapping of Chimpanzee Nests. *Current Anthropology* 33.2: 187–207.

Shafer, Harry J.
1995 Architecture and Symbolism in Transitional Pueblo Development in the Mimbres Valley, SW New Mexico. *Journal of Field Archaeology* 22.1: 23–47.

Shahack-Gross, Ruth, Fiona Marshall, Kathleen Ryan, and Steve Weiner
2004 Reconstruction of Spatial Organization in Abandoned Maasai Settlements: Implications for Site Structure in the Pastoral Neolithic of East Africa. *Journal of Archaeological Science* 31: 1395–1411.

Shahack-Gross, Ruth, Riona Marshall, and Steve Weiner
2003 Geo-Ethnoarchaeology of Pastoral Sites: The Identification of Livestock Enclosures in Abandoned Maasai Settlements. *Journal of Archaeological Science* 30: 439–59.

Shennan, Stephen
1994 (ed.) *Archaeological Approaches to Cultural Identity*. London: Routledge.
2009 Evolutionary Demography and the Population History of the European Early Neolithic. *Human Biology* 81.2–3: 339–55.

Sherratt, Andrew

1981 Plough and Pastoralism: Aspects of the Secondary Products Revolution. In *Patterns of the Past: Studies in Honour of David Clarke*, edited by I. Hodder, G. Isaac, and N. Hammond, pp. 261–305. Cambridge: Cambridge University Press.

1983 The Secondary Exploitation of Animals in the Old World. *World Archaeology* 15.1: 90–104.

Shott, Michael J.

2001 Crises in Forager Studies, Ethnographic and Archaeological. *Reviews in Anthropology* 29: 211–32.

Silberbauer, George

1982 Political Process in G/wi Bands. In *Politics and History in Band Societies*, edited by E. Leacock and R. Lee, pp. 23–35. Cambridge: Cambridge University Press.

Silverman, Eric K.

2001 *Masculinity, Motherhood, and Mockery: Psychoanalyzing Culture and the Iatmul Naven Rite in New Guinea*. Ann Arbor: University of Michigan Press.

Simmons, Alan H.

2011 *The Neolithic Revolution in the Near East: Transforming the Human Landscape.* Tucson: University of Arizona Press.

Simms, Steven R.

1988 The Archaeological Structure of a Bedouin Camp. *Journal of Archaeological Science* 15: 197–211.

Singer-Avitz, Lily

2011 Household Activities at Tel Beersheba. In *Household Archaeology in Ancient Israel and Beyond*, edited by A. Yasur-Landau, J. R. Ebeling, and L. B. Mazow, pp. 275–301. Leiden: Brill.

Sircar, Kanika

1987 The House as a Symbol of Identity. In *Mirror and Metaphor: Material and Social Constructions of Reality*, edited by D. W. J. Ingersoll and G. Bronitsky, pp. 298–309. Lanham, MD: University Press of America.

Small, David B., and Nicola Tannenbaum (eds.)

1999 *At the Interface: The Household and Beyond*. Monographs in Economic Anthropology No. 15. Lanham, MD: University Press of America.

Smith, Adam T.

2001 The Limitations of Doxa: Agency and Subjectivity from an Archaeological Point of View. *Journal of Social Archaeology* 1.2: 155–71.

2003 *The Political Landscape: Constellations of Authority in Early Complex Polities*. Los Angeles: University of California Press.

Smith, Andrew B.

2008 Is Absence of Evidence, Evidence of Absence? Problems in the Archaeology of Early Herding Societies of Southern Africa. In *The Archaeology of Mobility: Old World and New World Nomadism*, edited by H. Barnard and W. Wendrich, pp. 264–79. Los Angeles: Cotsen Institute of Archaeology, UCLA.

2005 *African Herders: Emergence of Pastoral Traditions*. Walnut Creek, CA: AltaMira Press.

Smith, Bruce D.

1978 *Mississippian Settlement Patterns*. New York: Academic Press.

Smith, Claire

1999 Ancestors, Place and People: Social Landscapes in Aboriginal Australia. In *The Archaeology and Anthropology of Landscape: Shaping Your Landscape*, edited by P. J. Ucko and R. Layton, pp. 189–205. London: Routledge.

Smith, David G., and Gary W. Crawford

1997 Recent Developments in the Archaeology of the Princess Point Complex in Southern Ontario. *Canadian Journal of Archaeology* 21.1: 9–32.

Smith, Michael E.

1987 Household Possessions and Wealth in Agrarian States: Implications for Archaeology. *Journal of Anthropological Archaeology* 6: 297–335.

2007 Form and Meaning in the Earliest Cities: A New Approach to Ancient Urban Planning. *Journal of Planning History* 6: 3–47.

2009 V. Gordon Childe and the Urban Revolution: A Historical Perspective on a Revolution in Urban Studies. *Town Planning Review* 80.1: 3–29.

2010 The Archaeological Study of Neighborhoods and Districts in Ancient Cities. *Journal of Anthropological Archaeology* 29: 137–54.

Smith, Monica L.

2003a (ed.) *The Social Construction of Ancient Cities.* Washington, DC: Smithsonian Institution Press.

2003b Introduction: The Social Construction of Ancient Cities. In *The Social Construction of Ancient Cities*, edited by M. L. Smith, pp. 1–36. Washington, DC: Smithsonian Institution Press.

Snellgrove, David L.

2004 *Angkor—Before and After: A Cultural History of the Khmers.* Bangkok: Orchid.

Snow, Dean R.

1995 Migration in Prehistory: The Northern Iroquoian Case. *American Antiquity* 60.1: 59–79.

1996 More on Migration in Prehistory: Accommodating New Evidence in the Northern Iroquoian Case. *American Antiquity* 61.4: 791–96.

Sobel, Elizabeth A., D. Ann Trieu Gahr, and Kenneth M. Ames (eds.)

2006 *Household Archaeology on the Northwest Coast.* Ann Arbor: International Monographs in Prehistory.

Sommer, R.

1969 *Personal Space: The Behavioral Basis of Design.* Englewood Cliffs, NJ: Prentice-Hall.

Souvatzi, Stella G.

2008 *A Social Archaeology of Households in Neolithic Greece: An Anthropological Approach.* Cambridge: Cambridge University Press.

2012 Between the Individual and the Collective: Household as a Social Process in Neolithic Greece. In *New Perspectives on Household Archaeology*, edited by B. J. Parker and C. P. Foster, pp. 15–43. Winona Lake, IN: Eisenbrauns.

Souvatzi, Stella, and Athena Hadji (eds.)

2014 *Space and Time in Mediterranean Prehistory.* New York: Routledge.

Sørensen, Marie Louise S.

2000 *Gender Archaeology.* Cambridge: Polity Press.

Spain, Daphne

1992 *Gendered Spaces.* Chapel Hill: University of North Carolina Press.

1993 Gendered Spaces and Women's Status. *Sociological Theory* 11.2: 137–51.

Spence, Kate

2004 The Three-Dimensional Forms of the Amarna House. *Journal of Egyptian Archaeology* 90: 123–52.

2007 A Contextual Approach to Ancient Egyptian Domestic Cult: The Case of the "Lustration Slabs" at El-Amarna. In *Cult in Context: Reconsidering Ritual in Archaeology*, edited by D. A. Barrowclough and C. Malone, pp. 285–92. Oxford: Oxbow.

Spencer, Charles S.

1993 Human Agency, Biased Transmission, and the Cultural Evolution of Chiefly Authority. *Journal of Anthropological Archaeology* 12: 41–74.

Speth, John D., and Katherine A. Spielmann

1983 Energy Source, Protein Metabolism, and Hunter-Gatherer Subsistence Strategies. *Journal of Anthropological Archaeology* 2: 1–31.

Spielmann, Katherine A.

2002 Feasting, Craft Specialization, and the Ritual Mode of Production in Small-Scale Societies. *American Anthropologist* 104.1: 195–207.

2009 Seip Mound State Memorial. Ross Country, South Central Ohio: Seip Earthworks and Mounds: Ancient Ritual Spaces. In *Archaeology in America: An Encyclopedia*, edited by F. P. McManamon, L. S. Cordell, K. G. Lightfoot, G. R. Milner, pp. 115–18. Westport, CT: Greenwood Press.

Spindler, Louise S.

1977 *Culture Change and Modernization: Mini-Models and Case Studies*. Prospect Heights, IL: Waveland Press.

Srejović, Dragoslav

1972 *Europe's First Monumental Sculpture: New Discoveries at Lepenski Vir*. New York: Stein and Day.

Stanish, Charles

2009 The Evolution of Managerial Elites in Intermediate Societies. In *The Evolution of Leadership: Transitions in Decision Making from Small-Scale to Middle Range Societies*, edited by K. J. Vaughn, J. W. Eerkens, and J. Kantner, pp. 97–119. Santa Fe: School for Advanced Research Press.

Stark, Miriam T.

1998 (ed.) *The Archaeology of Social Boundaries*. Washington, DC: Smithsonian Institution Press.

2004 Pre-Angkorian and Angkorian Cambodia. In *A Cultural History of Southeast Asia: From Earliest Times to the Indic Civilizations*, edited by P. Bellwood and I. Glover, pp. 89–119. New York: Routledge, Curzon.

Startin, W.

1978 Linear Pottery Culture Houses: Reconstruction and Manpower. *Proceedings of the Prehistoric Society* 44: 143–59.

Steadman, Lyle B., Craig T. Palmer, and Christopher F. Tilley

1996 The Universality of Ancestor Worship. *Ethnology* 35.1: 63–76.

Steadman, Sharon R.

1996 Recent Research in the Archaeology of Architecture: Beyond the Foundations. *Journal of Archaeological Research* 4.1: 51–93.

2000 Spatial Patterning and Social Complexity on Prehistoric Near Eastern "Tell" Sites: Models for Mounds. *Journal of Anthropological Archaeology* 19: 164–99.

2004 Heading Home: The Architecture of Family and Society in Early Sedentary Communities on the Anatolian Plateau. *Journal of Anthropological Research* 60.4: 515–58.

2005 Reliquaries on the Landscape: Mounds as Matrices of Human Cognition. In *Archaeologies of the Middle East: Critical Perspectives*, edited by S. Pollock and R. Bernbeck, pp. 286–307. Oxford: Blackwell.

2009 *Archaeology of Religion: Cultures and Their Beliefs in Worldwide Context.* Walnut Creek, CA: Left Coast Press, Inc.

2010 Agency, Architecture, and Archaeology: Prehistoric Settlements in Central Anatolia. In *Agency and Identity in the Ancient Near East: New Paths Forward*, edited by S. R. Steadman and J. C. Ross, pp. 27–46. London: Equinox.

2011 Take Me to Your Leader: The Power of Place in Prehistoric Anatolian Settlements. *Bulletin of the American Schools of Oriental Research* 363: 1–24.

Steadman, Sharon R., Gregory McMahon, and Jennifer C. Ross

2007 The Late Chalcolithic at Çadır Höyük in Central Anatolia. *Journal of Field Archaeology* 32.4: 385–406.

Steadman, Sharon R., Gregory McMahon, Jennifer C. Ross, Marica Cassis, Jeffrey D. Geyer, Benjamin Arbuckle, and Madelynn von Baeyer

2013 The 2009 and 2012 Seasons of Excavation at Çadır Höyük on the Anatolian North Central Plateau. *Anatolica* 39: 113–67.

Steadman, Sharon R., and Jennifer C. Ross (eds.)

2010 *Agency and Identity in the Ancient Near East: New Paths Forward.* London: Equinox.

Stefanović, Sofija, and Dušan Borić

2008 New-born Infant Burials Underneath House Floors at Lepenski Vir: In Pursuit of Contextual Meanings. In *The Iron Gates in Prehistory: New Perspectives*, edited by C. Bonsall, V. Boroneanţ, and I. Radovanović, pp. 131–74. BAR International Series 1893. Oxford: Archaeopress.

Stein, Gil J.

1999 *Rethinking World-Systems; Diasporas, Colonies, and Interaction in Uruk Mesopotamia.* Tucson: University of Arizona Press.

2002 Colonies without Colonialism: A Trade Diaspora Model of Fourth Millennium B.C. Mesopotamian Enclaves in Anatolia. In *The Archaeology of Colonialism*, edited by C. Lyons and J. Papadopoulos, pp. 27–64. Los Angeles: Getty Research Institute.

2005a (ed.) *The Archaeology of Colonial Encounters: Comparative Perspectives.* Santa Fe: School of American Research Advanced Seminar Series.

2005b The Political Economy of Mesopotamian Colonial Encounters. In *The Archaeology of Colonial Encounters: Comparative Perspectives*, edited by G. J. Stein, pp. 143–71. Santa Fe: School of American Research Advanced Seminar Series.

Stein, John R., and Stephen H. Lekson

1992 Anasazi Ritual Landscapes. In *Anasazi Regional Organization and the Chaco System*, edited by D. E. Doyel, pp. 87–100. Anthropological Papers No. 5. Albuquerque: University of New Mexico Maxwell Museum of Anthropology.

Stevens, Anna

2006 *Private Religion at Amarna: The Material Evidence.* BAR International Series 1587. Oxford: Archaeopress.

Stewart, Pamela J., and Andrew Strathern

2002 Power and Placement in Blood Practices. *Ethnology* 41.4: 349–63.

Stockett, Miranda K.

2005 On the Importance of Difference: Re-Envisioning Sex and Gender in Ancient Mesoamerica. *World Archaeology* 37.4: 566–78.

Stokes, Robert J., and Barbara J. Roth

1999 Mobility, Sedentism, and Settlement Patterns in Transition: The Late Pithouse Period in the Sapillo Valley, New Mexico. *Journal of Field Archaeology* 26.4: 423–34.

Stone, Elizabeth C.

1987 *Nippur Neighborhoods.* Studies in Ancient Oriental Civilization, No. 44. Chicago: Oriental Institute Publications.

2007 (ed.) *Settlement and Society: Essays Dedicated to Robert McCormick Adams.* Los Angeles: Cotsen Institute of Archaeology, UCLA.

Stone, Elizabeth C., and Paul Zimansky

2004 *The Anatomy of a Mesopotamian City: Survey and Soundings at Mashkan-Shapir.* Winona Lake, IN: Eisenbrauns.

Stopp, Marianne P.

2002 Ethnohistoric Analogues for Storage as an Adaptive Strategy in Northeastern Subarctic Prehistory. *Journal of Anthropological Archaeology* 21: 301–28.

Stordeur, Danielle

2000 New Discoveries in Architecture and Symbolism at Jerf el Ahmar (Syria), 1997–1999. *Neo-Lithics* 1/00: 1–4.

2003a Des crânes surmodelés à Tell Aswad de Damascène (PPNB–Syrie). *Paléorient* 29.2: 109–16.

2003b Symboles et imaginaire des premières cultures néolithiques du Proche-Orient (Haute et Moyenne Vallée d L'Euphrate). In *Arts et symboles du Néolithique à la protohistoire*, edited by J. Guilaine, pp. 15–36. Paris: Errance.

Stordeur, Danielle, and Frédéric Abbès

2002 Du PPNA au PPNB: Mise en lumière d'un phase de transition at Jerf el Ahmar (Syrie). *Bulletin de la Société préhistorique française* 99: 563–95.

Sullivan, Lynne P.

1995 Mississippian Household and Community Organization in Eastern Tennessee. In *Mississippian Communities and Households*, edited by J. D. Rogers and B. D. Smith, pp. 99–123. Tuscaloosa: University of Alabama Press.

Sumner, William M.

1989 Population and Settlement Area: An Example from Iran. *American Anthropologist* 91.3: 631–41.

Svoboda, Jiři, Sandra Sázelová, Pavel A. Kosintsev, Vlasta Jankovská, and Martin Holub

2011 Resources and Spatial Analysis at Actual Nenets Campsites: Ethnoarchaeological Implications. *Journal of Anthropological Archaeology* 20: 30–43.

Sweely, Tracy L.

1999a Gender, Space, People, and Power at Cerén, El Salvador. In *Manifesting Power: Gender and the Interpretation of Power in Archaeology*, edited by T. L. Sweely, pp. 155–71. London: Routledge.

1999b (ed.) *Manifesting Power: Gender and the Interpretation of Power in Archaeology.* London: Routledge.

Swidler, W. W.

1972 Some Demographic Factors Regulating the Formation of Flocks and Camps among the Brahui of Baluchistan. In *Perspectives on Nomadism*, edited by W. Irons and N. Dyson-Hudson, pp. 69–75. Leiden: E. J. Brill.

Sykes, Kay

1989 The Chief's House, Symbol of Power. In *Households and Communities: Proceedings of the Twenty-First Annual Conference of the Archaeological Association of the University of Calgary*, edited by S. MacEachern, D. J. W. Archer and R. D. Garvin, pp. 490–501. Calgary: University of Calgary.

Szabo, Albert, and Thomas J. Barfield

1991 *Afghanistan: An Atlas of Indigenous Domestic Architecture*. Austin: University of Texas Press.

Taçon, Paul S. C.

1999 Identifying Ancient Sacred Landscapes in Australia: From Physical to Social. In *Archaeologies of Landscape: Contemporary Perspectives*, edited by W. Ashmore and A. B. Knapp, pp. 33–57. Oxford: Blackwell.

Tedlock, Dennis, and Arthur Sze

2013 *An Archaeology of Architecture: Photowriting the Built Environment*. Albuquerque: University of New Mexico Press.

Terrell, John Edward, and John P. Hart

2008 Domesticated Landscapes. In *Handbook of Landscape Archaeology*, edited by B. David and J. Thomas, pp. 328–32. Walnut Creek, CA: Left Coast Press, Inc.

Testart, Alain

1982 The Significance of Food Storage among Hunter-Gatherers: Residence Patterns, Population Densities, and Social Inequalities. *Current Anthropology* 23.5: 523–37.

Thau, Michael

2002 *Consciousness and Cognition*. Oxford: Oxford University Press.

Theodoratus, Dorothea J., and Frank LaPena

1994 Wintu Sacred Geography of Northern California. In *Sacred Sites, Sacred Places*, edited by D. L. Carmichael, J. Hubert, B. Reeves and A. Schanche, pp. 20–31. London: Routledge.

Thomas, John S., and Robbins, Michael C.

1985 Social Status and Settlement Pattern Features: A Tojolabal Maya Example. *Human Organization* 44.2: 172–76.

Thomas, Julian

1996 *Time, Culture and Identity: An Interpretative Archaeology*. London: Routledge.

2008 Archaeology, Landscape, and Dwelling. In *Handbook of Landscape Archaeology*, edited by B. David and J. Thomas, pp. 300–306. Walnut Creek, CA: Left Coast Press, Inc.

Tilley, Christopher

1994 *A Phenomenology of Landscape: Places, Paths and Monuments*. Oxford: Berg.

2009 *Interpreting Landscapes: Geologies, Topographies, Identities; Explorations in Landscape Phenomenology 3*. Walnut Creek, CA: Left Coast Press, Inc.

Toll, H. Wolcott

2001 Making and Breaking Pots in the Chaco World. *American Antiquity* 66.1: 56–78.

Torrence, Robin
2008 Punctuated Landscapes: Creating Cultural Places in Volcanically Active Environments. In *Handbook of Landscape Archaeology*, edited by B. David and J. Thomas, pp. 333–43. Walnut Creek, CA: Left Coast Press, Inc.

Torrence, Robin, and Anne Clarke
2000 *The Archaeology of Difference: Negotiating Cross-Cultural Engagements in Oceania.* One World Archaeology 38. London: Routledge.

Trigger, Bruce G.
1967 Settlement Archaeology—Its Goals and Promise. *American Antiquity* 32: 149–60.
1985 *Natives and Newcomers: Canada's "Heroic Age" Reconsidered.* Montreal: McGill-Queen's University Press.
1990 Monumental Architecture: A Thermodynamic Explanation of Symbolic Behaviour. *World Archaeology* 22.2: 119–32.
2003 *Understanding Early Civilizations.* Cambridge: Cambridge University Press.

Tringham, Ruth E.
1991a Households with Faces: The Challenge of Gender in Prehistoric Architectural Remains. In *Engendering Archaeology*, edited by J. M. Gero and M. W. Conkey, pp. 93–131. Oxford: Blackwell.
1991b Men and Women in Prehistoric Architecture. *Traditional Dwellings and Settlements Review* 3: 9–28.
1994 Engendered Places in Prehistory. *Gender, Place and Culture* 1: 169–203.
2005 Weaving House Life and Death into Places: A Blueprint for Hypermedia Narrative. In *(Un)settling the Neolithic*, edited by D. W. Bailey, A. Whittle, and V. Cummings, pp. 98–111. Oxford: Oxbow Press.

Tuan, Yi-Fu
1974 *Topophilia: A Study of Environmental Perception, Attitudes, and Values.* New York: Columbia University Press.
1977 *Space and Place: The Perspective of Experience.* Minneapolis: University of Minnesota Press.

Turnbull, Colin M.
1961 *The Forest People.* New York: Simon & Schuster, Inc.

Turner, Victor
1967 *The Forest of Symbols: Aspects of Ndembu Ritual.* Ithaca: Cornell University Press.

Ucko, Peter J., and Robert Layton (eds.)
1999 *The Archaeology and Anthropology of Landscape: Shaping your Landscape.* London: Routledge.

Ucko, Peter, Ruth Tringham, and Geoffrey W. Dimbleby (eds.)
1972 *Man, Settlement and Urbanism.* London: Duckworth.

Uerkvitz, Ralf
1992 Settlement Size and Demographic Inferences: A Structural Approach. *Journal of Quantitative Anthropology* 3: 297–323.

Ujam, Faozi
2006 The Cosmological Genesis of the Courtyard House. In *Courtyard Housing: Past, Present and Future*, edited by B. Edwards, M. Sibley, M. Hakmi, and P. Land, pp. 95–107. New York: Taylor & Francis.

Upham, Steadman
1990 Analog or Digital? Toward a Generic Framework for Explaining the Development of Emergent Political Systems. In *The Evolution of Political Systems: Sociopolitics in Small-Scale Sedentary Societies*, edited by S. Upham, pp. 87–115. Cambridge: Cambridge University Press.

Ur, Jason
2003 CORONA Satellite Photography and Ancient Road Networks: A Northern Mesopotamian Case Study. *Antiquity* 77.1: 102–15.

Ur, Jason, and Emily Hammer
2009 Pastoral Nomads of the 2nd and 3rd Millennia A.D. on the Upper Tigris River, Turkey: The Hirbemerdon Tepe Survey. *Journal of Field Archaeology* 24: 37–56.

van de Mieroop, Marc
1999 *The Ancient Mesopotamian City*. Oxford: Oxford University Press.

van de Walle, Etienne, and Elisha P. Renne (eds.)
2001 *Regulating Menstruation: Beliefs, Practices, Interpretations*. Chicago: University of Chicago Press.

Van der Leeuw, Sander
1993 Giving the Potter a Choice: Conceptual Aspects of Pottery Techniques. In *Technological Choices. Transformations in Material Cultures since the Neolithic*, edited by P. Lemonnier, pp. 238–88. London: Routledge.
1994 Cognitive Aspects of "Technique." In *The Ancient Mind: Elements of Cognitive Archaeology*, edited by C. Renfrew and E. B. W. Zubrow, pp. 135–42. Cambridge: Cambridge University Press.

Van Dyke, Ruth M.
1999 Space Syntax Analysis at the Chacoan Outlier of Guadalupe. *American Antiquity* 64.3: 461–73.
2003 Memory and the Construction of Chacoan Society. In *Archaeologies of Memory*, edited by R. M. Van Dyke and S. E. Alcock, pp. 180–200. Oxford: Blackwell.

Van Gijseghem, Hendrik
2001 Household and Family at Moche, Peru: An Analysis of Building and Residence Patterns in a Prehispanic Urban Center. *Latin American Antiquity* 12.3: 257–73.

Van Gijseghem, Hendrik, and Kevin J. Vaughn
2008 Regional Integration and the Built Environment in Middle-Range Societies: Paracas and Early Nasca Houses and Communities. *Journal of Anthropological Archaeology* 27.1: 111–30.

VanPool, Todd L., and Christine S. VanPool
2003 Agency and Evolution: The Role of Intended and Unintended Consequences of Action. In *Essential Tensions in Archaeological Method and Theory*, edited by T. L. VanPool and C. S. VanPool, pp. 89–113. Salt Lake City: University of Utah Press.

van Sittert, Lance
2002 The Rural Enclosure Movement in the Cape Colony, c. 1865–1910. *Journal of African History* 43.1: 95–118.

Ventsel, Aimar
2012 Reindeer, Social Relations and Networks in a Post-Socialist Arctic Community: The Dolgan in Sakha. In *Who Owns the Stock? Collective and Multiple Property*

Rights in Animals, edited by A. M. Khazanov and G. Schlee, pp. 45–64. Oxford: Berghan Books.

Verhoeven, Marc

2002 Ritual and Ideology in the Pre-Pottery Neolithic B of the Levant and Southeast Anatolia. *Cambridge Archaeology Journal* 12: 233–58.

2006 Megasites in the Jordanian Pre-Pottery Neolithic B: Evidence for "Proto-Urbanism"? In *Domesticating Space: Construction, Community, and Cosmology in the Late Prehistoric Near East*, edited by E. B. Banning and M. Chazan, pp. 75–79. Studies in Early Near Eastern Production, Subsistence, and Environment 6. Berlin: Ex oriente.

2011a Retrieving the Supernatural: Ritual and Religion in the Prehistoric Levant. In *The Oxford Handbook of the Archaeology of Ritual and Religion*, edited by T. Insoll, pp. 795–810. Oxford: Oxford University Press.

2011b The Many Dimensions of Ritual. In *The Oxford Handbook of the Archaeology of Ritual and Religion*, edited by T. Insoll, pp. 115–32. Oxford: Oxford University Press.

Vidale, Massimo

2010 Aspects of Palace Life at Mohenjo-Daro. *South Asian Studies* 26.1: 59–76.

Vierich, Helga I. D., and Robert K. Hitchcock

1996 Kūa: Farmer/Foragers of the Eastern Kalahari, Botswana. In *Cultural Diversity among Twentieth-Century Foragers: An African Perspective*, edited by S. Kent, pp. 108–24. Cambridge: Cambridge University Press.

Vita-Finzi, Claudio

1978 *Archaeological Sites in Their Setting*. London: Thames and Hudson.

Voss, Barbara L.

2000 Feminisms, Queer theories, and the Archaeological Study of Past Sexualities. *World Archaeology* 32: 180–92.

Wadley, Lyn

1998 The Invisible Meat Providers: Women in the Stone Age of South Africa. In *Gender in African Prehistory*, edited by S. Kent, pp. 69–81. Walnut Creek, CA: AltaMira Press.

2000 The Use of Space in a Gender Study of Two South African Stone Age Sites. In *Gender and Material Culture in Archaeological Perspective*, edited by M. Donald and L. Hurcombe, pp. 153–68. London: MacMillan Press.

Waguespack, Nicole M.

2005 The Organization of Male and Female Labor in Foraging Societies: Implications for Early Paleoindian Archaeology. *American Anthropologist* 107.4: 666–76.

Waites, Margaret C.

1920 The Nature of the *Lares* and Their Representation in Roman Art. *American Journal of Archaeology* 24.3: 241–61.

Walde, Dale, and Noreen D. Willows (eds.)

1991 *The Archaeology of Gender: Proceedings of the Twenty-Second Annual Conference of the Archaeological Association of the University of Calgary*. Calgary: University of Calgary.

Walker, Susan

1983 Women and Housing in Classical Greece. In *Images of Women in Classical Antiquity*, edited by A. Cameron and A. Khurt, pp. 81–91. London: Croom Helm.

Wang, Shuo
2004 The Selection of Women for the Qing Imperial Harem. *The Chinese Historical Review* 11.2: 212–22.
Warrick, Gary
1989 Trends in Huron Family, Household and Community Size, A.D. 900–A.D. 1650. In *Households and Communities: Proceedings of the Twenty-First Annual Conference of the Archaeological Association of the University of Calgary*, edited by S. MacEachern, D. J. W. Archer, and R. D. Garvin, pp. 277–86. Calgary: University of Calgary.
1996 Evolution of the Iroquoian Longhouse. In *People Who Lived in Big Houses: Archaeological Perspectives on Large Domestic Structures*, edited by G. Coupland and E. B. Banning, pp. 11–26. Madison, WI: Prehistory Press.
2000 The Precontact Iroquoian Occupation of Southern Ontario. *Journal of World Prehistory* 14.4: 415–66.
Wason, Paul K.
1994 *The Archaeology of Rank*. Cambridge: Cambridge University Press.
2010 The Neolithic Cosmos of Çatalhöyük. In *Religion in the Emergence of Civilization: Çatalhöyük as a Case Study*, edited by I. Hodder, pp. 268–99. Cambridge: Cambridge University Press.
Waterson, Roxana
1990 *The Living House: An Anthropology of Architecture in South-East Asia*. Singapore: Oxford University Press.
1995 Houses and Hierarchies in Island Southeast Asia. In *About the House: Lévi-Strauss and Beyond*, edited by J. Carsten and S. Hugh-Jones, pp. 47–68. Cambridge: Cambridge University Press.
2000 House, Place, and Memory in Tana Toraja (Indonesia). In *Beyond Kinship: Social and Material Reproduction in House Societies*, edited by R. A. Joyce and S. D. Gillespie, pp. 177–88. Philadelphia: University of Pennsylvania Press.
Watkins, Trevor
1990 The Origins of House and Home? *World Archaeology* 21.3: 336–47.
2004a Architecture and "Theatres of Memory" in the Neolithic of Southwest Asia. In *Rethinking Materiality: The Engagement of Mind with the Material World*, edited by E. DeMarrais, C. Gosden, and C. Renfrew, 97–106. Cambridge: McDonald Institute for Archaeological Research.
2004b Building Houses, Framing Concepts, Constructing Worlds. *Paléorient* 30.1: 5–23.
2005 From Foragers to Complex Societies in Southwest Asia. In *The Human Past: World Prehistory and the Development of Human Societies*, edited by C. Scarre, pp. 200–233. London: Thames and Hudson.
2006 Architecture and the Symbolic Construction of New Worlds. In *Domesticating Space: Construction, Community and Cosmology in the Late Prehistoric Near East*, edited by E. B. Banning and M. Chazan, pp. 15–24. Berlin: Ex oriente.
2009 Ordering Time and Space: Creating a Cultural World. In *Proceedings of the 5th International Congress on the Archaeology of the Ancient Near East*, edited by J. M. Córdoba, M. Molist, M. C. Pérez, I. Rubio, and S. Martínez, pp. 647–59. Madrid: Centro Superior de Estudios Sobre el Oriente Próximo y Egipto.
2012 Household, Community and Social Landscape: Maintaining Social Memory in the Early Neolithic of Southwest Asia. In *As Time Goes By? Monumentality, Landscapes*

and the Temporal Perspective, edited by M. Furholt, M. Hinz, and D. Mischka, pp. 23–44. Bonn: Verlag Dr. Rudolf Habelt GmbH.

Watkins, Trevor, K. Dobney, and Mark Nesbitt

1995 *Qermez Dere, Tel Afar: Interim Report No. 3*. Project Paper No. 14. Edinburgh: University of Edinburgh.

Watson, O. Michael

1970 *Proxemic Behavior: A Cross-Cultural Study*. The Hague: Mouton.

Watson, O. Michael, and Theodore D. Graves

1966 Quantitative Research in Proxemic Behavior. *American Anthropologist* 68.4: 971–85.

Watson, Patty Jo

1978 Architectural Differentiation in Some Near Eastern Communities, Prehistoric and Contemporary. In *Social Archaeology*, edited by C. Redman, M. J. Berman, E. V. Curtin, W. T. Langhorne Jr., N. M. Versaggi, and J. C. Wanser, pp. 131–57. New York: Academic Press.

1979 *Archaeological Ethnography in Western Iran*. Viking Fund Publications in Anthropology 57. Tucson: University of Arizona.

Webb, Jennifer M.

2002 Engendering the Built Environment: Household and Community in Prehistoric Bronze Age Cyprus. In *Engendering Aphrodite: Women and Society in Ancient Cyprus*, edited by D. Bolger and N. Serwint, pp. 87–101. American Schools of Oriental Research Archaeological Reports 7. Boston: American Schools of Oriental Research.

Weber, Max

1968 *Economy and Society: An Outline of Interpretive Sociology*. New York: Bedminster Press.

Webley, Lita

2005 Hideworking among Descendants of Khoekhoen Pastoralists in the Northern Cape, South Africa. In *Gender and Hide Production*, edited by L. Frink and K. Weedman, pp. 153–73. Walnut Creek, CA: AltaMira Press.

2007 Archaeological Evidence for Pastoralist Land-Use and Settlement in Namaqualand over the Last 2000 Years. *Journal of Arid Environments* 70: 629–40.

Weedman, Kathryn

2005 Gender and Stone-Tools: An Ethnographic Study of the Konso and Gamo Hideworkers of Southern Ethiopia. In *Gender and Hide Production*, edited by L. Frink and K. Weedman, pp. 175–96. Walnut Creek, CA: AltaMira Press.

2006 Gender and Ethnoarchaeology. In *Handbook of Gender in Archaeology*, edited by S. M. Nelson, pp. 247–94. Walnut Creek, CA: AltaMira Press.

2010 Feminine Knowledge and Skill Reconsidered: Women and Flaked Stone Tools. *American Anthropologist* 112.2: 228–43.

Welch, John R.

2009 Reconstructing the Ndee (Western Apache) Homeland. In *The Archaeology of Meaningful Places*, edited by B. Bowser and M. N. Zedeño, pp. 149–62. Salt Lake City: University of Utah Press.

Welk, Terrance M.

2012 *The Archaeology of Anti-Slavery Resistance*. Gainesville: University Press of Florida.

Westgate, Ruth
2007 The Greek House and the Ideology of Citizenship. *World Archaeology* 39.2: 229–45.
Wheatley, David, and Mark Gillings
2002 *Spatial Technology and Archaeology: The Archaeological Applications of GIS*. Boca Raton: CRC Press.
White, Andrew A.
2013 Subsistence Economics, Family Size, and the Emergence of Social Complexity in Hunter-Gatherer Systems in Eastern North America. *Journal of Anthropological Archaeology* 32: 122–63.
White, Douglas R., Michael L. Burton, and Lilyan A. Brudner
1977 Entailment Theory and Method: Cross-Cultural Analysis of the Sexual Division of Labor. *Behavior Science Research* 12.1: 1–24.
Whitehouse, Harvey
2000 *Arguments and Icons: Divergent Modes of Religiosity*. Oxford: Oxford University Press.
2004a *Modes of Religiosity: A Cognitive Theory of Religious Transmission*. Walnut Creek, CA: AltaMira Press.
2004b Theorizing Religions Past. In *Theorizing Religions Past: Archaeology, History, and Cognition*, edited by H. Whitehouse and L. H. Martin, pp. 215–32. Walnut Creek, CA: AltaMira Press.
Whitehouse, Harvey, and Ian Hodder
2010 Modes of Religiosity at Çatalhöyük. In *Religion in the Emergence of Civilization: Çatalhöyük as a Case Study*, edited by I. Hodder, pp. 122–44. Cambridge: Cambridge University Press.
Whitehouse, Harvey, and Luther H. Martin (eds.)
2004 *Theorizing Religions Past: Archaeology, History, and Cognition*. Walnut Creek, CA: AltaMira Press.
Whitley, David S.
2001 (ed.) *Handbook of Rock Art Research*. Walnut Creek, CA: AltaMira Press.
2005 Religion. In *Handbook of Archaeological Methods and Theory*, edited by H. Maschner and A. Bentley, pp. 547–66. Walnut Creek, CA: AltaMira Press.
2006 *Introduction to Rock Art Research*. Walnut Creek, CA: Left Coast Press, Inc.
2008 Cognition, Emotion, and Belief: First Steps in an Archaeology of Religion. In *Belief in the Past: Theoretical Approaches to the Archaeology of Religion*, edited by D. S. Whitley and K. Hays-Gilpin, pp. 85–103. Walnut Creek, CA: Left Coast Press, Inc.
Whitley, David S., and Kelley Hays-Gilpin (eds.)
2008 *Belief in the Past: Theoretical Approaches to the Archaeology of Religion*. Walnut Creek, CA: Left Coast Press, Inc.
Whitley, James
2002 Too Many Ancestors. *Antiquity* 75: 119–26.
Whittle, Alasdair
1996 *Europe in the Neolithic: The Creation of New Worlds*. Cambridge: Cambridge University Press.
2003 *The Archaeology of People: Dimensions of Neolithic Life*. London: Routledge.

2009 The People Who Lived in Longhouses: What's the Big Idea? In *Creating Communities: New Advances in Central European Neolithic Research*, edited by D. Hofmann and P. Bickle, pp. 249–63. Oxford: Oxbow.

Whittlesey, Stephanie M.

2009 Mountains, Mounds, and Meaning: Metaphor in the Hohokam Cultural Landscape. In *The Archaeology of Meaningful Places*, edited by B. J. Bowser and M. N. Zedeño, pp. 73–89. Salt Lake City: University of Utah Press.

Wicker, Nancy L., and Bettina Arnold (eds.)

1999 *From the Ground Up: Beyond Gender Theory in Archaeology*. BAR International Series 812. Oxford: Archaeopress.

Wiessner, Polly

1974 A Functional Estimator of Population from Floor Area. *American Antiquity* 39.2: 343–50.

Wilk, Richard R.

1984 Households in Process: Agricultural Change and Domestic Transformation among the Kekchi Maya of Belize. In *Households: Comparative and Historical Studies of the Domestic Group*, edited by R. M. Netting, R. R. Wilk, and E. J. Arnould, pp. 217–44. Berkeley: University of California Press.

1989 *The Household Economy: Reconsidering the Domestic Mode of Production*. Boulder, CO: Westview Press.

Wilk, Richard R., and Wendy Ashmore (eds.)

1988 *Household and Community in the Mesoamerican Past*. Albuquerque: University of New Mexico Press.

Wilk, Richard R., and Robert McC. Netting

1984 Households: Changing Forms and Functions. In *Households: Comparative and Historical Studies of the Domestic Group*, edited by R. M. Netting, R. R. Wilk, E. J. Arnould, pp. 1–28. Berkeley: University of California Press.

Wilk, Richard R., and William L. Rathje

1982 Household Archaeology. *American Behavioral Scientist* 25.6: 617–39.

Wilkinson, Tony J.

2003 *Archaeological Landscapes of the Near East*. Tucson: University of Arizona Press.

Wilkinson, T. J., McGuire Gibson, and Magnus Widell (eds.)

2013 *Models of Mesopotamian Landscapes: How Small-Scale Processes Contributed to the Growth of Early Civilizations*. BAR International Series 2552. Oxford: Archaeopress.

Willey, Gordon R.

1956 *Prehistoric Settlement Patterns in the New World*. Viking Fund Publications in Anthropology No. 23. New York: Wenner-Gren.

Williams, Elizabeth

1985 Estimation of Prehistoric Populations of Archaeological Sites in Southwestern Victoria: Some Problems. *Archaeology in Oceania* 20.3: 73–80.

Williamson, Ronald F.

1990 The Early Iroquoian Period of Southern Ontario. In *The Archaeology of Southern Ontario to A.D. 1650*, edited by C. J. Ellis and N. Ferris, pp. 291–320. Ontario: Ontario Archaeological Society, Inc.

2012 What Will Be Has Always Been: The Past and Present of Northern Iroquoians. In *Oxford Handbook of North American Archaeology*, edited by T. R. Pauketat, pp. 271–84. Oxford: Oxford University Press.

Wills, Wirt H.

2001 Ritual and Mound Formation during the Bonito Phase in Chaco Canyon. *American Antiquity* 66.3: 433–52.

Wilshusen, Richard H.

2002 Estimating Population in the Central Mesa Verde Region. In *Seeking the Center Place: Archaeology and Ancient Communities in the Mesa Verde Region*, edited by M. D. Varien and R. H. Wilshusen, pp. 101–20. Salt Lake City: University of Utah Press.

Wilshusen, Richard H., and James M. Potter

2010 The Emergence of Early Villages in the American Southwest: Cultural Issues and Historical Perspectives. In *Becoming Villagers: Comparing Early Village Societies*, edited by M. S. Bandy and J. R. Fox, pp. 165–82. Tucson: University of Arizona Press.

Wilson, Peter J.

1988 *The Domestication of the Human Species*. New Haven, CT: Yale University Press.

Winkelman, Michael

2008 Cross-Cultural and Biogenetic Perspectives on the Origins of Shamanism. In *Belief in the Past: Theoretical Approaches to the Archaeology of Religion*, edited by D. S. Whitley and K. Hays-Gilpin, pp. 43–66. Walnut Creek, CA: Left Coast Press, Inc.

Wolf, Eric

1999 *Envisioning Power: Ideologies of Dominance and Crises*. Berkeley: University of California.

Woodburn, James

1982 Egalitarian Societies. *Man*, New Series, 17.3: 431–51.

Woolf, Greg

1998 *Becoming Roman: The Origins of Provincial Civilization in Gaul*. Cambridge: Cambridge University Press.

Wright, Bruce William

1979 *A Proxemic Analysis of the Iroquoian Settlement Pattern*. Calgary: Western Publishers.

Wright, Katherine I.

2000 The Social Origins of Cooking and Dining in Early Villages of Western Asia. *Proceedings of the Prehistoric Society* 66: 89–121.

Wright, Rita P.

1991 Women's Labor and Pottery Production in Prehistory. In *Engendering Archaeology: Women and Prehistory*, edited by J. M. Gero and M. W. Conkey, pp. 194–223. Cambridge: Basil Blackwell.

1996 (ed.) *Gender and Archaeology*. Philadelphia: University of Pennsylvania Press.

Wynne-Jones, Stephanie

2013 The Public Life of the Swahili Stonehouse, 14th–15th Centuries AD. *Journal of Anthropological Archaeology* 32: 759–73.

Yanagisako, Sylvia J.
1979 Family and Household: The Analysis of Domestic Groups. *Annual Review of Anthropology* 8: 161–205.
Yanagisako, Sylvia J., and Jane F. Collier
1987 Toward a Unified Analysis of Gender and Kinship. In *Gender and Kinship: Essays Toward a Unified Analysis*, edited by J. F. Collier and S. J. Yanagisako, pp. 14–50. Stanford, CA: Stanford University Press.
Yasur-Landau, Assaf, Jennie R. Ebeling, and Laura B. Mazow (eds.)
2011 *Household Archaeology in Ancient Israel and Beyond*. Leiden: Brill.
Yellen, John
1977 *Archaeological Approaches to the Present: Models for Reconstructing the Past*. New York: Academic Press.
Yesner, David R.
1994 Seasonality and Resource "Stress" among Hunter-Gatherers: Archaeological Signatures. In *Key Issues in Hunter-Gatherer Research*, edited by E. S. Burch, Jr. and L. J. Ellanna, pp. 151–68. Oxford: Berg.
Young, Biloine W., and Melvin L. Fowler
2000 *Cahokia, the Great Native American Metropolis*. Urbana: University of Illinois Press.
Young, William C.
1995 *The Rashaayda Bedouin: Arab Pastoralists of Eastern Sudan*. San Diego: Harcourt Brace College Publishers.
Zako, Reem
2006 The Power of the Veil: Gender Inequality in the Domestic Setting of Traditional Courtyard Houses. In *Courtyard Housing: Past, Present and Future*, edited by B. Edwards, M. Sibley, M. Hakmi, and P. Land, pp. 65–75. New York: Taylor & Francis.
Zarins, Juris
1992 Pastoral Nomadism in Arabia: Ethnoarchaeology and the Archaeological Record—A Case Study. In *Pastoralism in the Levant: Archaeological Materials in Anthropological Perspectives*, edited by O. Bar-Yosef and A. Khazanov, pp. 219–40. Monographs in World Archaeology, No. 10. Madison, WI: Prehistory Press.
Zedeño, María N.
1997 Landscape, Land Use, and the History of Territory Formation: An Example from the Puebloan Southwest. *Journal of Archaeological Method and Theory* 4: 67–103.
2008 The Archaeology of Territory and Territoriality. In *Handbook of Landscape Archaeology*, edited by B. David and J. Thomas, pp. 210–17. Walnut Creek, CA: Left Coast Press, Inc.
Zimansky, Paul E.
1998 *Ancient Ararat: A Handbook of Urartian Studies*. Delmar, NY: Caravan Books.
Zubrow, Ezra B. W. (ed.)
1976 *Demographic Anthropology: Quantitative Approaches*. Albuquerque: University of New Mexico Press.
Zubrow, Ezra B. W., Françoise Audouze, and James G. Enloe (eds.)
2010 *The Magdalenian Household: Unraveling Domesticity*. Albany: SUNY Press.
Zvelebil, Marek
1986 Mesolithic Prelude and Neolithic Revolution. In *Hunters in Transition: Mesolithic Societies of Temperate Eurasia and Their Transition to Farming*, edited by M. Zvelebil, pp. 5–15. Cambridge: Cambridge University Press.

Index

About the Author

Sharon R. Steadman is professor of anthropology and director of the Rozanne M. Brooks Museum at SUNY Cortland. In addition to her work at the university, Steadman is the field director and co-director of the Archaeological Project at Cadır Höyük, Turkey. She is author of the leading textbook *Archaeology of Religion: Cultures and Their Beliefs in Worldwide Context*, and co-edited the books *Agency and Identity in the Ancient Near East*, and *The Oxford Handbook of Ancient Anatolia*. A book by Steadman and co-author Jennifer Ross titled *Ancient Complex Societies* will appear soon from Left Coast Press, Inc.